Christoph Hanisch

Why the Law Matters to You

Practical Philosophy

Edited by
Herlinde Pauer-Studer, Neil Roughley,
Peter Schaber, and Ralf Stoecker

Volume 16

Christoph Hanisch

Why the Law Matters to You

Citizenship, Agency, and Public Identity

DE GRUYTER
ONTOS

ISBN 978-3-11-032395-5
e-ISBN 978-3-11-032456-3

Library of Congress Cataloging-in-Publication Data
A CIP catalog record for this book has been applied for at the Library of Congress.

Bibliografische Information der Deutschen Nationalbibliothek
Die Deutsche Nationalbibliothek verzeichnet diese Publikation in der Deutschen Nationalbibliografie; detaillierte bibliografische Daten sind im Internet über http://dnb.dnb.de abrufbar.

Druck und Bindung: Hubert & Co. GmbH & Co. KG, Göttingen
∞ Gedruckt auf säurefreiem Papier
Printed in Germany

www.degruyter.com

Acknowledgments

This book started as my doctoral dissertation at Bowling Green State University. I want to thank my committee at BGSU. Albert Dzur, Neil Englehart, David Shoemaker (now at Tulane University), and Michael Weber have provided invaluable feedback at various stages of the project. My deepest thanks go to my advisor Fred D. Miller, Jr. who supervised my work during a challenging time for the Philosophy department and during which he was in charge of coordinating the work of many graduate students. Also the participants of Professor Miller's research group have helped me tremendously to understand the very different perspectives concerning the issues dealt with in the dissertation and always reminded me that there is no such things as neutral intuitions that one can uncritically take as starting points in philosophical debates. A special thanks to Fred Miller's assistants Pamela Phillips and Jonathan Miller who compiled outstanding notes during the group meetings. I am indebted to Zeth Campe, my office mate, for important discussions on politics, history, as well as, philosophy. I also want to thank Herlinde Pauer-Studer (University of Vienna) who discussed drafts of my chapters during my stays in Austria. In particular, I want to thank my wife Medea for supporting me and my work when she was in much need of this kind of support herself. At later stages, work on the book manuscript was funded by the ERC Advanced Grant "Distortions of Normativity."

Contents

Introduction

This book defends a Neo-Kantian account of the modern state and legal institutions against an alternative view of social organization. This alternative view is exemplarily presented by Chandran Kukathas's ideal of a modern society, the "liberal archipelago."[1] While not explicitly committing himself to this school of thought, it is argued that Kukathas's theory ultimately collapses into an individualist anarchist critique of the Weberian state.[2] The Neo-Kantian rejoinder to this critique employs a constitutivist argument about individual agency. The argument concludes that anarchism is incompatible with the provision and maintenance of those very external conditions (first and foremost the law) that are necessary for the achievement of a high degree of individual self-constitution. Individualist anarchism (and Kukathas's ideal society) in its extreme form undermines its own prerequisites.

Kukathas attacks contemporary liberalism's[3] vision of political, social, and legal unity, understood as a prerequisite for the peaceful coexistence under modern conditions of thorough-going pluralism and diversity. The French *niqab*

---

1 Kukathas 2003. An important precursor of Kukathas's view is to be found in the often neglected third part of Nozick's *Anarchy, State, and Utopia.* (See Nozick 1974, pp. 297–334.) In a recent publication, Kukathas discusses Nozick's utopian framework explicitly and his conclusions lend further support to my claim that Kukathas's thought is much closer to individualist anarchism than he admits. According to Kukathas, Nozick's utopian framework (the minimal state) is too statist and Nozick fails to show that his utopia cannot be had under anarchistic conditions. In addition, Kukathas renews his main critique since "the purpose of the state is to limit rather than enable people's pursuit of diverse ends. It is a way of making the many live as one. To the extent that those who do not wish to conform are compelled to do so, the state suppresses rather than enables the pursuit of diverse ideals" (Kukathas 2011, p. 290).

2 Kukathas attempts to clarify his relationship to anarchism in a footnote: "My sympathies with (some forms of) anarchism are quite evident. However, it should be made clear that, to the extent that this work is about the nature of the state and its authority, it will be unacceptable to anarchists for failing to condemn the state as incapable of having any legitimacy" (Kukathas 2003, p. 8). The contention defended in Part 1 of this book will be that Kukathas underestimates the anarchistic implications of his own theory and the latter can, therefore, be used as a representative of the view that this essay argues against, i.e., a view that regards the state as neither necessary nor desirable. For an anthology of historical and contemporary classics of individualist anarchist thinking, see Stringham 2007.

3 The label "contemporary liberalism" refers to the work of Rawls, Kymlicka, Dworkin and others that are sometimes also referred to as "egalitarian liberals." Kukathas considers his alternative version of liberalism to be close to what is nowadays referred to "classical liberalism" and "cultural libertarianism." (See Mitnick 2006, p. 136.)

controversy[4] and the court proceedings regarding the Amish communities' educational policies[5] are the kind of cases that Kukathas presents in order to motivate his main claim that individual freedom and pluralism on the one hand and the modern state, with its central feature of enforced constitutional cohesion, on the other are necessarily in tension with one another. Kukathas's alternative ("liberal tolerationism") places an unconditional requirement of respecting individual conscience at the center of his account and puts it in place of what he believes to be an unnecessary and dangerous obsession with social unity and homogeneity, a pattern of thinking he sees exemplified in Rawls, Kymlicka, Dworkin and other contemporary political philosophers. If the right not to be forced to act against the dictates of one's conscience is taken seriously, the modern state necessarily seems to pose a threat to the former when it imposes controversial legal norms on all of its subjects. The first part of this book (Chapters 1–3) is dedicated to spelling out this particular kind of criticism directed at the modern state and, especially, its legal institutions. According to Kukathas, contemporary liberalism faces a dilemma and is torn between respecting thorough-going diversity and pluralism on the one hand and enforcing a stability-guaranteeing conception of social unity on the other. In critically assessing Rawls's version of political liberalism, Kukathas summarizes this central point of disagreement:

> Yet stability and social unity [...] can only be bought at the cost of toleration. This is because articulating a political conception of justice, and presenting it as the first principle governing conduct in the public realm, subordinates toleration, entrenches a particular comprehensive moral conception, and excludes certain moral ideals as unacceptable.[6]

The liberal archipelago is supposed to overcome this dilemma by rejecting the goal of unity and by assigning individuals an unconditional right to live in accordance with the dictates of their conscience. The monolithic status of freedom of conscience finds its political manifestation in an equally unconditional right to exit the (by definition) voluntary religious, cultural, social, and political associations one is a member of.

Kukathas and the individualist anarchists' vision of a world of maximum individual sovereignty (and of a parallel decrease of the importance of the state) is reflected in contemporary enthusiasm concerning globalization and the end

---

4 See Chrisafis 2011.

5 Concerning the decision to grant certain religious communities the privilege to opt out of the public school system after 8th grade, the landmark decision remains *Wisconsin v. Yoder*, 406 U.S. 205 (1972).

6 Kukathas 2003, p. 133.

of the nation state.[7] Kukathas's archipelago and the individualist anarchists' conceptions of an ideal society present a world of maximum individual freedom, it seems, a world in which relationships of citizenship are voluntarily engaged in and renounced, depending on whether or not shared membership in a particular legal order is deemed compatible with one's conscience. The picture of an archipelago (small islands "operating in a sea of mutual toleration") that Kukathas evokes in order to show the superiority of this social arrangement, the view of individuals freely floating around amongst voluntary associations, is a fitting illustration of the enticing vision of a borderless and globalized post-statist world. One of the first observations I will discuss with respect to these views is that states, as many take them for granted today, cannot establish any unconditional requirements vis-à-vis their subjects in such a world. More importantly, the lack of such unconditional requirements has an impact on the relationships among the individuals populating such a stateless environment. If individual freedom of conscience reigns supreme, the reach of a legal order (and the juridified relationships of its subjects vis-à-vis one another) rests on voluntary acquiescence on part of the subjects. Again, at first blush this might not be such a bad thing after all. On the contrary, liberty and freedom seem to be maximized in such a consent-based global condition.

This essay curbs this enthusiasm that many share with respect to a possible future of a borderless world of diminished (maybe even completely vanished) state sovereignty.[8] To some extent the following nine chapters present a seemingly conservative attempt to show that the modern Weberian state, with its characteristic feature of monopolizing the creation, enforcement, and administration of public norms that apply to all its citizens, is not a mere historical accident (in both senses of the word), itself the result of nothing else but plain violence, conquest, and war.[9] It is at this point that the Neo-Kantian defense of

---

7 For good discussions of this debate, see Douglas 1997, Wolf 2001, Agnew 2009, Holton 2011.

8 This enthusiasm is neither new nor firmly located exclusively on one extreme end of the political spectrum. In section 7.2 I show that the desire to see the (juridical) state "wither away," and to see it replaced by a global community of solidarity brotherhood (Marxism) or a completely privatized world of voluntary market-based relationships (Rothbardianism) has had lasting appeal. Moreover, certain varieties of communitarianism similarly complain that the juridification of all human relationships (typical of the modern state) endangers the authenticity of, especially, intimate social forms like marriage and friendship.

9 See Kukathas 2003, p. 164. The notion of "conservatism" must be understood in a distinct way here. As will become clear in presenting the detailed arguments for why the idea of a modern juridical state is inherently related to individual human agency (arguments that draw on ideologically diverse thinkers such as Hayek, Waldron, Pettit, and Korsgaard), this exploration does not defend any substantially conservative policies and legal arrangements. Rather,

the status quo (concerning the abstract and general idea of ordering the world) comes into play. In response to Kukathas, the individualist anarchist, and the globalization advocates, the following chapters show that a high degree of individual agency is critically dependent on certain external conditions being in place. The normative self-conception of modern citizens, their self-understanding as rights holders who lead a life under protecting and action-enabling public norms, is impossible in a condition of exclusively private relationships among individuals in a stateless world. The constitutivist view defended in Part 2 (Chapters 4–6) insists that it is ultimately the inescapability of the problem of action, the activity that constitutes us as persons with a stable identity across time, that necessitates our moving into a juridified condition and staying therein.[10] Put conversely, it will be argued that in its extreme form individualist anarchism undermines its own prerequisite, identity and individuality, by rejecting the conclusiveness of property, contract, and status relationships that only legal institutions and courts can claim to provide in their distinctively enforceable form.[11] In order to result in robust identities, self-constituting action has to take place under the modern law and constitutional

the state- and public-law based conservatism defended must be understood relative to the individualist alternative of complete statelessness. The main claim defended is one about (the public) structure, not content.

10 As will become clear at several points in the book, this introduction summarizes the book's conclusions and main claims in a simplified and catchy way. The stark contrast that is drawn between the state-based defense of the rule of law and the alternative stateless utopias should of course not be taken to imply an uncritical glorification of actually existing states. It should be obvious from the following discussion that this essay is highly aware not just of the imperfections of modern legal systems but of the specific dangers that come with the Weberian state. That there is a genuine relationship between the historical emergence of the modern state, with its characteristic bureaucratization of centralized power, and the catastrophes and atrocities of the twentieth century is not at all denied here. On the view that the enlightenment achievement of the juridical state carries within it the source of its own abuse in the name of totalitarian ideologies, see the accounts of Arendt 1976, Bauman 1989, Adorno and Horkheimer 2002 (1944).

11 It is important to note that the argument of this essay is an exercise in ideal theory, that is, it contrasts the *idea* of a rightful legal order with the *idea* of anarchism. It is, of course, not denied that some real world (Weberian) states have done a terrible job with respect to the task of providing the external conditions for self-constitution. (Moreover, no real world state can provide 100% assurance and juridification regarding our legal status.) Conversely, some fairly high degree of self-constitution might be (empirically) possible within social arrangements that leave the settling of private disputes in private hands. However, the point remains that only the juridified state can *claim* to solve property and contract disputes in a non-contingent and public fashion, which in turn constitutes part of a *sui generis* conception of independent individual agency.

arrangements. As will be spelled out in what follows, the notion of "agency" and a particular conception of "freedom" (as non-domination) can be used almost interchangeably as a result of the argument defended. Adapting one of Hayek's famous lines, the self-constitution of liberty is inextricably linked to the presence of institutions that are public in nature and that establish our status as agents independently of the private whims and desires of others.

Those who are familiar with Kant's political writings will most probably be surprised about the framework-choice hinted at in the previous paragraphs, given that the Kant of *Perpetual Peace* is the philosopher of "cosmopolitan right" and world citizenship (*Weltbürgerrecht*).[12] Is not a view like Kant's actually more congenial to Kukathas's liberal archipelago and even the individualist anarchists' position than the state-based alternative defended in this essay?[13]

One problem with this view is that Kant's *Perpetual Peace*, while invoking the idea of world citizenship, does not at all regard the sovereign state as an obsolete model. On the contrary, and this gets us closer to the main claim defended in the following three parts, the idea of a peaceful global order is inherently connected to the necessity of persons being members of distinct juridical states (i.e., republics in Kant's case). Whereas *Perpetual Peace* justifies the state indirectly as an instrument to secure international trade and peaceful coexistence, the argument pursued in this book looks at different Kantian sources that allow a more direct defense of why individuals share a universal need of membership in a legal order (and are actually under an unconditional normative requirement to enter it). While Kant's mature political writings, first and foremost the *Doctrine of Right*, play a significant role in the final third part (Chapters 7–9), it is the work of Neo-Kantian moral philosopher Christine Korsgaard that provides the initial steps for replying to the challenge posed by Kukathas's critique of the Weberian state.

---

12 On the notion of "cosmopolitan right," see PP 8:357–8:360 and MM 6:352–6:353. The idea of cosmopolitan right underwent a significant development within Kant's work. (See Byrd and Hruschka 2011, pp. 205–211.) A recent attempt to show that Kant's notions of cosmopolitan right and the idea of a republican constitution condition one another, see Anderson-Gold 2009. (See also Thomson 2008 and Kleingeld 2012.) Furthermore, I put aside the controversies about Kant's views concerning the possibility/desirability of a world state/republic. This work ignores the important point that a rightful condition, in order to be completely conclusive, must overcome, in one form or another, anarchism (between individual juridified states) on the global level. (See Pogge 1988.)

13 This impression might also be strengthened by the influential anarchist position by Robert Paul Wolff, a position heavily relying on a Kantian notion of autonomy. (See Wolff 1998 (1970).)

The choice of Korsgaard's work might also come as a surprise. Primarily interested in moral philosophical (as opposed to political and legal philosophical) issues, Korsgaard has developed a distinct view with respect to the sources of moral requirements (her account of practical identity) on the one hand and, more recently, an original argument about the self-constitution of individual agents on the other.[14] It is these two Kantian contributions that are combined and turned into a social and political thesis concerning the necessity of external public norms, required for completing the task of performing actions in the "societal condition" (a world populated by more than one individual who are aware of each other's existence). In short, it is the inescapability of action qua self-constitution, together with the claim that action (in the presence of other agents) necessarily requires certain external features in the environment (in which this self-constituting action takes place), that present a strong reply to the position that I see Kukathas committed to. The normative requirement to establish and maintain the rule of law has its ultimate origin in our human condition that consists in the task of leading a life as well-constituted agents. The liberal archipelago represents an unviable account of individuals-in-the-societal-condition because it fails to provide the specifically unconditional and public institutional framework, within which individuals act and, hence, in which they constitute themselves into agents successfully to begin with. Modern legal institutions are presented (especially in Chapter 8) as the paradigmatic instantiation of a principle-based structure that provides such a framework, which is required for practical deliberation and the reliable setting and pursuit of ends, both of which are essential features of the phenomenon of distinctively human action. Citizenship is then ultimately defined in terms of the principles (i.e., the laws etc.) that constitute the practical identity (the normative self-conception) of those who are subject to a legal system and perform their self-constituting actions under them. An agent's practical identity (the action-guiding principles that she employs in the course of her practical deliberation and choice) is at the same time a public identity (at least in the societal condition). In Kant's language, the public principles that clarify and establish one's "external freedom" vis-à-vis all those around oneself, are necessarily part of every action one performs and, hence, become part of one's normative self-conception. These latter issues are taken up in the final section of Part 3 of the book when we return to Kukathas's work afresh and present the final objections to it inspired by the self-constitution account.

14 See Korsgaard 1996 and Korsgaard 2009.

This conclusion concerning the necessity of legal institutions for individual agency will strike many as implausible and at several points in the essay the claims made will be qualified – without that suggesting a retreat from the claims stated in the previous paragraph. The two most important qualifications are, firstly, the concession that individual agency comes in degrees. The constitutivist argument employed in this essay does not submit that any form of human agency can only emerge and be maintained under modern legal institutions and within a Weberian state. The thesis rather is that a particularly high degree of unified agency requires for its possibility the existence of a modern legal system and the normative self-conception of those who are constituting themselves qua its subjects. Secondly, the constitutivist argument in support of modern political and social institutions does not purport to establish substantial moral arguments concerning justice and legitimacy. While such arguments are certainly compatible with the argument for the public identity claim (the essay's central argument presented in Chapter 5), the book's main arguments do not in and of themselves provide a rich set of criteria for evaluating legal and political systems in the form of all-things-considered judgments.

This second qualification becomes especially noticeable at two points: When reconstructing and employing Korsgaard's Neo-Kantian account, the essay stops half-way and does not endorse the substantial Kantian conclusions concerning criteria of moral rightness that Korsgaard establishes at later points in her two major works. Moreover, when reviving Lon Fuller's jurisprudence (in section 8.1), the interpretation of his views deliberately turns his "internal *morality* of law" into law's internal *rationality*.[15] The law, in order to play its role in the self-constituting activities of modern citizens, must indeed satisfy certain formal criteria that ultimately rest on the nature of the law's addressees and their capacities as agents; not any kind of publicly declared norm can count as law. However, these Fullerian standards of legality do not amount to any substantial moral criteria that provide a blueprint for an ideally just and legitimate political and legal system. A legal system that provides the external prerequisites for a high degree of individuality and self-constitution, might turn out to be a fairly unjust one. Even though some policies that fall within the sphere of morally unjust acts of legislation (like willy-nilly enacting retroactive laws) are simultaneously ruled out by the requirements of law's internal rationality, the essay does not take a definite stance on issues of substantive justice.

Despite the limited moral reach of this work's conclusions, the normative claims established (that those individuals who find themselves in the societal

---

15 See Fuller 1969.

condition face the inescapable challenge of having to publicly clarify their standing vis-à-vis one another in a reliable and stable way, etc.) provide the basis for ultimately rejecting Kukathas's and the individualist anarchists' alternative account of social ordering. In the final sections of the book, Kant's (among others) political and legal philosophical work takes center stage in substantiating the abstract argument for the public identity claim. Kant's idea of entering a "rightful condition" because of the (not merely contingently empirical) problems that confront the enjoyment of rights in the state of nature is combined with Philip Pettit's recent work on non-domination and republican freedom in Chapter 7. These ideas are used to show that the idea of a legal order requires, *pace* Kukathas, a form of unconditional membership in order to establish the relationships of citizenship that are identified as crucial for performing actions in the sense required for a high degree of successful self-constituting activity. Property, contract, status (family relationships, marriage...), are all identified as legal relationships that are undermined by what Kukathas calls an unconditional "right to exit" one's association(s). Since these legal relationships are necessary for attaining the status of an independent agent, undermining their unconditional nature at the same time threatens that very status. I conclude (in Chapter 9), that a legal order cannot be a voluntary association in Kukathas and the anarchist's sense, even if that claim implies that individual conscience, its undoubtedly high value notwithstanding, must be compromised at times. Despite these critical disagreements, the essay concludes with noticing a significant overlap (or at least compatibility) between the constitutivist account defended here and many of Kukathas's political recommendations. Neither a sophisticated structure of federalism nor a rather austere account of citizenship (one that is skeptical of notions such as thorough-going national and cultural homogeneity as a basis for the rule of law) is incompatible with the constitutivist defense of the modern state. Still, it is individuality and freedom themselves that conflict with individualist anarchism and the stateless world that many find so tempting in the face of the promises of a seemingly unregulated world citizenship as well as the historical record of state atrocities and governmental mismanagement of human affairs.

With respect to a slightly different context (though also influenced by Kant's political thought and addressing an issue relevant to Kukathas, namely the status of refugees), Hannah Arendt summarizes this essay's main claim very well, when she famously identifies the most basic human right as "the right to have rights."[16] The parallel between Kant and Arendt becomes evident when the former identifies the one fundamental right to external freedom ("the innate right of humanity"[17]) as the only one we have conclusively before we enter a rightful condition. Of course, Kant's argument in support of the juridical state (*Rechtsstaat*)[18] is cast in the language of an unconditional duty (to enter a condition in which public law reigns supreme), but Kant's and Arendt's points ultimately rest on the same insight, central to this work: The right and duty one has qua human agent is to create and maintain juridified relations with one another and to enter a condition in which rights can be enjoyed, as Kant puts it, conclusively and peremptorily (as opposed to merely provisionally). Enjoying rights conclusively means that one has them because public institutions enact, enforce and adjudicate disputes concerning them in the name of those who are subject to them and not merely because other individuals happen to let you do so conditionally and as a matter of private goodwill.

The demands of (private) morality on the other hand, themselves not dependent on the existence of a rightful condition (especially for someone like Kant), are not sufficient to constitute the agential spheres in a way that goes beyond remaining dependent on the private wills of all those with respect to which one "cannot avoid living side by side [...]."[19] One of the controversial claims defended in the following chapters is the "total law thesis" (section 7.2)

---

16 Arendt 1976, p. 296–297. "We became aware of the existence of a right to have rights (and that means to live in a framework where one is judged by one's actions and opinions) and a right to belong to some kind of organized community, only when millions of people emerged who had lost and could not regain these rights because of the new global political situation." For an excellent discussion of Arendt's idea of the right to have rights, in which it is defined as the right "to be a *legal person*," see Benhabib 2004, p. 3 and pp. 49–70. (See also Michelman 1996.)

17 For an excellent exegesis of Kant's complex notion of the innate right of humanity, see Ripstein 2009, pp. 30–56.

18 On the difficulty of translating the German word *Rechtsstaat* adequately into English, see Byrd and Hruschka 2011, p. 1 and pp. 25–26. Their preferred translation "juridical state" captures the moral austerity of the *Rechtsstaat* better than the conception of "a state under the rule of law." Still, the rule of law exhibits some extensive and important overlap with the meaning of *Rechtsstaat* and will be used in this essay to denote the kind of public condition that is defended as necessary for a high degree of individual agency.

19 See Kant's postulate of public right: "when you cannot avoid living side by side with all others, you ought to leave the state of nature and proceed with them into a rightful condition, that is, a condition of distributive justice" (MM 6:307). Importantly, the notion of "distributive justice" does not refer to what is understood as such in contemporary discussions. Rather, it refers to the necessity of a system of public courts that conclusively determine mine and thine. (See Byrd and Hruschka 2011, pp. 38–39.)

that develops Kant's and Arendt's argument into a distinct direction. Following Jeremy Waldron and others, the distinctive feature of life within modern institutions has taken on a thoroughly legal form. Contrary to trends, related to the one mentioned at the outset concerning globalization and privatization, that often bemoan the "overlegalization"[20] of affairs that are considered "personal" and "private," this essay attempts to show that the casting of our personality in legal terms is the expression of a distinct historical achievement, dedicated to realizing an ideal of individual independence that the principles and norms of individual morality cannot capture in all its importance. Again, the following pages do not defend this and other claims in the form of all-things-considered judgments; it is very likely that an "over-juridification" of our lives will impact them negatively, by undermining the spontaneity of human activities or by criminalizing harmless acts for example. However, it will be submitted as the central conclusion that a constitutivist account of our identity as temporarily extended and unified agents (and of the process of how we become and maintain who we are) shows that *some* level of life under and within such public institutions is the foundation of successfully completing the task of a high degree of self-constitution and, eventually, of a free life.

20 Baumgartner 1993, p. 336.

Part 1:
A Challenge for Citizenship

> The erroneous belief that all human relationship must be in terms of purposes pursued and actions performed has persuaded many that all human associations must be composed either of persons transactionally related in seeking individual satisfactions, or of persons cooperatively related in seeking common satisfactions, and consequently that the character of a state *must* be identified as some sort of substantive condition of human circumstance.
>
> Oakeshott[21]

> In a well-ordered society each person understands the first principles that govern the whole scheme as it is to be carried out over many generations; and all have a settled intention to adhere to these principles in their plan of life. Thus the plan of each person is given a more ample and rich structure than it would otherwise have; it is adjusted to the plans of others by mutually acceptable principles. [...] [T]he collective activity of justice is the preeminent form of human flourishing. For given favorable conditions, it is by maintaining these public arrangements that persons best express their nature and achieve their widest regulative excellences of which each is capable.
>
> Rawls[22]

In his book *The Liberal Archipelago* Chandran Kukathas criticizes varieties of contemporary liberalism (the paradigmatic cases being Rawls, Dworkin, and Kymlicka). According to Kukathas, these theories of social and political justice fail to reconcile two central liberal values, tolerance of thorough-going diversity on the one hand and the maintenance of a unified and stable liberal society on the other. These two values constitute the horns of a dilemma that Kukathas sees egalitarian liberals struggling with. Rawls *et al.* resolve this dilemma by emphasizing the value of social stability and unity too much. They sacrifice tolerance when they invest the modern state with the authority to enforce a unifying conception of social/political/legal justice – even on those members of society who reject that particular conception. Kukathas's work is an attempt to address this dilemma in a more satisfying way. Liberalism, in Kukathas's more "classical" sense, abandons the idea of a liberal state that is in charge of securing social unity in the name of substantial political aims. Liberal tolerationists like Kukathas embrace a radical solution to the dilemma, namely the unconditional endorsement of the value of tolerance while giving up on the idea that a liberal society must exhibit cohesion in the form of the state and shared legal institutions.

The first chapter, "Kukathas's Challenge To Contemporary Liberalism," reconstructs *The Liberal Archipelago*'s critique of contemporary liberalism. It does

21 Oakeshott 1975, p. 318.
22 Rawls 1999 (1971), pp. 462–463.

so by outlining the particular value-dilemma that Kukathas thinks befalls this influential branch of liberalism, viz. the tension between tolerating diversity on the one hand and achieving social stability and unity on the other (section 1.1). The chapter then presents Kukathas's positive view of liberal toleration and its practical implementation in the form of the liberal archipelago, a liberal society that honors individual freedom of conscience by allowing its members to freely associate with (and dissociate from) all others (section 1.2).

The second chapter, "The Liberal State and Liberal Citizens," argues that Kukathas's argument against contemporary liberalism rests on Max Weber's influential conception of the modern state. Weber's three concepts of "power," "authority," and "state" underlie Kukathas's worry that the state necessarily conflicts with thorough-going diversity and the value of tolerance. At the end of section 2.1 it is shown, however, that Weber's conceptual framework can be interpreted differently and that the Weberian state is compatible with Kukathas's own thin requirement of legitimacy ("acquiescence" to *de facto* regimes). The second chapter continues with a discussion of the diminished role that citizenship and membership in shared institutions play in Kukathas's vision of a liberal society. The context of individual agency and identity is perceived differently in the liberal archipelago than in the case of contemporary liberal theory and practice (section 2.2). Kukathas's picture suggests that the citizens of the liberal archipelago are not related to political and legal institutions in a particularly significant way. Moreover, Kukathas claims that if individuals wish to exit a specific association, because its public norms conflict with the demands of their conscience, they are unconditionally permitted to do so.

The last point concerning the categorical right to exit plays a central role when I commence my own reply to Kukathas in Chapter 3. The liberal archipelago, with its uncompromising adherence to the value of tolerance and freedom of individual conscience, dissolves contemporary liberalism's dilemma at too high a price. In fact, the liberal archipelago exhibits its own dilemma (section 3.1). If developed fully, Kukathas's liberal archipelago will either see its cultural etc. associations turn into "mini-states" or his ideal society will collapse into individualist anarchism. Elaborating on an argument presented by Michael Walzer, it is concluded that Kukathas's premises (especially the right to exit) commit him to endorsing the second horn of the dilemma – individualist anarchism understood as the rejection of any stable and unified public authority over individuals.

Chapter 1: Kukathas's Challenge to Contemporary Liberalism

Kukathas's main opponent is contemporary liberalism, especially the "political" variety represented by Rawls and Kymlicka. This brand of liberalism takes as its starting point the problem of reconciling two values, namely tolerance of thorough-going diversity and maintaining a certain degree of social, political, and legal unity necessary for a public order's stability. According to Kukathas, Rawls and other liberals fail to realize that these two values cannot be reconciled. Kukathas points out that recent liberal political philosophy has been insensitive to the inherently dilemmatic nature of this problem. Why, asks Kukathas, do liberals assume that diverse cultural and religious communities need to join an "overlapping consensus," committing all citizens to submitting to a shared political conception of justice in the first place? The question is pressing given that any realistic prospects for achieving and maintaining such a consensus must rely on the eradication of diversity, Kukathas argues. The discussion of this dilemma (tolerance vs. unity) is the task of the first half of this chapter.

The Liberal Archipelago presents an alternative vision of liberalism. An open and tolerant society takes on the form of an archipelago, consisting of a number of diverse religious, cultural, and social associations (the archipelago's islands) that are loosely connected by their shared membership in one overarching but extremely narrowly conceived political association, *viz.* the liberal state. The liberal state plays the role of a mere "umpire" that guarantees the peaceful coexistence amongst the associations on the one hand and enforces, if necessary, each individual's "right to exit" these associations on the other. Kukathas's theory of liberalism is briefly summarized and its underlying "minimal moral conception," that identifies freedom of conscience as the only universal value and interest, is reconstructed (1.2). The end of this chapter begins to look at the conceptual framework that Kukathas uses in his theory and that accounts for his worries concerning contemporary liberalism, i.e., Max Weber's influential conception of the modern state.

1.1 The Liberal Dilemma (Tolerance vs. Unity)

Before we look at Kukathas's positive view, we need to make sure that we comprehend his critique of contemporary liberalism. His main objection takes on the form of a dilemma that contemporary liberals fail to deal with in a satisfying way. Kukathas formulates the central question of all liberal political theory as follows: "what is the principled basis of a free society marked by cultural diversity and group loyalties?"[23] The distinction between Kukathas's (liberal) archipelago and the alternative accounts of liberal society, presented by Rawls and others, lies in the distinct answers to this question. In particular, the disagreement between Kukathas and his opponents consists in the conflicting formulations of the objectives a liberal political theory should strive to achieve. Whereas Kukathas's liberalism claims to return to the traditional *political* problem of authority, most contemporary liberals are concerned with the *moral* question of justice (a result of contemporary political philosophy being heavily influenced by the work considered responsible for its revival, Rawls's *A Theory of Justice*).[24]

However, even the traditional "political" approach, focusing on the question of authority instead of justice, rests on a problematic assumption that Kukathas wants to reject. Also most traditional contractarians (such as Locke and Rousseau) take the existence of nations or dominions as a starting point for their accounts of legitimate authority. States are conceived of as *closed* territorial entities, enclosed by rigid borders. In this tradition, it is always a determinate subset of the global populace that finds itself in need of settling the issue of political authority. The existence of national communities is taken as an unquestioned assumption in much classical as well as contemporary political theorizing: "Political philosophy [...] has generally begun with the assumption that the nation-state is the appropriate starting point for reflection on the political order."[25] Kukathas refers to numerous examples illustrating this assumption.[26] Plato's metaphor of the "ship of state," the modern notion of the "body politic," and Rawls's "well-ordered society" are just a few instances of this starting point of political thought. All these metaphors have in common their reference to the conception of a "closed society," a conception lying at the heart of Rawls's construction of the original position. As we will see Kukathas rejects this assumption and claims that a liberal society has to be an "open society."

Especially in the work of contemporary liberal thinkers, the assumption of closeness finds its expression in a longing for social and political unity. In fact, once societies are conceived of as being closed social entities (letting anybody neither in nor out) achieving the political goal of unity becomes an urgent and seemingly inescapable task. Social unity and political stability are considered

---

23 Kukathas 2003, p. 4.

24 See Kukathas 2003, p. 7.

25 Kukathas 2003, p. 257.

26 See Kukathas 2003, p. 8.

political values on a par with the traditional liberal values of individual freedom and equality *because* settling on *one* shared normative public framework is now a practical problem that cannot be escaped from.[27] John Rawls's work (especially his *Political Liberalism*[28]) and Will Kymlicka's *Multicultural Citizenship*[29] provide the foil for the negative part of Kukathas's project, i.e., his critique of contemporary liberalism. Replying to Rawls's account of the good of a "social union" in *A Theory of Justice* Kukathas presents a clear formulation of his disagreement:

> This conception of a political order [Rawls's "social union"; C.H.] expresses a wish for a degree of social unity which is simply inconsistent with the extent of diversity, mobility, and disagreement in the modern world. It can only be achieved, in the end, by suppressing diversity, or reducing freedom of movement, or stifling dissent.[30]

Another example of how contemporary liberals' occupation with defending social unity conflicts with diversity is illustrated by Kukathas's discussion of Dworkin's rejection of "checkerboard solutions" to questions of law.[31] Dworkin defends the idea of a principled *unity* and emphasizes the need for a certain level of *integrity* that a legal order must exhibit in order to secure the stability of the constitutional state's authority. When it comes to the most fundamental moral and legal issues (such as criminal justice) legal pluralism must be circumscribed in order to avoid the disintegration of the political order necessary to establish and maintain the rule of law. Dworkin goes so far as to reject arbitrary compromises between an option identified as correct and an incorrect one

---

27 Christine Korsgaard claims that it is a widespread misunderstanding concerning Rawls's project to interpret it as the attempt to justify the liberal state to illiberal individuals and populations (this point is made most explicitly in *The Law of Peoples*, but is also true of Rawls's earlier works). Rather, according to Korsgaard, "he is concerned about a parallel problem that arises when we try to justify policies *within* the liberal state, for even within the liberal state, we must use the coercive mechanisms of the state to enforce liberal policies" (Korsgaard 2008, p. 318). The particular practical problem Rawls is concerned with is therefore not the justification of why his theory assumes a closed society. Both *A Theory of Justice* and *Political Liberalism* attempt to develop a solution to the problem of what people are supposed to do who already have accepted that they are going to share one political community; the more general issue of whether or not to have such a society in the first place is no longer on the agenda once the process of constructing conceptions of liberal justice is engaged in.

28 Rawls 1993.

29 Kymlicka 1995.

30 Kukathas 2003, p. 258.

31 Kukathas 2003, p. 179–80. (See Dworkin 1986, pp. 178–86.) The fully developed reply to Kukathas in section 9.2 deals extensively with Dworkin's account of a legal system's integrity.

as being worse than going with the second, incorrect, option.[32] When it comes to fundamental legal norms, the state's authority must take on the form of a sovereign monopoly: "Integrity is a value which stands beside justice and fairness; and systems which do not possess this integrity stand condemned for failing to live up to this ideal."[33] Dworkin's conclusion is that states accepting checkerboard solutions at the constitutional level (the "basic structure of society") disintegrate and end up acting in an unprincipled manner.[34]

These are just two examples of how liberals' longing for social and political unity conflicts with the other important liberal value of tolerance with respect to diversity and pluralism according to Kukathas. As Dworkin's account illustrates the aim of securing integrity (or in Rawls's case "stability for the right reasons") is not a by-product of mainstream liberal theory. Social unity is identified as a genuine political value, the efficacious realization of which is considered a criterion of success for a theory of liberal political institutions.

In addition to discussing how contemporary liberal theory celebrates social and political cohesion and homogeneity, Kukathas presents a plethora of examples that illustrate his main worry. In these examples the coercive state apparatus interferes with the practices and customs of ethnic, religious, and cultural minorities. The coercive imposition of the policies in question result in members of these communities having to act contrary to the dictates of their conscience, the gravest rights violation there is according to Kukathas. Kukathas describes the case of the Amish and Hutterites in North America and the way in which their views concerning educational policies have conflicted with compulsory schooling requirements imposed by centralized governments in the name of a shared conception of free and equal citizenship (and of what is required to become such a citizen).[35] Drawing on his own background, Kukathas presents the cases of Australian and Malaysian Aborigines, in the case of which children were separated from their families to make sure the cultural heritage

---

32 "In fact, Dworkin maintains that, if there were two alternative solutions, A and B, such that he viewed A as right in principle and B wrong in principle, he 'would rank the checkerboard solution not intermediate between the other two but third, below both'" (Kukathas 2003, p. 180).

33 Kukathas 2003, p. 180.

34 I have decided to discuss Kukathas's critique of Dworkin's position despite the fact that *The Liberal Archipelago* puts more emphasis on other representatives of liberalism such as Rawls, Raz, and especially Kymlicka. The reason for this choice will become clearer in part two of this book where authoritative integrity (as well as stability and predictability) is connected with successful individual self-constitution.

35 Kukathas 2003, p. 181.

(deemed incompatible with modern society) died out.[36] Not mentioned by Kukathas, but important to complete the enumeration of the kind of scenarios that motivate his critique of liberalism, is the case of European debates concerning the wearing of the *niqab* by Muslim women.[37] The recent French decision to ban full-face veils from public places is especially relevant for understanding Kukathas's objections to the value of social unity, because the republican ideals (inspired by Rousseau's notion of the general will and the ideals of the French Revolution) explicitly refer to the laicisitc values incorporated into the state and *its* interests. The ultimate motivation of the French "burqua-ban" is "unveiled" when one considers the punishment for breaking the law in question: "Women wearing *niqab* will be fined €150 (about $200) and be given a citizenship class to remind them of the republican values of secular France and gender equality."[38]

Returning to the theoretical underpinnings of these political controversies, Kukathas's challenge against contemporary liberalism can be summarized in the form of a dilemma. The dilemma results from liberals' continued adherence to the liberal values of tolerance while simultaneously attempting to safeguard the aforementioned goals of state-based unity and principled legal integrity. The dilemma's two horns are as follows. The first horn of the dilemma threatens to undermine the value of tolerance. In order to achieve the level of unity required for a Rawlsian social union or Dworkin's "community of principle," pluralism about the right and the good has to be confined within limits that are backed-up by state coercion. If pluralism gets too deep then an overlapping consensus and legal integrity are threatened, causing the liberal state to respond to this threat to its existence. By pointing to empirical cases, Kukathas illustrates his claim that even liberal states resort to force in order to keep thorough-going pluralism in check. Resorting to this kind of force, however, conflicts with the liberal ideal of tolerance requiring the liberal state to abstain from intervention into individuals' and communities' internal affairs.

The second horn of the dilemma results from taking the value of liberal tolerance (too) seriously. Insofar as contemporary liberals value tolerance, this attitude threatens, according to Kukathas, the other central value they cherish

---

36 Kukathas 2003, p. 136.

37 See Chrisafis 2011. The decision to ban clothing that covers a person's entire face from all public places (with the exception of places of religious worship, carnival parades, etc.) must be distinguished from the earlier French ban of the headscarf that applies in the context of state institutions only (e.g. public schools). I briefly return to this case at the very end of my replies to Kukathas in section 9.2.

38 Chrisafis 2011.

(social unity) and diminishes the prospects of sustaining an overlapping consensus on fundamental political issues. Insofar as the liberal state allows cultural and religious communities to develop unconstrained diversity and does not interfere into their internal affairs (by means of, for example, compulsory public education) the social unity necessary for such a state's continuous operation will erode, or so Kukathas predicts. Rawls, Dworkin and Kymlicka on the other hand consider it problematic when support for the state's institutional structure is weakened beyond a critical point as a result of lack of agreement among those who are subject to its authority. These liberals therefore cannot accept the second horn of the dilemma either and cannot value tolerance to the extent that Kukathas thinks liberalism should. Unchecked tolerance of pluralism will result in undermining the kind of political unity and stability that contemporary liberalism wants to see maintained in the form of the modern constitutional state.

In summary, then, contemporary liberals' project of establishing a just liberal state must fail because it is the two values of tolerance and social unity that turn out to collide if implemented together under circumstances of diversity and pluralism. Establishing and strengthening social, political, and legal unity conflicts with tolerance concerning diverse conceptions of justice as well as with respect to conceptions of the good life. Equally problematic, at least for Rawls *et al.*, is a liberal conception overemphasizing tolerance since it unavoidably leads to the eradication of any agreement even with respect to the most basic matters of justice. This dilemma shows, according to Kukathas, that there is something fundamentally wrong with contemporary liberalism. As long as a unified liberal society and state is considered a good of high value and a goal, the promotion of which justifies the imposition of coercive policies, tolerance will be restricted in genuinely illiberal ways.

There are two ways to deal with a dilemma. Contemporary liberals endorse one of its horns, according to Kukathas, when they are willing to sacrifice a good deal of tolerance in the name of social and political unity in the liberal polity. Alternatively, and this is Kukathas's strategy, one can dissolve a dilemma by showing that, upon closer examination, we are not really confronted with a genuine dilemma. If one of the values involved in the dilemma (social unity) is of considerably smaller importance than the other value (tolerance of diversity) then the dilemma loses its force. In order to understand why Kukathas believes that the value of social unity plays an exaggerated role in contemporary liberal thought and should, therefore, be put in its place, we need to have a brief look at his alternative conception of liberalism. Kukathas's central proposal is to award tolerance of individual and group diversity unconditional priority over all other supposed values that liberals might care about.

1.2 The Liberal Archipelago and Kukathas's State

Kukathas's version of liberalism rests on a specific conception of human nature informed by David Hume's moral psychology.[39] This conception of fundamental assumptions concerning human interests and motives (governing human conduct) is a moral, however at the same time, strictly "minimal" one. Kukathas accepts Rawls's claim that even a political version of liberalism cannot do entirely without normative assumptions and arguments. However, these assumptions must be as minimal as possible in the sense of "uncontroversial": "The theory advanced in this work defends a kind of political liberalism [...]. [I]t tries to account for what is important for all human beings in order to explain why a liberal political order [...] is one that all persons can have sufficient reason to accept."[40] Kukathas believes to have identified such a universally acceptable minimal moral conception in Hume's account of motivation: "Human beings are the same the world over, [...]. Hume's thought suggests three primary motives that account for human action: *(self-) interest, affection,* and *principle.*"[41]

A critical analysis of these assumptions is put to one side here and we move on to the normative conclusion Kukathas draws from this particular conception of human agency. Of all the possible human interests that political theory may be concerned with, it is the interest not to act contrary to one's conscience that Kukathas singles out as the most fundamental one: "The most important source of human motivation is principle – or, better still, *conscience*. [...] [C]onscience is what not only guides us (for the most part), but what we think *should* guide us. [A]ll humans have a sense of propriety or, more broadly, a moral sense which governs their conduct."[42]

Far from resting on a relativistic conception of basic interests then, Kukathas takes the interest of not being forced to act against one's conception of right and wrong as the universal foundation of his liberal political theory. Other interests, such as leading an autonomous (self-determined) life or pursuing a particular religion, are too controversial and cannot provide the basis for justifying the liberal archipelago. Only our interest in living in accordance with

---

39 See Kukathas 2003, pp. 41–73.

40 Kukathas 2003, p. 17.

41 Kukathas 2003, p. 43.

42 Kukathas 2003, p. 48. Spinner-Halev is right when he says: "Unfortunately, Kukathas does not say much about where conscience comes from. In a surprisingly brief passage, [...], Kukathas does say that it may be that the commands of conscience have a social origin and can be taught. [...] Saying more about the origins of conscience would help the reader determine how important conscience ought to be to liberalism" (Spinner-Halev 2005, pp. 595–596).

the dictates of conscience is shared universally enough to provide an uncontroversial starting point for answering Kukathas's central question of what a liberal society must look like in the face of perpetual diversity and pluralism.

Kukathas justifies the exclusive status of the value of individual freedom of conscience on the basis of his exposition of fundamental human interests and motives. A liberal society that takes the value of tolerance seriously cannot commit itself to anything more than to the enforcement of rights, liberties, and obligations that are necessary to protect the universally shared interest in living in accordance with one's conscience. Liberal states that attempt to promote (and enforce) more substantial conceptions of social and political justice (on the basis of a more controversial set of human interests) are incompatible with the kind of cultural, religious, and social diversity that emerges in a truly free society.[43] Kukathas, in rejecting contemporary liberalism's commitment to such more substantial views, further justifies this narrow focus on freedom of conscience by reminding us of the historical roots of classical liberalism. Referring to Locke and Bayle's writings on religious toleration, Kukathas formulates his political theory around the idea that the freedom to live and act in accordance with one's conscience is the crucial condition for the peaceful coexistence of fundamentally diverse cultural, religious, and social associations within one liberal society. Contemporary liberals have more or less ignored this basic liberal commitment when they invest the state with a much richer and more active political agenda that presumes, unrealistically, an overlap of interests that goes beyond freedom of conscience.[44]

Kukathas goes on to point out how freedom of conscience implies a specific requirement for any viable liberal political order. Freedom of conscience (combined with the assumption that human life takes on the form of social relationships) makes necessary a derived freedom, namely the freedom to associate with and (more importantly) the freedom to dissociate from others:

---

43 As mentioned in the text, Kukathas presents his work as being primarily directed at Will Kymlicka's theory of multicultural citizenship. While Kymlicka is certainly the focus of Kukathas's attack (the latter's opposition to minority and group rights is a central theme in *The Liberal Archipelago*) Rawls's *Political Liberalism*, with its focus on the issue of legitimacy in the face of diversity, often provides the better foil. This becomes especially clear when Kukathas describes contemporary liberalism's dilemma of reconciling a minimum of social cohesion ("overlapping consensus") with classical liberalism's commitment to individual liberties. For a good account of the way in which Rawls came to appreciate as the most important ones the very issues that Kukathas deals with, see Estlund 1996.

44 See Kukathas 2003, p. 262.

> In general terms, freedom of association exists when individuals are free to leave the group or community or enterprise of which they are a part. This is important because, ultimately, what matters is that people not be required to live in or be a part of ways they think wrong, or to participate in practices which (morally) they cannot abide. People should be free to live as conscience dictates; and not be required to violate conscience.[45]

Freedom of association does, of course, have its place in contemporary liberal theory in a similar way as freedom of conscience does. However, Kukathas's emphasis on these two freedoms, and especially his claim that *only* those two are the cornerstones of a viable liberal theory, render the liberal archipelago into a distinct representative of liberalism.[46] This distinctness becomes even more visible once some of the policy recommendations and the archipelago's institutional design are examined in more detail.

As mentioned above, the liberal archipelago is also a kind of political community and even admits the necessity of a state – Kukathas grants his opponents that much. The particular social, cultural, and religious associations (the archipelago's islands) are loosely connected with each other by populating "a sea of mutual toleration," at other points described as "a sea of indifference."[47] This society is liberal because the state, guaranteeing the peaceful coexistence among these associations, fulfills the function of a mere "umpire."[48] Kukathas says: "[T]he point about an umpire is that his concern is not to determine the outcome of the game; it is simply to keep the game going by adjudicating when conflicts or disputes arise."[49] Kukathas is quick to emphasize that the state is just one among many umpires populating the archipelago (and one with an especially restricted set of powers). Moreover, the liberal state must not be misconceived as occupying a superior position in a hierarchical system of authorities (and this non-specialness of the liberal state will be of great importance for the critical evaluation of Kukathas's right to exit and the consequences it has for the realizability of the liberal archipelago). Moon sums up Kukathas's view succinctly, employing Max Weber's language that will be discussed in a moment: "[T]he state, or the larger political community, is just one among the various partial associations of society and is not superior to the others – it certainly does not possess sovereign authority. [...] Evidently, then, in his view the state

45 Kukathas 2003, p. 95.

46 For two criticisms of this overly narrow focus on the freedoms of conscience and association and Kukathas's neglect of other, possibly overriding, classical liberal liberties, see Klosko 2005, p. 146 and Moon 2005, pp. 423–424.

47 Kukathas 2003, p. 22 and p. 137.

48 See Kukathas 2003, pp. 212–214.

49 Kukathas 2003, p. 213.

will not have a monopoly of the legitimate use of violence."[50] The diminished liberal state is defined in terms of a small number of functions it is supposed (and restricted) to perform, namely securing peace between the associations on the one hand and protecting and enforcing one individual right, namely the right to exit these associations on the other.[51]

According to Kukathas, the right to exit one's association is the only "inalienable right" the protection of which is the liberal state's task.

> Recognition [of an association's authority by not electing to leave it; C.H.] in these austere terms would, of course, be meaningless without the individual having one important right against the community: the right to leave the community. If there are any fundamental rights, this has to be that right. It is an inalienable right, and one which holds regardless of whether the community recognizes it as such. It would also be the individual's only fundamental right, all other rights being either derivative of this right, or rights granted by the community.[52]

The right to exit then ensures that individual members can leave an association's jurisdiction if they wish to do so – it is a corollary of freedom of association (and disassociation) mentioned above. And even with respect to this already unusually narrow scope of state-enforced rights, Kukathas imposes further qualifications. The negative right to exit is to be secured in purely formal terms. For example, that the costs of leaving illiberal associations can be extremely high (materially and otherwise) does not nullify an individual's freedom to leave: "[E]xit may, indeed, be costly; but the individual may still be free to decide whether or not to bear the cost. The magnitude of the cost does not affect the freedom."[53] Moreover, not wishing to leave as the result of indoctrination and manipulation is of no concern to the liberal umpire supervising the liberal archipelago. Were the state to interfere with the internal affairs of its associations in order to secure their members' right to exit in a more positive and proactive manner and were it to enforce more comprehensive rights and liberties (speech, religion, education, health etc.), it would pursue the kind of social

---

50 Moon 2005, p. 424.

51 For the criticism that Kukathas's state is too thin to successfully perform even those two functions see my discussion of Levey and Spinner-Halev's objections at the end of section 2.2.

52 Kukathas 2003, p. 96.

53 Kukathas 2003, p. 107. Kukathas's Humean assumptions are also noticeable in his purely instrumentalist conception of agency, resulting in his strict rejection of judging even clear-cut cases of indoctrination as objectionable: "Freedom is a matter not of what preferences [people; C.H.] have but of whether they may act in accordance with them" (Kukathas 2003, p. 109). Freedom of conscience is neither concerned with the moral status of agents' ends nor with how they acquired and developed them.

unification and engineering that Kukathas thinks unavoidably results in intolerance and oppression.

Amongst the many issues that critics find noteworthy about Kukathas's vision of liberalism, the implementation of the right to exit has provoked most disagreement. In particular, the case of children, who find themselves oppressed in totalitarian associations, has irritated commentators.[54] We need to keep in mind that as long as individuals "acquiesce" to the authority of whatever association they are subject to, and as long as they do not actively attempt to disassociate, the only workable liberal requirement of legitimacy is satisfied. Kukathas's thin notion of legitimacy is a corollary of the fundamental right to exit. This is the only right that every inhabitant of the archipelago has, independently of her membership in its specific associations. An authority that does not honor the right to exit and physically prevents its subjects from leaving is illegitimate. About the right to exit Kukathas therefore says: "The right to exit is, in fact, nothing more or less than the right to repudiate authority. [...] No authority has the right to prevent anyone from dissociating from the community and seeking to leave it."[55] Moon's summary is well-taken: "[S]o long as the groups involved (including the state itself) are successful in commanding the 'acquiescence' of their members, they are legitimate, and this rather undemanding notion of legitimacy trumps considerations of justice."[56]

Kukathas does not spell out the specific policies reigning in the liberal archipelago explicitly, but it is clear that the liberal umpire can only interfere with associations when individual members are physically prevented from leaving. Acquiescing to an association's authority because one is merely threatened with sanctions by an authority still counts as conferring legitimacy on the specific authority-relationship between this association and the individual member.[57]

54 See Klosko 2005, pp. 145–146 and Moon 2005, p. 424.

55 Kukathas 2003, p. 97. Also see the following passages, extensively discussed when Kukathas's notion of legitimacy is compared with Weber's: "[A]ssociations have authority over their members, for as long as those members recognize as legitimate the terms of their associations, and the authority that upholds them. All that is necessary as evidence of such recognition is that members elect not to leave" (Kukathas 2003, p. 96).

56 Moon 2005, 422. Moon's quote is important for my purposes for two reasons. Firstly, it makes clear how similar Kukathas's criterion of legitimacy is to Weber's thin standard of when a social relationship counts as one of "legitimate authority." (See section 2.1.) Secondly, and this point will be crucial for the final critique of Kukathas, notice that Moon rightly counts "the state itself" as an institution, to the authority of which one can acquiesce and that is therefore on a par with all the other partial associations that Kukathas talks about. (See section 9.1.)

57 It remains a puzzling question what Kukathas would say about an association that successfully ensures that, let us say, its female members are not even aware of having the right to exit

Liberals criticized by Kukathas object that such an interpretation of freedom of association (and disassociation) is not robust enough since the liberal archipelago rules out any more substantial public provisions intended to guarantee the right to exit, such as compulsory public (and civic) education.[58] For Kukathas, on the other hand, to live in accordance with the dictates of one's conscience, which is every individual's most fundamental interest, is sufficiently secured in his ideal society as long as the liberal umpire protects the right of each individual to leave her association. Universal acquiescence to *de facto* authorities, for whatever reasons, is a necessary and sufficient condition for requiring the liberal state to remain completely passive with respect to associations' internal affairs.

In concluding this exposition of Kukathas's theory of liberal toleration I want to draw attention to the extent to which Max Weber's framework provides a conceptual basis for the liberal archipelago and Kukathas's worries concerning contemporary liberalism. As will be spelled out in more detail in the next chapter, Kukathas formulates his critique of contemporary liberalism with reference to a specific conception of the modern state, understood as a monopoly of the legitimate use of violence within a so-called "compulsory association." The main reason why the liberal state (as envisioned by Kukathas's adversaries) clashes with tolerance is that it monopolizes coercion and uses this monopoly to enforce substantial views of justice. One thing to note first though is that Kukathas's liberal umpire also remains well within this definition of the state. Kukathas's state claims to successfully monopolize coercion with respect to the enforcement of the right to exit. If an individual wants to leave her association and is physically prevented from doing so, the state is required to make use of its monopolized power and must protect the individual's freedom of (dis-) association by enforcing the right to exit.

---

their suppressive associations. Kukathas's discussion of the example of the Muslim woman Fatima is especially relevant here. (See Kukathas 2003, p. 113.) After all, Kukathas rejects a policy permitting the liberal state to actively spread this information amongst members of such communities. Under these circumstances acquiescence can certainly be secured and, in accordance with Kukathas's readiness to accept quite radical policies that are hostile to autonomy, one expects the liberal archipelago to accept such a case as one of genuine acquiescence. Kukathas discusses why the costs of exiting, even if very high and taking on the form of harsh sanctions, do not impact the freedom to leave one's association, see Kukathas 2003, pp. 107–114. Of additional interest is Kukathas's recent exchange with Pettit concerning Hobbes's definition of freedom. (See Kukathas 2009, p. 193 and Pettit 2009.)

58 See Barry 2001, pp. 238–249.

Viewed from this angle Kukathas does not necessarily invoke a substantially different conception of the liberal state than the one that mainstream liberals do, who similarly presuppose Weber's highly influential conceptual framework. Rather, the liberal archipelago's state is merely "quantitatively" different since it is invested with a minimal set of public powers with respect to which it holds a monopoly of enforcement. Since even the liberal umpire claims at least this monopoly, however, Kukathas cannot avoid the problem of achieving some *minimal* degree of social unity and overlapping acquiescence on the part of the individual associations (and their members) in question.

It is not entirely clear what Kukathas would propose to do with respect to associations and their members that refuse to acquiesce to the liberal umpire's authority. If he accepts the other main feature of the Weberian state, namely its compulsory nature, then Kukathas would actually have to allow the liberal umpire an exclusive and strong privilege. This privilege would consist in coercively prohibiting dissenting associations (and their members) from leaving the authority of the umpire's jurisdiction and from forming their own states. Individuals can leave their associations if they wish to do so, but associations cannot leave the "sea of tolerance" itself. The problem with this asymmetrical application of the right to exit is that it would create exactly the kind of hierarchical inequality between the state on the one hand and all other associations on the other that Kukathas promised to avoid. By allowing the monopolization of the enforcement of the right to exit *combined* with the state's compulsory character, the liberal archipelago would fail to provide a principled (as opposed to a merely gradual) solution to contemporary liberalism's struggle with tolerating thorough-going diversity. By granting the state not to have to apply the right to exit to itself, so to speak, Kukathas runs into the same problems that contemporary liberals are confronted with when they try to solve the puzzle of how a diverse society can exist within *one* political and legal framework. Oppression of at least some diversity and pluralism will be the result, even in the liberal archipelago when the liberal umpire is invested with the privilege of monopolizing legitimate violence with respect to the right to exit. The liberal umpire is then enforcing individual freedom of conscience and the right to exit with respect to those associations that consider such policies unacceptably liberal and individualistic, while at the same time forcing these illiberal associations to stay within its jurisdiction. In other words, also Kukathas seems to have to allow his version of the liberal state to enforce some level of legal unity and it is this public activity that conflicts with unrestricted respect for individual and associational diversity in the liberal archipelago.

Alternatively, Kukathas might conceive of the liberal state as just another voluntary association[59] (a *Verein* in Weber's terminology) in which every association can leave the archipelago (and escape the reach of the umpire's authority) whenever they want to do so. This reading puts the umpire on a par with all other partial associations and citizenship in the liberal state does not stand out as a unique element of the Archipelagoans' identity – exactly as Kukathas thinks it should be in a truly liberal society.[60]

The problem with this non-compulsory conception is that the state is now so thin and weak that it cannot even enforce the right to exit on behalf of "its citizens." Associations can declare independence, leave the archipelago, and "lock up" their members in their newly established sovereign states in case the umpire threatens to enforce the right to exit by invading the associations' jurisdictions. This is especially likely given the kind of totalitarian and illiberal associations that Kukathas allows to flourish within the liberal archipelago.[61] Moreover, as one commentator points out in a similar vein, "there is no reason to think that some states won't divide around just a few ethnic or national lines, which is common enough today."[62] There seems to be little reason for an association not to take this small but decisive final step, i.e., to leave the archipelago's jurisdiction altogether and become a sovereign state.

Again, it is not clear what Kukathas's thoughts are concerning the state's compulsory nature. I shall discuss it in more detail below and show that Weber's conceptual framework allows more nuanced conceptions of the state-citizen relationship. Clearer is Kukathas's suggestion that in the liberal archipelago a diversity of overlapping jurisdictions and political authorities will be present. Translated into Weber's terms, the liberal society envisioned is an oligopoly of legitimate violence. The examples of the United States and the European Union are mentioned in order to illustrate this aspect of the archipelago.

---

59 Since Weber is explicit that the state is an exemplar of "compulsory associations" this alternative would be a distinctively un-Weberian rendering of Weber's definition of the state. As will be made clear at many points in this investigation, Weber (like Kant) insists on the compulsory nature of modern states for good reasons, above all it being a necessary condition for the rule of law.

60 The conception of citizenship that emerges from Kukathas's theory will be discussed in section 2.2.

61 Seceding from the archipelago will be especially tempting to illiberal associations which face the threat of many members wanting to make use of their right to exit. Such societies would then quickly declare their independence, erect impervious borders, and prevent their members from leaving. Problems like these generate additional (not merely practical) concerns regarding Kukathas's ideal society.

62 Spinner-Halev 2005, pp. 596.

Given the diminished role that the liberal state is supposed to play, Kukathas's view suggests that the determination of what counts as legitimate use of violence is located to a larger extent with the associations populating the archipelago. Another question that will be addressed below is, to what extent a multiplication of such authorities really constitutes a successful strategy to alleviate Kukathas's worries about individuals' freedom being threatened by coercive institutions.

Chapter 2: The Liberal State and Liberal Citizens

So far we have seen Kukathas present his vision of an ideal liberal society as a more satisfying response to contemporary liberalism's value dilemma. His solution puts the values of political unity and stability into, he believes, their right place by emphasizing that a liberal society can and should basically do without them. Given thorough-going diversity and pluralism this is the only way to provide "a principled basis of a free society" that does not clash with the value of tolerance and freedom of individual conscience. A closer look at Max Weber's conceptual framework (state-power-authority) helps to better understand Kukathas's objection to the goal of unifying diverse populations into a political society. It is Weber's influential definition of the state as the possessor of the monopoly of legitimate force that drives Kukathas's skepticism concerning the prospects that contemporary liberalism can resolve the tension between the two values of tolerance and social unity. In response to Kukathas this chapter's first section (2.1) argues that Weber's conceptual framework is compatible with a liberal state not exhibiting intolerance. Neither the feature of "monopolizing legitimate force" nor "compulsory organization" render the liberal state necessarily incompatible with the value of tolerance.

Implications concerning the issue of citizenship are then extracted from Kukathas's critique of contemporary liberalism and from his positive theory (2.2). *The Liberal Archipelago* does not discuss this issue extensively but many of the topics that are addressed (the role of state-institutions, the conceptions of community, membership and identity) provide the basis for a conception of shared citizenship (or lack thereof) in the liberal archipelago. Kukathas rejects David Miller's conception of "modest nationalism" and critically examines the work on national sovereignty by Raz and Margalit. These discussions are an important source for explicating a Kukathasian account of citizenship. This chapter concludes by discussing a couple of critical responses to Kukathas. His extremely thin conception of citizenship generates some problems that foreshadow the comprehensive reply presented in Chapter 3.

2.1 Weber's Conceptual Framework Revisited

One might ask in response to the dilemma presented in the previous chapter, what exactly is so problematic about advocating a minimal degree of social unity concerning the basic structure of liberal societies? Why does the project of achieving political cohesion in the form of the liberal state necessarily lead to intolerance? In order to answer these questions one has to have a closer look at *The Liberal Archipelago's* conception of the liberal state. Investing the state (even a liberal one that honors constitutionally guaranteed civil rights, institutional checks and balances, and a democratically legitimized government) with the authority to achieve the goal of social unification is regarded as problematic by Kukathas because enforcing social unity becomes a self-serving task for the state. Constricting pluralism becomes a matter of the state's own "survival" and integrity (in Dworkin's sense discussed above). Kukathas suggests that the state's response to this threat of factionalization is the use of force to level out cultural, ethnic, and political diversity. Kukathas's view of the modern state, as an institution that necessarily exhibits these tendencies for unification, homogenization, and, eventually, oppression is informed by Max Weber's influential account.

Kukathas mentions Weber only once in *The Liberal Archipelago*. The reference in question comes, however, at a crucial point, namely in the concluding discussion concerning the prospects of his vision of a liberal society to get realized under real-world conditions.[63] Kukathas agrees that

> [t]he march of the twentieth century has been down the road of rationalization, heading in a direction Max Weber thought unalterable, towards the creation of the modern sovereign state. This is an entity which is not only territorial but also internally sovereign, recognizing no higher authority within its borders, and maintaining its right to hold a monopoly of violence.[64]

Kukathas does not agree with Weber's judgment about the unalterable character of the historical trajectory. The liberal archipelago is a true political option even though its realization is unlikely in the near future given the expansionist tendencies of real-world (liberal) states and governments. Even so, Weber's definition of the state, mentioned in the quoted passage, is clearly providing the

63 With respect to Kukathas's *The Liberal Archipelago* it is interesting to discover significant parallels with Nozick's *Anarchy, State, and Utopia*. Nozick is even more explicit in relying on a Weberian definition of the state. (See Nozick 1974, pp. 23 & 117–118.) Kukathas's worries about the liberal state are strongly reminiscent of Nozick's discussion of "protective associations" and whether or not they match the definition of the state as an institution based on monopolizing physical force. Even more striking is the extent to which Kukathas's positive view of the liberal archipelago, discussed in section 1.2, echoes *Anarchy, State, and Utopia*'s third and final part ("Utopia"), often overlooked in discussions of Nozick. Just one suggestive passage: "Though the framework is libertarian and laissez-faire, *individual communities within it need not be*, and perhaps no community within it will choose to be so" (Nozick 1974, p. 320).
64 Kukathas 2003, p. 269.

background for Kukathas's critical assessment of mainstream liberalism and the latter's reliance on the democratic state to implement conceptions of political and social justice.

Kukathas's skepticism concerning social unity in the form of the liberal state is better understood once Weber's influential definitions of core sociological terms are revisited. There are, however, more reasons for engaging in this task. Weber's definitions of core concepts such as "state," "power," and "authority" have had a strong influence on political theorists and philosophers not just social scientists. In fact, this influence is so thoroughgoing that Weber's framework (similar to Hobbes's conception of sovereignty) is often tacitly assumed in theories employing the concept of the Westphalian state.[65] Moreover, Kukathas's discussion of contemporary liberalism rests on the assumption that such a homogeneous conception of the state is shared by the otherwise diverse theories of liberalism that he attacks. This homogeneity makes it possible to criticize the major representatives of contemporary liberalism on similar grounds and by means of employing similar arguments. The ubiquitousness of Weber's seminal descriptive definition of the state provides a common ground that contemporary liberals and their critics such as Kukathas share.

The central feature of Weber's conceptual framework is his definition of the state. The modern state "successfully upholds the claim to the *monopoly* of the *legitimate* use of physical force in the enforcement of its order."[66] The monopoly concerning the determination of who is and who is not entitled to coerce members of society (i.e., who can do so "legitimately") is what Kukathas refers to when he quotes the territorial and internal sovereignty characteristic of the modern state.[67] It is especially this feature of a sovereign monopoly of physical

65 This is not a criticism of Kukathas but rather a more general observation about the use of Weber's terminology and conceptual framework.

66 Weber 1978 (1921), p. 54. For an important Anglophone clarification of Weber's complex definition of the state and its elements, see Dusza 1989.

67 See Morris 1998, pp. 43–44. This monopoly is compatible with other institutions in society (e.g., the family) enforcing orders. The crucial point is that these other institutions' permission to use physical force is contingent on the state issuing and upholding this privilege. Weber's example concerns parents' permission to physically castigate their children: "[T]oday the use of force is regarded as legitimate only so far as it is either permitted by the state or prescribed by it. Thus the right of a father to discipline his children is recognized – a survival of the former independent authority of the head of a household, which in the right to use force has sometimes extended to a power of life and death over children and slaves. The claim of the modern state to monopolize the use of force is as essential to it as its character of compulsory jurisdiction and of continuous operation" (Weber 1978 (1921), p. 56). We will come back to this important observation concerning the family in section 7.2.

coercion that underlies Kukathas's argument that the liberal state, which after all is such a modern state, necessarily stands in a strained relationship to the value of tolerance when it enforces a unifying set of norms on a heterogeneous group of individuals and associations.

In the course of presenting the response to Kukathas's state-skepticism and its relationship to Weber's conceptual framework, two claims will be made. Firstly, and this will be shown in the third chapter, the feature of having to settle the question of what counts as a legitimate use of force is an inescapable characteristic of every social structure (even Kukathas's social, cultural, and religious associations) insofar as they face the task of confronting certain challenges that emerge whenever individuals live in proximity to each other. Secondly, and this is the task of the remainder of this section, it is not entirely clear that a Weberian conceptual framework necessarily implies the state's incompatibility with the value of liberal tolerance – especially when the latter is regarded as being honored sufficiently when individuals merely acquiesce to authorities in the way Kukathas supposes. In what follows we have to distinguish two possible instantiations of Weber's state-conception: one is based on sheer "power," the other manifests "authority." In order to see that Kukathas's attack on the liberal state is convincing only if the first of these two state-conceptions is assumed, we have to look at Weber's analysis of "power" (*Macht*) on the one hand and "legitimate authority," "domination," and "rule" (all three different translations of *Herrschaft*) on the other, and apply them to the "state" as defined above.

Weber distinguishes sheer "power" from "legitimate authority." The former constitutes the most brute (in both senses of basic and violent) form of how a social order can be established and maintained. "Power" is defined as "the likelihood that one person in a social relationship will be able, even despite resistance, to carry out his own will [...]."[68] A successful instantiation of power does not require any proactive compliance, let alone consent (or acquiescence), on the part of those who are subject to the party exerting power. The exercise of sheer power is a one-directional process. Individuals and groups that are at the receiving end of a power-relationship can be entirely passive in their practical deliberation leading up to the performance of the dictated behavior.

---

68 Weber 2005, p. 179. A thoroughgoing analysis of the difficulties involved in finding an adequate English translation of Weber's conception of "power" is presented in Wallimann et. al. 1980.

"Legitimate authority" (or "rule") is distinguished from power.[69] Authority is conditional on subjective attitudes of obedience and, hence, some level of "cooperation" (rather, non-resistance) on part of the parties subject to the command-issuing entity. We need to keep in mind at this point that Weber's conceptual framework lies at the heart of a strictly "value-free" analysis of social relationships. Accordingly, the definition of authority reads as follows: Authority (*Herrschaft*) "is defined as the probability [*Chance*; C.H.] that a command with a given specific content will be obeyed by a given group of persons."[70] A social relationship counts as one based on authority only if the individuals or groups asked to obey its orders regard this authority as minimally justified, in the sense of "worth obeying." As soon as addressees refuse to obey the authority but the orders are nevertheless efficaciously imposed, the relationship in question turns into one based on sheer power. Hence, Weber's conception of "authority" adds an element of voluntariness and legitimacy to the social relationship in question. However, one should not expect a normatively rich conception of legitimacy at this point. It is, of course, *compatible* with Weber's conception of authority that subjects attribute a significant degree of legitimacy to the source of commands. For example, citizens' attitudes might amount to them reflectively endorsing those commands as being well justified from a sophisticated justificatory viewpoint of political morality and some shared substantial theory of justice.

Even so, Weber's notion of legitimacy is certainly not restricted to such scenarios of actively endorsed and supported authority. Weber has something much less demanding in mind when he distinguishes power from authority: "In general, it should be kept clearly in mind that the basis of every authority, and correspondingly of every kind of willingness to obey, is a *belief*, a belief by virtue of which persons exercising authority are lent prestige."[71] Whether this belief (and the compliance based on it) on the part of the subjects is the result of tradition, outright manipulation and indoctrination, or some process of autonomous self-legislation is of no relevance to the notion of legitimacy in play here.

---

69 As Kalberg emphasizes, Weber's term "*Herrschaft*" is perhaps the concept most difficult to translate adequately into English. (See Kalberg 2005, p. 177, n. 1.) Earlier translations tended to use the concept "domination," which, because of its rather negative connotation, neglects the crucial fact that authority, according to Weber's definition discussed in the text, rests on legitimacy-granting subjective beliefs held by the subjects. In order to preserve this element of legitimacy the concepts of "rule," "rulership," and "legitimate authority" are preferable translations of "*Herrschaft*."

70 Weber 1978 (1921), p. 53.

71 Weber 1978 (1921), p. 263.

Stephen Kalberg summarizes Weber's distinction between power and authority succinctly: "Because they are rooted in a belief, legitimate authority relationships to Weber are more enduring and stable than power relationships, which rest on force alone."[72]

It is especially at this point that we can see why exploring Weber's influential framework is relevant for evaluating Kukathas's project. Remember how *The Liberal Archipelago's* central notion of "acquiescence" is concerned with how the individual members sustain an association as a legitimate authority simply by deciding not to leave its jurisdiction. As in Weber, the content of the associations' constitutive norms (whether they are just, in the egalitarian liberals' sense for example) is not at all necessary for determining whether this minimal standard of legitimacy is satisfied; what matters for both Weber and Kukathas is that the relationship between an authority and its subjects takes on a certain form, characterized by the presence of prestige granting subjective beliefs and the absence of a subjective desire to exit respectively. All that matters for this form of social ordering to be successfully instantiated are certain subjective attitudes towards the ruling authority. In order to clarify the claim that Weber's and Kukathas's notions of legitimacy are similar and similarly thin (despite the fact that Weber employs his notion in a purely descriptive analysis of social relationships and Kukathas does so with respect to a normative account of authority[73]), Weber's notion of "legitimate authority" must be further contrasted with "power." In addition, these two notions will be conjoined with Weber's definition of the state. The purpose of this exploration of Weber's conceptual framework is to prepare an objection to Kukathas (fully developed in Chapter 3), namely, that the modern state itself (and not only the archipelago's associations) can be the object of acquiescence. In other words, nothing in Weber's account of the state (and its monopolization of coercion) necessitates the emergence of the dilemma that Kukathas sees contemporary liberalism confronted

---

72 Kalberg 2005, p. 174.

73 At first sight, it might appear confused to argue for a strong resemblance between Weber's and Kukathas's notions of legitimate authority because the former is employed in a purely non-normative context. I assume in the text that this important difference is no hindrance to identifying a significant conceptual overlap between the two that allows to develop the critical question that will eventually be directed at Kukathas, i.e., why cannot the modern state itself be the proper subject of acquiescing attitudes on part of its citizens and, hence, be a legitimate authority? The presence of certain subjective beliefs vis-à-vis an authority that lead its subjects to stay put (by not making use of their right to exit in Kukathas's theory) is a legitimacy criterion that can be employed in both descriptive and normative analyses. I thank Jonathan Miller for asking me to clarify this point.

with. On the other hand, and this simply is the flip side of this objection, all the problems that come with such a monopolization of force will be an issue in the independent associations of the archipelago too (at least once they are as sovereign as Kukathas wants them to be).[74]

First, however, let us refine our understanding of Weber's and Kukathas's accounts of legitimate authority. According to Kukathas, as long as individuals do not actively resist their association's sovereignty and do not attempt to exit its jurisdiction they count as acquiescing to the authority in question and thereby legitimize it: "[A]ssociations have authority over their members, for as long as those members recognize as legitimate the terms of their associations, and the authority that upholds them. All that is necessary as evidence of such recognition is that members elect not to leave."[75] The particular source of acquiescence (fear, manipulation, reflective endorsement) does not matter – neither for Kukathas nor for Weber. All that matters is the presence of subjective beliefs and attitudes on part of the subjects. In addition, with respect to individual freedom of conscience (and the justification of an individual who appeals to the right to exit) it is irrelevant whether or not, in a 100-person society, 99 persons acquiesce to the state's authority. The one dissenting individual stands in a Weberian relationship of mere "power," not legitimate authority, to her state or association. How many of her co-citizens are and are not in this same kind of relationship does not have an impact on the quality of hers.

With this contrast between legitimate authority and power in mind, let us now return to the liberal archipelago's critique of contemporary liberalism and its reliance on a Weberian state. Remember, it has been contemporary liberals' presupposing the modern state (understood as a monopoly of violence) combined with their commitment to pluralism and tolerance that caused the initial dilemma that Kukathas sees liberals confronted with. Let us begin by stating Weber's seminal definition of the state in its entirety: "A compulsory political organization with continuous operations (*politischer Anstaltsbetrieb*) will be called a 'state' insofar as its administrative staff successfully upholds the claim to the *monopoly* of the *legitimate* use of physical force in the enforcement of its order."[76] For the purpose of applying Weber's framework to Kukathas's debate

---

74 This exercise is going beyond a mere interpretation of Weber. The application of the notions of "legitimate authority" and "power" to his account of the state (resulting in two different manifestations of the latter) is supported by remarks in Pakulski 1986. I am indebted to Fred Miller for asking me to clarify the nature of this extension of Weber's framework.

75 Kukathas 2003, p. 96.

76 Weber 1978 (1921), p. 54.

about the liberal state and social unity, two issues, implicit in this definition, are worth closer examination.

Firstly, with respect to the assumption, apparently shared by most contemporary liberals that societies are assumed to be "closed," Weber's conception of a "*politischer Anstaltsbetrieb*" is relevant.[77] Immediately before introducing his definition of the state, Weber draws an important distinction between two categories of social institutions. There are "voluntary associations" (*Verein*) on the one hand and "compulsory associations" (*Anstalt*) on the other, the state being the prime example of the latter.[78] The potentially problematic nature of the state, with respect to tolerance of internal diversity, finds one of its clearest suggestions (though Weber does not explicitly deal with the non-descriptive issue of tolerance in the way Kukathas does) in the exposition of the distinction between voluntary and involuntary associations:

> [I]nsofar as an organization has rationally established rules, it is either a voluntary or a compulsory association. Compulsory organizations are, above all, the state with its subsidiary heterocephalous organizations, and the church insofar as its order is rationally established. The order governing a compulsory association claims to be binding on all persons to whom the particular relevant criteria apply – such as birth, residence, or the use of certain facilities. It makes no difference whether the individual joined voluntarily; nor does it matter whether he has taken any part in establishing the order. It is thus a case of imposed order in the most definite sense. Compulsory associations are frequently territorial organizations.[79]

Kukathas's critique of the liberal state reflects the feature of involuntariness (e.g., membership by birth) emphasized in Weber's descriptive account of a compulsory association. *Insofar* as the contemporary liberals' conception of the state overlaps with this understanding of compulsion it finds itself in the strained relationship with tolerance concerning internal diversity. Compulsory membership, subjecting groups and individuals to an *inescapable* monopoly of force, seems to conflict with the liberal values of tolerance and freedom of conscience. And since Kukathas's target, the liberal state, seems to share this feature of Weber's definition it follows that the contemporary liberal state too must conflict with tolerance.

---

77 See Dusza 1989, pp. 76–77.

78 Weber, 1978 (1921), p. 52. The *Anstaltsbetrieb*'s conceptual component "*Betrieb*" is defined as "[c]ontinuous rational activity of a specified kind." An *Anstaltbetrieb* is therefore such a continuous rational activity executed within a compulsory association.

79 Weber 1978 (1921), pp. 52–53.

But does the liberal state necessarily exhibit this feature of a compulsory association? And does Weber's "compulsory membership" neatly fit with, for example, Rawls's notion of a closed well-ordered society, the latter being a crucial example of the kind of liberal society that Kukathas rejects? The issue of "compulsory membership" will be discussed in more detail below, when attention is drawn to the fact that real-world liberal states allow their citizens to emigrate. Kukathas's objection from intolerance is weakened already when we keep in mind that even imperfect real-world liberal states do not prevent those who are initially singled out for citizenship by "birth, residence, or the use of certain facilities" from leaving. For the moment let us just submit the observation that the "compulsion" in Weber's state-definition is a less dramatic (and literal) property in the case of liberal states. The latter do not erect Iron Curtains around their borders.[80]

The second state-feature that is worth closer examination concerns the monopolization of force. It is not the case that Weber's definition implies that the state necessarily involves sheer power as opposed to exhibiting legitimate authority relationships. Notice that even if membership in the modern state were strictly compulsory (as Kukathas seems to assume) that would not render legitimate authority in Weber's sense impossible. Why should not those individuals, subject to the liberal state of Rawls et al., share the kind of subjective beliefs necessary for Weberian legitimacy (and Kukathasian acquiescence)? A closer look at how the three Weberian conceptions discussed above (power, authority, and state) relate to one another clarifies this point. This closer look suggests that Kukathas's skepticism concerning contemporary liberalism rests on merely one instantiation of Weber's state-conception, namely the one based on power and power alone. Kukathas cannot object to the other instantiation, i.e., a state

---

80 Kukathas's argument against liberals striving to achieve "social unity" seems to lose a lot of its initial force once citizens of liberal democracies have the permission to leave their country in case they cannot reconcile the commands of their individual conscience on the one hand with the basic legal and constitutional norms of the state they live in on the other. The "right to exit" one's association (the single most basic right in Kukathas's liberal archipelago) *is* honored by liberal states. This is also the point of Walzer's reply to Kukathas saying that the liberal archipelago already exists, namely in the form of the international state system. In addition, it will be shown at the end of this part (section 3.2) that Kukathas's Weberian worry about closeness/compulsion of contemporary liberalism's state strongly rests on Rawls's notion of "closeness" built into the design of the original position. It must be noted, though this cannot be argued here in detail, that this Rawlsian closeness is, contrary to what Kukathas seems to suggest, *not* a recommendation concerning whether or not emigration should be an option for the citizens of a well-ordered society.

that stands in relationships of authority to its individual subjects wherein citizens develop and maintain prestige-lending attitudes.

To sum up more concisely, combining Weber's concept of the "state" on the one hand with "power" and "authority" on the other results in two possible state-conceptions: a) a state that rests on power alone and enforces policies and norms even in case its subjects do not maintain subjective beliefs that amount to regarding this state as minimally justified and resist, without success, this enforcement. And b) a state that rests on authority and enforces norms on individuals who, while not always necessarily agreeing with the content of every specific norm so enforced, hold a general subjective belief that lends the state the standing to successfully uphold its monopoly of legitimate violence across time.[81]

In concluding this discussion it is submitted that Kukathas's attack on the contemporary liberal state rests on "a" while it ignores the possibility of "b", a possibility that shows that the modern state is compatible with Kukathas's own criterion of legitimate authority, i.e., acquiescence. A state falling under description "b" can be an extremely unjust state but still be the object of acquiescing attitudes and beliefs. Remember that the feature that Kukathas's and Weber's notions of legitimate authority share is the undemandingly thin criterion that determines (descriptively and normatively respectively) when an institution counts as one that creates and enforces norms without relying on sheer power. All that is needed is subjective beliefs lending the authority prestige on the one hand and choosing not to leave the authorities reach on the other. The question then is, why does Kukathas readily grant the liberal archipelago's associations and their authorities that they can stand in such a relationship vis-à-vis their subjects while at the same time ruling out that modern states can do so as well and thereby become states like "b"? The dilemma outlined above (the tension between the two liberal values of tolerance and social unity) assumes that liberal states *unavoidably* conflict with the value of tolerance because they enforce norms against the commands of at least some individuals' conscience. The problem with this picture is not that it misrepresents real-world liberal poli-

81 I am indebted to David Shoemaker for urging me to clarify these two possible state-conceptions. It is important to note that the second conception, while based on an individual's affirmative attitude towards the source of the commands and norms that are addressed at her, does not make the enforcement of these commands and norms redundant. The issue of compliance with specific (legal) norms needs to be kept distinct from the question of general acquiescence to an authority. Hence, an individual can maintain prestige-granting beliefs with respect to her state, while still struggling with certain weaknesses of will on the one hand and uneasiness with how particular norms are formulated and enforced on the other.

tics (yes, the US government enforces the prohibition against polygamy also on those who would prefer to practice this life-style); rather, it leaves out the *possibility* of "b", i.e., a liberal state that does not conflict with the value of tolerance because its members' subjective beliefs render Weber's condition for legitimate authority satisfied. In order for the conception of the liberal state to *necessarily* conflict with tolerance, Kukathas has to presume an interpretation of Weber's definition, according to which the state is an institution based on power and not on legitimate authority. The target of Kukathas's critique is the liberal state understood as a compulsory and closed association which is ruled by sheer power, imposing norms on groups and individuals that consider these norms as violating their conscience. However, as was argued above, Kukathas takes from Weber's definition of the state the property of "compulsion" without at the same time acknowledging the possibility that such a compulsory association can be a legitimate authority in Weber's (and his own) thin sense.

Overall then, Kukathas's criticism of mainstream liberalism rests on a Weberian conception of the state – however, only partially so. Having reconstructed Weber's intricate conceptions of "power," "legitimate authority," and "the state" one sees that the conception of the liberal state, criticized by Kukathas, does not straightforwardly fit with these three definitions in all of their relevant combinations. It is true that the closeness of Rawls's well-ordered society *seems* to correspond well to one feature of Weber's definition of the state, namely its compulsory nature. However, even granted this assumption, Kukathas attributes a sheer power-based "monopoly of physical force" to the entity he describes as the modern liberal state when he introduces the conflict between political unity and tolerance. Unsurprisingly, this kind of state necessarily conflicts with individual freedom of conscience when it denies those subjects, who would rather leave the authority's reach completely than comply with its commands, the right to exit.[82] For example, Kukathas says about

82 In their reviews of *The Liberal Archipelago*, J. Donald Moon and George Klosko make a good methodological point about Kukathas's way of approaching political philosophy. (See Moon 2005, pp. 425–426 and Klosko 2005, p. 148.) Kukathas focuses on examples of radical pluralism in order to generate a situation of irresolvable conflict that renders feasible only a state based on sheer power: "[I]t is striking how infrequently he [Kukathas; C.H.] discusses the cultural practices of liberal societies. One reason his view would be inimical to the inhabitants of such societies is that he does not argue *from* their views. [...] [T]here should be some limit on the intuitions and examples that are considered. [...] If we accord equal weight to examples from all cultures, disagreement must result. It is in large part because Kukathas neglects the sensibilities of contemporary liberal citizens that his theory departs so sharply from them" (Klosko 2005, p. 148).

Dworkin's ideal liberal state (defended in Chapter 9 against Kukathas's objections) that "[i]t is a goal that could *only* be reached by suppressing diversity in a way that involved the 'oppressive use of state power'."[83] But why should this necessarily be the case?

Of course a state can be an instance of such an institution based on the suppressive use of power alone (type "a" above) – but it need not be. If legitimacy, in the descriptive sense of the presence of certain prestige-granting subjective beliefs (Kukathas's "recognizing as legitimate"), is absent in such a state then it will, as Kukathas envisages, necessarily suppress internal diversity and violate the liberal value of tolerance. However, the mainstream definition of the state is compatible with a conception of legitimate authority to an extent that Kukathas does not consider. More importantly, this version of legitimacy is achieved when citizens stand in the same relationship to their liberal states as acquiescing members of Kukathas's liberal archipelago do with respect to their associations. In other words, the conceptual framework employed in *The Liberal Archipelago* does not in and of itself suggest that what is good enough for the archipelago's social, religious, and cultural associations cannot equally well apply to citizens of contemporary liberal states. The members of the latter, despite significant political disagreements, in most cases *decide not to leave* their country of citizenship.

Thus, in the same way in which the liberal archipelago's cultural, religious, and social associations are dependent on their members' acquiescence, so is the modern state, especially the liberal one that Kukathas is attacking. It is, therefore, difficult to identify a qualitative difference between Kukathas's target on the one hand and the ideal associations of his liberal archipelago on the other, once the Weberian conceptual framework incorporates the difference between sheer power and legitimate authority. Insofar as this is the case, however, Kukathas's in-principle worries about state-intolerance are significantly tamed. And insofar as these worries remain a valid concern, it will be shown (after having talked about the liberal archipelago's views on citizenship) that they apply to the constituents of his preferred social arrangement (i.e., associations) too.

2.2 Liberal Citizenship as a Thin Public Identity

We now need to turn to Kukathas's account of how he conceives of the individual constituents populating his ideal liberal society. Kukathas's views about

83 Kukathas 2003, p. 181 (my emphasis).

citizenship must be reconstructed on the basis of dispersed arguments and discussions in his book. There is no explicit section on the status of citizenship. The gist of Kukathas's approach to liberal citizenship, however, is quite straightforwardly derivable from his theory of liberal toleration presented in the previous chapter and the exposition of his Weberian views on individuals' relationship to the public authority. To the same extent to which the liberal state plays a diminished role in structuring the lives of the liberal archipelago's inhabitants, the identity-constituting status of liberal citizenship gets reduced to a minimum. In fact, whether or not the inhabitants of the archipelago share a common self-understanding as citizens at all is not clear given the liberal state's role as a mere umpire that supervises the external dealings amongst the associations on the one hand and protects the individual right to exit on the other. Since mere acquiescence is required for associations to count as not violating their subjects' freedom of conscience, even individuals who are not fully aware of their membership in a wider liberal society (or know what such membership implies) do not therefore count as being subject to an illegitimate authority.

The standard case in the liberal archipelago will have individuals maintaining their identities primarily within the framework of their local associations' norms and values. The minimal liberal umpire, on the other hand, does not provide a rich enough basis of practical principles and norms for developing the normative self-conception (what will be called the "practical identity") of its citizens.[84] Spinner-Halev, whose reply to Kukathas focuses on the issue of citizenship, sums up: "Some liberals may object that we need some sort of unity in the liberal state in order to inculcate a sense of common citizenship. Kukathas goes on to argue, however, that there is no need for a common citizenship."[85] According to *The Liberal Archipelago* then, the public dimension of an agent's practical identity (the principle-governed and publicly established context within which her actions are performed) is developed and maintained primarily within the cultural and religious communities constituting the archipelago. Since these associations may be illiberal and undemocratic ones, the individuals living in Kukathas's maximally tolerant society will not necessarily perform actions in a context of the rule of law and other features central to liberal institutions.

In discussing recent work on this topic Kukathas indicates that this diminished role of citizenship is a welcome feature of the liberal archipelago. Spinner-

84 See Part 2 in which the conceptual framework employed in this paragraph gets developed in more detail.
85 Spinner-Halev 2005, p. 595.

Halev reminds us of the moral-philosophical rationale underlying Kukathas's critical stance towards modern citizenship: "The problem with concentrated power, and with the quest for unity, autonomy and a common citizenship is that they all too readily allow for the violation of individual conscience."[86] One particularly good illustration of contemporary liberals' project of designing a stable political society (by means of fostering shared values and norms in the form of citizenship) is David Miller's "modest nationalism."[87] Kukathas rejects Miller's claim that some degree of national unity and solidarity among citizens is necessary for a modern society's stability. Miller maintains that the inhabitants of liberal societies (and nations) are committed to realizing comprehensive conceptions of social and political justice. According to Kukathas's interpretation, in order to achieve this political goal, and the "shared ethos that provides for a deep social unity" necessary for achieving it, Miller's liberal state commits itself to the "effort to change the way people think and live – to create new kinds of people: citizens."[88] Kukathas notes that Miller subscribes to a (problematic) liberal tradition of civic education dating back to Mill and Rousseau.[89]

Given the monolithic role that freedom of conscience plays in his theory, it is not surprising that Kukathas is highly critical of Miller's ideal nation-state. In addition, the emphasis Miller puts on strengthening national solidarity by means of, for example, citizenship-education is unmasked as a mere instrument that gets utilized to push a partisan project, namely implementing a specifically egalitarian conception of social and economic justice. The national "community should take precedence because social justice is itself the more important value, and the relevant form of social justice is one that subordinates diversity to a form of social life which creates citizens for a particular kind of society."[90] Most importantly, then, Kukathas is critical of Miller's approach because it licenses states to enforce partisan norms and values (manifested in a homogeneous conception of citizenship) on diverse communities and associations. What about associations that reject this liberal conception of citizenship? According to Kukathas's reading, Miller is committed to the view that "those who disagree about this cannot withdraw from citizenship, and cannot withdraw from the

86 Spinner-Halev 2005, p. 595.
87 See Kukathas 2003, pp. 205–209 and Miller 1995.
88 Kukathas 2003, p. 205 and p. 208.
89 "In this, he [Miller; C.H.] is at one with John Stuart Mill who was similarly concerned with the issue of the effect of political institutions on character formation. On this understanding, a liberal regime must be one made up of liberal individuals – liberal citizens" (Kukathas 2003, p. 209).
90 Kukathas 2003, p. 208.

nation-state. If there is to be a nation-state, there has to be education for citizenship; and other considerations must be subordinated to this end."[91] As was discussed in the first chapter, the liberal archipelago rejects such political aims because they necessarily conflict with the value of tolerance. Since not every association endorses the normative framework expressed in the idea of liberal citizenship (in Miller's substantial sense) a state dependent on the widespread endorsement of the latter must sooner or later rely on state-enforced conformity for its continuous existence.

Underlying these criticisms of liberal citizenship is Kukathas's requirement of acquiescence (applied to the state, not associations, in this case), which seems to get readily violated in Miller's nation-state. In another discussion, dedicated to Raz and Margalit's conceptions of the liberal nation-state and national self-determination, Kukathas further illustrates why his theory of liberal toleration rejects the view of society as unified by a shared conception of citizenship and national identity.[92] Kukathas is highly critical of the strongly nonvoluntaristic and collectivistic account of group membership that Raz and Margalit assume. According to them, stable groups are the basic and primary entities around which the world is organized (and with respect to which individuality is constituted). In discussing the problem of whether such collectives qua cultural groups have a right to collective self-determination, Raz and Margalit acknowledge, however, that "[m]embership in the group is, in part, a matter of mutual recognition [and members of such groups; C.H.] are aware of their membership and typically regard it as an important clue in understanding their tastes and their manner."[93] Kukathas stresses the importance of this qualification concerning "mutual recognition" and he uses it to show that Raz and Margalit incorrectly attribute rights of self-determination to culturally defined collectives. They are also mistaken to attribute to cultural and national groups a conceptual priority over the individual. Kukathas summarizes: "Raz and Margalit are conceding that individual members must not only be viewed by others as belonging to the group but must also view themselves as members. It will not do for others to deem them to be members: individuals must acquiesce

91 Kukathas 2003, p. 208.

92 See Kukathas 2003, pp. 196–205 and Raz and Margalit 1990. It should be noted that my own arguments do not defend the theories of national identity presented by Miller and Raz and Margalit. The exposition focuses on the discussed passages because *The Liberal Archipelago*'s criticisms of the nation state incorporate Kukathas's most explicit objections to the importance of citizenship. My defense of citizenship does not commit me to an endorsement of liberal nationalism.

93 Raz and Margalit in: Kukathas 2003, p. 201.

in that description."[94] This general account of group membership can be applied to the special case of the modern nation state. Accounts of citizenship that ignore the requirement of acquiescence to political authority are rejected by Kukathas.[95]

In summary, we must keep in mind two features of Kukathas's assessment of (liberal) citizenship. Firstly, insofar as shared citizenship plays a role for the archipelago's population at all, it will be a drastically diminished element in the individuals' self-understanding. Citizens will associate with one or more of the archipelago's associations and it is the latter that are going to provide a sufficient basis for their members' identities, or so Kukathas assumes. The liberal umpire is not playing a significant enough role in the process of developing and maintaining the normative self-conceptions of its subjects. Secondly, this diminished role notwithstanding, the requirement of passive acquiescence (necessary for conferring legitimacy on the authorities that individuals are subject to) also applies to citizenship in the liberal archipelago. As will be discussed in the final chapter below, the fact that the archipelago's associations and even individual persons can in principle leave the archipelago creates a problem for Kukathas's view, especially concerning the exit rights that the liberal umpire is supposed to enforce.

A bit more needs to be said concerning the second feature of Kukathas's account of citizenship. He adds an interesting twist that should be discussed, also because it fleshes out the above suggestion according to which Kukathas's view shares a lot with Weber's sociological account of power- and authority-relationships. In discussing the problem of political obligation, Kukathas claims that the individuals' obligations regarding the liberal umpire will

> be *indirect* inasmuch as they emerge not out of an immediate claim the political community has upon the individual but out of the fact that other communities to which the individual belongs are party to the convention or settlement which creates or sustains the po-

94 Kukathas 2003, p. 201.

95 How can acquiescence (in the sense of Weber's "subjective beliefs") be a requirement of legitimacy when it is in principle possible that those who are subject to an authority could be unaware of its very existence? It must be noted that Kukathas often switches from using the notion of "acquiescence" understood as holding some positive belief (in the authority being worth staying put) on the one hand to merely exhibiting a pattern of behavior that is the result of *not* holding the belief of wanting to exit on the other. Remember the passage quoted above: "All that is necessary as evidence of such recognition is that members elect not to leave" (Kukathas 2003, p. 96). The issue of performing actions under an authority, the existence of which one is not aware of, will be revisited in section 8.2. Thanks to Jonathan Miller for pointing out this tension in Kukathas's view.

> litical society. Political obligation stems from our acquiescence in the authority of those associations which have themselves accepted the authority of the state.[96]

It is in considering this argument about indirect legitimacy that two objections to Kukathas's vision of a liberal society must be mentioned briefly. Both objections are critical of the overly "thin" conception of citizenship that emerges amongst the inhabitants of the liberal archipelago. Firstly, employing Weber's conception of power, Jeffrey Spinner-Halev notes that

> Kukathas too is oddly facile when it comes to issues of power. What will prevent an association from trying to gain too much power for itself, and imposing its will on others? Kukathas's rather thin state probably won't be able to prevent its being taken over by a large group. With no conception of citizenship, it's not clear why anyone would be loyal to the state, since we all live our lives through our association of choice.[97]

Spinner-Halev is quoted extensively because his argument is reminiscent of my own line of criticism, which rests on a similar assumption concerning the nature of the archipelago's associations. Contrary to Spinner-Halev, however, the argument presented here is not primarily concerned with powerful associations taking over the archipelago's liberal state (which is not to deny that Spinner-Halev's *is* a well-taken objection to Kukathas's view). Rather, my objection focuses on the problem of secession and the latent threat of dissolution that the liberal archipelago is likely to be confronted with when its overarching institution (the umpire) fails to provide the institutional background required for citizenship in it. Hence, one worry with Kukathas's picture is that it seems rather unlikely that associations, once in charge of all the state-like coercive powers, immunities, and privileges[98] won't take the final step, *viz.* seceding from the archipelago and establishing their fully sovereign "mini-states" with a much richer basic institutional structures which in turn engender a sense of shared citizenship.[99]

---

96 Kukathas 2003, p. 210.

97 Spinner-Halev 2005, p. 596.

98 See Hohfeld 1978 (1913).

99 This line of argument is similar to Walzer's main reply to Kukathas, discussed in the next chapter. It is true that Kukathas, at one point, says that "the institutions of the state – which, typically, assume powers of policing, lawmaking, and war-making, among others – [...] affect other communities [i.e., the archipelago's associations] very profoundly" (Kukathas 2003, p. 209). Kukathas's presentation of the liberal archipelago sometimes seems to allow for a "thicker" state, with more powers than the umpire-state, discussed in the text. Still, the passage just quoted is an exception and takes place in a critical discussion of the "typical" (historical)

As mentioned above, a related worry is that this tendency to secede will be especially strong in the case of illiberal and totalitarian associations – and their leaders. Given that these associations will be farthest removed from the ideal of liberal citizenship, we cannot expect their inhabitants to exhibit much adherence to the liberal umpire and the prime value it incorporates, tolerance. In other words, if the overarching liberal state is not at all engaged in the business of "creating citizens," the value of internal as well as external tolerance might rest on an extremely fragile foundation when it comes to the illiberal associations of the archipelago. Whereas Spinner-Halev is worried that the instability of the associations' external relationships and their expansionist tendencies undermine the archipelago's stability, Geoffrey Brahm Levey criticizes the theory of liberal toleration with respect to the degree of internal intolerance that it allows to develop within illiberal associations. The two lines of criticism rest on the same underlying worry though, i.e., that the very value of tolerance dies off, so to speak, amongst the citizens of the archipelago:

> Yet one might well argue that tolerating gross intolerance, as a matter of principle, only throws into doubt one's commitment to the principle of toleration. There is also raised here a question as to how, in the absence of social unity, overarching political authority, and shared institutions and values, and in the likely presence of myriad group tyrannies, the liberal archipelago *transmits* and *reproduces* the value of toleration.[100]

Levey and Spinner-Halev's objections are reminiscent of Rawlsian stability-arguments.[101] Once the liberal archipelago is realized, the radical *laissez faire* attitude towards the internal development of associations will not reproduce the tolerant political structure that made possible this unconstrained development in the first place. In short, the liberal archipelago does not seem to be capable of reproducing itself across time.

Kukathas concludes his discussion of citizenship by admitting that historically it has been indeed the case that people have developed strong attachments to their "political communities": "Indeed, it would be surprising if they did not, since governments and political elites have always found it useful to foster, encourage, and play upon such sentiments."[102] Kukathas is right when he stresses that these historical explanations do not amount to a sufficient norma-

---

manifestation of the state and it therefore remains consistent with Kukathas's ideal umpire that leaves lawmaking, policing, etc. to the associations.

100 Levey 2004, p. 574 (my emphasis).

101 Rawls 1999 (1971), ch. IV. Especially relevant for Levey's critique of Kukathas is section 35, "Toleration of the Intolerant." (See Rawls 1999 (1971), pp. 190–194.)

102 Kukathas 2003, p. 210.

tive justification of why one *should* value citizenship.[103] At several points Kukathas insists that his view "sees political association and, so, political authority, as something which is the product of accident and which amounts to a conventional settlement which we should respect only to the extent that 'innovation' threatens to produce something worse."[104] The thought pursued in the final section of this first part (3.2) will be that exactly the same points about "historical accidents" and "conventional settlements" can be made with respect to the various associations of the archipelago and not just concerning modern citizenship. Why, for example, are religious communities conventional constructs to a lesser degree than modern nation states, as Kukathas's approach seems to assume? In addition, is it true that the process of monopolizing the legitimate use of violence is a mere accidental historical event without any normative and value-based rationale to it? Or are Kant's and Hegel's accounts of the state more plausible than Kukathas's when they say that the modern state and legal institutions (and a life as a citizen in and under them) are necessary because individual freedom requires them?

103 However, it should be noted that the quoted passage is uncharitable in suggesting that every instance of national solidarity and patriotic sentiment is the result of indoctrination.
104 Kukathas 2003, p. 210.

Chapter 3: Initial *Ad Hominem* Reply to Kukathas

It is now time to begin evaluating Kukathas's critique of contemporary liberalism and his alternative theory of liberal toleration. A dilemma is presented, the two horns of which are, firstly, that the archipelago's associations turn into state-like entities themselves once the liberal state gets reduced to a mere umpire in Kukathas's ideal liberal society. If Kukathas accepted the dilemma's first horn he would face anew the conflict between an association's enforceable public (especially legal) norms and freedom of individual conscience. Upon trying to avoid this conflict Kukathas is led back, secondly, to an absolutism concerning freedom of conscience. However, unconditionally endorsing this freedom (and the right to exit associational jurisdictions) leads to the undermining of any public authority and eventually to individualist anarchism. Insofar as freedom of conscience is regarded as the only cornerstone of a liberal society, the question arises why individuals are not going to regard *any* association's (not just the contemporary liberal state's) longing for social unity as potentially intolerable.

In order to show how this dilemma presents an irresolvable problem for Kukathas, arguments presented by Michael Walzer and others are revisited. Walzer's remarks support the claim that the possibility of any type of society and association (understood as a continuous engagement of individuals in shared social practices[105]) is threatened by the merely provisional character of *all* of its public norms that would result if a radically unqualified right to exit were always in place. The discussion of the dilemma is completed by pointing out that by accepting that associations might well turn into mini-states, Kukathas's critique of contemporary liberalism is severely weakened. The archipelago's associations find themselves in a need of their members' acquiescence that is very similar to the one that contemporary liberal states have to achieve in order to count as legitimate authorities. This chapter concludes by discussing some rejoinders that can be put forward in response to the foregoing critique of Kukathas.

---

105 This is, of course, a mere working definition. A more nuanced account of the "societal condition" (the fact of the minimum of inescapable interdependence amongst individual agents) will be presented in the essay's next two parts. In order to present the initial reply to Kukathas in this chapter, however, a more mundane account of what a society is can be assumed.

3.1 "Mini-states" vs. Individualist Anarchism

In his "Response to Kukathas"[106] Michael Walzer argues that the liberal archipelago, far from being a radically new idea, presents a domestic version of the international state system. According to Walzer, "the regime he [Kukathas; C.H.] describes with conditional verbs already exists. International society is a regime of that sort, a maximally tolerant regime, where all the presumably intolerable practices that Kukathas lists are in fact tolerated."[107] The international system is "maximally tolerant" because it incorporates a strong conception of sovereignty, allowing states (liberal and illiberal alike) to run their internal affairs as they please almost without limits.[108] According to Walzer, the question that must be asked is whether we should prefer that domestic societies turn into small-scale versions of the international system. Kukathas's answer to Walzer's question leaves the reader puzzled. He says,

> [t]he response to this is to say that, if the image of a society of mutual toleration presents domestic society as a kind of international society, this is because that is indeed what domestic society is like. It is much more like international society than has, perhaps, been conceded. It should be recognized and accepted as such, and demands to view it as something 'thicker' should be resisted.[109]

Commenting on this exchange between Kukathas and Walzer, Spinner-Halev notes that one wonders what actually existing states Kukathas refers to: "Kukathas oddly argues that both domestic and international society are much like that [the liberal archipelago; C.H.] now [...]. It is hard to know which domestic society Kukathas has in mind, or what this means internationally in this age of globalization and interdependence."[110]

---

106 Walzer 1997.

107 Walzer 1997, p. 106.

108 Walzer mentions the issue of humanitarian intervention as one of the few policies that have recently called into question absolute state sovereignty. (See Walzer 1997, pp. 106–107.) Kukathas's liberal umpire can be interpreted as circumscribing associations' sovereignty in a similar way. After all, assuming that victims of genocide and ethnic cleansing (the prime justifications for humanitarian intervention) would have preferred *exiting* their societies instead of getting tortured and murdered, members of the archipelago's associations rely on the liberal umpire to intervene with associations' internal policies and affairs *insofar* as the latter conflict with the right to exit. Enforcing the right to exit in the archipelago is therefore similar to humanitarian intervention sanctioned by the United Nations.

109 Kukathas 2003, p. 164.

110 Spinner-Halev 2005, p. 596.

Important about Walzer's observation is not primarily that it reveals the extent to which a globalized version of the liberal archipelago already exists. Rather, the line of argument pursued here focuses on another corollary of Walzer's observation. If it is true that the liberal archipelago will turn out to look very much like the current international system then the entities populating the former will likely resemble sovereign states. In the same way in which a weak United Nations possesses only minimal authority to intervene in the dealings of its member states, the liberal umpire (as discussed in section 1.2) adopts a passive stance with respect to associations' internal affairs. The associations of the liberal archipelago are sovereign entities and actors in a very traditional sense then.

Someone persuaded by Kukathas's view will resist this conclusion concerning associational sovereignty. After all, the liberal archipelago apparently honors freedom of conscience more than contemporary liberal states do because the archipelago's population acquiesces to religious, cultural, and social associations, the jurisdiction of which they can leave when they wish to do so. Moreover, the archipelago appears to do a superior job with respect to toleration than the liberal state does because the former abstains from imposing a conception of shared citizenship upon potentially resisting individuals.

However, when we develop Walzer's point about the liberal archipelago's resemblance to the international system further, these claims about the superior prospects of acquiescence become far less obvious. The archipelago's associations will have to assume many of the functions currently executed by the state, once the liberal umpire is installed and replaces the liberal state as we know it. Every association of (potentially as well as actually) interacting individuals has to set up *some* publicly acknowledged and enforceable arrangements of property, contract etc. Importantly, even if it were possible to coexist without settling on a comprehensive conception of public norms, this is itself a settlement that has to be publicly acknowledged and sustained.[111]

One example of these societal core-functions is criminal punishment. Kukathas briefly talks about this issue in order to illustrate the associations' independence. Among the wide-ranging privileges that associations enjoy in

111 These are, of course, the prominent themes driving Kant's political philosophy. Unless one can guarantee (and is guaranteed) a lifelong existence in *complete* isolation (not even potentially interacting with a single other human being) one is under a duty to enter a "rightful condition" with others, the latter being *some* public regime of property and contractual right ensuring that individual freedom and rights are conclusively, as opposed to provisionally, established. (See MM 6:344.) Parts 2 and 3 of this book will return to these issues. (See Ripstein 2009.)

the liberal archipelago is the authorization to inflict cruel and unusual forms of punishment without the liberal umpire being justified in interfering with those practices.[112] In other words, Kukathas seems to realize that the associations themselves establish coercive institutions that enforce norms on its members in a quite traditional (Weberian) sense of monopolized violence. I will have to say more about why these core-functions are necessary in section 3.2 and in the remainder of this essay that identifies public norms as constitutive of individual agency.

Walzer's remarks on the international system support the suspicion that sovereign associations will resemble modern states to an extent that significantly undermines the libertarian appeal of Kukathas's vision of a liberal society. Kukathas fails to consider that the hypothetical cultural and religious associations of the archipelago are very likely to differ significantly from the actually existing associations at home in real-world states. Only the neglect of this difference allows him to depict the associations of the archipelago in a much more favorable light than actually existing liberal states. When we look at cultural and religious associations as they *are* in actual liberal states, they indeed appear highly successful in securing acquiescence and they seem to achieve social unity and homogeneity *naturally* and *spontaneously*.[113] Real-world states, by contrast, appear to be *artificial* constructs, coercively imposing unity on subjugated associations and their members. What Kukathas does not pay attention to

112 Kukathas sums up: "[T]here would in such a society be (the possibility of) communities which bring up children unschooled and illiterate; which enforce arranged marriages; which deny conventional medical care to their members (including children); and which inflict cruel and 'unusual' punishment. All of this is possible in the name of toleration" (Kukathas 2003, p. 134).

113 It was argued above that Kukathas's remarks on the nature of these associations are not always clear. Sometimes he seems to suggest that they are "voluntary associations," at other times he explicitly says that associations are not "necessarily voluntary" ones. An interesting paper by Paul Harrison 1960 applies Weber's notion of voluntary associations to the specific empirical case of the Baptists in the United States. Much of what Harrison says there supports the criticisms of Kukathas presented in the text. Especially noteworthy is Harrison's claim that voluntary associations often develop a tendency to be much more authoritarian than the Weberian state with its codified legal and bureaucratic institutions. This is so because "[i]ronically, since this power [present when ordering voluntary associations, C.H.] is undefined and covert, it often exceeds that which ordinarily accrues to leaders of authoritarian and hierarchical institutions" (Harrison 1960, p. 232). In addition, Harrison's Weberian picture emphasizes another point, crucial for replying to Kukathas: "It is misleading to call these systems [i.e., voluntary associations, C.H.] 'non-authoritarian.' No social system can operate on a continuous basis without support from some mode of authority, no matter how informal and inadequately defined it may be" (Harrison 1960, p. 233).

is that actual states are taking care of all the institutional prerequisites necessary for enabling the peaceful coexistence among these associations. In addition, and that is the more important point, the state provides the background-conditions for the associations' *internal* dealings.[114] Of course, it is these monopolized prerequisites that are the reason for the state being in so much more need of a robust public justification than the more or less voluntary associations are.

Associations are more successful in securing acquiescence only because a stable rule of law is provided by the state's monopoly of violence. Taking real-world states and real-world associations as a blueprint unduly romanticizes the archipelago's version of the latter because the "dirty work" of force and coercion is taken care of by the state. Kukathas takes associations as they present themselves under conditions of the rule of law and simply transfers them to the liberal archipelago where securing exactly this rule of law is not taken care of by the liberal umpire. Kukathas overlooks that shifting sovereignty away from the state also shifts the burden of taking care of societal functions towards the associations.[115]

Remember that in the liberal archipelago the monopoly of violence stays with the liberal state (the umpire) with respect to *only* two capacities: the enforcement of the right to exit and ensuring peace between the associations. What institutions are going to take care of all the other core-functions related to the associations' internal dealings? And do these associations now continue to appear as attractive as they did in real-world circumstances – now that they have to take care of the unattractive business of using force and coercion to render its internal affairs stable and predictable for its individual members? Do associations continue to attract acquiescence more easily than actual liberal

---

114 This thought is an important motivation for the "total law thesis," presented in section 7.2.

115 Christopher W. Morris presents a similar argument, criticizing romantic views of utopian socialist and anarchist communities. The success and continued existence of Israeli kibbutzim, for example, is often used to show that communism works, i.e., a condition where the state and its coercive legal institutions "withered away." Morris points out that "[m]ost of the decentralized, noninstitutional forms of cooperation that we are familiar with take place in states. These are really experiments in *semi*anarchy. Kibbutzim are protected against hostile neighboring states and peoples by the Israeli army, [...]. States can provide assurance that the larger social framework will not unravel and thus facilitate semianarchy" (Morris 1998, pp. 98–99). I add that the Israeli state is not merely necessary for the kibbutzim's continuous existence because it protects these communities from *external* threats; unless the kibbutzim engage in what Morris calls "secondary state formation" (i.e., become monopolizers of force themselves) the Israeli state also provides the preconditions for peace *inside* such "anarchist" communities, above all the rule of law.

states do? It is one thing to imagine the liberal archipelago as the negation of contemporary liberals' vision of the state because of historical and contemporary episodes that show it clashing with freedom of individual conscience. It is quite another to deal with the power-vacuum that is generated by reducing the liberal state to the role of the archipelago's umpire. Once the state is no longer in charge of the rule of law the associations will have to do so.

We are now in a position to conclude this argument from "mini-states." We can thereby show that its conclusion constitutes the first horn of a dilemma that *The Liberal Archipelago* cannot escape. That Kukathas does not object to Walzer's claim concerning the parallel between the international state-system and the domestic liberal archipelago has weighty consequences: The associations populating the archipelago stand in a very similar relationship to their members as contemporary liberal states do with respect to their citizens. Achieving acquiescence to liberal states has been identified as problematic by Kukathas because of the coercive implementation of norms that might conflict with individuals' conscience. Now the first horn of the dilemma is that once associations become sovereign entities they face the very same problem. In the face of this discovery, the liberal state seems to have the same (good and bad) chances to secure acquiescence as the archipelago's associations have. Why then privilege one over the other and expect the liberal archipelago to provide a better way of dealing with *individual* diversity and pluralism? According to the first horn of the dilemma, the liberal archipelago reproduces the tension that contemporary liberalism is confronted with (social unity vs. tolerance of (individual) diversity) merely on the level of cultural, religious and social associations.

In response to this horn of the dilemma, Kukathas will most likely reemphasize the central and uncompromising role that individual freedom of conscience plays in his theory of toleration. If it is really the case that, as a consequence of reducing the liberal state to an umpire, associations turn into ministates then why not apply the requirement of acquiescence at this lower, more local, level of monopolized coercion? The solution to the problem of associations qua mini-states is to split-up the mini-state in question into its constitutive sub-associations, the members of which then freely acquiesce to these local authorities. As with the step from the liberal state to the liberal umpire we again reduce the original association to the role of a mere watch dog and enforcer of the right to exit. Comprehensive sovereignty now lies with the sub-associations. In particular, formulating, enforcing, and adjudicating foundational norms is now a (democratic or nondemocratic) task for these local collectives.

Insofar as the argument made above has some force, however, we are now encountering the same problem again. The new sub-associations, in order to count as associations in the liberal archipelago's sense, will have to exhibit a degree of independence and sovereignty very similar to modern nation states. Given the mini-state's diminished role relative to the sub-associations in question, the latter must take on functions formerly executed by the mini-state. Acquiescence to these sub-associations' public norms will then be as difficult to secure (now and, especially, in the form of a commitment extending into the future) as in the case of contemporary liberal states. Still, Kukathas might hope to avoid the problem of the coercive imposition of social unity by a public authority by further localizing the institutionalization of these core functions. He might hope that such small-scale social arrangements get him both: an association constituted by certain public norms on the one hand and the non-violation of anybody's free conscience on the other. Let us simply push back the requirement of acquiescence yet another level and so on until associational organization and order are fully compatible with individual freedom of conscience.

This thought experiment leads to the second horn of Kukathas's dilemma, i.e., a version of individualist anarchism. The foundational role of the right to exit makes necessary this formulation of individualist anarchism as the only form of "social organization" fully compatible with Kukathas's unconditional individual freedom of conscience. In avoiding the first horn of the dilemma (acquiescence to sovereign associations runs into exactly the problems that the liberal archipelago wanted to avoid), Kukathas's argument gravitates towards the second horn. Acquiescence to associative norms can only be conditional and remains subject to the caprice of individual choice. While some will shrug their shoulders and even welcome this conditionality as an expression of true freedom, one of the main arguments pursued here is that the availability of an unconditional right to exit undermines the necessary conditions of the possibility of those future-directed norms by means of which membership in an associations is constituted and organized. In the liberal archipelago, individuals can (if at all) conclusively and unconditionally acquiesce to only one authority, namely their own conscience.

Given the absolute status of *individual* freedom of conscience that Kukathas adheres to, any instance of acquiescence to an association's authority can merely have a conditional form. The reason for this conditionality is that we can simply not predict what associative norms our fellow association members (or, in the nondemocratic case, authoritarian rulers) are going to legislate in the future and how, for example, judges will apply and interpret them. As members of an association we can only subscribe to the following "commitment": "I stick to my association's decisions, norms, and policies – unless I declare that they conflict with the dictates of my conscience and choose to exit the norms' reach." Unless we develop clairvoyant powers, allowing us to exactly predict how our association is going to further specify and develop norms in the course of its existence, the categorical enforceability of appeals to one’s conscience makes the establishment of those institutions impossible that were referred to under the heading of core societal functions. Those societal functions like property and contract are not just important for instrumental reasons (e.g., enhancing security or maximizing well being). Rather, the most basic function that public norms fulfill is that they involve the stable and enduring public recognition of the association-members as such. An association’s public norms, in other words, are constitutive of an individual counting as being a member of it. And if exiting the reach of these norms, that are supposed to maintain this status, is readily available to all members at all times then this very status (and all the normative properties associated with it, e.g., certain rights and obligations) remain subject to the choices based on individual conscience (or on what individuals believe to be such dictates).[116]

Kukathas has to choose between two options then (the two horns of the dilemma). On the one hand, he might allow the archipelago’s associations to take over many of the functions that are now executed by the (liberal) state. This concession, however, results in the same problems concerning acquiescence that befall the liberal state, i.e., sub-groups and/or individuals whose absolute individual right to freely associate and dissociate gets violated in the name of maintaining some degree of social unity. On the other hand, Kukathas might allow freedom of conscience and the right to exit to take on its absolutist form. The unrestricted prerogative of exiting legal arrangements and obligations, however, leads to the rejection of any conclusively established public authority – a situation tantamount to what Kant calls “savage (lawless) freedom”[117] that individuals have in the state of nature, i.e., the absence of a “rightful condition”[118] (of the rule of law). It is concluded that, given the unconditional nature of freedom of conscience, Kukathas has to go with the second horn. Insofar as freedom of conscience reigns supreme, the *individual* herself is the only authority she can unconditionally acquiesce to. The individual, and not cultural, religious etc. associations, is then sovereign in the same way as states are in today’s international arena. We will return to the possibility of individual

116 It is important to keep in mind that we are currently discussing an initial reply to Kukathas. The developed strategy in Part 2 will make the more nuanced claim that maintaining a high degree of individuality is threatened by the second horn of the dilemma. At the current stage of the discussion, Kukathas might still reply by calling into question the importance of the societal functions listed in the text. On the problem of making appeals to conscience the basis for public policy decisions like religious exemptions, see Maclure and Taylor 2011, Part 2.
117 PP 8:357.
118 MM 6:306–6:308.

secession (and Kukathas's unsatisfactory response to it) in section 9.2. At one point Kukathas answers affirmatively the question of "what of individuals who choose to reject the authority of the wider society or the state and withdraw into communities as small as a single family (or individual). Are they not licensed, under the present defense of toleration, to reject the authority of the law and to do entirely as they please?"[119]

3.2 The Unavoidability of Public Authority

Before discussing a couple of objections to the dilemma one has to say more about associations turning into mini-states in the liberal archipelago. This is important in order to motivate the conclusion of this first part, namely that public norms and authority are necessary for associations to provide certain core-functions. These norms are at the same time constitutive of the associations (once the state is no longer in charge of providing those background conditions, above all some kind of rule of law).

J. Donald Moon submits a claim that is similar to the conclusion defended here. He observes that one feature of Kukathas's archipelago is that the liberal umpire must not interfere with associations when the latter impose "internal restrictions"[120] (also harsh and illiberal ones) on their members. A couple of examples were already mentioned that have provoked much indignation on part of Kukathas's critics.[121] Moon's argument is worth discussing for a further reason though. With respect to the associations' authority to inflict punishment, Moon identifies a tension with the right to exit. Moon says,

> [I]f cultural and religious groups have the authority to inflict even cruel and unusual punishment on members who violate their norms, we have to ask what the right to exit amounts to. Although Kukathas denies that groups have the right to force individuals to remain in the group, what does this restriction mean if groups are free to coerce their members to abide by their norms?[122]

Moon, like most commentators, focuses on one apparent consequence that follows with respect to the individual right to exit, once associations become entities that enforce collective norms. He objects to Kukathas's theory because of all the illiberal policies that the liberal archipelago's groups have authority to

119 Kukathas 2003, p. 135.
120 Kukathas 2003, p. 184.
121 See fn. 112.
122 Moon 2005, pp. 424–425.

impose on their members. Moon concludes that there is a tension here between the groups' authority to "enforce" and "coerce" on the one hand and the individual right to exit on the other: "Since exiting the group typically involves actions that violate group norms [...], and if one may be punished for such violations, then the supposed freedom of exit would appear to be nugatory."[123]

Without wanting to downplay this objection to Kukathas, Moon's critique is used in a different way – and the exact opposite conclusion is arrived at. Moon's premises (that there is a tension between the unqualified right to exit and the enforcement of the shared norms defining an association) can be used to establish the conclusion that the liberal archipelago undermines the foundations of the kind of associations it wants to see flourishing. Any kind of public authority dissolves exactly because the liberal umpire enforces the individual right to exit *for any reason whatsoever* (at least as long as this reason can somehow be linked to an agent's conscience). In other words, whereas most commentators worry about Kukathas's right to exit becoming "nugatory," the argument presented here claims that this right is too strong since it renders the archipelago's associations (even highly liberal ones) impossible because the associations' authority becomes utterly "nugatory" in the face of that right.

Again, the problem is the vacuum that ensues when the liberal state is taking on the role of a mere umpire. In the archipelago associations are in charge of things such as criminal law and punishment – replacing the liberal state's monopoly of legitimate violence with respect to these social tasks. Now it is a rather disconcerting outcome of Kukathas's view that individuals, convicted of a crime (as defined by their association) and awaiting punishment from their association's authority, can say something like: "Well, I guess I make use of my right to exit now. Liberal umpire, please enforce this right and compel my association to release me from unjustified incarceration." Scenarios like these are not restricted to the case of criminal punishment. Contracts amongst association members become unpredictable, unstable, and actually incoherent if associations cannot *conclusively* maintain the respective legal norms by asserting to use *inescapable* enforcement mechanisms.[124] Keep in mind Kukathas's definition of the right to exit (and what it means for his view's potential to collapse

123 Moon 2005, p. 425.

124 The language of conclusively (as opposed to provisionally) entering legal relationships (by means of establishing a *public* authority legitimizing and enforcing property rights, contracts, etc.) is Kant's. (See MM 6:255–257.) For an important analysis concerning the question of whether Kant leaves enough space for a genuine and freestanding sphere of private right, see Brudner 2011.

into some variety of anarchism): "The right to exit is, in fact, nothing more or less than the right to repudiate authority."[125]

But was not the restricted role of the liberal umpire supposed to forestall exactly this outcome, i.e., that the liberal state has such a strong impact on associations' internal affairs? And is not it implausible to expect the umpire to bail out prison inmates? In response it is claimed that this is not implausible at all. This outcome follows from the way Kukathas conceives of the liberal umpire. Keep in mind that the umpire has to practice a strict policy of "benign neglect" when it comes to substantial issues of justice, social morality etc. that reign supreme within a particular association. What triggers the umpire's function of enforcing the right to exit is only one thing, namely an individual's expressed and articulated desire to leave and her appealing to her conscience that she sees infringed by a certain public decision or policy that she is subject to. Whether a prison inmate is locked-up by her association's force-monopoly for criticizing the prophet in public, for having sex with fourteen year olds, or for assassinating a politician...it all simply does not have to matter for whether or not the umpire enforces the right to exit. The individual "criminal" in question, by having to face (what she perceives as) an unjust trial and by having to suffer penal measures, is forced to endure a kind of treatment that violates her conscience.[126]

Might not Kukathas reply by drawing a distinction here between appeals to conscience that are justified and those that seem to be crazy and inauthentic like the ones seemingly put forward by the "criminals" just mentioned? The liberal umpire simply has to determine whether an individual *really* appeals to her conscience or just pretends to do so because she wants to escape punishment, a contractual obligation, etc. We could then restrict the umpire's interventions to cases in which individuals *rightly* petition the liberal state to rescue them from the reach of their associations' monopoly of violence.

---

125 Kukathas 2003, p. 97.

126 The scenario described in the text presupposes a certain conception of criminal punishment, namely that the criminal has to either pay a fine to her association's authority or has to serve a prison sentence on the association's territory. There is another, at least conceivable, alternative consisting in punishment going hand in hand with "banishing" the criminal from the association's jurisdiction. This alternative is of limited relevance for the liberal archipelago (as well as for the actual world) because all the other associations are under no enforceable obligation to admit the banished individual. Unless the liberal archipelago reserves some space for these outlaws, the associations have to deal with *their* criminals within their own territory. I thank Ben Dyer for directing me to these issues.

The answer is "no." Kukathas cannot take that route. First of all, the liberal umpire would have to appeal to a robust normative conception of justice and norms if it distinguished between groups that justifiably imprison individuals and those that do not. Remember that Kukathas is worried when a comprehensive liberal state (since it endorses substantial and disputed political, legal, and social norms) receives "carte blanche to intervene in the practices of all kinds of associations."[127] Allowing the state to appeal to controversial moral judgments in order to justify its policies and actions even to a minimum degree, results in a slippery slope toward state tyranny. However, Kukathas overlooks that this strict neutrality on part of the liberal umpire *combined* with the absolute status of freedom of conscience (and the right to exit) undermines the very prerequisites of every association and legal order that attempts to exists as a self-determining collective across time.

Another strategy seems to remain for Kukathas in order to show that the unconditional right to exit does not undermine all the necessary conditions for the possibility of life in stable and enduring associations. This strategy tries to define individual conscience in a way that relativizes this notion to each individual agent. In other words, an appeal to one's conscience is genuine only if that appeal reflects and fits with the agent's "valuational system."[128] Why cannot the liberal state/umpire use a kind of "sincerity detector" that allows it to distinguish between convicts who appeal to freedom of conscience (and the right to exit) merely to escape their (even from their own viewpoint justified) punishment from those who sincerely try to escape what they honestly believe to be unjustified prosecution on part of their association's authority?[129]

Unfortunately, pumping up the notion of conscience in this way won't help Kukathas either. Or rather, this strategy could help Kukathas only if he allowed the liberal state to do exactly what he, "in the name of toleration," does not allow it to do. The controversies in the philosophy of mind and action (What counts as a sincere intention to exit one's jurisdiction?) and the conceptual problems related to the construction of a sincerity detector (On what basis does the detector distinguish an appeal to one's conscience from an honest appeal to self-interest if self-interest is part of the conscience of a cunning egoist?) are all issues that the liberal umpire has to avoid in deciding whether or not to enforce the right to exit in a particular case. Under conditions of thorough-going diversi-

---

127 Kukathas 2003, 147.

128 Watson 1975, p. 215.

129 I am indebted to Corwin Carr and Peter Jaworski for pressing me on this point and for coming up with the idea of a sincerity detector.

ty there will be many associations and individuals (certain dualists, for example) that outrightly reject the natural scientific paradigm and will, consequently, consider a "sincerity detector" a highly controversial and inadequate means for the umpire to determine genuine appeals to conscience. Most importantly, taking sides in all the normative and substantial moral debates on the nature and source of conscience would make the liberal umpire subject to the criticism that it privileges certain theoretical and practical conceptions of conscience over others. It seems, Kukathas has no choice but to adopt a view that is similar to the one Kant endorses in his political and legal (as opposed to his moral) philosophy. This view is strictly concerned with the external side of actions only. In the liberal archipelago it must be enough, therefore, that an individual expresses her desire to exit and attempts, unsuccessfully because hindered by others, to do so. The quality of the agent's will (the internal side of action) must never be of any concern for the liberal state/umpire. Keep in mind Kukathas's own formulation of the right to exit as an essential part of his theory does "not sanction the forcible induction into or imprisoning of any individual in a community. No one can be *required* to accept a particular way of life."[130] And earlier: Associations "are not entitled to force individuals to remain, even if the consequence of those individuals leaving might be the destruction of the association."[131]

Also Michael Walzer's "Response" substantiates the argument against *The Liberal Archipelago* currently under discussion. Following the analogy discussed in section 3.1, Walzer summarizes Kukathas's project as follows: "do we want [...] to make domestic society into something much more like the already existing international society?"[132] Walzer answers that the difference between these two kinds of society "isn't an eradicable difference; it arises out of and is manifest in a profound asymmetry between the two."[133] A look at real-world political and social realities shows, according to Walzer, that there is exactly one international society that sharply contrasts with a plethora of domestic societies *because* only the latter exhibit a shared historical, cultural, and national identity.[134] The genuine equality and looseness that is present in the in-

130 Kukathas 2003, p. 103.
131 Kukathas 2003, p. 97.
132 Walzer 1997, p. 107.
133 Walzer 1997, p. 107.
134 It is of course true that Walzer submits an exaggerated claim here himself. The actually existing states (that Walzer contrasts with the international society) are far less homogeneous concerning their ethnic and national makeup than he claims. This is the main reason why my adaptation of Walzer's critique of Kukathas shifts away from its communitarian underpinnings

ternational system (and that Kukathas wants to apply to the relationship between associations) is possible only in the international arena since "member states participate equally in international society because none of them has to adapt to someone else's rules and practices."[135]

Walzer draws attention to the fact that, and here Kukathas's term is used deliberately, associations have to rest on future-directed settlements of some common rules and social practices. In order to count as an association some shared normative principles need to be endorsed by *its* members. The state is the paradigmatic example of such a settlement but Walzer's general point can be extended to all associations, defined as social forms governed by shared constitutive rules and practices. Also a society of hermits must execute shared practices of indifference and noninterference in order to enjoy their lives and freedoms qua members of the one hermit community. Walzer's insight is that an association's internal settlements regarding rules and practices result in the phenomenon that

> every domestic society [develops; C.H.] a 'common moral standpoint,' a set of shared understandings that is much thicker than that of international society, even if it is (as it always is) internally disputed, uncertain in its extent and coverage, allowing room at the margins for deviant or simply diverse practices. Religious difference and cultural pluralism are entirely compatible with this kind of commonality; indeed, they are likely to make for social conflict and civil war without it.[136]

The argument defended in the remainder of this exploration will rely on the necessity of a "common standpoint" that agents in society must share – a claim that Kukathas criticizes on grounds of potential violations of freedom of conscience. My reading of Walzer's argument will support the argument that some shared *political* and *legal* (not necessarily moral) standpoint is a necessary condition of a high degree of independent individual agency. The conclusion of Walzer's "Response" is a good place to concentrate this discussion and to foreshadow the argument from how identities are constituted within law-governed societies. Expanding on the point concerning people's attachments to their associations' normative settlements he claims that "[t]he domestic society that Kukathas wants us all to live in would, therefore, have to be inhabited by *beings*

---

and towards a purely legal and constitutional basis of the state in the style of Rawls and Dworkin. I thank Jonathan Miller for bringing this issue to my attention.

135 Walzer 1997, p. 107.

136 Walzer 1997, p. 108.

of some other sort. Or, it would simply break up in the radical way suggested by its international analogue. The analogy would become an identity."[137]

This conclusion echoes the dilemma presented in the previous section. There it was suggested that, insofar as individual conscience is the (only indisputable) basic value underlying the liberal archipelago, nothing prevents Kukathas's ideal society from "breaking up" into sovereign "one-man associations." This is individualist anarchism understood, in Walzer's terms, as the rejection of any settlement requiring a sustained commitment to some shared rules and practices – what he calls "the common standpoint." Walzer explains the implausibility of such a "society" by emphasizing the attachments that association-members actually develop. The line of argument pursued here agrees with Walzer's observation and also with his claim that Kukathas's theory (if pursued conclusively all the way down to individualist anarchism) would have us imagine *agents* that are very different from us. However, the upcoming chapters will present a different argument for why Kukathas's picture finds itself in this strained relationship with our self-understanding and why the public settlements that Walzer talks about exhibit a certain stability and predictability.

137 Walzer 1997, pp. 110–111 (my emphasis).

Part 2:
Public Identity and Self-Constituting Action

> Is what we call "obeying a rule" something that it would be possible for only *one* person, only *once* in a lifetime, to do? [...] To follow a rule, to make a report, to give an order, to play a game of chess, are *customs* (usages, institutions).
>
> Wittgenstein[138]

> The significance for the individual of the knowledge that certain rules will be universally applied is that, in consequence, the different objects and forms of action acquire for him new properties. [...] The effects of these man-made laws on his actions are of precisely the same kind as those of the laws of nature: his knowledge of either enables him to foresee what will be the consequences of his actions, and it helps him to make plans with confidence. [...] Like the laws of nature, the laws of the state provide fixed features in the environment in which he has to move.
>
> Hayek[139]

This part presents the first installment of the major argument in response to Kukathas's challenge against liberal citizenship. The following defense of citizenship and the rule of law employs the Neo-Kantian accounts of practical identity on the one hand and self-constituting action on the other, both presented by Christine Korsgaard. At first Korsgaard's two arguments are reconstructed as concisely as possible (Chapter 4). These two arguments are then connected in Chapter 5. This task requires considerable constructive work because Korsgaard does not explicitly connect her earlier with her more recent work in the way this is needed for the argument presented here.

Connecting the argument from practical identities with the one from self-constituting action is, however, just the first step of the argument concerning the relationship between the possibility of action on the one hand and the predictability that is provided by norm-governed social practices and institutions on the other (section 5.2). It is argued that action (in Korsgaard's demanding sense inspired by Aristotle and Kant and discussed in section 5.1) and especially the practical activity of setting and willing particular ends have to take place in a rule-governed context. The practical identities that are constituted under public norms and rules are therefore also *public* identities. In order to establish this conclusion, the argument for the public identity claim is presented in the course of a seven stage argument. In addition, section 5.2 closes with some reflections on how this new argument can help the constitutivist to overcome the so-called "paradox of self-constitution."

Section 6.1 further elaborates on the argument for the public identity claim and focuses especially on what it means to set and pursue ends in the course of

138 Wittgenstein 2009 (1953), section 199, pp. 87.
139 Hayek 1960, p. 153.

performing self-constituting actions. A radicalized version of the state of nature scenario is presented, namely one that is devoid of *any* interpersonal rules and norms whatsoever. It is submitted that action (and therefore successful self-constitution) is possible in such a speculative world only to an extremely diminished degree. The identities that are constituted in such hypothetical circumstances do not incorporate any public norms that structure the interpersonal status of individuals as agents. Part 2 ends with a discussion of two objections to the argument for the public identity claim in section 6.2, the first calling into question whether the actual performance of any actions is necessary for having a well-constituted identity and the second questioning the necessity of social practices and institutions for performing actions.

Chapter 4: Korsgaard's Two Arguments

The purpose of this chapter is primarily exegetical. The plethora of critical objections to Christine Korsgaard's ethical theory are for the most part put to one side here.[140] This chapter presents a charitable and internally coherent summary of Korsgaard's views on the origins of normative requirements and the nature of action. Her major works, *The Sources of Normativity*[141] and *Self-Constitution*[142], present two arguments that cover and combine a wide range of issues in moral philosophy, psychology, metaethics, and action theory. Korsgaard's Neo-Kantian approach is first and foremost concerned with explaining the phenomena of (moral) obligation and the authority of practical reason. In *The Sources of Normativity* she argues that practical requirements have normative force because they are expressions of our practical identities (as citizens, students, fathers, etc.), i.e., our reflectively endorsed self-conceptions that consists of practical principles (which in turn provide reasons for action).

In *Self-Constitution* Korsgaard shifts attention towards issues of agency and the theory of action. Claiming that "action is self-constitution" Korsgaard shows that certain constitutive principles of practical reason (formal versions of the categorical and hypothetical imperatives) set standards for good actions, i.e., actions that successfully unify the agent who performs them. Good actions are those that fulfill their function well, which is to constitute individual agents as autonomous and efficacious causes of their movements. The normative force of practical requirements is here ultimately derived from the constitutive standards of action.

4.1 Practical Identity and *The Sources of Normativity*

In the third lecture of *The Sources of Normativity*, entitled "The authority of reflection," Korsgaard assigns herself the task of solving "the normative problem" which consists in the puzzle of why and how normative requirements obligate us.[143] Human beings are equipped with a unique mental capacity in the

140 See Cholbi 1999; Clayton Coleman 2005; Gert 2002; Gibbard 1999; Norman 2000; Shelton 2003; Skorupski 1998.

141 Korsgaard 1996.

142 Korsgaard 2009.

143 See Korsgaard 1996, pp. 90–130.

form of self-consciousness. What makes this capacity so unique is its reflective nature, i.e., the feature that allows only humans to distance themselves from their immediate impulses, desires, and urges: "[W]e human animals turn our attention on to our perceptions and desires themselves, on to our own mental activities, and we are conscious *of* them. That is why we can think *about* them."[144] This complex form of self-consciousness is also the grounds for an equally unique phenomenon, namely a peculiar first-personal point of view concerning practical deliberation and action. Only human beings are confronted with the challenge of having to choose whether or not to take emerging incentives as reasons for action. We must choose whether or not to perform actions intended to attain the desire's object as opposed to merely being caused by this desire to act in a determined way. This phenomenon of inescapable choice, and the related self-understanding as a being confronted with this challenge, is what we experience as the freedom to endorse or reject desires:

> [O]ur capacity to turn our attention on to our own mental activities is also a capacity to distance ourselves from them, and to call them into question. [...] It is because of the reflective character of the mind that we must act, as Kant put it, under the idea of freedom. [...] [T]he reflective mind must endorse the desire before it can act on it, it must say to itself that the desire is a reason.[145]

The normative problem is the first-personal manifestation of this human condition of necessary choice and action. According to Korsgaard's conception of the latter, actions have to be performed by an agent on the basis of reasons, which in turn arise from normative principles that an agent endorses as part of her normative self-conception: "Reflective distance from our impulses makes it both possible and necessary to decide which ones we will act on: it forces us to act for reasons."[146] The normative problem consists in the puzzle of how these abstract practical principles that guide our choices can have a grip on us. Why are we obligated to direct our choices and actions in one direction rather than another? Why do normative requirements, for example moral ones, obligate us? Korsgaard sums up the normative problem in the following way: "'Reason' means reflective success. So if I decide that my desire is a reason to act, I must decide that on reflection I endorse that desire. And there we run into the problem. For how do I decide that?"[147]

---

144 Korsgaard 1996, p. 93.
145 Korsgaard 1996, p. 93 and p. 94.
146 Korsgaard 1996, p. 113.
147 Korsgaard 1996, p. 97.

Korsgaard's original contribution consists in the introduction of the notion of an agent's "practical identity" which refers to the individual self-conception that guides our choices and actions. Korsgaard describes a practical identity "as a description under which you value yourself, a description under which you find your life to be worth living and your actions to be worth undertaking."[148] Our particular practical identities are contingent. Being a parent, a friend, a citizen of a particular state, Roman Catholic, a teacher and all the specific normative requirements associated with these identities (the "dos and don'ts") are not necessarily attached to the individual agent in question. One can give up one's particular practical identities, especially when these identities conflict with each other or conflict with our moral identity as a human being. In a nutshell then, the solution to the normative problem, the problem that originates in our reflective capacities and the distinctly human condition of deliberative detachment, lies in our individual self-conceptions and the reason-providing normative principles defining them. Having at least one such practical identity is necessary in order to have any principled basis for endorsing desires as reasons for action.

Take the simple example of a spouse. According to standard conceptions, being a spouse and being exclusively engaged to another person in the framework of the institution of marriage, is a self-conception that is defined in terms of certain normative principles that regulate the relationship with one's partner but also with all others. A person with such a practical identity, when confronted with certain inclinations like the feeling of sexual attraction towards another person, takes up these inclinations in a specific way that is determined by the spouse-identity's constitutive principles. "Do not cheat on your partner" is such a constitutive principle, defining the practical identity "spouse." In the context of the current example this normative principle's role with respect to the popping-up inclination of sexual attraction is that it blocks actions based on it (unless the practical identity becomes a scam, but then one is not really valuing oneself under the description in question). If the identity of being a spouse constitutes you (and you value yourself *qua* agent falling under that description), then the desire to flirt and sexually unite with persons other than your partner

148 Korsgaard 1996, p. 101. Korsgaard's "practical identity" is implicit in John Rawls's and Robert Nozick's work. Here is just one example from *Anarchy, State, and Utopia*: A human is a "being able to formulate long-term plans for its life, able to consider and decide on the basis of abstract principles or considerations it formulates to itself and hence not merely the plaything of immediate stimuli, a being that limits its own behavior in accordance with some principles or picture it has of what an appropriate life is for itself and others, and so on" (Nozick 1974, p. 49). Also see his notion of a "formed self-conception." (See Nozick 1981, p. 307.)

does not qualify as a reason for action. Rather, the result of a spouse's practical deliberation in this case is an obligation not to act on the inclination that presents itself as a potential reason for action.

Normative requirements (like not cheating on your spouse) have a grip on us because they are a constitutive part of how we see ourselves as persons and as the authors, not the mere causes, of our actions. This normativity ultimately originates in the problem we are inescapably confronted with, i.e., action. Only an individual who was able to stop performing any actions at all would overcome this problem without endorsing any practical principles. This, however, would amount to an incoherent conception of "leading" a human life though and would constitute a kind of practical, i.e., agential, suicide.

What work do practical identities exactly do in confronting the genuinely human challenge of choice and action in the face of reflective detachment from immediate desires? Korsgaard answers: "It is necessary to have *some* conception of your practical identity, for without it you cannot have reasons to act. We endorse or reject our impulses by determining whether they are consistent with the ways in which we identify ourselves."[149] Practical identities differ from each other in prescribing different ways in which we legislate for ourselves – to put it in Kant's language. Whenever a desire (incentive) presents itself as a potential grounds for action the agent has to ask herself whether somebody with her particular practical identity can will the subjective principle of acting on this impulse (the proposed action's maxim) as a law that would apply to her were she to find herself in a similar enough situation again. Take again the example of the spouse: The question she has to ask herself when feeling sexual attraction towards a stranger involves the maxim of taking this inclination (sexual attraction) as a reason for action (flirting). The maxim describes the proposed course of action: "I shall chat up this person in order to prepare the grounds for a sexual adventure." In order to identify the normative status of this maxim it has to be examined from the deliberative standpoint of the spouse. Does the specific maxim and action "fit" and cohere with the description under which she values herself or not? Depending on the answer, we end up with moral reasons and obligations: "If it can be willed as a law it is a reason, for it has an intrinsically normative structure. If it cannot be willed as a law, we must reject it, and in that case we get obligation."[150]

149 Korsgaard 1996, p. 120.

150 Korsgaard 1996, p. 113. Already in *The Sources of Normativity* Korsgaard presents the outline of an Aristotelian/Kantian action-theory that underlies the quoted claim concerning a law-like maxim having "an intrinsically normative structure" and form. This claim needs clarification and will be revisited in section 5.1 when the conception of action that underlies

As Korsgaard is quick to admit this conception of practical identity does not yet get us into genuine moral territory. So far the only thing established is that a coherent first-personal deliberative perspective, held together by normative principles, is required to exist as a unified person across time.[151] Moreover, there remains a strong element of relativism here because the process of choosing and acting described in terms of practical identities only requires the agent to legislate for herself in accordance with these identities' specific norms and principles – constrained only by the categorical imperative in its most abstract and formal version. The categorical imperative so conceived[152] simply consists of the formal requirement to endorse *some* autonomously chosen practical laws, i.e., a personal policy that guides the choice of actions in similar enough circumstances. Again, the example of the spouse-identity illustrates how practical identities provide such laws and principles: legislating for oneself as a spouse means to take oneself to be the kind of person who not only resists the urge for sexual adventures here and now, but values oneself as someone who will do so in the future and not just on this one occasion without that having any ramifications for the similar situations and actions to come. Engaging in this minimal level of self-legislation is necessary for consistent and coherent willing and acting as an agent. Without living up to even this minimal requirement one practically "dissolves," "falls apart," and ceases to exist as an agent. Such an individual would

---

Korsgaard's view is examined more closely. In short, the normativity of a maxim of acting on a certain impulse that fits the criterion of being a universal law lies in its successfully constituting and unifying an agent's faculty of volition. A maxim has this property because of its form (it relates an act to an end in a way that makes it fit as a universal law) not because of its matter. On the latter point see Korsgaard's helpful discussion of "Plato's example of the three maxims." (See Korsgaard 1996, pp. 107–108.)

151 For an earlier statement of Korsgaard's view on personal identity, and its opposition to Parfit's empiricist/utilitarian account, see Korsgaard 1996a, pp. 363–397. A thorough reply is presented in Shoemaker 1996.

152 In a nutshell, the categorical imperative (in its highly abstract universal law formula that Korsgaard contrasts with the more substantial "moral law"/Kingdom of Ends version) is a constitutive principle of action that requires you to endorse *some* subjective principle of action (maxim) and to legislate for yourself, which in turn necessarily involves an appeal to the possible universalizability of your maxim. The hypothetical imperative establishes your "causal efficaciousness," i.e., it commands to take the means necessary to realize the ends you will (not just wish or desire). (See Korsgaard 2009, pp. 59–80.) On Korsgaard's distinction between the categorical imperative and the moral law, see Korsgaard 2009, p. 80; Korsgaard 2002, p. 61; Korsgaard 1996, pp. 98–100.

not perform actions. One becomes a mere bundle of impulses that results, from time to time, in unrelated bodily movements.[153]

We need not go into all the complex details here, but the basic, though not uncontroversial,[154] thought that Korsgaard takes straight out of Kant is that a free will is a kind of causality, i.e., the rational uncaused cause as that we see ourselves from our deliberative and practical standpoint.[155] In order not to be/become a complete wanton, a free will, like any other cause, acts in accordance with *some* law and *some* rational principle. Freedom is not "lawlessness." On the contrary, "Kant says: 'Since the concept of a causality entails that of laws [...] it follows that freedom is by no means lawless [...].'"[156] Since the law in question, in order to be autonomously given, must not have its source outside the will it must be the will's own law: "The categorical imperative merely tells us to choose a law. Its only constraint on our choice is that it has the form of a law. And nothing determines what the law must be. *All that it has to be is a law.*"[157] Korsgaard admits that Hegel's "empty formalism objection" is adequate when directed against this highly abstract version of the categorical imperative. The imperative, requiring us to adopt *some* principle/law in order to autonomously determine our (first-personally conceived) faculty of volition, does not tell us what *particular* principles/laws are to be endorsed. This is exactly the job of a practical identity. However, the notion of legislating in accordance with one's practical identity does not yet drive a wedge between morally permissible laws and impermissible ones: "[T]here is still a deep element of relativism in the system. For whether a maxim can serve as a law still depends upon the way that

153 The scenario of an agent who completely fails to endorse any practical principles and identities is, of course, a limiting case. However, the syndrome of a psychological breakdown and certain cases of extreme psychosis suggest that this limiting case does not amount to a mere armchair philosophical claim (though the latter is more important for the conceptual investigation of agency undertaken in the text). Concerning the loss of efficaciousness of unprincipled agents, see the example of Jeremy discussed in the next section. Thanks to Fred Miller for posing the question of whether Korsgaard has actual persons in mind here.

154 Nagel 1996, p. 202.

155 It is important to stress that Kant's argument discussed by Korsgaard, does not establish a theoretical/metaphysical argument about the existence of a self and its free will. The point to keep in mind is the distinction between an empiricist (third-personal) approach to the peculiar human condition described in the text on the one hand and an approach that looks at the same phenomenon form the perspective of the deliberating agents (first-personally) on the other. For a critique of this Kantian move as employed by Korsgaard, see Risse 2007.

156 Korsgaard 1996, p. 97.

157 Korsgaard 1996, p. 98.

we think of our identities. [...] [D]ifferent laws hold for wantons, egoists, lovers, and Citizens of the Kingdom of Ends."[158]

As was said above, the next argumentative steps in *The Sources of Normativity* are supposed to establish standards that identify particular practical identities as morally permissible ones.[159] We can put most of these complex thoughts to one side because it is only the initial steps of her argument, those concerned with action *simpliciter*, that we need in order to develop the reply to Kukathas.

What we need to take with us from *The Sources of Normativity* is that the principles guiding our choices are not isolated normative facts but are the constitutive features of who we are: "A view of what you ought to do is a view of who you are."[160] Our so-called "moral identity," the only identity we universally share qua human being, consists of only one specific and highly abstract such requirement and principle, namely to adopt and endorse a (in most cases more than one) set of principles in the form of a practical identity.[161] We must endorse particular identities in order to have any substantial reasons and obligations. Without valuing a practical identity as the source of practical reasons, we cannot perform actions because acting involves attributing value to the objects of our choice (the ends of our actions). We would be mere unstructured bundles of desires and impulses, resulting in events in the world but not actions, if we conferred this value in accordance with highly particularistic and incoherent "principles" lacking any law-like form whatsoever.

Another way this point is conveyed in *The Sources of Normativity* is that reasons for action, and the underlying normative principles, are "expressive" of our identities. Practical identities "give rise" to reasons and obligations by providing a kind of filter that allows certain impulses to pass the test of reflective endorsement (guided by the identity's constitutive principles). These identities are conceptions an agent has of herself, consisting in what she can and cannot see herself doing insofar as she endorses the identities in question. As the argument in *Self-Constitution* will show, however, the relationship between actions on the one hand and our practical identities on the other is far more

158 Korsgaard 1996, p. 113.

159 These arguments concerned with obligations towards other human beings (and animals) occupy much of the fourth and final lecture in *The Sources of Normativity*. (See Korsgaard 1996, pp. 131–166.)

160 Korsgaard 1996, p. 117.

161 Korsgaard 1996, pp. 121–125.

complex than Korsgaard's "expressivist"[162] interpretation suggests. Our actions are not merely the expression of our reflectively endorsed normative self-conceptions and the practical principles that are the latter's building blocks. Rather, it is in the course of practical deliberation and by means of performing actions that we create and *constitute* those very identities and, hence, ourselves.

4.2 Action and *Self-Constitution*

In her recent book *Self-Constitution. Agency, Identity, and Integrity* Korsgaard focuses on questions of practical reason, rationality, and the normative force of rational requirements.[163] Drawing on the work of Plato, Aristotle, and Kant she defends a version of the "Constitutional Model of the soul"[164] that she attributes to all three of them. This model is used to solve the problem of agency and rests on a teleological account of performing actions that is also present in both Aristotle and Kant. As in *The Sources of Normativity*, Korsgaard presents her view as an alternative to, on the one hand, empiricist conceptions of normativity (especially those of Hume, Bentham, Mill) and rationalist/realist conceptions (such as those of Ross, Clarke, Price, and Prichard) on the other. While the former cannot explain why normative requirements, like the instrumental principle, can rationally guide our practical deliberation and actions, the latter fail to account for how these requirements can motivate us.

162 The term "expressivism" does not refer to the metaethical view that claims that moral judgments express non-cognitive attitudes regarding moral norms and rules. (See Gibbard 1990.)

163 Moral philosophical questions do, of course, remain a crucial concern for Korsgaard. The conclusions established in *Self-Constitution* are basically the same ones as those in *The Sources of Normativity*, namely substantial Kantian ones defending a conception of autonomy as the source of moral obligation. However, the arguments leading up to these conclusions are different ones in the two works respectively. As is made clear in the text, the exegetical sections (4.1 and 4.2) do not attempt to summarize the two works' entire scope. The focus lies instead on the first couple of initial steps in Korsgaard's two arguments (her conception of practical identity and her action-theory), thereby leaving out the genuinely moral philosophical stages, especially her arguments from the publicity of reasons.

164 Korsgaard 2009, pp. 133–158. The Constitutional Model is contrasted with the Combat Model of the soul that Korsgaard ascribes to the empiricist tradition. The Combat Model rests on the assumption that the soul consists of the two separate and competing forces of reason and passion. The virtuous person is the one that follows reason. Korsgaard criticizes this view because it cannot make sense of agency. Put simply, the Combat Model cannot answer the question of *who* is choosing to follow reason here? (See Korsgaard 2009, p. 134.)

Self-Constitution's central thesis is that "[t]he function of action is self-constitution."[165] Restating the starting point of her earlier work, Korsgaard claims that human beings are a special kind of creature because of the reflective structure of their consciousness. We are not passive in the face of urges and desires; we have to choose and decide on the basis of principles whether or not to endorse incentives and thereby awarding them the status of reasons for action.[166] The new facet that Korsgaard adds to this picture is that she now describes the "human plight"[167] (the *Expulsion from the Garden of Eden* by Thomas Cole is on the front cover of her book) as the inescapable challenge that consists in human beings having to turn the dispersed parts of their mental lives into unified agents who author their actions: "We must act, and we need reasons in order to act. And unless there are *some* principles with which we identify we will have no reason to act. Every human being must make himself into someone in particular, in order to have reasons to act and to live."[168] The source of our distinctly human freedom consists in the problem that our self, our agency, is not unified and held together automatically by instincts and "naturally" as in the case of the other animals. We would remain in this condition of disunity if we did not engage in the activity that Korsgaard describes in her book, and the constitutive standards of which she identifies as the categorical and hypothetical imperatives, namely action.

The way out of the particular human predicament is to be found in the phenomena of practical deliberation, choice, and a conception of action that defines the latter as "acts-done-for-the-sake-of-ends." Korsgaard develops a version of Aristotle and Kant's theories of action that puts much weight on the notions of "*logos*" and "maxim" employed in their two accounts respectively.[169] For both thinkers practical deliberation is directed at the principle describing the functional arrangement of a supposed action's necessary parts, i.e., its act and its end.[170] Aristotle and Kant do not reduce the object of practical deliberation and choice to the possible consequences and effects that are brought about by means of performing a particular act. Rather, agents choose a "whole pack-

---

165 Korsgaard 2009, p. 32.

166 This claim, concerning the relationship between practical principles and reasons (the latter are not conceivable in isolation from the former) is itself controversial and challenges the prominent view that reasons are "foundational normative entities" defended by Scanlon, Raz, and Parfit. (See Pauer-Studer 2009, p. 400.)

167 Korsgaard 2009, p. 2 and p. 23.

168 Korsgaard 2009, pp. 23–24.

169 For a valuable clarification of Korsgaard's use of Aristotle, see Broadie 2010, pp. 705–707.

170 Section 5.1 further clarifies this conception of action.

age" of "to-do-this-act-for-the-sake-of-this-end" when they employ their identity-constituting practical principles in the process of practical deliberation.[171] Korsgaard claims that when agents choose *logoi*/maxims, and perform the actions described by them, humans thereby adopt and endorse conceptions of themselves as individual agents. *The Sources of Normativity* presented a phenomenology of these practical identities and an account of the way in which these sets of principles are the source of our reasons for action. Korsgaard now puts the spotlight on the question of the necessary conditions of the possibility of acquiring and sustaining such practical identities. She continues to claim that an action must "be expressive of *myself*"[172] and must be authored by a sufficiently-well constituted agent *in order to* count as a proper instance of action; however, she now emphasizes at the same time "that you constitute yourself *as* the author of your actions in the very act of choosing them."[173] As a result, in *Self-Constitution* the notion of practical identity is not playing the same, central, role as in her earlier work.[174] Now the problem of agency takes center stage and with it the (Platonic[175]) question of how the dispersed elements of our mental lives get unified into one coherent practical standpoint, occupied by a deliberating and acting individual agent.

According to Korsgaard's view, the two fundamental Kantian principles of practical reason, the categorical imperative (the requirement to choose maxims in accordance with some self-legislated practical principles) and the hypothet-

---

171 Korsgaard 2008, p. 218.

172 Korsgaard 2009, p. 19.

173 Korsgaard 2009, p. 20. If that sounds a bit paradoxical, Korsgaard agrees. We will come back to this so-called "paradox of self-constitution" below.

174 Only a short section in *Self-Constitution* attempts to clarify the relationship between the argument in *The Sources of Normativity* and Korsgaard's more recent work: "The argument from my earlier work [...] says that in order to be a person–that is, to have reasons–you must constitute yourself as a particular person, and that, in order to do that, you must commit yourself to your value as a person-in-general, that is, as a rational agent. In this book I will argue for the same conclusion, but with a more direct focus on agency–on what is necessary to constitute yourself as the author of your actions" (Korsgaard 2009, p. 25).

175 Korsgaard's recent work is more "Platonic" than her earlier (very Kant-focused writings) in the sense of identifying as the prime task of practical philosophy the challenge of unifying ourselves as agents. The metaphysical assumption underlying this project is that a human being's mental life (her "soul") consists of dispersed forces (reason, passion,...) that do not come in the form of a harmonious unity by default. The genuinely human challenge consists in putting these diverse parts under the rule of constitutional norms; a task which is confronted in the course of practical deliberation and action. Korsgaard says: "I call it the Constitutional Model, because its clearest appearance is in Plato's *Republic*, where the human soul is compared to the constitution of a polis or city-state" (Korsgaard 2008, p. 101).

ical imperative (the principle of instrumental rationality that requires agents to will the means necessary to realize an end that they will), are the general principles constitutive of every action.[176] Every agent engaged in the activity of willing and acting (again this is something that humans are inescapably confronted with) must try to follow these principles in order to count as performing actions at all. Korsgaard believes that her account can solve the problems haunting empiricist and rationalist conceptions of normativity: the two Kantian imperatives are rationally binding and guiding (contra empiricism) because their constitutive role makes any attempt to perform actions conditional on trying to conform to them. The two imperatives have authority over our choices and actions because we cease being able to will *anything* if we systematically violate them. Actually, *systematically* violating them (making this violation one's deliberately willed policy) already presupposes the presence of their normative force. Similar to the skeptic who cannot avoid employing the principle of non-contradiction in the course of presenting his skeptical propositions, the willing wanton, simply by following her policy of constantly destroying and recreating her identity by means of performing incoherent patterns of action, *follows* a meta-principle and policy of acting and constitutes herself in accordance with it.[177] The categorical and hypothetical imperatives are, at the same time (contra rationalism), solving the problem of how we can be motivated to follow them, because we cannot escape the problem for which they are providing the solution, i.e., our human condition of being condemned to choose and act.[178]

---

176 For additional clarification concerning Korsgaard's usage of the categorical and hypothetical imperatives, see fn. 152.

177 This paradox is also relevant regarding much more wide-ranging issues that cannot be addressed here and that have to do with the value of maintaining a unified self. German romanticism (especially Schlegel), Buddhism, and Parfit's views on personal identity have called into question the very view that is assumed as a framework in this essay. However, the quick reply in the text suggests that the constitutivist seems to have the last word in these debates. Even if overcoming the enlightenment ideal of individuality were preferable all things considered (because individuality produces suffering and/or restricts authentic freedom), would not the romantic and Buddhist agent need to successfully unify herself first, i.e., *before* she engages in the project of overcoming the constraining condition of clearly defined agency and identity? (See also fn. 552 in the conclusion.)

178 One common criticism of constitutivist models like Korsgaard's is that they seem to prove too much. After all, if choice and action are unavoidable features of every human life, and the two Kantian imperatives are necessary conditions for engaging in these activities, then presenting the imperatives as *normative requirements* (that *can* get violated by free agents) might appear dubious. Normativity seems to presuppose the possibility of failing to comply with the imperatives in question. On this problem, see Lavin 2004 and FitzPatrick 2005. Korsgaard's reply to these worries (Korsgaard 2009, pp. 159–176) has not convinced all critics. (See Gowans

In order to forestall misunderstandings it is important to note that Korsgaard takes highly abstract and formal versions of the two Kantian imperatives to play this role. Hence, one must not expect her theory of action and agency to straightforwardly deliver substantial moral conclusions. Take the categorical imperative first. Basically, what Korsgaard's interpretation and defense of the universal law formula amounts to is the negative claim of rejecting the possibility of, what she calls, "particularistic willing."[179] When agents perform actions, and thereby determine their faculty of volition by choosing this specific act for that particular end, they cannot avoid willing universally and, hence, legislating for themselves (not necessarily in a morally substantial mode and "for the Kingdom of Ends" though). Recall the example of the spouse. Rejecting the desire for a sexual adventure as an illegitimate reason for action is the result of examining the normative status of that desire. To do this, and in order to take up this desire as having any normative significance for possible courses of action, the spouse has to engage with this desire from her deliberative standpoint. In other words, she has to consider the possibility of acting on this desire from the perspective of her practical identity and the principles that constitute it. When the spouse chooses not to act on this desire and rejects it as an insufficient grounds for action, this is seen by her as implying something *for her* future choices were she to find herself in exactly the same circumstances again. This minimal sense of a reason's universalizability distinguishes it from a mere whim, which, according to the view defended here, amounts to a desire that circumvents or "sneaks through" one's deliberative standpoint so to speak. Acting on a whim, however, is exactly not the same as performing actions for a reason in the sense assumed here.[180]

2010, pp. 124–126 and Broadie 2010, p. 710.) Strong support for Korsgaard's position is presented in Tenenbaum 2011, pp. 451–453. For another defense of the constitutivist approach that deals with the issue of bad action, see Schapiro 2001, pp. 103–104.

179 Korsgaard 2009, pp. 72–77.

180 Acting on a whim, therefore, can constitute an agent only in a retrospective process of deliberation, so to speak. Only once an agent looks back on this behavior and endorses it from her deliberative standpoint does it function like self-constituting actions do. Of course, this remark opens the flood gates regarding the complicated issues of moral responsibility that I cannot address here. However, it is important to note that the fact that many of our "actions" are not the result of the highly cognitivist processes, described in the text, *at the very moment of performing them* does not in itself undermine the self-constitution account. There might be an important sense in which an action is "completed" only once it is reflective incorporated into one's practical identity – and this can happen *after* a whim has expressed itself in a certain pattern of behavior. I am indebted to David Shoemaker for pressing these and many other

An agent who endorses a particular maxim could avoid this minimum degree of self-legislation only if she were "willing a maxim for exactly this occasion without taking it to have any other implications of any kind for any other occasion."[181] Korsgaard claims that particularistic willing is impossible. Even an agent who determines her volition in accordance with the maxim "I shall do the things I am inclined to do, simply because I am inclined to do them" legislates for herself; she deliberates and acts on the principle that her inclinations are always to be taken as reasons. With respect to the categorical imperative Korsgaard concludes: It "is a constitutive principle of acting, [...], because conformity to it is constitutive of an exercise of the *will*, of the determination of a person *by himself* as opposed to his determination by something within him."[182]

Even more obvious[183] is the case of the hypothetical imperative, Korsgaard's version of the instrumental principle that consists in the requirement to take the means necessary to achieve an end you will (as opposed to merely desiring it[184]). That conformity to this rational principle is constitutive of willing and performing actions is brought out by Korsgaard in discussing the example of college student Jeremy. The story goes as follows:

> Jeremy, a college student, settles down at his desk one evening to study for an examination. Finding himself a little too restless to concentrate, he decides to take a walk in the fresh air first. His walk takes him past a nearby bookstore, where the sight of an enticing title draws him in to look at the book. Before he finds it, however, he meets his friend Neil, who invites him to join some of the other kids at the bar next door for a beer. Jeremy decides to have just one, and he goes with Neil to the bar. While waiting for his beer, however, he finds that the loud noise in the bar gives him a headache, and he decides to return home without having the beer. He is now, however, in too much pain to study. So Jeremy doesn't study for his examination, hardly gets a walk, doesn't buy a book, and doesn't drink his beer.[185]

Now the obvious problem with a character like Jeremy is that he does not get anything done – he is a completely inefficacious pseudo-agent. For Jeremy every temptation presents itself as a sufficiently strong stimulus to change his behavior and it is hard to accept that he is committed to the end(s) in question since he permanently fails to take up the necessary means for achieving them.

problems that a fully developed constitutivist picture would have to address. Something that is far from satisfyingly done.

181 Korsgaard 2009, p. 75.

182 Korsgaard 2009, p. 76.

183 See Gowans 2010, p. 119 and Roth 2011.

184 On the distinction between willing and desiring/wishing an end, see section 6.1 below.

185 Korsgaard 2009, 169.

In extreme scenarios like Jeremy's it becomes clear what Korsgaard has in mind when she makes apparently radical statements depicting characters like Jeremy as behaving like wantons who fail to constitute themselves into proper agents and fail to *lead* proper lives: "The reason that I must conform to the hypothetical imperative is that if I don't conform to it, if I *always* allow myself to be derailed by timidity, idleness, or depression, then I never really *will* an end."[186]

Korsgaard's account of self-constituting action consists in the following then: Because of the unique condition of being reflectively distanced from immediate desires on the one hand and the resulting necessity of deliberation, choice, and action on the other, human beings are confronted with the inescapable challenge of having to develop a unified self-conception as agents. The latter provides the principles on the basis of which some incentives are singled-out as reasons for action and others are rejected.[187] Such a unified self-conception is, however, not only the *basis* for practical deliberation and action. It is at the same time the *result* of performing actions and of making these actions' principles (their *logoi* and maxims) one's own: "In choosing in accordance with the principles of a form of practical identity, I claim, we make that identity our own."[188]

Korsgaard is well aware that her view appears paradoxical. On the one hand, she describes our practical identities as sets of normative principles that provide reasons for action. As stressed in *The Sources of Normativity* our actions are the *expression* of our already endorsed practical identities. The "I do" must necessarily attach to my actions and a sufficiently unified agent (the "I") has to be present in order to perform them. On the other hand, however, Korsgaard rejects the view that actions are merely expressions of the contingent practical identities that we happen to have. This side of her view is central to the argu-

186 Korsgaard 2009, p. 69. In the face of critical responses, Korsgaard has considerably altered her views concerning the hypothetical imperative. They now differ from the argument presented in "The Normativity of Instrumental Reason." (See Korsgaard 2008, pp. 27–68.) Most importantly Korsgaard no longer believes that the hypothetical imperative is a freestanding and independent second rational principle; rather "[t]here is only one principle of practical reason, and it is the categorical imperative [...] it [the hypothetical imperative; C.H.] picks out an *aspect* of the categorical imperative: the fact that the laws of our will must be practical laws, laws that constitute us as agents by rendering us efficacious" (Korsgaard 2008, p. 68).

187 The picture is even more complicated because Korsgaard presents a dynamic (two-way) interpretation of the Kantian notion of incentives. Incentives are not merely passively received inputs but are themselves formed/conceptualized versions of these inputs. Practical identities play a significant role here: "They are standing sources of incentives, as well as principles in terms of which we accept and reject proposed actions" (Korsgaard 2009, p. 22).

188 Korsgaard 2009, p. 42.

ment in *Self-Constitution*. She says "that in the relevant sense there is no *you* prior to your choices and actions, because your identity is in a quite literal way *constituted* by your choices and actions."[189] In other words, there is no prior agent (a person who has unified her practical identities conclusively) who performs self-constituting actions; rather, by means of performing such actions (in the complex Aristotelian and Kantian sense) that agent unifies herself by means of endorsing specific practical principles that in turn define her identity. Actions fulfill a function: by choosing and performing them, you become an agent with a particular practical identity. However, and that makes the whole picture appear paradoxical, since non-arbitrary choosing and acting (in Korsgaard's demanding sense) presupposes an already sufficiently unified agent one will ask: "How can you constitute yourself, create yourself, unless you are already there?"[190] Korsgaard calls this objection to her view the "paradox of self-constitution."[191]

Korsgaard's solution to the paradox of self-constitution is rather swift.[192] She dissolves the paradox by introducing an Aristotelian (but at the same time Kantianized, i.e., non-ontological) example of teleological explanation. When we observe the development of certain physiognomic characteristics and patterns of behavior, specific to the species of giraffes, we thereby understand the question of how a particular animal constitutes itself and becomes a giraffe: "No one is tempted to say: 'how can the giraffe make itself into itself unless it is already there?' The picture here is not of a craftsman who is, mysteriously, his own product. The picture here is of the self-constitutive process that is the essence of life. The paradox of self-constitution, in this context, is no paradox at all."[193] Similarly, in the human case, a person becomes a specific individual by performing actions that at the very same moment constitute herself as well as express herself. That is just what it means to be a person. According to this dynamic picture it does not make sense to insist on any conceptual priority among the constituting agent on the one hand and the agent-to-be-constituted on the other. "[W]hat it is to be a person, or a rational agent, is just to be engaged in the activity of constantly making yourself into a person – just as what it is to be a giraffe is to be engaged in the activity [*sic.*] constantly making yourself into a

189 Korsgaard 2009, p. 19.

190 Korsgaard 2009, p. 20.

191 "The Paradox of Self-Constitution" is presented in Korsgaard 2009, pp. 41–44.

192 The reviewers of *Self-Constitution* agree that more needs to be said to solve the paradox of self-constitution. See Gowans 2010, Doomen 2010, Chappell 2010, Ketcher 2010, Tenenbaum 2011, Schlosser 2011, Schlösser 2011.

193 Korsgaard 2009, p. 42.

giraffe."[194] That the process of self-constitution appears paradoxical is due to the misconception "that the endorsement of our identities, our self-constitution, is a state rather than an activity."[195] This misunderstanding leads to the false dichotomy according to which we either have to be fully developed agents in order to perform actions (in which case our agency is already determined and our will is heteronomous) or we are entirely empty selves (having no reasons whatsoever guiding our initial "actions" and, hence, not getting the process of self-constitution going in the first place).

Korsgaard's response – self-constitution simply is the activity of performing actions – remains puzzling. Her reply suddenly allows an example taken from the animal kingdom (giraffes) to provide the basis for the analogy that lies at the heart of her response. Up to the point where she discusses the paradox of self-constitution (and for most of the remainder of the book) she insists that self-constitution in the case of human beings has a different quality because human action is not determined by instincts. The self-constituting activity of animals is not the result of confronting the specifically human plight that motivates Korsgaard's entire project and that was discussed above. Moreover, the highly individualized activities of practical deliberation and of setting ends (dependent on the reflective self-consciousness that is unique to humans) are responsible for successful human self-constitution being dependent on very different internal and external (cultural, social etc.) conditions than are necessary in the case of animals. Korsgaard's giraffe-analogy underestimates the qualitative differences that she elaborates on so impressively at other points. Granted, a giraffe, by doing what it does as a representative of its species, teleologically executes "what it means to be a giraffe." But the same is not true in the case of humans, teleologically executing "what it means to be a person." What makes the human case special, even upon granting the general and abstract species-specific *telos* of "being a person," is the characteristic feature of having to construct one's practical identity in a qualitatively (not merely gradually) different way than a giraffe that becomes an exponent of its species.[196]

---

194 Korsgaard 2009, p. 42.

195 Korsgaard 2009, p. 43.

196 Korsgaard acknowledges this point to some extent when discussing the exclusively human features of agency. (See Korsgaard 2009, pp. 125–132.) Contrary to animals, whose self-constitution is guided by instincts, human beings face the challenge of having to lead a "way of life" and have to construct what Rawls calls "a conception of the good." (See Korsgaard 2009, p. 128.) And a bit later: "[I]t [human identity; C.H.] is more essentially individual than a non-human animal's, because he is free" (Korsgaard 2009, p.129). Here Korsgaard acknowledges that self-constitution into a person is different from animal self-constitution because, "the form

In the next chapter an alternative response to the paradox of self-constitution will emerge that focuses on these specific features of human action (and, therefore, human self-constitution). Only human self-constitution is a social and historical phenomenon. Action (especially the task of setting ends) is conditional on the presence of some rules, norms, and practices, providing a minimum degree of predictability concerning the effects that one's actions have in the world. The solution to the paradox of self-constitution, spelled out in section 5.2, argues that the process of setting ends (a necessary component of any action that constitutes its author) incorporates these interpersonal norms, which in turn renders the resulting practical identities into public ones (the practical principles that define an identity cannot subsist in the abstract, i.e., without getting applied to concrete, world-directed, actions). The starting point for the process of self-constitution is therefore always a social and public one. Kantians will object to this solution to the paradox because of its seemingly heteronomous character. Chapter 6 will come back to this issue after having presented the conception of why a practical identity is also always a public one in the next one.

---

of the human is precisely the form of the animal that must create its own form" (Korsgaard 2009, p. 130). However, as continued in the text, even granting this admission by Korsgaard I still think that a) spelling out the socio-political preconditions for creating one's individual form and b) showing that a seemingly heteronomous starting point of this process does not necessarily render autonomy impossible, are two significant and necessary additions to Korsgaard's attempt to solve the paradox of self-constitution. (See the interlude in section 5.2.)

Chapter 5: Public Actions and Public Identities

In a critical commentary David Enoch expresses puzzlement concerning Korsgaard's overall view. He says: "the relation between the views expressed in the Locke Lectures [now published as *Self-Constitution*; C.H.] and in *Sources* is not entirely clear to me."[197] There is something to that complaint because Korsgaard only briefly addresses the question of how her argument from practical identities fits with her recent project of grounding the normativity of principles of practical reason in what is constitutive of action.[198] This chapter is an attempt to connect the two arguments. Establishing the relationship between the conception of an agent's practical identity (a necessary prerequisite for performing actions) on the one hand and Korsgaard's account of action (and the way in which good actions constitute agency) on the other, will highlight the role that rule- and norm-governed practices play in the process of individual self-constitution. This claim concerning the central importance of social practices for individuality is the conclusion of this chapter.

The chapter is divided into two sections. Section 5.1 makes good on the promise of dedicating more attention to Korsgaard's Neo-Aristotelian and Neo-Kantian theory of action. Contrasting her view with Mill's (and consequentialist/empiricist conceptions more generally) Korsgaard regards actions as more than mere instruments, utilized to produce states of affairs. Actions are complex items that are chosen and performed for their own sake. Their end/purpose is just one important element of them. The second section (5.2) presents this chapter's main argument for the public identity claim, which consists of seven stages. Starting with the claim that the constitution of agency always also amounts to the constitution of particular practical identities, the argument concludes that these practical identities are always also public ones. One central move in the argument consists in further developing the point that the process of self-constituting action necessarily involves (among other things) the setting of ends. The latter task is dependent on a natural and social environment of norms and rules that put an agent's status as an end-setter on a reliable and predictable basis. Since "action is self-constitution" this in turn implies that the possibility of self-constitution requires such public norms.

197 Enoch 2006, p. 171, fn. 3.
198 Korsgaard 2009, p. 25.

5.1 The Structure and Form of Action

Korsgaard considers the broad question of what accounts for a thing's goodness.[199] What sets the standards for a particular thing being a good instance of something? (Why is this car a good car?) Korsgaard's answer refers to the thing's "functional nature": "A thing is good when it has the properties that make it good at being what it is, or doing what it does."[200] Korsgaard applies this general account of goodness to actions. In order to determine whether a particular action is a good one, we need to ask whether it is good *qua* action, whether it lives up to the standards that determine what an action is. Korsgaard complains that contemporary moral philosophy has been dominated by a specific answer to these two closely related questions of what an action is on the one hand and what makes an action a good one on the other. She has in mind the conception of action that has its origins in Bentham and Mill. According to utilitarianism's underlying consequentialist and empiricist account, actions are devices and instruments, employed in order to produce specific outcomes, namely those states of affairs that maximize the good along a scale defined in some commensurable unit (e.g., happiness).[201] The consequentialist view conceives of actions as events that, first and foremost, effect a measurable change in the world external to the will of the agent performing it. Only the external end/purpose of an action (the state of affairs resulting from its performance) constitutes the reason for choosing and performing it on the one hand and for the action's moral quality and value on the other. In other words, "action is essentially production, and accordingly its function is to bring something about. Whether an action is good depends on whether *what* it brings about is good, or as good as it can be."[202]

---

199 In addition to the sections in *Self-Constitution* my exposition and discussion of Korsgaard's action-theory relies on her recent paper "Acting for a Reason." (See Korsgaard 2008, pp. 207–229.)

200 Korsgaard 2008, p. 216.

201 A terminological clarification is necessary: In the text the terms "consequentialism" and "empiricism" are used almost interchangeably. Were the current argument concerned with moral-philosophical issues in a narrow sense, this would of course be an unacceptable convention. The reason the two labels are used together is not just the historical affinity between British empiricism and consequentialism/utilitarianism but also the substantial point that the consequentialist paradigm rests on a view of action that treats the latter in a way similar to treating objects of an empirical, but at the same time evaluative, investigation. The empiricist account is third-personal, whereas the account of action presumed by many non-consequentialists addresses the agent's standpoint. To what extent these two views really exclude each other is an issue I cannot pursue here. (See Korsgaard 1996a, p. xii–xiii.)

202 Korsgaard 2009, p. 8.

According to Korsgaard, the Benthamite/Millean account of the nature of action (and of how actions are to be evaluated) reduces actions to events that result in more or less desirable states of affairs. This account underdescribes the phenomenon of action and conflates the two very different activities of action and production, a distinction essential to Aristotle: "making and acting are different [...] so that the reasoned state of capacity to act is different from the reasoned state of capacity to make. [...] while making has an end other than itself, action cannot; for good action itself is its end."[203] In conflating mere acts and their consequences with comprehensively described actions (a distinction defined promptly), the consequentialist approach also ends up reducing the reasons for action to its purposes and ends. True, Korsgaard admits, giving an account of an action's purpose is an important feature of its description (even Kant's maxims must include it); however, properties critical to the internal structure of the action (its "form" of, first-personally, relating acts and ends in a particular way) are neglected by the account adhered to by Bentham and Mill.

The deficiencies of reducing a practical reason to an action's purpose is brought out by Korsgaard's example of Jack from Indianapolis, who goes to Chicago in order to buy a box of paperclips.[204] That merely citing the purpose of the action (successfully acquiring paperclips) is not sufficient to provide the reason for it is clear in Jack's example: "You will say 'that can't be the reason,' not because the purpose isn't served by the action, but because going from Indianapolis to Chicago just to buy a box of paperclips is so obviously not worthwhile."[205] It is important to note that the point of the paperclip-example is not a narrow moral-philosophical one. Of course, consequentialists have the resources to identify Jack's act as suboptimal and, depending on what is at stake overall, even morally inferior. Jack's trip to Chicago is not worthwhile since the overall consequences are affected by the inefficiency of the means he takes to realize his ends. Korsgaard's more general point, supposed to be illustrated by the example, is the conceptual distinction between a reason for an action and its purpose. That the purpose-focused account of reasons for action as paradigmatically at work in contemporary consequentialism does not rule out that consequentialism can be used to evaluate many aspects of our lives. Rather it fails as a comprehensive enough account of what a reason for an action is.[206]

203 Aristotle in Korsgaard 2008, p. 216.

204 Korsgaard 2008, p. 221.

205 Korsgaard 2008, p. 221.

206 For Korsgaard's critique of the way moral theories are often categorized (into consequentialism, deontology, etc.), see Korsgaard 2008, pp. 194–195. I thank my commentators who

In order to sharpen the criticism that a reason for an action is not exhaustively accounted for by merely quoting the state of affairs that it is intended to produce, Korsgaard introduces the distinction between acts/act-types on the one hand and actions on the other. Examples of acts and act-types are things like "lying" and "breaking promises." Actions, on the other hand, are more complex items like, "Breaking a promise in order to make some ready cash." According to the Benthamite/Millean action-theory, the reason for a specific *act* (like lying) is exhaustively accounted for by putting forward the effect that the act is expected to produce (say, rescuing a potential murder victim, to use the utilitarian's favorite example). The grounds for choosing the particular act is, again, the state of affairs that the proposed act is directed at. Importantly, the reason (the purpose/end) is something external to and separated from the act so defined. According to the Benthamite/Millean paradigm, practical deliberation amounts to the choice of a specific act that gets employed as a means to bring about an end that has been identified as worth producing. According to the alternative view, that will be presented promptly, a reason is nothing external to a chosen *action*; rather, "the kind of item that can serve as a reason for action [is] the maxim or *logos* of an action, which expresses the agent's endorsement of the appropriateness of doing a certain act for the sake of a certain end."[207] But I jump ahead of myself.

In order to put a more satisfying theory of action at the heart of her project, Korsgaard goes back to Kant as well as Aristotle, who share "precisely the same" account. This alternative account defines an action (as opposed to an act) as a "whole package" always including an act done for the sake of an end. Actions always have the form of "to-do-this-act-for-the-sake-of-this-end."[208] Aristotle and Kant understood that the object of practical deliberation and choice (remember our discussion of human beings' plight and the inescapability of this kind of choice and action) are whole actions understood as such "packages." Importantly, the aim/purpose/end *is* an essential part of this package; Korsgaard agrees that much with her adversaries. In Aristotle and Kant this view of action is connected with the notions of "*logos*" and "maxim" respectively: "What corresponds in Aristotle's theory to the description of an action is what he calls a *logos* – as I will render it, a principle. [...] Kant thinks that an action is described by a maxim, and the maxim of an action is also of the 'to-do-this-act-

urged me to clarify the Jack and the paperclips example and its function in Korsgaard's overall argument.

207 Korsgaard 2008, p. 226.

208 Korsgaard 2009, p. 10.

for-the-sake-of-this-end' structure."[209] Hence both Aristotle and Kant are (for the most part) very clear that the object of practical deliberation and choice is never an act alone but always an act done for the sake of a certain end. Not paying attention to this subtle difference also underlies, for example, the widespread misunderstanding (that Kant himself was not totally immune against, as well be discussed promptly) that the categorical imperative rules out certain acts and act-types like "breaking a promise," "lying," or "killing oneself." What the imperative is supposed to test is whole actions, e.g., breaking a promise (act) in order to get some ready cash (end).[210] The categorical imperative identifies the performance of a certain act in order to achieve a certain end as not conforming to the exclusively formal standard of maxims having a lawlike form.

More has to be said about Korsgaard's distinction between acts and act-types (e.g., "lying," "committing suicide") on the one hand and actions (e.g., "lying in order to avoid an inconvenient personal encounter") on the other. Korsgaard introduces a distinction internal to the notion of act-types (not whole actions!) which is of importance for the argument that follows.[211] In discussing a mistake that she sees Kant and Aristotle committing (both are guilty of the "slip" of declaring some mere act-types to be inherently morally wrong), Korsgaard admits that the categorical imperative works better or worse, depending on which one of two kinds of act-types is involved in a particular action.

---

209 Korsgaard 2008, p. 217 and p. 218.

210 In his proper ethical writings ("The Doctrine of Virtue" in *The Metaphysics of Morals* and the *Lectures on Ethics*), Kant presents a number of moral puzzles that indicate his sensitivity concerning the intricacies of moral life. Whether it is permissible (even obligatory?) to kill yourself when you have been infected with rabies and can foresee that you will turn into a violent threat to your fellow humans, is a perfectly legitimate and difficult question. (See MM 6:423 – 424.) There is a plethora of essays dedicated to the puzzles related to Kant's infamous "On a Supposed Right to Lie from Philanthropy." For two especially promising attempts to make sense of what is going on in the murderer-at-one's-door example, see Wood 2008, pp. 240–258 and Weinrib 2008a. Both authors point out that it is a fundamental mistake to situate the infamous essay in an ethical context. It is rather a legal-philosophical argument about the legal status of the "right" to lie. This also explains why Kant considers an agent's responsibility for lying to the murder in explicitly consequentialist terms. This only makes sense when one considers that Kant does not talk about moral responsibility here but about issues of liability.

211 Korsgaard 2008, p. 223. The distinction between the two kinds of act-types (spelled out in detail below) was first presented in Korsgaard 1996a, pp. 84–85 and 97–101. The distinction between the two act-types will be critical in discussing the Anarchia thought experiment in section 6.1. There it will be shown that even Korsgaard's natural acts depend for their possibility on social norms and practices. In other words, at least insofar as one is considering a world that one does not populate alone, the set of natural acts is an empty one.

With respect to the first kind of act-type the test "works almost too well" and this is responsible for an error that Kant makes when he declares certain act-types as being inherently wrong, i.e. wrong regardless of what end/purpose they are conjoined with. Members of the first kind of act-type "depend for their possibility not just on natural laws, but also on the existence of certain social practices and conventions."[212] Actions involving such act-types (e.g., act-types like writing a check, running for office, but also promising, honoring a contract etc.) are those that work best with the categorical imperative test. Representatives of these act-types find themselves caught up in a practical contradiction insofar as the possibility of performing them depends on the stability of social practices. If such an act is at the same time part of an action that, if practiced as a universal policy, would undermine these very practices a practical contradiction results because "practices and conventions are unlikely to survive their universal abuse."[213] The act in question would be an ineffectual means to achieve the chosen end because the act itself becomes impossible. Since *almost* all actions involving this first kind of act-type lead to a practical contradiction, Kant was tempted to regard representatives of the first act-type as inherently morally wrong. This last step constitutes the "slip" since, according to Korsgaard's account, only whole actions, not mere acts, can have the property of moral wrongness: "Even if Kant were right in thinking that any action involving the act-type 'false promise' will fail the test, that would not show that the act-type is inherently evil. It would only show that members of the class of actions involving that act-type are inherently evil."[214]

Korsgaard contrasts the first kind of act-type with the one comprising acts like "[w]alking and running, slugging and stabbing, tying up and killing – these are act-types that are made possible by the laws of nature, and accordingly, *one can do them in any society*."[215] The categorical imperative test does not work that well in cases of actions that involve act-types of this second kind. This is so because the possibility of performing these acts cannot be undermined by the universal violation of any specific background norms and practices that make that act-type possible in the first place. Importantly for our purposes, Korsgaard claims that act-types depending only on the reliability of the laws of nature are not dependent on any man-made institutional background. Only "where an action involves an act-type that must be sustained by practices and conven-

212 Korsgaard 2008, p. 223.
213 Korsgaard 2008, p. 223.
214 Korsgaard 2008, p. 223.
215 Korsgaard 2008, p. 223 (my emphasis).

tions, and at the same time violates the rules of those very practices or conventions, it is relatively easy to find the kind of contradiction that Kant looks for in the universalization test."[216] Hence, there are two kinds of act-types: those that are dependent for their possibility on the laws of nature alone and those that are dependent on social practices and institutions as well as on the laws of nature.

We do not need to delve into the genuine moral-philosophical context within which Korsgaard's distinction between the two kinds of act-types is presented.[217] What needs to be kept in mind is the grounds of the distinction, i.e., the two different kinds of necessary external conditions for the possibility of acts that Korsgaard mentions here (natural laws and social conventions). The major argument defended in this essay will make extensive use of these external conditions.

Let us conclude and summarize the exposition of Korsgaard's action theory. The starting point of Korsgaard's account was a critique of empiricist views on two, related, questions: what is an action and what is a good action. The empiricist account reduces an agent's reason for choosing a particular action to the action's purpose, its aimed-at effect. A Neo-Aristotelian and Neo-Kantian action theory rests on the conviction that the notion of a reason for an action has its source in the relationship between an act and an end, not merely in the latter. This relationship is described by the action's subjective principle, its *logos* and maxim. When an agent acts for a reason, she practically deliberates and chooses such an action description, not merely a purpose. A good instance of a *logos* and maxim exhibits the properties of "nobility" and "moral worth" respectively. "A good action is one that embodies the *orthos logos* or right principle – it is done at the right time, in the right way, to the right object, and – importantly for my purposes – with the right aim."[218]

216 Korsgaard 2008, p. 223.

217 Korsgaard concludes the rectification of the slip that she sees in Kant and Aristotle (that certain act-types ("lying," "murder," "adultery" etc.) are singled-out as inherently morally wrong) in the following way: Only actions, as defined in the text, can have the property of moral wrongness. Take for example the act-type of "murder": "To say that murder is wrong is not to say that there is an act-type, murder, that is wrong no matter what end you have in view when you do it. Rather, 'murder' is the name of a class of *actions*. A murder is a homicide committed for *some end or other* that is inadequate to justify the homicide. We don't call execution or killing in battle or killing in self-defense 'murder' unless we believe that those actions are not justifiable, that punishment or war or self-defense are not ends that justify killing" (Korsgaard 2008, p. 224).

218 Korsgaard 2009, p. 10.

What we need to keep in mind for our purposes is that Korsgaard's account of action, despite its anti-consequentialist tone,[219] does assign a central role to an agent's aims, purposes, and ends. Korsgaard admits that it would be incorrect "to say that Kantian agents do not care about or are not interested [...] in the consequences of their acts. It would be impossible even to formulate a maxim without attention to the intended consequences of an act."[220] Aims, ends, and purposes are essential parts of actions and their description in the form of subjective principles (*logoi* and maxims). Korsgaard's insistence that "the *aim* is included in the description of the action, and that it is the action as a whole, *including the aim*, which the agent chooses" emphasizes that a necessary feature of every action is some end/purpose/aim. Connecting this point concerning ends with Korsgaard's overall argument about the role that action plays in the process of self-constitution, we now see that, since action (formulating and choosing *logoi* and maxims) is only possible insofar as ends can be set and pursued, the possibility of self-constitution itself depends on successfully setting and pursuing ends. The next section argues for a particular account of what is involved in setting ends and in pursuing purposes and it explains why this feature of Korsgaard's account of action deserves privileged attention.

5.2 The Public Conditions of Self-Constitution

This section finally shows how the conception of action just developed is related to Korsgaard's views concerning practical identity and agency. As discussed above, Korsgaard argues that by means of performing actions, human beings constitute themselves as agents. The choice of an action is at the same time the endorsement of a particular normative self-conception, a view of ourselves as bearers of those specific practical principles that guide us in this particular process of choosing. It is in this process of practical deliberation and action that

219 This anti-consequentialism takes on a pretty strong form at times: "Consequentialism, as I see it, is not actually a moral theory because it supposes that the value of 'doings' just amounts to the productive value of acts – that all we have to care about is the effects of our acts. And that is refusing to assign value to actions as such. So, if you think with Kant and Aristotle that what morality is all about is actions as a whole, then consequentialism doesn't seem to be a moral theory. Consequentialism is a kind of technological vision, something proposed as a replacement for morality. It is a social engineering project" (Korsgaard 2002, p. 57).

220 Korsgaard 2002, p. 57.

we achieve the unity necessary to count as the author (not the mere cause) of our bodily movements. But how exactly does this process work?[221]

The argument for what is labeled from now on "the public identity claim" consists of seven stages. The task of this section is to present these seven stages successively and briefly explain them. The comprehensive justification and illustration of the argument for the public identity claim is the project of the remainder of this book. The seven stages are: 1. Performing actions does not merely constitute agents in the abstract but at the same time always also constitutes a particular individual with a specific and unique practical identity. 2. In this process the higher order principles defining such a practical identity get applied to concrete actions in order to actually constitute the individual as described in stage 1. 3. Every such application of higher order principles to a concrete action must involve the identification and setting of an end. 4. In order to set ends certain publicly acknowledged social practices and institutions must be in place (in addition to the regularities of the natural world that are not the prime concern now).[222] 5. These practices and institutions (themselves arrangements of practical rules and principles) are therefore always part of the full descriptions (the maxims/*logoi*) of the concrete actions chosen and performed by the agent. 6. The higher order practical principles that are the building blocks of a particular practical identity (and that guide the choice of all concrete actions) are therefore too always incorporating these public principles that make setting any ends possible. 7. Hence, a practical identity is always also a public identity. Let us look at each of these stages in turn and let us use the concrete example of a father and one of his identity-constituting actions in order to render the seven stages less abstract. The example envisages a father (the agent) visiting his sick daughter at the hospital (the concrete action).

Stage 1: *Performing actions does not merely constitute agents in the abstract but at the same time always also constitutes a particular individual with a specific and unique practical identity*. As the quote by David Enoch at the beginning of this chapter pointed out, the relationship between *The Sources of Normativity* and *Self-Constitution* is not clear. However, in the latter work Korsgaard summarizes its main thesis in the following way: "[W]e human beings constitute our own personal and practical identities – and at the same time our own agency – through action itself."[223] The qualification "at the same time" is crucial here but

221 When this chapter looks at the "mechanics" of self-constituting action this does not refer to a psychological or otherwise empirical investigation.

222 The first of the two thought experiments discussed in section 6.1 will focus on the role that natural regularities play as necessary preconditions of self-constituting action.

223 Korsgaard 2009, p. 45.

also ambiguous. It either refers to action achieving two separate states (unified agency on the one hand and a practical identity on the other) that emerge at the same time. Or it refers to a substantial and necessary connection between two, conceptually congruent, items. The second reading is the one we should endorse. Where there is a practical identity there is agency, and the other way round. This claim becomes clearer when we introduce another concept: In the case of human beings the constitution of agency is always also the constitution of individuality. Individuality consists in the development and maintenance of a *particular* practical perspective on the world. Put negatively, the scenario of a human who performs an action and thereby maintains her agency *without* also maintaining some practical identity is a conceptual non-starter. An abstract concept of agency (simply referring to the unified first-personal perspective of an action's author) cannot in and of itself occupy an individual human's practical standpoint and fails to provide what is necessary to engage in self-constitution, i.e., deliberating on and choosing actions. In order to choose actions' maxims and *logoi* (as discussed in the previous section) more has to be present than agency *simpliciter*.[224] The "at the same time" therefore refers to action as constituting not just agents. The performance of actions always also constitutes an individual with some specific practical identity.[225] Of course, at this initial stage of the argument, the content and quality of this identity (its practical principles of choice and action) remain totally unspecified. However, this indeterminacy is compatible with the claim that every action constitutes an agent with at least some such practical identity.

Application to the father example: When an agent practically deliberates and performs the concrete action of "I drive to the hospital in order to pay a supportive visit to my sick daughter" he does not merely constitute himself as an abstract agent; rather, he constitutes himself as an agent with the particular practical identity of a father at the same time.

---

224 This reading of Korsgaard's quote will certainly remind many of the communitarian critique of liberalism's empty self. (See Sandel 1998.) However, I resist to align my interpretation with this kind of criticism. Whereas communitarians require individuals to develop fairly thick community-based attachments in order to make meaningful choices, the line of argument pursued in this essay is compatible with (though it does not imply) quite radical versions of self-centered lives of hermits as discussed below.

225 This view does not imply pluralism amongst individuals. Given what is said in the text, it might turn out that all individuals endorse the same practical principles and, hence, have the same practical identity. Still, this is a different claim from the one that says that all individuals are the same because they are all abstract agents.

Stage 2: *In the process of individual self-constitution the higher order principles defining a practical identity get applied to concrete actions in order to actually constitute the individual as described in stage 1.* We need to have a closer look at the "mechanics" of self-constitution. In line with the action-theory discussed above, the choice of actions takes on the form of choosing their maxims and *logoi*. When an agent engages in the process of practical deliberation she looks at the description of the proposed action, which consists of a combination of an act and an end. The formulation of such a description is therefore necessary for engaging in the activity of practical choice. The feature of this picture that needs to be stressed at this point is how the abstract and general practical principles that are the building blocks of one's practical identity apply in the course of the choice of these descriptions of actions.[226] Let us call the abstract, identity-constituting, practical principles "higher-order principles." Introducing this terminological complication is necessary because maxims and *logoi* too have been referred to as principles above, namely "subjective" ones.[227] Subjective principles of action are lower-order principles, describing particular actions, which are chosen in the complex process of practical deliberation involving the higher-order principles that define what kind of agent oneself is. Let us therefore keep in mind that particular action-descriptions (maxims/*logoi*) refer to a specific combination of an act and an end (e.g., "I cheat on today's econ quiz (act) to get an A on it (end).") and that they therefore differ from the higher-order principles ("I don't use unfair means to obtain educational goals.") that define a practical identity ("graduate student"). In order to play their reason-giving and action-guiding role ("Should I cheat on today's econ quiz to get an A?"), the identity-constituting principles have to exhibit a certain level of abstraction and generality. (Practical identities unify us across time and if their principles were too specific then they would apply to only a few particular actions and therefore fail to provide the basis for sustained individuality.) However, and this is the substance of stage 2, these abstract principles can only play

226 This hierarchical view of principles will remind readers of Frankfurt and Watson's influential views respectively. (See Frankfurt 1988, pp. 11–25 and Watson 1975.) Especially Watson's view, with its emphasis on a platonic structure of the will, must certainly be acknowledged as a precursor of Korsgaard's theory and of the account presented here. A suggestive passage: "The free agent has the capacity to translate his values into action; his actions flow from his evaluational system. One's evaluational system may be said to constitute one's standpoint, the point of view from which one judges the world. The important feature of one's evaluational system is that one cannot coherently dissociate oneself from it *in its entirety*. (See Watson 1975, p. 216.)

227 See G 4:400–4:401, where Kant defines a maxim as a "subjective principle of volition."

their role in the process of self-constitution when they get applied to and actualized in concrete action – there is a relationship of mutual dependence between the two. Altering one of Kant's famous lines, stage 2 submits that "Practical principles without actualization in (concrete) actions are empty."[228] Higher-order practical principles that never get applied in the course of concrete actions cannot be the elements out of which normative self-conceptions are made.[229] This claim is not spelled out by Korsgaard, but it is my interpretation of her slogan that "action is self-constitution" (and, according to stage 1, "action is identity-constitution"). *Concrete* actions are the medium in which self-constitution must take place, exactly because the practical identities that figure in this process consist of *abstract* but practical principles and norms. In the same way in which, for example, the (abstract) pure category of causation cannot subsist independently of any empirical manifold that it gets applied to in the process of unifying cognition, so practical principles cannot compile identities when they never get actualized in concrete, worldly, actions. It is by means of deliberating about a concrete action and in the process of choosing it that an agent endorses those abstract principles that guide this deliberation and choice in this particular case – but also in cases that are relevantly similar. That is how our practical identity unifies us in a forward-looking way.

Application to the father example: The father's practical identity is composed of abstract principles such as, "A father has the publicly recognized right to visit his daughter at the hospital when she is sick." In order to constitute himself as a father, he has to be the kind of agent who applies this, and many other, abstract principles in the course of choosing what to do *if* the concrete situation arises in which his daughter is admitted to a hospital and he needs to decide whether to go the hospital in order to visit her.

Stage 3: *Every application of higher order principles to a concrete action must involve the identification and setting of an end.* Let us zoom in yet another level and analyze in more detail the basic unit of self-constitution, i.e., concrete actions. The objects of practical deliberation and choice are maxims and *logoi*. As

228 The other part of this statement, "Actions without principles are blind," is part of stage 6.

229 This point gets us close to one of Hegel's most perplexing views, i.e., his view on intentions and how actions must be completed. An agent's intentions fully reveal themselves to others, but also to the agent, only upon completion of an action. Pippin summarizes this view: "[T]he deed and the reception and reaction to it are considered a *constitutive element* of the deed, of what fixes ultimately *what was done* and *what turned out to be* a subject's intention" (Pippin 2008, p. 152). Why (at least in the human case) a practical identity that never gets applied in the course of concrete actions fails to be a *practical* identity is also the point of the objection discussed in section 6.2.

discussed in section 5.1, these descriptions of proposed actions necessarily involve acts and ends plus an arrangement of the two (the "subjective principle"). (When agents choose specific actions they choose such arrangements of acts plus ends.) At the end of the previous section it was pointed out that even this Neo-Aristotelian and Neo-Kantian conception of actions must exhibit what one might call a "minimally consequentialist structure."[230] Deliberative choice and action necessarily involve the activity of aiming at certain consequences, purposes, and ends. A narrow focus on intended purposes and ends certainly underdescribes actions (and the reasons for and against performing them). However, the eventual effect in the world (the desired state of affairs) that an agent determines herself to bring about by performing a particular action plays a necessary role in the agent's process of formulating the proposed action's maxim. Action involves, to put it in Kant's terms, the "setting of an end." Setting ends is part of what Korsgaard described as the agent choosing the "whole package" of action – the agent commits herself to the execution of an act for the sake of bringing about a certain end.[231]

Application to the father example: When the father is confronted with the news that his daughter is sick and was brought to a hospital, his process of practical deliberation has to identify the ends of possible actions first. One of these ends is to be with his daughter and to support her. If he was not able to set the end of supporting his daughter in this way, the father's practical deliberation about what to do (i.e., what action to choose) in response to the news cannot get off the ground, since setting at least one end is a necessary component of every action in the technical sense presented in the previous section.

---

230 The notion "consequentialist structure" is mentioned in the interview discussed above. (See Korsgaard 2002, p. 56.) With respect to this particular formulation Korsgaard explicitly rejects the idea that every workable moral theory has to have a robust consequentialist/utilitarian structure – despite her admitting that an action's consequences do matter for being able to formulate any maxims at all. This acknowledgment is part of the reason for me claiming that even Korsgaard's account of action has to have a *minimally* consequentialist structure.

231 Especially stage 3 makes the argument sound overly cognitivist in the sense that it requires people to be extremely self-transparent in order to count as agents at all. However, the account of action defended here merely tries to isolate the feature of choice that renders human action distinct from *exclusively* instinct-determined behavior. Action, in the technical sense employed, always involves at least some non-instinctual element of reflective activity. It seems legitimate to focus on the more complex instances of action in order to isolate this specific rational element without supposing that every action exhibits this maximum degree of practical deliberation and reflective endorsement. Still, the account presented is a demanding view of (free) agency and this issue is discussed in section 8.2.

Stage 4: *In order to set ends certain external and public practices and institutions must be in place.* It is at this stage that the argument for the public identity claim becomes controversial, if it has not become so already. Even if setting ends is a necessary feature of every action deserving that label, is not the task of identifying and determining ends a straightforward and trivial task, many will ask? The line of argument pursued here disagrees with the view, underlying this apparently rhetorical question. The point at which the seemingly private activity of action as self-constitution reveals its necessary public dimension is this one: at least in what will be called the "societal condition" (in which more than one individual exists and the individuals are aware of that fact) the process of setting ends requires the acknowledgment of public norms, which establish and maintain the individuals' standing as end-setters vis-à-vis one another in a reliable way. (The interpersonal predictability and reliability that is secured by this public recognition comes on top of the other group of external conditions for setting ends, viz. regularities in the natural world.) We just said that an individual engaged in the activity of self-constituting action is necessarily also engaged in the activity of setting ends (she mobilizes and determines her will in order to bring about some change in the world). Now in order to do *that* an agent must conceive of herself as being situated in an environment with certain features, the central one of which is a minimal degree of predictability regarding the efficacy of her proposed actions. A world that is characterized by the *complete* absent of any predictability whatsoever (such a world is described in the next chapter) does not allow to determine and constitute one's faculty of volition in a robust way by *setting* ends. In such a world it is consequently also difficult to formulate, let alone reflectively endorse, a maxim with an end in view. It is hard to conceive of oneself as "doing this act for the sake of *that* end" (there is nothing to refer to) and, therefore, also inconceivable how a successful and well-unified agent might consistently employ those abstract higher-order principles that would define her practical identity (see stage 2 above). The possibility of setting ends, therefore, requires not just that an agent's faculty of volition is internally constituted and unified in a particular way (the "internal" aspect of the story that Kantians focus on); moreover, the possibility of successfully formulating and choosing a maxim depends on the world being constituted and unified in a particular, namely predictable, way. The definition of public practices and institutions in play here is broad and permissive. It allows for both, the latter being deliberately constructed (this is the case with respect to the rule of law, the constitutional order, legal contracts, treatises, etc.) on the one hand and such regimes being the product of unplanned, "spontaneous"[232] encounters between persons (custom, mores, and (some people claim) the market). The important thing is that the notion of rule- and principle-governed practices and institutions employed here is so comprehensive because it defines all of them in terms of the one feature they have in common. They provide a necessary part of the external structure within which agents must set their ends and perform self-constituting actions.[233]

Application to the father example: In order to set the end of supporting his daughter by visiting her in the hospital, the father must understand himself as having the status of someone who can do so. For that to be the case certain external prerequisites have to be in place. At first sight it might seem like a trivial point,[234] but simply the legally and socially established facts that restrain all others from interfering with the father's realization of the end of supporting his sick child is necessary for this end to be identified as one that the father can will (and not merely wish for or desire). The special privileges and rights that parents have (and that protect access to their children in medical institutions) condition the end that is a necessary part of the action that we are currently investigating and in the course of the performance of which the father constitutes himself as a father.

Stage 5: *The practices and institutions (themselves arrangements of practical rules and principles) are always part of the full descriptions (maxims/*logoi*) of the concrete actions chosen and performed by the agent.* After having zoomed in onto acts and ends (the two basic elements of actions) the last three stages of the argument zoom back out. The two probably most controversial steps of the argument follow when we move back to the level of maxims and *logoi*. If it is in fact the case that certain public norms and institutions have to be in place for successfully setting ends in a robust fashion, then they are also necessary for

232 See Michael Polanyi 1951 and Hayek's 1960 for the idea of a "spontaneous order."

233 The qualification (that practices and institutions provide only a part of the conditions necessary for setting ends) is important for two reasons. Firstly, practices and institutions (rendering our interdependence with other agents stable and predictable) are necessary conditions for the conception of action as it presents itself to a person who populates the world with others. This point is crucial when discussing Robinson Crusoe scenarios in which there simply is only one person and, consequently, no need for any such practices and institutions. Secondly, even in the societal condition it is the combination of natural regularities and institutions/practices (not the latter alone) that constitute the necessary external conditions for the possibility of setting ends (and performing actions).

234 The extent to which even mere non-interference with one another's actions is a non-trivial achievement and social (and legal) practice is central to the discussion of the non-interference claim in section 7.1.

formulating maxims that are the objects of an agent's practical deliberation and choice that unify her in a high degree. The resulting maxims, if fully and comprehensively formulated, are describing actions the predictable possibility of which depends on these norms and institutions being in place. The Aristotelian and Kantian conception of action acknowledges the comprehensive nature of action-descriptions that always incorporate more than just an act and an end: When an agent deliberates about performing a certain action "[h]e considers promoting a certain end by means of a certain act done in a certain way at a certain time and place."[235] A central element of the argument for the public identity claim is that these maxims therefore also incorporate their publicly acknowledged prerequisites that stage 4 identified as necessary for our status as successful and well-established end-setters amongst other end-setters.[236] Also with respect to the current stage it is important to keep in mind that the notions of "practices" and "institutions" are construed very broadly. They refer to sets of public[237] rules and principles that provide the standards for determining whether or not an action counts as participation in it.[238] The crucial point for stage 5 is that these practices and institutions are themselves sets and arrangements of action-guiding and choice-enabling practical principles – hence something that can figure in an agent's practical deliberation.[239] In order to figure in an agent's process of setting ends these public principles must be general enough to allow different individuals to incorporate them into their practical deliberation. The classical analogy and example of such a rule- and norm-governed practice is

235 Korsgaard 2008, p. 225.
236 "Acknowledgment," "recognition," and even "acceptance" are used in a way that does not imply "consent" or "enthusiastic approval." Here I follow Searle's discussion of collective intentionality. (See Searle 2010, p. 8.) According to Searle, acceptance "need not take the form of an explicit speech act and can range all the way from enthusiastic endorsement to grudging acquiescence" (Searle 2010, pp. 103–104).
237 Also the term "public" is here used in a much wider sense than in most of contemporary political and legal philosophy. It refers to the societal fact that the existence of the standards, defining a practice or institution, is known and understood by those subject to them.
238 For another view that makes extensive use of the idea of practices in order to account for the phenomena of action and agency, see Schapiro 2001.
239 Especially the initial presentation of stage 5 is too abstract, of course. I ask the reader for patience until Chapter 8 where the specific institution of a legal system will be presented as the paradigmatic illustration of the third part's main claim that (non-dominated) human agency and the presence of non-private institutions that guarantee the enforcement of public principles are two ideas that are connected. The point about external norms and principles figuring in an agent's practical reasoning figures prominently in Raz's analysis of law. See section 8.2.

games like chess.[240] The practical principles (the rules) are constitutive of the game. They account for what participants do when they participate in such a practice. The rules are at the same time normative insofar as they impose normative requirements on those persons playing the game. Stage 5 defends a holistic view of action, reflected in the idea that maxims which are formulated within a broader system of public norms, necessarily incorporate these public norms. It is at this stage that a look at post-Kantian views on agency become highly relevant and underline the point of stage five. When Robert Pippin summarizes Hegel's "empty formalism objection" to the categorical imperative, the focus on what goes into a subjective principle of action is critical: "Kant's Categorical Imperative […] leaves a very large domain of moral experience undetermined, including the social context (itself quite normatively rich) necessary for there to be the act-descriptions plugged into the test […]."[241] In summary, actions performed within the societal condition differ from those performed outside of it. Even the seemingly purely private action of Robinson Crusoe splitting a coconut falls under a different description when performed in a world that he shares with Friday. Some public principles of non-interference, making Crusoe's end of successfully splitting the coconut possible, *are* part of the description of the "whole package" that he chooses in the course of practical deliberation.[242]

Application to the father example: Since (as was argued in stage 4) the father's end of supporting his daughter can only be set when certain minimal external prerequisites are secured, it follows that the whole action, of which that end is a necessary part, depends for its possibility at least on those same prerequisites (like a regime of parental rights). Hence, when the father chooses the action of driving to the hospital to pay his daughter a supportive visit, he chooses a (long) conjunction of normatively relevant properties (like the rights that establish him as someone who is privileged to perform the action in question without getting interfered with by anybody).

---

240 See Wittgenstein 2009 (1953), sections 31, 33, 197, 205 (pp. 18, 19–20, 86, 88). The usefulness of Wittgenstein's language-game approach for the account of practical deliberation and action (and their public prerequisites), defended in the text, is illustrated by passages like this one: "An intention is embedded in a setting, in human customs and institutions. If the technique of the game of chess did not exist, I could not intend to play a game of chess. To the extent that I do intend the construction of an English sentence in advance, that is made possible by the fact that I can speak English" (Ibid., section 337, pp. 115). A number of studies have closely investigated the relationship between Wittgenstein's later philosophy and social and political philosophy. (See Pitkin 1985, Crary 2000a, Heyes 2003, Robinson 2009.)

241 Pippin 2008, p. 69.

242 See especially section 6.2.

Stage 6: *The higher order practical principles that are the building blocks of a particular practical identity (and that guide the choice of all concrete actions) are always incorporating the public principles that make setting any ends possible.* Before submitting the final stage of the argument we need to present an additional step, zooming back out to the higher level of the abstract principles that define practical identities.[243] At stage 2 the claim was that these practical principles must get traction with concrete actions in order to fulfill their unifying and coherence-providing function for our normative self-conceptions. Unless they are applied in practical deliberation, directed at specific actions, they remain "empty" forms. However, there is a flip side of this view, which can be stated by, again, using Kant's dictum about how different levels of principles (more and less abstract) condition each other. Even if the identity-defining abstract principles remain "empty" unless they are actualized in concrete actions, it is also the case that "Actions without principles are blind," or more adequately put, "Concrete actions (as opposed to mere acts, discussed in the previous section) without higher-order principles that govern their choice are impossible." The process of formulating the particular action-descriptions, which are the objects of practical deliberation and choice, would be impossible without any abstract principles that define the deliberative standpoint from which this formulation is undertaken. The higher-order principles that define one's identity provide the conceptual framework that is needed to conceive of mere facts as eligible ends that one can set. When Kant talks about "incentives" as the starting point of any process of practical deliberation, he has something along these lines in mind. The abstract practical principles that compose our normative self-conceptions do not enter the picture only when fully formulated maxims are considered and chosen; they play a role already when those maxims are formulated and the proposed action's end is identified. The ends an agent identifies do not present themselves as ready-made items in the agent's experience. While human beings have natural needs and desires like hunger and sexual drives these do *not* in and of themselves suffice to constitute purposes and ends. In order to do that, and to have any practical significance, these incentives have to be identified as ends by the identity-describing higher-order principles. The issue is one of conceptualizing the world, one's body included. Korsgaard too alludes to this double-role of practical identities and their principles: "our practical identities [...] are standing sources of incentives, as well as principles in

243 Especially stage 6 of the argument for the public identity claim will be dealt with in the next chapter, in which the notion of willing an end gets contrasted with merely wishing/desiring it.

terms of which we accept and reject proposed actions."[244] For the abstract principles of one's identity to provide a basis for the process of self-constituting action they must "fit" the range of possible concrete actions (and their ends). These principles then, in order to be capable of figuring in concrete action, cannot take on any form whatsoever. This leads to the conclusion of this stage of the argument: The abstract practical principles that get employed in practical deliberation must incorporate the action-enabling external regularities and principles encountered in an agent's engagement with the institutions surrounding her (and, of course, with the natural environment and its regularities, discussed in section 6.1). Otherwise they would not be fit to confront the task of guiding the choice of concrete actions.[245]

Application to the father example: Not only the concrete maxim/*logos* of the action of "driving to the hospital in order to pay my daughter a supportive visit" incorporates the public practices such as non-interference guaranteed by legal regimes of parental rights; there must be a sufficient fit between these concrete maxims on the one hand and the abstract, higher order, principles that are used in the deliberation that declares the specific maxim permissible on the other. In our example this higher order principle, that defines part of the practical identity of a father, was "A father has the rights and obligations to visit his daughter at the hospital when she is sick." The general and abstract practical principles that define the practical identities of fathers, incorporate the social practices and institutionalized norms that make the concrete action possible that was described at the earlier stages of this seven stage argument.

Stage 7: *Hence, a practical identity is always also a public identity.* Insofar as the actualization of the higher-order practical principles in the course of action is constituting agents in the societal condition, the former are therefore necessarily also public principles. This follows from the objects to which they apply, i.e., actions in the world that is populated by more than one. The building

244 Korsgaard 2009, p. 22.

245 The biggest worry arising at this stage is that the move towards taking the external conditions of agency seriously overreaches and leaves us with a conventionalism about practical identities and a form of social determinism. I cannot discuss these issues in full detail here, but I will do so to some extent in the interlude following the argument for the public identity claim and in my discussion of Raz's account of reasons for action in section 8.2. Raz's work on "Social Dependence [of values, reasons, etc.] without Relativism" would certainly be the first source one would turn to, in order to address the worry about social relativism. Suffice it to say at this point that a holistic view of individual agency (one that pays attention to the interdependence of the activity of individual self-constitution and its external prerequisites) does not commit one to the view that human freedom cannot be conceived of in non-relativistic terms. (See Raz 1986, pp. 307–313 and Raz 2003.)

blocks of our practical identities must always be sensitive to the public norms and principles that make concrete actions possible in the first place. Given the Kantian and Aristotelian framework presumed, the final stage of the argument follows: practical identities are always also public identities (unless one is the only human populating the universe). The practical principles that constitute our identities are directed at actions, the possibility of which depends on what others do and do not do. Our standing vis-à-vis all others (even if it merely consist in the practice of non-interference) is a norm-governed institutional artifact.[246] Practical principles that are necessary for both, formulating a concrete action's maxim and to decide whether to perform it, are directed at actions that always incorporate such a public element. For example, the social "fact" that Friday does not interfere with Crusoe's action of splitting the coconut is reflected in the public nature of Crusoe's practical identity. His practical identity is a public one, which had not been the case as long as he lived a life on his own.[247]

Application to the father example: Since the practical identity of the father is a structure of abstract and higher-order normative principles that guide his choices of proposed actions' maxims and *logoi*, the fit between the two levels of practical principles translates into a fit of his identity with the external prerequisites of these concrete actions that constitute him as a father. His practical deliberation and choice of the concrete action of driving to the hospital and paying his daughter a supportive visit is conducted from the perspective of someone who has the practical identity of a father, an identity, the defining principles of which incorporate certain public practices and norms.

Bringing to the fore the critical role that rule-governed practices and institutions (together with the laws of nature) play in the form of a necessary condition for setting ends is contributing to the current discourse concerning action, agency, and practical reason.[248] In the absence of any rule-governed normative practices (and agents conceiving of themselves as being subject to their authori-

---

246 This claim is defended in section 7.1.

247 In the Friday-Crusoe scenario of non-interference there is a norm involved and not merely a "fact." The non-interference of a lion is exactly not the same as the social practice of non-interference, upheld amongst human individuals. There is a certain ambiguity here concerning the notion of "interference," an ambiguity that has to do with that notion being employed in normative as well as descriptive contexts (only according to the latter can a lion and a tornado "interfere" with a human agent). For more on this difficulty, see the beginning of the discussion of the non-interference claim in section 7.1. Thanks to Fred Miller for pointing out the need for making clearer that the Friday-Crusoe situation involves the emergence of norms.

248 For a review of the current general trend to address issues of practical reason by means of highlighting their relation to action-theory, see Milgram 2009.

ty) a potential agent sees herself confronted with a social universe that lacks its "cement," its minimal degree of predictability.[249] Such an anarchic world is hostile to self-constituting action because it is hostile to practical deliberation that identifies and aims at changes of states of affairs in the world. The latter task requires the ability to minimally estimate the effects and consequences of a proposed and reflected-upon course of action.[250]

Interlude: The paradox of self-constitution revisited

Before we look at a couple of objections to the argument for the public identity claim, we should make good on a promise given in the previous chapter.[251] How does the, for lack of a better word, "socialized" version of the self-constitution story deal with the paradox of self-constitution? Does the argument provide the constitutivist with the resources to handle the paradox more successfully than Korsgaard's own version does? Even if we accept the seven stages, culminating in the claim that every practical identity is also a public one, the question of

---

249 Hume's remark in *An Abstract of a Treatise of Human Nature* that causality constitutes "the cement of the universe" (Hume 2000 (1739), p. 404) and, to put it in the language preferred in the text, of the "natural world" can be applied to the notion of the "social world." The latter is characterized by an unavoidable minimal degree of interdependence of individuals (they potentially impact on each others lives). In the action-theoretical sense, spelled out in Chapter 6, practices and institutions structure the social world in a way analogous to the regularities that structure the physical environment. (On Hume's cement-metaphor, see Mackie 1980, pp. 3–28.)

250 Is this *minimal* predictability of consequences not itself setting an extremely demanding standard of what must be present in order to successfully set ends? After all, even if the laws of nature and practices/institutions are stabilizing the world, we always seem to lack a *full* guarantee of what is going to happen in response to our actions. It should be mentioned that Korsgaard is aware of the problem discussed in the text and that is taken as the cornerstone for this exploration's main argument. (See Korsgaard 2009, pp. 84–87.) Under the heading "The Possibility of Agency" she considers a forward looking version of the determinism problem and considers that it poses a "threat" to our sense of free agency. The "relation between the content of our wills, and the effects of our willings, seems completely contingent" because action means to "become hostage to the causal network, to the forces of nature, and the actions of others." Korsgaard does not develop further this important observation "that the meanings of our actions are determined, not just by what *we* mean by them, but by the way the world takes them up," into the action-theoretical direction that is pursued here. (Instead she uses this observation to present an interesting moral-philosophical discussion of Kant's philosophy of religion and why good actions sometimes generate bad consequences.)

251 See section 4.2.

who/what comes first (the agent vs. her actions) in the process of self-constitution remains pressing. We still seem to struggle with the problem of how an agent can constitute her identity by means of performing actions (in Korsgaard's demanding sense) without already being a unified agent. Either the agent is already there (but "who" performed the actions that constituted that very agent then?) or the activity that takes place is not performed by an agent (not resulting in proper actions and, hence, not successfully constituting an agent).

Let us begin by reminding ourselves of one of the explanations for why Korsgaard (and Kantians more generally) worry about the paradox of self-constitution, namely the issue of autonomy vs. heteronomy. When an agent involved in the process of self-constitution is already unified in accordance with the principles of a particular practical identity, then this process seems to be pre-determined, heteronomously shaped, and unfree. This is one reason for why Kant's moral philosophy puts emphasis on the internal and formal characteristics of practical reasoning. A moral agent determines her will in the process of practical deliberation, without referring to the empirical (historical, social etc.) contingencies of her current situation. This is not to say that an agent can practically deliberate by completely ignoring the particularities she finds herself confronted with. What Kantians mean when they insist on the *aprioricity* of practical reasoning is that the normative force of practical conclusions must not be dependent on anything tainted by impure and empirical elements. Both the necessity and the universality of unconditional moral requirements cannot have their source in contingent internal and/or external influences on the will. Inclinations (desires) count as impermissible internal determinants in the same way as custom, culture, and positive law are considered heteronomous external sources of practical requirements. A free agent conceives of herself (first-personally) as the source of a causal process resulting in the achievement of an end. Since she understands herself as a cause, a free will must act according to a practical law that, in order to be non-heteronomous, must be a self-legislated one. Only the categorical imperative, requiring the agent to impose *some* such law on her will, satisfies the necessary independence from internal and external contingencies.[252]

---

252 This feature of Kant's moral theory has provoked two standard objections. On the one hand, Hegel complains that the categorical imperative is an "empty formalism" and does not give specific enough direction for human conduct. (See Hegel 1991 (1821), p. 162.) On the other hand, Mill believes that the universal law formula allows the derivation of more substantial imperatives only if a robust (utilitarian) conception of the good is already assumed to be a necessary feature of all rational willing – something Kant cannot do. (See Mill 1998 (1861), pp.

Now the argument for the public identity claim might appear to present an account of agents that does not leave enough room for autonomous agency in this strong Kantian sense. After all, stages 4-7 put emphasis on the external prerequisites of the process of self-constitution. In addition to the agent-independent regularities of the natural world (discussed in more detail in the next chapter), it is public norms and institutions that need to be in place for successfully engaging in the activity of setting ends. The practical principles constituting an agent's practical identity incorporate these external norms and they make a coherent self-conception possible in the first place. However, if agents are "the result of their environment" in the sense of internalizing external norms, what happens to autonomy, understood as the option of radically self-creating one's identity? On first sight, the argument defended here seems to suggest the exact opposite: a deterministic vision of identity that avoids the paradox of self-constitution at a price too high. Why is that?

It is true that a response to the paradox of self-constitution that is based on the argument for the public identity claim cannot avoid heteronomy in the above sense. However, similar to Hegel's development of Kant's conception of autonomy, the heteronomy involved in self-constitution does not necessarily conflict with the prospects of leading a self-determining life; rather it only conflicts with an existentialist formulation of self-constitution, which at the same time leads to the paradox.[253] The alternative presented above suggests a developmental account of what is happening when an agent constitutes herself. Korsgaard moves somewhat in that direction when her recent reply to the paradox states that we have to look at successful self-constitution as "an activity" (rather than an end-state) and that we won't understand this process properly if we treat the paradox as a causality-dilemma or as exemplifying a chicken-and-egg debate ("Who comes *first*? The agent or her actions?"). The account presented here is sympathetic to the direction in which this recent amendment by

51–52.) Both objections are related to the motivation underlying the argument for the public identity claim, i.e., the necessity of external features that have to be in place for agents to set any ends.

253 In Korsgaard's case this existentialism is most noticeable in the fourth lecture of *The Sources of Normativity*. (See Korsgaard 1996, pp. 160–164.) The observation concerning Korsgaard's existentialist leanings has been observed by Nagel 1996 (p. 203) and Wallace (forthcoming). In a recent interview Korsgaard replies: "Why should I want to avoid an existentialist conclusion? Say that an existentialist believes that human beings are the creators of all meaning and value, and, while we are at it, in a way also the creators of ourselves. This is something I firmly believe is true, partly because I don't think any other hypothesis makes any sense, and partly because I don't think any other hypothesis does any philosophical work" (Korsgaard 2003, p. 786).

Korsgaard turns. However, it remains an incomplete reply to the critics of the self-constitution model. It must be further developed into a direction that Kantians, however, won't feel comfortable with because it introduces an element of heteronomy and even luck into the picture of self-constitution.[254]

This element of luck follows from the developmental approach's basic claim: our identity is something we "grow into," so to speak, and only when we are lucky enough to constitute ourselves under sufficiently stable and coherent public norms and institutions, we have the chance to pass the threshold of autonomous agency.[255] Even those of us who are lucky in this way perform self-constituting actions that are heteronomously determined for a significant amount of time. This is simply what it means to grow up. An individual human starts her "career" as a self-constituting agent within a framework of certain public norms and institutions.[256] There is no particular point in time at which the action-performing individual suddenly turns into a fully unified and autonomous agent. This happens gradually and is not an irreversible process; just because a certain threshold of autonomy is passed at some point, an agent can fall below it at a later point in time.[257]

Even the grown-up and well-constituted agent remains subject to the external determinants in the sense that they continue to provide the background for any action. The thing that a developmental process sees changing is how an agent sees the public principles figure in her practical reasoning. A different way to formulate this point is that the gradual process in which agency develops is one in which, under suitable conditions, the role of the external conditions of

---

254 A clarification is in place here: I have been emphasizing a lot that my main concern is *not* with Korsgaard's substantive moral philosophical arguments. Why do I talk about autonomy then? Firstly, it seems important to defend my reply to the paradox of self-constitution in a way that leaves at least room for a morally substantial conception of autonomy (without positively defending one myself). Secondly, since Korsgaard connects the notions of agency and autonomy very tightly, many of the arguments that express worries about heteronomy apply automatically to the ones concerning threats to agency. (See Tenenbaum 2011, p. 454.)

255 Of course, we need to remind ourselves that these external conditions are not sufficient for successful self-constitution. The seven stages establishing the argument for the public identity claim present a necessary condition only. If I am weak willed or otherwise *internally* handicapped, the finest external conditions won't constitute me into an agent.

256 For the claim that especially the modern family is not a private institution, see the total law thesis presented in section 7.2.

257 Jonathan Miller has suggested that, at least at this point, my view is more Aristotelian than Kantian. This sounds absolutely right and, as briefly mentioned at the end of this interlude, John McDowell's conception of "second nature" has been largely responsible for the move away from the existentialistic reading of autonomy and towards the socially conditioned one.

action are becoming more and more transparent to an agent over the course of her life. Autonomy so understood has more to do with achieving a certain level of self-*understanding* rather than self-*creation*.

The paradox of self-constitution is dissolved then by making room for imperfectly unified agents (with incomplete, partly incoherent, in other words, developing sets of practical principles) to perform deficient actions. As will be discussed in the next part, good (in the morally neutral sense) social institutions are those that facilitate the development of individual agency. The idea of a legal system, for example, cannot be understood without assuming and employing certain ideas of its addressees as minimally self-directed agents.

This response to the paradox of self-constitution will disappoint advocates of more radical conceptions of self-created identity. If authentic self-constitution is believed to involve practical identities that are completely detached from the external conditions of their possibility, then the argument for the public identity claim undermines any hope that an agent with such a self-perception emerges. Such an autonomous agent cannot be the starting point of the process of self-constitution. However, the argument from public identity does not regard this kind of heteronomy as a lamentable feature of human life that must be avoided.[258] It leaves room for individuals to develop into agents given that the world around them satisfies certain minimal criteria of stability and predictability. Admitting that an agent's normative self-conception is dependent on the presence of external features is the price that a constitutivist has to pay to avoid the paradox of self-constitution.[259]

---

258 There are, of course, other conceptions of heteronomy that are (more) problematic and the account presented in the text is not supposed to block the criticism of those. If heteronomy refers to deliberate manipulation and deception by others, for example, then this is very different from heteronomy, abstractly understood as the necessary dependence of any action on some public norms. Still, the self-creation and existentialist view of a truly authentic self (that underlies the paradox of self-constitution) is incompatible even with the second conception of heteronomy.

259 In a dispersed but decisive way, my suggestion for overcoming the paradox of self-constitution has been heavily influenced by John McDowell's Aristotelian conceptions of acquiring a "second nature" and getting initiated into conceptual capacities in the process of *Bildung*. (See McDowell 1996, pp. 78–86.)

Chapter 6: Clarification and Objections

In the introduction to her recent collection of essays, *The Constitution of Agency*, Korsgaard makes the following remark:

> The case [of an individual seeing herself required to engage in an act of revolution; C.H.] vindicates Plato's view that we cannot be fully unified as individuals if the state in which we live is unjust and therefore is itself disunified. To the extent that that is true, our efforts at self-constitution may be affected, even limited, by what goes on in the world around us. This is an aspect of the subject about which I have written little.[260]

Insofar as the foregoing interpretation and further development of her action theory (Chapter 5) are adequate, Korsgaard's conjecture in the quoted passage is well-justified: Yes, our efforts at self-constitution are affected, even limited, by what goes on in the world around us. In order to show that the degree of successful self-constitution is dependent on the condition of certain features of our environment (natural and social), this chapter asks us to imagine a world that is very different from the one we inhabit. A thought experiment further supports the argument for the public identity claim and focuses in particular on its controversial fourth stage that was concerned with the external prerequisites for the activity of successfully setting ends.[261] The thought experiment asks us to imagine a world that lacks these external conditions necessary for the formation and maintenance of our identities: in the absence of a minimum level of external predictability, provided by the laws of nature (Chaotica version of the thought experiment) and practices and institutions (Anarchia version), the task of setting ends (and, consequently, the performance of self-constituting actions) is possible only to a very diminished extent. Fully maintaining the status of an "end-setter" (a necessary component of being a well-constituted agent) is an activity that cannot be engaged in in Chaotica and Anarchia because *setting* ends is almost impossible there.

The final section replies to two objections that can be put forward against the argument for the public identity claim and the thought experiments intended to support it. Again, the two objections are primarily directed at the argument's fourth stage. One might ask, on the one hand, whether the laws of na-

260 Korsgaard 2008, p. 21.

261 Stage 4 (of the argument for the public identity claim): *In order to set ends certain external and public practices and institutions must be in place.*

ture and man-made institutions really have to be present for completing the task of setting ends. Why cannot a Chaotian/Anarchian "agent" construct a purely speculative self-conception, one that conceives of her identity as it would be like, were she situated in stable and predictable external conditions? On the other hand, and this objection focuses on the social conditions of agency, what about Robinson Crusoe? After all, there is simply no need for any *social* institutions in a world that is populated by only one individual? Does it follow that Crusoe does not set ends, fails to perform any actions, and, hence, lacks an identity?

6.1 An Extreme State of Nature

The initial presentation of the argument for the public identity claim involved the introduction of the distinction between the regularities of nature on the one hand and social practices and institutions on the other as two distinct kinds of external conditions of agency. The previous chapter talked about these external preconditions for setting ends in a rather abstract and undifferentiated manner. Up to this point, the presentation of these conditions has been too crude also because the minimal predictability required for setting ends was presented as primarily being dependent on artificial social institutions. Despite the prime importance of these man-made rule-governed structures for this essay's main argument, there are other external action-enabling features that are independent from human choices and practices, *viz.* the laws of nature.[262] What these two groups of external conditions have in common is that they provide the stable and predictable context that is necessary to set ends and to design the purposes of our actions in the course of practical deliberation. However, these two types of external conditions fulfill this task in different ways.

---

262 According to some readings of Kant's theoretical writings, the "world" (in the external sense I am concerned with) is "unified" and "well-constituted" by means of the conceptualizing powers of the human understanding. Therefore, one might conclude, the predictability (causal laws etc.), required for setting ends and for self-constituting action, has its ultimate source in the forms of the human understanding. However, unless this kind of Kantianism is prepared to defend the radical claim that the empirical world is subject to the active powers of the understanding *in exactly the same way* as the realm of social practices and institutions is, the bifurcated argument in the text retains its legitimacy. That Kant himself did not draw such a radical conclusion is noticeable at many points, above all when he describes humans as being conceivable from two very different standpoints, namely as empirical beings (*subject* to the causal laws of nature) and as noumenal beings (free agents – as they conceive of themselves first-personally).

Chaotica: A world without natural laws

Putting metaphysical and epistemological discussions in the philosophy of science (concerning causality, induction, etc.) to one side, the notion of "laws of nature" employed here is hoped to be relatively uncontroversial. It refers to the general propositions in terms of which we refer to the invariable regularities that structure the environment we find ourselves in. When one attempts to perform the action of "walking in order to climb this mountain" certain external regularities are in play that condition the end one sets (reaching the peak) and the acts one engages in to achieve it. These regularities enable one to set one foot in front of the other, this pattern of movements resulting in the aimed-at state of affairs of one having successfully changed one's location. Achieving this state of affairs depends on the world "behaving" in a particular way rather than others.

Put negatively, the performance of actions (in the demanding sense of choosing an "act-done-for-the-sake-of-an-end" discussed above) would be constantly frustrated in an environment that is characterized by the complete absence of any minimal predictability regarding the world's "responses" to our actions.[263] The notions of regularity and predictability employed in this action-theoretical argument are referring to what is necessary for agents to expect and foresee how their actions are going to affect the condition of the world. The ends one sets and the acts one engages in to realize these ends, in short the actions one performs in the process of constituting oneself as their author, depend for their possibility on these external regularities. Since self-constitution has been conceived of, first and foremost, as the process of reflective deliberation about (and the endorsement of) the subjective principles describing the actions we perform (Kant's maxims, Aristotle's *logoi*), self-constitution always involves a reference to these external regularities. Action is related to the world in the form of figuring out how an act is a suitable instrument for achieving an end (that is practical reasoning's "minimal consequentialist structure" introduced above). For example, a comprehensive description of the action of one "walking in order to climb this mountain" includes all the natural regularities that make the performance of this self-constituting action possible.[264]

263 The terms "behavior" and "responses" must, of course, not be misunderstood as assuming that nature is some kind of agent, somehow actively responding in one way rather than another. The same is not true (to the same extent) in the context of the second version of the thought experiment dealing with the non-natural prerequisites of agency.

264 I am indebted to Jonathan Miller for pointing out to me that more has to be said concerning the following issue: It seems overly rationalistic and demanding to expect all well-unified

The issue under discussion is a subtle (some might say trivial) point. Standard cases of successfully setting ends and endorsing the related principles of actions, like "walking in order to climb this mountain," seem unproblematic and one might overlook the quite complex necessary preconditions of their possibility quite easily. What should get in the way of formulating this maxim in a meaningful way (because the possibility of setting the end of "climbing this mountain" gets somehow undermined)? In order to answer this question we need to look in more detail at how the fact that the world rests on a particular configuration of regularities, that make it respond in specific ways, informs our self-conception as its inhabitants. The non-trivial nature of this claim becomes more evident when we leave behind the standard cases in which agents set ends and act without paying attention to how the laws of nature make action possible.

Imagine a (potential) archer who finds herself in, what we call from now on, Chaotica.[265] Chaotica is a world devoid of the kind of external regularities that characterize and constitute the conception of the world available in the standard cases of action, such as the principles of classical mechanics. Our would-be archer attempts to engage in the process of practical deliberation regarding the possible end of targeting and hitting a mark. Remember at this point that, according to Korsgaard's account of self-constituting action, having the specific practical identity of an archer consists in two aspects. On the one hand, an

agents all the time to formulate the maxims of their proposed actions (and, hence, the objects of their practical deliberation and choice) in the comprehensive sense described in the text. It is true, it should be stressed in reply, that an *explicit* enumeration of all the external prerequisites (descriptive and normative) that make one's end-setting and action possible would amount to a bizarre requirement. However, firstly, in our more reflective moments we do take into consideration these external conditions (especially when we are confronted with ends that might conflict with those of other agents or push the limits of the physical world). And, secondly, given what was said in the interlude on the paradox of self-constitution, it is submitted that those who are more reflective concerning the necessary preconditions of their actions do in fact achieve a higher level of transparency and, hence, self-unification than those who do not. I have no problem insisting that in the sense of freedom and autonomy discussed above, a physicist and a legally well-informed citizen are more free to the extent to which they understand the world (naturally and socially) better than others. We return to the well-informed citizen in section 8.2.

265 There are a number of issues involved in the following thought experiment that must be ignored in order for it to illustrate the points concerning self-constituting action. A world in which absolutely no laws of nature whatsoever are present would also be a world in which human brains were not subject to any natural regularities. The experiment's set up has therefore to be qualified: the (potential) agent, trying to set ends and perform actions in this chaotic world, has a brain capable of functioning similarly enough to ours.

archer expresses her practical identity in the course of performing certain, archer-specific, actions (involving ends of the kind just mentioned). On the other hand, it is in the course of deliberately performing these specific actions, that an agent with an archer's self-conception is supposed to perform, that an individual maintains the practical, action-guiding, principles defining such an archer-identity. In line with what was established in the argument for the public identity claim, performing the specific actions that define an archer is necessary to become, be, and remain one. In the archer's case the "whole action package" of "firing-the-bow-in-order-to-hit-the-mark" would be the object of the potential agent's choice. This act of choice, on the other hand, necessarily involves setting the end of hitting the mark and, importantly, the stable self-conception of an individual that is capable of doing so. Without successfully identifying an end (as the attainable object of her rational pursuit) the agent's choice remains conceptually incoherent because the subjective principle describing the action (the *logos* and maxim) lacks one of its indispensible parts.

Now apply this view of what is involved in the task of setting ends (and, consequently, in the performance of action) to the case of the archer. The critical point of the thought experiment is not primarily that it would not be a rewarding or satisfying task for our archer to engage in the action in question in a world that consists of constantly and erratically moving marks and targets. Looking at Chaotica in this way makes it sound as if we are dealing with an already well unified archer, one with the relevant coherent practical identity, who suddenly finds herself in an erratically behaving environment. Her frustration with not attaining an endorsed and pursued end presupposes that the archer has already successfully identified a coherent end and is aiming (though in a futile way) at this attainable end. This interpretation misses the point of the thought experiment insofar as it attempts to separate the agent and her identity on the one hand from her actions on the other – a view that would fail to understand the complex relationship of mutual dependency between the two elements.[266]

266 In their discussion of liberal vs. republican conceptions of freedom, Kukathas and Pettit agree that the former (Hobbesian) conception conceives of freedom as the property of actions, whereas the republican model regards freedom as a property of persons (citizens). (See Kukathas 2009 and Pettit 2009.) Despite their diametrically opposed evaluation of these two traditions, Kukathas and Pettit do not question this separation between actions and their authors. Apart from some brief remarks in section 7.1, this book does not explicitly deal with substantial conceptions of freedom but it seems clear that the overall approach pursued leads to a rejection of the attempt to drive a wedge between free agents and free actions.

Rather, in Chaotica the problem starts "earlier" (conceptually, not temporarily speaking) in the process of performing the action in question. The complete lack of any pattern of predictability makes it impossible to coherently *set* the end of hitting the mark *as an end* that can be pursued by taking the adequate means (the act of firing the bow). In the thought experiment we are not trying to imagine something on a par with a living target like an animal that is also difficult to aim at. (Apparently it is this difficulty that makes the whole activity of hunting interesting in the first place.) We are trying to imagine a different variety of unpredictability here, one that is so extreme that it renders the task of *setting* the end of hitting the mark not just practically unstable but conceptually incoherent.

Importantly, the claim here is not that actually *hitting* the mark is a complete impossibility and that this impossibility is as such acknowledged by the potential agent (that would undermine the set-up of the thought experiment). It is rather that hitting the target is a matter of pure coincidence and therefore becomes a state of affairs that cannot be set as an end and as something that can be attained in the course of one's deliberate action. An action's end asks for specific means and acts to be undertaken in order to attain it and it is this feature of an end (as a necessary element of any self-constituting action) that cannot get off the ground in Chaotica. Whether or not the archer is attempting to deliberately aim in some particular direction or fires her bow just randomly does not make a difference concerning the prospects of hitting the target. The context within which this attempted action takes place fails to provide the minimum stability and predictability necessary for setting the end of "*that* target being hit by me aiming and firing the bow at it." Randomly firing the bow and accidently hitting some mark does not involve the *setting* of an end in the sense employed in the account of self-constituting action under investigation. The individual in question therefore fails to perform an action in the sense that is necessary for constituting a unified agent in the course of practical deliberation, choice, and action.

Setting the end of hitting a mark is impossible in Chaotica because of the complete lack of predictability and stability normally guaranteed by the laws of nature. Since we have assumed that an action-description necessarily involves an end, it follows that action is impossible in Chaotica.[267] Last but not least,

---

267 It must be admitted that a potential agent must at least have desires (to aim and hit a target, in the case of the potential archer). However, the mere occurrence of desires (in the absence of practical principles that conceptualize and organize them) falls short of what is presented as a well-constituted individual with a practical identity in the text. On why desiring

since "action is self-constitution," it follows that successful self-constitution is impossible when the natural environment lacks any predictability whatsoever. Our (potential) archer will not be an archer – she cannot be because no such things as regularities of dynamics and optics are in place in the form of natural laws. In the same way in which certain specific practical identities (like being an alchemist) are impossible to maintain in an authentic and coherent way because the natural world is law-governed in a specific way and not another, the more radical scenario presented in the thought experiment undermines the possibility of any practical identity. Consider the identity of an alchemist and what we think about the related normative self-conception that such a person "endorses."[268] Given the way our world is structured in terms of natural regularities, being an alchemist is an incoherent self-conception to maintain because the world is simply not structured in the way that such an identity and its constitutive actions require (*successfully* transmuting lead into gold etc.).[269] Generalizing this line of argument we can conclude that, given that no ends whatsoever can be set and pursued in Chaotica, maintaining a practical identity is impossible in the circumstances depicted in the thought experiment.

It is not some internal deficit, some failure to properly unify one's faculty of volition due to weakness of will or the presence of some overpowering desire, that undermines one's identity; under certain (very unusual) circumstances, external conditions are sufficient to undermine the phenomenon of individual agency. Since, as has been argued in further developing Korsgaard's arguments in section 5.2, the self-constitution of agency always is at the same time the self-constitution of a particular individual (with a particular practical identity) it follows that Chaotica's incompatibility with setting ends and purposes results in the impossibility of individuals as we know them.[270] Individuals like us have a sufficiently coherent and stable normative self-conception, which consists of

something is not enough for successfully confronting the task of self-constituting action, see the first objection in section 6.2.

268 For a more detailed discussion of the extent to which such a "practical identity" is possible as a "fancied" one, given that the alchemist-specific actions are not conclusively performable in our world, see the speculative soldier example that is part of my discussion of the first objection in section 6.2.

269 I am indebted to Fred Miller and Jonathan Miller for suggesting the alchemist-analogy.

270 The "as we know them" qualifier is supposed to convey the admission that I do not believe my argument can establish, on *a priori* grounds, that every kind of individuality is impossible in Chaotica. I am, however, quite confident (as will be argued in the next section when discussing Robinson Crusoe) that insofar as alternative manifestations of individuality are possible, they lie far outside of our conceptions of individuality and remain inconceivable for us.

those practical principles that we employ when choosing how to act. Chaotica, since it is characterized by a complete lack of "natural principles" that an agent can incorporate into the comprehensive description of the object of her choice (i.e., the proposed action's maxim/*logos*), undermines what is necessary for maintaining such a self-conception across (as well as at a particular point in) time.

Anarchia: A world without social practices and institutions

One implicit assumption made in the first thought experiment is that the potential archer finds herself *alone* in Chaotica. There the laws of nature are the only external condition necessary to identify purposes and to set ends. Things change, however, when we construct an alternative Chaotica, let us call it Anarchia, which is populated by more than one individual.[271] This section uses Anarchia to show how the setting and pursuit of ends depend for their possibility not just on the laws of nature, but also on the stability and predictability provided by social practices and institutions.[272] This discussion, like the one in the previous section, will appear a little bit bizarre because the world depicted in the experiment is far removed from our own. However, this initial puzzlement and reaction can be taken as an indication that we (the more or less well-unified agents that we are) simply take for granted the presence of much of the rule- and law-governed background that enables us to set ends and perform ac-

---

271 The name "Anarchia" is chosen because of the interpersonal chaos that characterizes it. All parallels notwithstanding, Anarchia is different from traditional state of nature scenarios on the one hand and the narrow concept of anarchy (defined as the absence of government) as political philosophers have used it on the other. Anarchia lacks social institutions of all kinds – not just political and legal ones. It therefore differs from Locke's version of the state of nature and even from Hobbes's. I thank David Shoemaker for asking me to clarify Anarchia's distinct features.

272 It follows from this way of contrasting the two types of external action-enabling conditions (laws of nature and social practices/institutions) that setting ends always depends on the presence of a stable physical environment. Only a subcategory of these cases does in addition also depend on the reliable presence of at least some social practices and institutions rendering the actions/reactions of other individuals predictable. However, the second set of cases will be almost fully congruent with the larger first one, given that agents find themselves in the societal condition (i.e., the fact that there exists more than one individual and both are aware of one another's existence). The question of possible agency outside the societal condition (Robinson-Crusoe-style scenarios) will be discussed below.

tions.[273] That others do not interfere with our attempts to set ends in unpredictable ways seems “natural,” “self-evident,” and hardly in need of any explanation. The difficulty of engaging in these thought experiments does not, however, diminish the conceptual force of the claim made. On the contrary, the difficulty of imagining how attempts at self-constituting action fail in Anarchia’s completely disordered societal world supports the claim that certain minimal features about interpersonal relations are necessary conditions for the possibility of setting ends, performing actions, and maintaining a principle-based normative self-conception similar enough to ours.[274]

We need to keep in mind that the notion of a “social institution,” employed here, is a very broad one. The working definition conceives of these institutions as “rule-governed practices,” the normative demands of which are acknowledged by those individuals who are subject to these institutions’ constitutive norms (e.g., chess players relationship to the rules of chess). The broad character of this definition allows us, as was suggested in the previous chapter, to incorporate Korsgaard’s discussion of Kant’s *Groundwork* example of the action of making a false promise (act) to get some ready cash (end) into the framework of social practices and institutions. There we had a closer look at the distinction between two act-types, namely the one instantiated by “natural” and the other one instantiated by “conventional” acts. Parallel to this distinction we considered two kinds of action, namely those involving representatives of these two distinct act-types respectively. Recall that, according to Korsgaard’s view, natural acts (e.g., killing, walking, stabbing) depend for their possibility *only* on the laws of nature, whereas conventional ones (e.g., keeping a promise, playing a card game) presuppose established and well-maintained social practices and institutions.[275]

---

273 For a social-scientific and historical account of how we have begun to take social and political order for granted, see Fukuyama 2011, pp. 10–14.

274 Hayek similarly refers to our tendency to underestimate what is in play when individuals deliberate and act: “Many of the ‘mere habits’ and ‘meaningless institutions’ that we use and presuppose in our actions are essential conditions for what we achieve; they are successful adaptations of society that are constantly improved and on which depends the range of what we can achieve. While it is important to discover their defects, we could not for a moment go on without constantly relying on them” (Hayek 1960, p. 34).

275 See section 5.1. It was brought to my attention (by Fred Miller) that the discussion of Korsgaard’s two act-types (and the two kinds of actions) that follows in the text seems to lose sight of the distinction between acts and actions. I admit that there is a shift going on that I had not made explicit enough. However, I do not think that this shift of focus pertains to the distinction between acts and actions. Rather, what needs to be justified is a shift from a focus on an action’s end (and what is necessary for setting it) towards an action’s act (and what is nec-

Now with the two categories of external conditions introduced as features of the argument for the public identity claim, we can return to Korsgaard's distinction between natural and conventional acts. I submit that natural acts in Korsgaard's sense do not exist. And, *a fortiori*, no actions ("*acts*-done-for-the-sake-of-ends") that involve such purely natural acts exist either. This might appear to be a pretty extreme claim at first sight. How can acts like walking or eating (paradigmatic examples of natural acts according to Korsgaard's classification) be acts that depend for their possibility on more than the presence of the laws of nature? The claim defended here is that these acts, like their conventional cousins, do in fact depend on a background of norm- and rule-governed practices and institutions – at least when these acts are taking place in the societal condition. It follows, in line with the technical definition of self-constituting actions endorsed above, that whole actions (acts plus ends) too depend on a background of norm- and rule-governed practices and institutions. Since every act depends for its possibility on X, it follows that every action too depends on X, since an instance of the latter always incorporates an instance of the former.

The societal condition is defined as a world inhabited by more than one individual who acknowledge each other's existence as beings who are capable of interfering with one another's attempts at acting (they conceive of themselves as being radically free in the sense mentioned above).[276] Moreover, however,

essary for performing it). However, this shift is less dramatic than it might seem. Keep in mind the difference between acts and act-types on the one hand and whole actions on the other: According to the technical definition of actions introduced above, acts (and ends) are a necessary component of all actions. They are not themselves constituting whole actions. An action is the combination of an acts and an end. Now in the text it is argued that "natural *acts*" do not exist. According to the definition of whole actions, however, this implies that there cannot be "natural actions" either. True, the main argument of this essay is concerned with self-constituting *actions*, not acts (acts cannot, after all, fulfill the self-constituting function, only whole actions can). However, by showing that the two necessary components of actions (acts and ends) are dependent for their possibility on those external factors that are completely absent in Chaotica and Anarchia, it is at the same time shown that whole actions too depend for their possibility on the very same factors.

276 It is crucial that Anarchia is characterized by the presence of at least two *human* beings (and not, for example, one human and some animals). The challenge of unpredictability that human agents confront one another with is different from the potential unpredictability that other natural beings and events present. The fact that only humans are conceiving of themselves as unconditionally free to interfere with one another's actions is enough to get the challenge concerning a coherent normative self-conception (of exactly these free beings) going. Constant actual interference is not the primary issue; it is the way in which non-interference remains in limbo, due to the absence of any publicly established norms that agents can incorporate into their processes of self-constituting action, that has the impact on the degree of

when individuals acknowledge each other's existence in that way, they do not do so as mere forces of nature that are unsusceptible to subjecting themselves to external public norms. In other words, while actual social norms and institutions are completely absence in Anarchia, the potential agents populating it identify one another as similar enough beings who are capable of restricting their freedom to interfere with one another by practically deliberating and choosing not to interfere in such a way. The same is, of course, not true of our encounters with animals and other forces of nature.[277] The central claim defended here is that, unless we are considering the case of merely one individual populating the universe, acts (and, therefore, self-constituting actions) and a high degree of agency that depend for their possibility only on the laws of nature form an empty set.[278] Let us take a look at one of the actions mentioned above that seems to incorporate a clear-cut case of a purely natural act in order to see why this is the case. Assume that our potential archer from the first thought experiment finds herself in a world that conforms to natural regularities and laws and, hence, in a world that secures the predictability necessary to conceive of oneself as being able to set the specific end of hitting a mark and to perform the act of firing the bow.[279] However, while the presence of the laws of nature provides one set of the necessary conditions of the possibility of setting ends and performing acts, the potential archer now finds herself in a world populated by other individuals. And apart from being aware of each other's existence as externally unconstrained potential agents nothing like structured interaction, communication etc. is going on between them.

---

successful agency the argument in the text is concerned with. Why the enduring possibility of arbitrary interference has this impact will become clearer in Part 3 when the law is presented as the social institution that frees non-interference (and agents) from this state of limbo.

277 I am indebted to Jonathan Miller for urging me to clarify this point concerning what the objects and subjects are in the process of mutually acknowledging other potential agents as such in the societal condition. It must also be admitted that the contrast between humans and (higher order) animals as stated in the text is exaggerated – at least with respect to dogs, primates etc. and their behavior (though not with respect to the self-conception of radically free beings).

278 More on the possibility of action and agency in Robinson-Crusoe cases will be said in section 6.2.

279 In the example the archer's action is "firing-the-bow-to-hit-this-mark." This action can be dissected into its two constitutive parts, the act of firing the bow on the one hand and the end of hitting the mark on the other. In order to show that the action as a whole is conditional on the presence of environmental features, it is sufficient to show that any one of its two constitutive parts is.

The main claim is that setting ends and acting (and ultimately the constitution of a self) must take place within some interpersonal constraints here. More precisely, the non-interference with other individuals' projects, plans, and actions *is* conceived of as such a rule- and norm-governed social practice, however self-evident they appear to us. Hence, also acts that seem completely "natural" and independent from any artificial norms and rules are in fact not. This abstract claim might still sound strange and fantastic. It seems so obvious (let alone morally required) that no one is going to corrupt another individual's process of setting trivial ends like walking in a public space or aiming at and hitting a mark. However, this response rests on uncritically stipulating a default condition of non-interference. The claim defended here is that this pattern of non-interference, since it is itself a social practice, always remains under the nontrivial requirement of explanation and justification, addressed to beings like us, who conceive of themselves as free in the sense of potentially interfering with one another's actions.[280]

From the perspective of free beings, a state of non-interference by others is a precondition also for those acts that are termed "natural" by Korsgaard. Their possibility depends at least on the stability and predictability guaranteed by, in this case, a seemingly negative practice, namely the practice of abstaining from invading an agent's attempts to perform self-constituting actions. In other words, as soon as individuals find themselves in the societal condition they face a unique practical problem that they would not face were they alone. One cannot simply assume that individuals in the societal condition do not interfere with each other's attempts at setting ends. That there is an overwhelming number of substantially normative and non-normative arguments supporting such things as "negative rights" etc. is not denied here at all – it is simply not the issue. (However, the fact that there are these arguments indirectly vindicates the view defended here, according to which freedom from others interference is something that can and must be justified and explained in a way that the regularities of nature obviously need not be.)

Support for this view comes from James Buchanan's discussion of why anarchy (in a sense very similar to the one employed in our thought experiment) must be considered a "conceptual mirage."[281] Admittedly, there are many im-

280 The political implications of this critique of the "non-interference claim" are discussed in Chapter 7.

281 Buchanan 2000 (1975), p. 5. The way the label "individualist anarchism" is used, might appear idiosyncratic (especially when mentioning Rothbard et al.) and it is pointed out several times in the text that in this second part of the book "anarchism" does not merely refer to the absence of modern state institutions but, more broadly, to a condition without any social

portant differences to the argument presented here. For example, Buchanan is following the traditional social contract approaches and considers what happens when (already well-unified) individual agents come together and have to figure out how to arrange their coexistence by setting up a regime of mutual constraints. Buchanan's discussion is useful, however, because he presents his conceptual objections against individualist anarchism by looking at an act that clearly falls into Korsgaard's category of natural acts, namely letting one's hair grow. He argues that even actions involving acts like this one are subject to potential interference if certain external conditions are not secured. Buchanan says,

> What if one person is disturbed by long-hairs while others choose to allow their hair to grow? Even for such a simple example, the anarchist utopia is threatened, and to shore it up something about limits must be said. At this point, a value norm may be injected to the effect that overt external interference with personal dress or hair style should not be countenanced. [...] If there is even one person who thinks it appropriate to constrain others' freedom to their own life-styles, no anarchistic order can survive in the strict sense of the term.[282]

It is noteworthy to see Buchanan calling into question what can be labeled the "default assumption." Buchanan suggests that we better establish *some* public norms that secure and guarantee that individuals can engage in the seemingly natural act of letting their hair grow. As soon as there is more than one individual, norms and rules are needed that are acknowledged by agents (and thereby become part of the action-descriptions, with respect to which the agents' identity-constituting principles get actualized in these concrete actions).

There is an important distinction that has to be mentioned in connection with this discussion of Buchanan's critique of anarchism.[283] The hair-growing example is concerned with what we can call "permissive," as opposed to, "enabling" public norms. The latter type of norms makes cooperation between individuals possible, e.g. the norms constituting the institutions of contract and promising. In the case of enabling norms it is obvious that they are instances of social practices and institutions. After all, they enable actions that simply can-

---

practices and institutions. However, in Part 3 we will focus on the distinctively modern manifestation of legal norms and structures as a special case of the broader category of social institutions. This discussion will fit better into conventional debates between individualist anarchists and their critics.

282 Buchanan 2000 (1975), p. 6.

283 I thank Fred Miller for directing me to this distinction between two kinds of norms that present two distinct social conditions of the possibility of individual agency.

not be engaged in outside of the societal condition. This seems much less clear in the case of the other type of norms, i.e., permissive ones that merely consist in the non-interference with each others lives and actions. Letting one's hair grow is part of an action that can be performed even if nobody else was around and permissive norms merely ensure that these "natural" actions (in Korsgaard's sense) can get engaged in without the interference of all the others who might do so.

However, the crucial point with respect to this distinction is that it is significantly less decisive in the framework presented here. Firstly, when Hayek says, in the passage quoted at the beginning of this part, that "the different objects and forms of action acquire for him new properties [when these actions are performed under the law; C.H.],"[284] this observation gets extended to supposed "natural actions." In short, letting one's hair grow when no one else is around is a different act than letting one's hair grow when others are around and do not interfere with this act. These two acts fall under different descriptions and are, therefore, parts of two different objects of self-constituting choice in the sense established in section 5.2 and in my critique of Korsgaard's distinction between natural and conventional act-types.[285]

Secondly, and this is one way to interpret Buchanan's point in the discussed passage, also permissive norms are public norms in the sense identified as necessary for a high degree of unified agency in the presence of others. Of course, permissive norms play a very different role in "enabling" individual action and agency – they do so in a seemingly purely negative way. Still, and this is the controversial claim submitted here, even non-interference is a non-trivial achievement and is itself a social, interpersonal, practice and institution. In this important respect then, the difference between permissive and enabling public norms is merely one of different degrees of "social involvement," so to speak. Permissive norms are only minimally social forms of cooperation, but they still are. The remainder of our discussion of public norms focuses on the permissive variety, simply because if it can be shown that even permissive norms of non-interference are social ones, then the same point will apply, to at least the same degree, to enabling public norms.

Buchanan does not explicitly connect his observations with issues having to do with action-theory and the possibility of individual agency. As mentioned above, he seems to assume (with classical contractarians) an unquestionable

284 Hayek 1960, p. 153.

285 This claim concerning action descriptions will also play a crucial role in the discussion of Robinson Crusoe in the next section.

conceptual priority and self-sufficiency of individual agency.[286] However, at some points Buchanan comes very close to endorsing this chapter's main claim, and here is just one good example: "Without some definition of boundaries or limits on the set of rights to do things and/or to exclude or prevent others from doing things, *an individual, as such, could hardly be said to exist.*"[287]

Let us summarize. We have modified Korsgaard's distinction between natural and conventional acts by, firstly, drawing the distinction differently, namely by means of distinguishing between individuals in and those outside of the societal condition. Natural acts are possible but only in the hypothetical scenario of a one-man universe. (The practical, non-public, identity of such a Robinson-Crusoe-type individual will be discussed below.) Secondly, it was claimed that such purely natural acts are impossible in the societal condition. The performance of acts that, at first sight, seem to depend solely on the laws of nature turn out to be very much dependent on the presence of social practices and rules, namely those establishing (at least) practices of non-interference with agents' setting and pursuing ends. However, despite almost eliminating Korsgaard's distinction in its entirety, one must not forget that the two types of external conditions play two independent conceptual roles and are of a fundamentally different nature. The rules, norms, and laws, constituting man-made institutions and practices, are themselves normative constructions in a way that the laws of nature are not.[288]

It is this claim that eventually leads us back to the argument for the public identity claim. Our highly individualized practical identities are constituted by performing self-constituting actions. It was argued that the abstract practical principles that are the building blocks of our practical identities must be actualized in concrete actions in order to retain their role as such building blocks (abstract practical principles without their application to concrete actions are empty). It is concrete actions, more specifically their descriptions in the form of

---

286 As will become clearer in Chapter 7, advocates of individual rights do not need to worry that the claims made in the text imply anything like a moral priority/superiority of the collective over the individual. That the concept of the individual cannot be coherently constructed in complete isolation from a concept of interpersonal norms does not undermine the idea of robust individual rights. This is also a common misunderstanding concerning Hegel (but probably not of Fichte and Herder). (See Pippin 2008, p. 26.)

287 Buchanan 2000 (1975), pp. 14-15 (emphasis in original). A bit earlier, Buchanan also distinguishes his view form Rothbard's, whose "approach fails to come to grips with the problem of defining rights initially, the issue that is central to my discussion" (Buchanan 2000 (1975), p. 9). (See also Chapter 7 below.)

288 I put aside discussions concerning moral realism on the one hand and constructivism about laws of nature on the other (despite the former's prominent role in Korsgaard's project).

maxims and *logoi*, that are chosen (or rejected) on the basis of those abstract principles that describe who we are from our first-person, deliberate, standpoint (concrete actions without them being chosen on the basis of abstract practical principles are mere happenings).

In the societal condition a full description of these concrete actions' maxims cannot ignore the normative principles that define and limit an individual agent's relationship to all others who potentially impinge on her action-attempts. In a world like ours, these relationships are put on a predictable and firm foundation by public norms, practices, and institutions. As was argued at stage 5 of the argument for the public identity claim, an agent who chooses and performs an action *under* these norms, therefore, always deliberates about and chooses maxims that include these public principles. Furthermore, the identity of this agent is a public one, because it consists of all the abstract practical principles (internal and external) that guide the choice of these particular action-descriptions. Since Anarchia, by stipulation, completely lacks any of these stable and predictable (law/principle like) interpersonal features, it follows that there simply is not anything that can complete the action-descriptions that are needed to perform self-constituting actions in the presence of others. The radical and complete absence of public norms, which makes the *setting* of ends hardly possible and that renders the successful performance of the acts directed at these ends into a matter of chance, goes hand in hand with incomplete maxims, which in turn accompany disunified agency and crippled identities.

6.2 Two Objections and Towards the Rule of Law

Before the argument for the public identity claim can be rendered more concrete (by looking at how legal institutions can be better understood by applying it), a number of potential objections to the account defended here must be discussed. It has been admitted all along that the two thought experiments ask us to imagine a world that is radically different from ours, firstly with respect to its physical constitution (and its laws) and secondly concerning its man-made practices and institutions. The main contribution of the previous chapters consists in an account of action that identifies conditions external to individuals as ones that are necessary for setting ends and, hence, for performing actions. But does the argument defended here really say that individuals fail to constitute themselves into individuals because they cannot complete the performance of actual actions in the extremely unstable and unpredictable environment that characterizes the thought experiments? Why are not potential agents able to identify and set ends in the complete absence of natural regularities and public rules, norms, and laws in a weaker sense than the argument for the public identity claim requires for maintaining full-fledged agency? Cannot they, from their first-personal perspective, do so at least "speculatively" and, hence, independently of what is going on "in the world around them?" A second objection calls into question the specific claim that some *social* and *public* practices and institutions have to be in place for ends to be conclusively set and willed. What about individuals outside of the societal condition, such as Robinson Crusoe? Does not he perform actions?

First objection: Why not constitute oneself in a speculative, non-anarchic, world?

Why cannot the whole business of self-constituting action be taken care of purely internally and independently of what is going on "outside" of an agent's will? This seems especially true since the lynchpin of the action-theoretical argument defended here is primarily concerned with what is happening when a practical reasoner confronts the task of deliberating, choosing, and setting ends, understood as the particular initial elements involved in the composite phenomenon of action. The thought experiments were supposed to show that not even this task can be taken up successfully in Chaotica and Anarchia. But why do actions have to be performed in and shared with the world, so to speak, in order to play the role in the process of individual self-constitution that Korsgaard assigns them? Why cannot a potential agent, who finds herself in Anarchia, constitute herself by means of retreating into a speculative but non-chaotic private world? Is not this process of practical deliberation, despite its fancied character, getting close enough to actual action so that it successfully constitutes the deliberating individual into an agent with a well-unified practical identity? Put less technically: Why cannot individuals, who find themselves in Anarchia, envision what an ordered world *would be* like and thereby establish a reference point that stabilizes their self-conception as an end-setter in this way?[289]

In response to this objection it is insisted that the *setting* of ends and the *performance* of acts are tasks that have to be executed in the demanding sense

289 It is true, as Jonathan Miller has pointed out to me, that conversely, the actual presence of natural or social laws might not enable a cognitively defective person to attain agency. It is important to keep in mind that what is missing in Chaotica and Anarchia are *necessary* conditions for a high degree of agency, not *sufficient* ones. This is also the reason for why my view remains compatible with Korsgaard's story about the two Kantian imperatives and their role as the *internal* constitutive principles of willing.

presented above. As was stressed in the initial presentation of especially the second stage of the argument for the public identity claim, in order for practical deliberation and action to fulfill their functions (i.e., constituting those who perform them as agents with a particular practical identity) they cannot be conducted in terms of maxims/*logoi* that describe actions that are known (by the individual reflecting on them) to be and remain merely speculative ones. Maxims have to be endorsed in a truly practical manner, i.e., with the aim of actually resulting in actions that have at least the realistic potential of making a specific, aimed-at, difference in the world. It is this world-directedness that cannot be provided by the purely speculative and fancied "actions" of Anarchian individuals. A potential action is not really an action because the function of self-constitution is not successfully fulfilled when, in the course of practical deliberation, ends are "set" in a merely dreamed-up world of stable and predictable external conditions.

Support for this claim comes from Kant's distinction between willing an end on the one hand and merely desiring/wanting it on the other.[290] Only willing an end counts as having conclusively "made up" one's mind and as having concluded a process of *practical* deliberation with a mental act of commitment (i.e., choice) that amounts to actually taking the first step(s) on the way to completing the whole action. This is also the reason for why it makes sense to incorporate the setting of the end into the description of the whole action-package. By contrast, there remains a reflective gap between my desire on the one hand and the worldly execution of the action required to obtain the desire's object on the other. The same gap is not an issue in case I will the very same object; in the latter case my willing the object already counts as part of the action in question

290 Kant's distinction between willing an end and merely desiring it is most clearly stated in his definitional discussion of hypothetical imperatives: Hypothetical imperatives "represent the practical necessity of a possible action as a means to achieving something that one wills (or that it is at least possible for one to will)" (G 4:414). It is problematic that some (older) translations of the *Groundwork* replace the "wills" and "will" in this quote by "desires" and "desire." The hypothetical imperative does exactly not apply to those agents who merely desire a certain end, they must will it. Robert Johnson sums up the distinction very well: "'[I]f you want pastrami, try the corner deli' is also a command in conditional form, but strictly speaking it too fails to be a hypothetical imperative in Kant's sense since this command does not apply to us in virtue of our *willing* some end, but only in virtue of our *desiring* or *wanting* an end. For Kant, willing an end involves more than desiring or wanting it; it requires the exercise of practical reason and focusing oneself on the pursuit of that end. Further, there is nothing irrational in failing to will means to what one desires. An imperative that applied to us in virtue of our desiring some end would thus not be a hypothetical imperative *of practical rationality* in Kant's sense" (Johnson 2008).

and I, the agent, count as already being engaged in it. Willing amounts to a kind of internal mobilization of myself ("resolving to do X") that is absent in the case of merely wishing a state of affairs to obtain. As was argued above, self-constitution requires actions that involve this robust kind of willing and end-setting which in turn is hardly possible in an environment that lacks any predictable patterns and refuses to award us the status of end-setters at all.

Next, consider an underappreciated dimension of the very notion of "deliberation" that further illustrates this difference between bringing the process of practical reasoning to an end by means of determining one's will as opposed to merely wishing to do something. The idea of "*de*-liberation" captures an element of self-determination understood as restricting one's own, lawless, freedom.[291] Determining one's will in a certain way (and thereby excluding all the other available options) always means to restrict one's own "liberty" to pursue whatever end one might want to choose. Hobbes's understanding of the notion of "deliberation" is closely related to what has been said: "And it is called *deliberation*; because it is putting an end to the *liberty* we had of doing, or omitting, according to our own appetite, or aversion."[292] The similarities between this notion of deliberation and the process of self-constitution that was laid out in seven stages above are apparent.

The reply to the first objection from speculative action rests on the distinction between a demanding conception of willing and merely desiring an end. Instances of aiming at outcomes in complete detachment from external conditions (something that seems, at first sight, readily available to individuals in Anarchia) do not count as willing an end. Action involves a degree of determination of the will that cannot be attained, unless the aiming at the action's end is accompanied by a subjective attitude identifying the end as one that can actually be achieved. This element of one's deliberative standpoint can be called the "attitude of realizability."[293] Potential agents in Anarchia cannot sustain this attitude towards their possible ends because of the external detriments depicted in the thought experiments. Merely desiring the occurrence of certain states of

291 See Frankfurt 1988, pp. 174–175.

292 Hobbes 1994 (1651), p. 33.

293 The notion of an "attitude of realizability" resembles R. Jay Wallace's claim that intending an end and desiring it are two distinct attitudes an agent can take on with respect to an end. Importantly, according to Wallace, the difference in question is ultimately based on (theoretical) beliefs concerning the end's realizability: "One specific respect in which these attitudes [desiring vs. intending; C.H.] differ is that the commitment to realize an end is constrained by one's beliefs about the possibility of realizing the end, whereas desires are not similarly constrained" (Wallace 2001, p. 20).

affairs, and imagining what it would possibly be like to bring them about, might well be possible for these individuals – that much must be granted.

However, constituting one's identity by means of performing proper actions (and engage in the process of practical deliberation about them) requires circumstances that allow individuals to set ends conceived of as states of affairs that can actually be brought about – not accidentally and by chance, but because certain acts are deliberately considered plausible means to do so. The role of external public norms is to allow individuals to sustain this attitude of realizability towards their ends. This attitude comes in degrees, of course, and these degrees are reflected in the levels of successful self-constitution. Not all sets of external conditions are equally conducive to constituting agents and no realistic arrangement can guarantee absolute realizability all the time.[294] As will be argued in the final part of this book, the ultimate justification of a prominent set of such public norms (i.e., the modern law) is best understood in terms of how good a job it does in facilitating the self-constitution of individual agency.

The following example will help to illustrate this line of argument by presenting a slightly different scenario, potentially put forward by someone who is still not fully convinced by my reply to the first objection.[295] Imagine a person who *wants* to join the US armed forces and serve in Afghanistan. Now let us grant, for the sake of argument, that this person has somehow coherently identified this end, understood as a certain state of affairs involving her in a specific position and situation. In addition, she comes up with all kinds of speculative

---

294 See again Korsgaard 2009, pp. 84–90, who uses the expression "attitude of trust towards the world" to describe something similar to the attitude of realizability.

295 Fictional literature turns out to be a rich source for cases that illustrate the problem with the first objection that considers speculative action to be sufficient for successful self-constitution. The example of Walter Mitty, who leads an imaginary life, is similar to the case of the speculative soldier discussed in the text. (See Thurber 2008 (1939).) However, the case of Don Quixote is different because we can hardly say that the latter does not perform any "real" actions whatsoever when he tilts at windmills. The case of Don Quixote presents another problem with agency that is out of touch with reality. It does, however, support the conclusions established in the text. After all, Don Quixote is a tragic figure and a "failed agent" (similar to the speculative soldier). (See Cervantes 1979 (1605).) Another example is the story "An Occurrence at Owl Creek Bridge" by Ambrose Bierce, about a man who is being hanged and imagines the rope breaks, when in fact it does not. (See Bierce 2008 (1890).) What all these stories about delusion and daydreaming highlight, and this point is discussed in the text, is that there are limits to an exclusively first-personal account of self-constitution as employed in this essay. Genuine self-constitution requires not merely an internally coherent normative self-conception but has to be the result of actions that "track" the world in a specific way and make a difference therein. This thought also necessarily seems to lead us to a third-personal dimension of agents mutually acknowledging one another as agents.

paths of action, consisting in her doing all the things she believes soldiers are doing while on duty. In this sense of "wanting to be a soldier" even an individual finding herself in Anarchia seems to be capable of desiring certain states of affairs that result from her acts. Insofar as these instances of practical deliberation count as genuine ones, the objector concludes, we can imagine that the individual in question is actually successful in somehow constituting herself into an imaginary, though unified, agent. Sure, her ends and actions are purely speculative ones and so is her practical identity as a soldier; but she still seems to endorse a (internally) coherent self-conception, right?

The modified version of the argument from self-constitution and the underlying theory of action blocks this move. First, consider that the would-be soldier in our example differs from other potential agents in Anarchia in one important respect: she exhibits, we stipulate, the attitude of realizability, regardless of whether or not actual external conditions warrant it. The individuals in Anarchia, discussed above, were aware of the unpredictability and instability of the context within which they attempted to set ends and perform actions. That they were not able to develop the accompanying attitude, saying to themselves wholeheartedly that the desired ends can actually be brought about, was the reason for them not being able to will them and to develop a coherent identity as an end-setter. The soldier-case is different in this respect and at first sight the presence of the attitude of realizability seems to help the objector who defends the possibility of speculatively constituted agency.

However, this apparent victory of the objector comes at a price too high. Just ask yourself what we think about people who constitute themselves in the thoroughly speculative way described, in a kind of "dream world" that allows their "actions" to have the effects that they want them to have? Do not we think that such an agent, who "successfully" constitutes herself in these circumstances, is an instance of failed agency because she does not exhibit a minimal connection to the external world? It does not seem to be an unwelcome corollary of the action-theory defended here that "agents," such as the "soldier" described, are considered pathological. Our soldier seems to have fantasized herself into something self-delusional when she exhibits the attitude of realizability with respect to her ends and aims. She lost (or never properly developed) her grip on reality and she is simply *self*-deceived when regarding herself as having endorsed the practical identity of a soldier by means of performing the actions that are constitutive of this very identity. The soldier-case then illustrates that speculatively setting ends is insufficient for willing them and for performing actions *even if* such fancied actions were thinkable (*for* some practical reasoners) in the radical Anarchia presented in the two thought experiments.

Second objection: Is not Robinson Crusoe performing actions?

The second objection to the argument for the public identity claim rests on the idea that a conceptual wedge can be driven between the role that the laws of nature play as a necessary prerequisite for action and the role that normative social structures play.[296] True, the objector continues, a world in which gravity acts completely erratically and unpredictably is not at all conducive to the activity of individual self-constitution. Setting and pursuing ends is an inconceivable option in the absence of any regularities that structure the world surrounding a potential agent and it is correct to claim that the concept of action is an incoherent one in Chaotica so imagined. However, things seem to be different with respect to the predictability provided by social practices and institutions. We can show this, the objector claims, by envisioning a character like Robinson Crusoe.[297] It seems quite a stretch to claim that a character like Crusoe does not

---

296 Insofar as the argument in the text claims that the presence of some public norms is necessary for a high degree of self-constitution amongst human beings, one might wonder if it leads us to accepting the more general claim that all possible kinds of agents (e.g., Martians) are necessarily social beings. In other words, is it (conceptually) possible to envision agents who are aware of each other's existence but are not necessarily social beings in the minimal sense defended here? As Jonathan Miller put it in response to an earlier draft: "Might there be non-human agents that are not social beings?" These questions are complex and this note can only hint at a reply. A crucial assumption seems to be one that Hart's and Kant's political and legal philosophy share, namely that beings who are similar enough to us (i.e. they are vulnerable to interference, harm, etc. by one another) share a problem, even if they are not members of the human species. As long as potential agents are beings who are vulnerable to this kind of threat to their status as functioning agents, then these beings, while non-human, must be "social" in the sense defended in the text. They share the universal need to establish and maintain some regime of public norms. Things are different, of course, if our nature (or the nature of those beings who share the problem of potential interference) were to change in the way Hart envisions: "suppose that men were to become invulnerable to attack by each other, were clad perhaps like giant land crabs with an impenetrable carapace, and could extract the food they needed from the air by some internal chemical process" (Hart 1958, p. 623). Only if non-human agents are of the kind envisioned by Hart, might the requirement to settle on some kind of publicly acknowledged social regulation of behavior become optional. But, again, much more would have to be said about agency among beings who are that different from us.

297 The Robinson Crusoe mainly discussed in the text is different from the one described in Defoe's novel and most likely not a psychologically possible one. After all, the character we are supposed to imagine has not, like the original Crusoe, lived amongst other human agents before ending up on the lonely island. The conceptual point raised in the objection must assume a different scenario, namely a Crusoe who has never lived in the company of others at all and, *a fortiori*, has never experienced what it is like to live under the normative conditions defined by public norms. Actually, we need to describe our Crusoe in even more radical terms.

perform any actions and, hence, fails to constitute himself into a unified agent with a specific practical identity. Since Crusoe does exist in a world necessarily devoid of any man-made *social* practices and institutions (he lives on the lonely island on his own after all) but still goes about doing things (e.g., splitting a coconut in order to eat it) and successfully completes these actions, this seems to imply that the former institutions are not necessary for performing meaningful actions. Crusoe appears to do fine when he identifies and sets ends. The status of an end-setter can be ascribed to him and, more importantly, he can coherently award himself this status without other agents acknowledging him as such and these others letting him set and pursue his ends and plans. Crusoe appears to be efficacious when he chooses "whole action packages" (acts-done-for-the-sake-of-ends), exactly as this essay's demanding account of practical deliberation and action requires it for an agent's self-constitution to be conducted successfully.

Let us begin our discussion of this objection by briefly looking at the example of Robinson Crusoe as it is originally presented in Defoe's famous novel.[298] This version of Crusoe is different from the one I'll focus on below in that it presents an agent who successfully constituted himself in the societal condition before arriving on the island. Defoe's Crusoe knows and understands what action descriptions look like when other individuals are around and public principles regulate their standing vis-à-vis one another; this understanding cannot be assumed to simply disappear upon arrival on the island. When Defoe's Crusoe strands on the island, he does so as an agent who once was familiar with the process of incorporating maxims and *logoi* into his process of developing and maintaining a practical identity that, if fully formulated, include certain public action-enabling norms. However, once alone on the island (and having involun-

We must imagine an individual outside the societal condition who *knows* that he is the only individual in the universe and this belief informs her self-conception. There is some historical and empirical evidence related to "language deprivation experiments" indicating that such a Crusoe is psychologically impossible. But these empirical problems do not diminish the second objection's conceptual challenge to the account of action presented in the text. For a historical account of language deprivation experiments, see Shattuck 1994. For the claim that basically all reported cases of "feral children" do not withstand scrutiny, see Aroles 2007. (See also Newton 2004.)

298 The following paragraphs distinguish between "Defoe's Crusoe" and "Robinson Crusoe." I'll focus on the second case, i.e. the Crusoe who populates the universe alone and acknowledges that fact in the course of his self-constituting activities. However, also the original version presents enlightening features of what is happening when an agent, who previously lived in a highly developed society, suddenly finds herself outside of the societal condition (and later returns to the former when encountering Friday).

tarily exited the societal condition) Defoe's Crusoe performs actions in a significantly different context. And even those acts that were discussed under the label of "natural" (as opposed to "conventional") ones, like "letting one's hair grow," take on a different meaning and play a different role in the course of self-constitution once engaged in an environment outside of the societal condition. It is for this reason that Crusoe's identity indeed changes once he realizes that there are no others around who could potentially interfere with his action attempts (permissive norms), let alone others who might cooperate with him and set and pursue ends that only collective endeavors can yield (enabling norms). The actions he chooses fall under different descriptions on the island and this change is reflected in an altered normative self-conception. More on this aspect of the Crusoe cases below.

The kind of change that is referred to is also an issue when Defoe's Crusoe (re)enters the societal condition later in the novel. There is one particularly striking passage that nicely illustrates the Hayekian point about how the "objects and properties" of actions take on a new form *for* the agents who perform them when features of their environment change. Defoe describes the moment that Crusoe encounters the abstract and unknown "other" (who later turns out to be Friday) in the form of footsteps in the sand:[299]

> I stood like one Thunder-struck, or as if I had seen an Apparition; I listen'd, I look'd round me, I could hear nothing, nor see any Thing; [...] how it came thither, I knew not, nor could in the least imagine. But after innumerable fluttering Thoughts, like a Man perfectly confus'd and out of my self, I came Home to my Fortification, not feeling, as we say, the Ground I went on, but terrified to the last Degree, looking behind me at every two or three Steps, mistaking every Bush and Tree, and fancying every Stump at a Distance to be a Man; nor is it possible to describe how many various Shapes affrighted Imagination represented Things to me in, how many wild Ideas were found every Moment in my Fancy, and what strange unaccountable Whimsies came into my Thoughts by the Way.
>
> When I came to my Castle, for so I think I call'd it ever after this, I fled into it like one pursued; whether I went over by the Ladder, as first contriv'd, or went in at the Hole in the Rock, which I call'd a Door, I cannot remember; no, nor could I remember the next Morning, for never frightened Hare fled to Cover, or Fox to Earth, with more Terror of Mind than I to this Retreat.[300]

Note the way in which Defoe describes the impact that Crusoe experiences (first-personally and autobiographically) upon encountering the trace of another

299 Thanks to Fred Miller for directing me to this and many other literary examples and cases that deal with agency under unusual conditions.
300 Defoe 1994 (1719), p. 112.

being that he immediately categorizes as similar enough to himself (and, hence, as entertaining similar processes of practical deliberation as he does). Crusoe is "confused" and he is "out of himself." The unpredictability that comes with the arrival of another agent has a thorough-going effect on Crusoe's self-understanding and practical identity as an agent. His actions, and the environment in which they take place, take on a different significance exactly in the way that Hayek describes when individuals overcome the lawless condition and put their freedom under the rule of public laws. In the face of the potential interference by others, the very same object that used to be regarded as a dwelling suddenly becomes a "castle" and a "fortification." According to the main line of argument pursued here, this point about changing actions and environments eventually translates into a different normative self-conception of Crusoe. The actions that Crusoe performs after having discovered the footprint are different from seemingly similar actions performed earlier because of the acknowledged presence of another human. The confusion and anxiety that Defoe so nicely describes can be interpreted as the effect of finding oneself in the societal condition that is at the same time a completely unregulated one concerning one's relationship to this other individual. The discovery of the footprint shakes the core of Crusoe's stable self-understanding ("out of myself") because there is yet no principled public basis established between himself and the unknown stranger.

It must be admitted that what we have shown so far merely is that actions and identities change in a case like the one described by Defoe. In the original Crusoe, an already well-constituted agent is confronted with the presence of another agent. Even for such an agent, who used to live in a rule-governed society before, this event significantly alters his self-conception. This is a substantial and important conclusion in and of itself; however, we still need to address the second objection directly, according to which action and agency is well possible in the complete absence of any public norms (even if we're talking about a Crusoe who does not know what life in the societal condition would be like). In other words, we still need to answer the question of whether or not a practical identity is possible in the first place in the case of life outside of the societal condition and, if that is the case, what such a normative self-conception would look like.

In order to spell out more fully what Crusoe's actions (and, hence, his practical identity) are like outside of the societal condition let us move on to this slightly adapted version of the story. In this version, Crusoe has not experienced self-constitution in the societal condition before. In response to the second objection two points should be emphasized. Firstly, the fact that Crusoe is the only individual and potential agent around (and, again, he is aware of that fact) does indeed change the problem with respect to which the account of action and identity defended here is supposed to submit a solution. There are challenges with respect to the problem of agency and self-constitution that simply do not emerge when an agent finds herself in a one-man world. The point made here can be illustrated by an analogy, based on Tim Scanlon's remarks on why modern moral philosophy tends to restrict the scope of morality to the realm of what he calls "what we owe to each other."[301] Scanlon distinguishes morality in a "broad sense" (that concerns itself with the permissibility of self- as well as other-regarding actions) from the "morality of right and wrong."[302] The latter defines the scope of Scanlon's contractualist moral theory narrowly and it rests on a notion of morality that refers "to a particular normative domain including primarily such duties to others as duties not to kill, harm, or deceive, and duties to keep one's promises."[303] Now the morality of right and wrong cannot apply to individuals like Robinson Crusoe because regard for others is not a demand that can be a part of his normative conceptual framework. Robinson Crusoe, simply because of his peculiar circumstances outside of the societal condition, is not potentially confronted with legal, political, and moral issues in the way Scanlon defines them. Insofar as an agent's practical identity incorporates practical principles that concern her relation to all other agents, these kind of practical principles (the ones that were called "public" in a wide sense) do not and cannot figure in Crusoe's practical deliberation and identity. Following the main argument of this chapter, Crusoe does indeed not have a public identity but, nevertheless, does have a practical one determining his self-conception as a successful coconut-splitter etc. The maxims he endorses in the process of actualizing his practical principles are exhaustively described – even if these descriptions lack end-setting norms that would require others to let him go about his coconut-splitting undisturbed. These others are simply not an issue in his case and this has an impact on the actions he performs and, hence, on the identity that results and is maintained in the course of performing these actions.

Now exactly this societal condition materializes when Friday enters the picture and Crusoe is confronted with the existence of another person. His situation concerning the external conditions that are necessary for confronting the task of setting ends and performing actions has changed. It is also now that the need for some man-made practices emerges in order to impose a normative form on the unavoidable interdependence between the (two) individuals. As empha-

301 Scanlon 2000, pp. 171–187.
302 Scanlon 2000, p. 6
303 Scanlon 2000, p. 171.

sized in the previous chapter, even if Friday and Crusoe *grant each other* the maximum amount of individual non-interference, and acknowledge each other as individuals who go on living as hermits, *this* already counts as a practice in the sense that the argument presented here is concerned with. That Friday abstains from constantly and erratically impacting on Crusoe's setting of ends (and *vice versa*) is not the "natural" and "default" mode of coexistence in the societal condition populated by beings who are "free" (in a self-ascriptive sense) to do exactly that.

The way in which all of this has an impact on Crusoe's practical identity again follows from what was said when presenting the argument for the public identity claim. The description of even a banal, and seemingly private and self-regarding, action such as splitting a coconut in order to eat it has changed due to Friday's arrival. The interpersonal norms between him and Crusoe are now part of the action that the latter chooses in accordance with those practical principles that define what person he is. When Friday is present, Crusoe constitutes himself into an agent with a public practical identity. Crusoe before Friday's arrival was indeed a different individual compared to the one he is now.

In summary, then, it can be granted that Robinson Crusoe's actions are possible qua actions (in the self-constituting mode) even in the absence of social practices and rules (as long as the natural regularities are not like those in Chaotica). It is true then that the argument for the public identity claim is restricted in scope, at least when our concern in dealing with the second objection only is the possibility of *any* (even fairly minimal) degree of individual agency whatsoever.[304] The argument applies to those agents who live in an environment populated by at least one other individual. As soon as agents are mutually aware of each other's existence the game changes and the activity of setting ends requires practices and institutions that render predictable the actions and responses on part of the others.[305]

---

304 In other words, when granting the objector that Robinson Crusoe is an agent with a non-public practical identity that should not be taken to imply that Crusoe exhibits agency to the same degree as agents in the (well-ordered) societal condition do. Crusoe's agency is diminished because the repertoire of possible actions that he can potentially engage in is much smaller than the one that is at the disposal of those who are in the societal condition with other agents. I am indebted to Fred Miller for pointing out that the difference between Crusoe's and our agency can be described in two distinct ways: according to degrees of one overarching conception of agency and according to two distinct manifestations of agency.

305 Let us ignore here that, of course, a two-person world cannot set-up an arbitrator or Leviathan.

However, and let us conclude with this second point, one must not concede too much to the objection, notwithstanding its valid point that agents like Robinson Crusoe cannot be ruled out as impossible qua agents by the argument presented here. There is a couple of questions one should ask, namely what kind of agent this isolated Robinson Crusoe would be? What would his practical identity look like? Is it an identity sufficiently similar to ours or is Crusoe engaged in a very different activity when he practically deliberates and endorses principles of action?

The second objection underestimates the extent to which Crusoe, even if we grant that he is some kind of agent, must be an individual exhibiting a very unique and alien kind of practical identity and is likely to exhibit agency to a significantly lower degree as we do.[306] There are two ways of looking at Crusoe's case. Firstly, he seems to partake in our form of life – to a very diminished degree though. Or, secondly and maybe more radically, he might be regarded as partaking in a different form of life.[307] It does not seem completely outlandish to compare our relationship to such an individual with the one we have to the internal "point of view" of a bat in Thomas Nagel's famous essay.[308] Analogously to Nagel's argument, that we cannot exhaustively comprehend the phenomenological content of the consciousness of a being with a physical constitution that radically differs from ours, we face a challenge when we attempt to characterize the normative self-conception of a being in a non-societal environment that is radically different from our own. And similar to the task of trying to imagine what our self-conception would be like if we were, let us say, immortal beings, we can ask "What is it like to be Robinson Crusoe?"

306 This is one of the many points in this book at which an exploration of Hegel's theory of mutual recognition and of the social preconditions of modern agency would be indicated. Hegel claims that individuals realize a higher degree of agency and freedom through participating in the life of modern societies (and modern states) and thereby achieve a form and degree of freedom that had been inaccessible under earlier historical conditions. Underlying his philosophy of history is the much less controversial assumption that humans become, *ceteris paribus*, *more* self-aware and autonomous through their interaction with and mutual recognition of others. Hence, one might conceive of Crusoe's diminished degree of agency in analogy to individuals who constitute themselves under pre-modern conditions. These claims cannot be fully investigated here but the political and legal-philosophical issues dealt with in Part 3 will probably remind one of some of Hegel's theses. See Pippin 2008 and Honneth 2010 for an accessible contemporary account of Hegel's social thought. I am indebted to Michael Weber and Jonathan Miller for pointing out the resemblance of my view to Hegel's.

307 See Wittgenstein 2009 (1953), sections 19, 23, 241 (pp. 11, 15, 94).

308 Nagel 1979, pp. 165–180.

These questions cannot be answered swiftly by simply "subtracting" the property of mortality from our current self-understanding and construct the alternative self-conception by adding the feature of immortality to the result of the foregoing subtraction.[309] Crusoe's case presents a problem that is puzzling in a similar way. Simply taking our conceptions of agency and identity as they present themselves to *us* and subtract from it the existence of all others around us will not do in order to grasp what life outside the societal condition would be like for such a unique agent. Admitting that some kind of action is possible in the case of Crusoe does therefore not straightforwardly imply that his agency and the related normative self-conception (Crusoe's practical identity) are fully comprehensible to us. As Charles Taylor summarizes, in expanding on a famous remark of Aristotle's, "as humans this separation [between individual and society; C.H.] is unthinkable. On our own, as Aristotle says, we would be either beasts or Gods."[310]

309 In addition to Nagel's picture, discussed in the text, the claim that Robinson Crusoe is a radically different "person" relative to us draws on John McDowell's attack on the common sense view, according to which we can easily conceive of what it means for animals to be in pain by just "stripping off" what is special about us (i.e., conceptual capacities) and thereby arrive at a "residue" (i.e., non-conceptual content) that we share with other sentient beings. The common sense view underestimates the extent to which our perception (of pain) is already deeply conceptualized and therefore of a radically different nature than an animal's. (See McDowell 1996, pp. 63–65.)

310 Taylor 1985, p. 8. Taylor states his conclusions in terms similar to mine: "The community is also constitutive of the individual, in the sense that the self-interpretations which define him are drawn from the interchange which the community carries on. [...] Outside of the continuing conversation of a community, which provides the language by which we draw our background distinctions, human agency of the kind I describe above is not just impossible, but inconceivable." My view's relationship to communitarianism will be clarified at several points in the next part. Reviewers have expressed worries that this conclusion is too strong and that our relationship to Crusoe is not really comparable to the internal phenomenology of Nagel's bat. It is admitted that the claim, as stated in the text, sounds exaggerated and also relies on a good deal of speculation (about Crusoe's inner life). The argument seems to exploit our ignorance about Crusoe's mental states (an epistemological claim) and uses it to establish an ontological conjecture about the existence of Crusoe as an agent. In the text I weaken the claim by granting Crusoe the status of an agent. In addition, one might prefer to describe Crusoe's practical identity as merely attenuated in comparison to ours. I am open to these suggestions but do not want this openness to be misunderstood as retreating from this essay's methodological focus on the first-personal, phenomenological, dimension of agents and practical deliberation and its crucial role for understanding the nature of agency.

Part 3:
Self-Constituting Action and the Law

> As against the coercion applicable by individual to individual, no liberty can be given to one man but in proportion as it is taken from another. All coercive laws, therefore...and in particular all laws creative of liberty, are 'as far as they go' abrogative of liberty.
>
> Bentham[311]

> And one cannot say: the human being in a state has sacrificed a *part* of his innate outer freedom for the sake of an end, but rather, he has relinquished entirely his wild, lawless freedom in order to find his freedom as such undiminished, in a dependence upon laws, that is, in a rightful condition, since this dependence arises from his own lawgiving will.
>
> Kant[312]

In this part we finally return to the issue that motivated this project in the first place, namely Chandran Kukathas's critique of citizenship and liberal socio-political institutions. The previous chapters presented Neo-Kantian and Neo-Aristotelian accounts of agency, identity, and self-constituting action. The following three chapters make good on the promise, submitted in Chapter 3, that the aforementioned accounts can be applied to political and legal philosophical issues. This application allows us to present a reply to Kukathas's challenge.

Before this final reply to Kukathas is introduced (Chapter 9) this part begins with a general discussion of how the action-theoretical lessons of the Chaotica and Anarchia thought experiments can be applied to the phenomenon of law. In order to show how self-constituting action is related to the ideas of juridified predictability and stability, two lines of argument are pursued in Chapter 7. The first line calls into question the so-called "non-interference claim," which consists in the following postulate: *Human beings in the societal condition are not necessarily in need of any shared social practices and institutions because, by default, they are not interfering with each other's actions. Hence, since "action is self-constitution," the possibility of successful self-constitution too does not necessarily require that such practices and institutions are in place – not even in the societal condition.* The critical portion of the confrontation with the non-interference claim calls into question its central assumption that the *obvious* default condition in interpersonal relationships is that we do *not* interfere with one another's actions. This critique of the non-interference claim argues that in the case of free beings like us, the shared practice of non-interference is a non-trivial achievement. The constructive part of section 7.1, on the other hand, introduces the notion of "non-domination" in order to extend the non-interference claim. Only non-dominated action is action under the law and takes place within the framework provided by the public institutions that legis-

311 Bentham 1843, p. 503.
312 MM 6:316.

late and execute legal norms. Non-domination is a relationship-status amongst agents whose actions are not interfered with as a matter of right. This element of non-domination, crucial for a high-degree of practical agency, is not paid enough attention to in the non-interference paradigm.

The second line of argument that will be discussed in Chapter 7 concerns the "total law thesis." The total law thesis, however, will not be refuted but defended. It consists in the following claim: *In the modern state* every *action falls under a description that includes those public principles and norms (i.e., the law) that make its non-dominated performance possible.* In other words, the total law thesis attacks another intuition (and objection to my overall project), namely that successful self-constitution is first and foremost a private and non-public task and, consequently, takes place outside of modern legal institutions. Both with respect to individual agents and social organization, this common-sense intuition claims, public identity and public institutions come *after* individuals have fully constituted themselves as agents in non-public spheres. It is argued, in response, that there is no such thing as a "legal vacuum" in modern societies. What we cherish as the private sphere (and the freedom we enjoy when performing actions within it) is itself circumscribed and infused by the law.

Chapter 8 illustrates these considerations by looking at a prominent conception of the law. It is shown that Lon Fuller's jurisprudence can be incorporated into the self-constitution framework of agency and thereby can explain why the law purports to have reason-providing authority over citizens. Fuller's eight principles of legality (canonizing his "internal morality of law") are presented as illustrations of how the law structures interpersonal relationships in terms of stability and predictability (and how non-law fails to do so). Law has to satisfy certain formal standards of rationality and these standards have their ultimate source in what is necessary for the possibility of sustaining the unified agency of its addressees. The remainder of Chapter 8 replies to the worry that the conception of citizenship under public law, resulting from the previous arguments, is an overly demanding one. Is not it too much to ask ordinary citizens to "incorporate" the norms and principles that structure their interpersonal standing into their practical deliberation and actions?

Having concluded the argument for the connection between legal security and stability on the one hand and how agents develop and maintain their normative self-conceptions by performing actions conclusively (i.e., under coercive legal institutions) on the other, Chapter 9 allows us to revisit Kukathas's liberal archipelago afresh. In section 9.1, Kukathas's ambiguous treatment of the term "society" is taken as a starting point for arguing that the associations, populating the archipelago, will themselves be small scale legal jurisdictions (thereby sufficiently resembling Weberian states, which in turn renders Kukathas's main thesis vacuous).[313] The ultimate reason for this unavoidability of legal ordering does not (only) lie in the law's instrumental benefits; rather a legal system plays a constitutive role in the process of free agents' self-constitution. The same thought underlies the defense of Dworkin's notion of a legal system's integrity, presented in section 9.2. Federalism and separation of powers is perfectly compatible with the self-constitution account of the law.

---

313 The claim is that the liberal archipelago's associations will "*sufficiently resemble* Weberian states," as opposed to saying that all these associations will *be* Weberian states in all relevant respects. In order to be a horn of a genuine dilemma, the small-scale law communities in question need only share the most important feature of Weber's conception of states (i.e., the centralization and monopolization of coercion with respect to setting and promoting public norms concerning a particular issue/problem that applies to a specific agent). This connection between law and coercion remains controversial and I'll say more about it in the text, especially in the very last section, 9.2. I thank Jonathan Miller for asking me to clarify that my dilemma is not a false dichotomy that Kukathas could easily avoid.

Chapter 7: Action and the Law

This chapter introduces the two main arguments in support of the claim that the argument from self-constituting action supports a particular view of how we should conceive of our interpersonal relations and their institutional underpinnings. These two arguments are a critique of the "non-interference claim" and a defense of the "total law thesis" respectively.

The first argument attacks the non-interference claim that, if it were persuasive, would be a strong objection to the view that public norms and practices are necessary for a high degree of individual agency in the presence of others. The non-interference claim states: *Human beings in the societal condition are not necessarily in need of any shared social practices and institutions because, by default, they are not interfering with each other's actions. Hence, since "action is self-constitution," the possibility of successful self-constitution too does not necessarily require that such practices and institutions are in place – not even in the societal condition.* The initial plausibility of the non-interference claim has its origin in the intuition that the overly legalistic and institutionalist view of human relationships, defended in this essay, neglects the fact that non-interference with one another's action-attempts is the "default" and "natural" setting in the societal condition. I will argue that this common-sense intuition is mistaken and that, for example, the legal structures that enable citizens of modern states to engage in self-constituting action (without interference by others) are a non-trivial part of the solution to the inescapable problem of human beings having to constitute themselves in the societal condition. The conclusion of this discussion of the non-interference claim suggests that the notion of "non-domination" is needed to capture this first argument's basic insight in a way that is not fully achieved by an undifferentiated focus on actual non-interference.

Section 7.2, further strengthens the constitutivist account of agency by calling into question another view that seems intuitively plausible. Is not it, psychologically, sociologically, and historically speaking the case that individuals first constitute themselves within the intimacy and privacy of the extra-legal realms of life? An argument like the one defended here, insisting on the priority of public norms and on the claim that their particular modern instantiation in the form of a legal system is this all-encompassing and all-infusing ("total") thing, seems mistaken. The strategy pursued in replying to this view consists in calling into question the conceptual and normative coherence of a purely private realm. The total law thesis rejects the view that a high degree of self-constituting action can take place in an exclusively extra-legal setting, i.e., in the complete absence of the interpersonal practices of institutionalized non-interference that lie at the heart of the idea of the rule of law. The total law thesis states: *In the modern state* every *action falls under a description that includes those public principles and norms (i.e., the law) that make its non-dominated performance possible.*

7.1 Against the Non-Interference Claim

Let us recall the conclusion that we established in the previous part. There we imagined Chaotica and Anarchia, far-removed worlds where the necessary conditions of setting ends and performing actions are absent in their entirety. Anarchia, the more important version for our purposes, while not chaotic with respect to the natural world, exhibits radical caprice on the part of its inhabitants. As a consequence, individual agency is a highly contingent and fragile matter in such a societal condition because conclusively *setting* ends is impossible there. Conclusively setting ends and plans of action amounts to a practical commitment that has to have an "attitude of realizability" attached to the intention of the action that aims at realizing these ends. A world of radical insecurity and unpredictability undermines the conditions of exactly such a commitment that we also refer to as "willing" (as opposed to merely desiring or wanting) an end and its action. Social practices and institutions have to be in place to regulate interpersonal relations in a way that, from the agent's perspective, justifies the expectation that the ends she sets *can* be realized and achieved in a way that is not chancy and subject to all others' private choices and actions.[314]

314 An important qualification has been suggested in the course of discussing an earlier draft of this chapter. What about war? It seems that an essential feature of war exactly is that the parties to the military conflict actively try to thwart each other's ends. Does war, then, diminish agency? The case of war raises complicated issues for the account presented in this part, but I do not at all want to shrink back from incorporating the case of war into the self-constitution framework. That war has been referred to (at least today) as a "dehumanizing" activity can be vindicated when we keep in mind that the state of nature (and Anarchia) has been compared, most famously by Hobbes of course, to a war-like condition. Later in this chapter, the case of slavery is presented as a paradigmatic example of external conditions that fail to provide the kind of external conditions that robust agency requires. Being in war (especially a civil war that renders one's own domestic legal norms void) can be compared with slavery so understood. In addition, the modern development (unfortunately only partly successful) of juridifying warfare can be understood as an attempt to civilize war's anarchistic dimension. This is not to deny that these attempts to make war less barbarous have as their most explicit motivation concerns

A general objection to this picture is based on a claim that most people will find initially very plausible. The thought is that the argument for the necessity of social regulation rests on an implausibly pessimistic picture of how individuals in the societal condition "behave." Anarchia depicts individuals who necessarily (compulsorily?) undermine each other's agency. When we, the real-world people, look at the world it seems hard to imagine that "the others" abstain from interfering with our actions only because some legal norms explicitly outlaw such interference. Even more clearly becomes the case, the objection continues, when we carefully investigate our own mental lives, intuitions, and motivational states with respect to why we abstain from such interference. In order to pose the constant threat to others' attempts at self-constituting action, we would have to invest an enormous amount of time, energy, and resources. What flock of individuals would be disposed to actually interfere (or pose the plausible threat of interference) with others' lives in such a radical manner?

Non-interference and pre-institutional liberty

Let us summarize and label this group of responses to the Anarchia thought experiment the "non-interference claim." It states: *Human beings in the societal condition are not necessarily in need of any shared social practices and institutions because, by default, they are not interfering with each other's actions. Hence, since "action is self-constitution," the possibility of successful self-constitution too does not necessarily require that such practices and institutions are in place – not even in the societal condition.* The fundamental idea expressed in this claim is that questions concerning interpersonal relations can be answered on the basis of accepting a certain, uncontroversial, starting point and baseline.[315] This starting point is that potential agents "enter" this world as individuals that are not interfering with one another's lives and actions. Interference with others, on the other hand, is a positive and active step that has to be

that do not have (at least at first sight) much to do with agency, such as human suffering and welfare.

315 The critique of the non-interference claim pursued in this section somewhat resembles an argument by Barbara Fried, in which the option of complete social and economic non-cooperation in the state of nature is identified as being very much a kind of social arrangement in need of justification: "[T]he Crusoeian solution, adopted by Gauthier and others, of imagining no social interaction at all doesn't solve the problem. It merely substitutes a different set of arrangements characterized by no social interaction rather than a particular form of social interaction" (Fried 2003, pp. 67–68).

triggered by some desire or reason. Only when specific desires or reasons are present, does interference occur and, on the normative level, might be justified under certain circumstances. In social and political philosophy this intuition plays a prominent role, namely in certain conceptions of the state of nature.

First let us introduce a working definition of "interference." Interferences are those actions that a) involve the initiation of physical force on the part of agents, understood as beings who could have abstained from engaging in this interfering behavior by means of engaging their volitional capacities, and that b) result in the frustration of another agent's actions and projects. Feature "a" is pointing out that animals and natural events (though this is controversial[316]) do not qualify as "interferers" because volitional control (in the demanding sense involved in the notion of practical principles) could not have prevented the interfering events from happening in these cases. And feature "b" too must be understood in the context of the action theory stipulated in this book and defended in Chapter 5: Interference refers to all those instances of the initiation of physical force that undermine what is externally (i.e., external to the interfered-with agent's will) necessary for successfully performing actions. According to this definition, A preventing B from winning a foot race by simply outpacing her, does not count as interference, even though A's action undermines B's pursuit of successfully realizing the end of winning the race (B is not subject to a physical hindrance initiated by A). If A trips B, on the other hand, B's not finishing the race first counts, according to our working definition, as the result of interference initiated by A.[317]

The non-interference claim that will be critically examined in this section assumes that the absence of interference, as defined in the previous paragraph, is the default state of affairs in the societal condition. Since interference is an activity (the initiation of force directed at others) its instantiations are in need of explanation and justification. The same is not true of non-interference amongst human beings, the defender of the non-interference claim insists. Non-interference comes to us "naturally." Translated into moral language this intuition finds its prominent expression in Hobbes, Bentham, and in Isaiah Berlin's

---

316 Cannot animals interfere with me and my actions? Cannot hurricanes do so? Strictly speaking, I do not think so or, at least, it would be preferable to have an alternative concept available for these cases in which non-human causes distort our activities of choice and action. The notion of interference used in the text is tied to the kind of agency currently discussed, i.e., adult human agency. Concerning the status of animals as agents in the sense defended in the text, see Korsgaard 2009, pp. 104–108.

317 I am indebted to Fred Miller for providing this example and for urging me to render the working definition more precise and less broad.

notion of "negative liberty."[318] Freedom, properly understood, simply consists in *non*-interference with an agent's choices and actions. Notice that freedom so conceived is envisioned as a base-line and starting point for the further arguments and justifications presented by these thinkers. The individual's condition of "not-being-interfered-with" is something natural in both senses of pre-social and pre-legal. Deviations from this natural state of liberty, in the form of putting this freedom under coercive public laws (as well as by the violent interference of private parties), then necessarily infringe and diminish the former: "Law is always a 'fetter', even if it protects you from being bound in chains that are heavier than those of the law, say arbitrary despotism and chaos."[319] Also the content of the above quote by Bentham ("every act of regulation emanating from a sovereign [is; C.H.] destructive of liberty"[320]) illustrates this normative rendering of the non-interference claim. Each individual *is* free by default and the introduction of any legal norms, coercively regulating interpersonal relations, necessarily takes away some of this baseline quantity of freedom, which is at the same time conceived as a "natural" maximum. Laws generating good social consequences do so to a lesser degree and compensate for this deprivation of liberty by, for example, enhancing well-being; bad laws infringe more on this pre-institutional sphere of freedom. However, both kinds of law reduce an individual's liberty.

A much more complex view concerning this default condition of freedom is found in Locke's *Second Treatise of Government* and the conception of the state of nature presumed there. The latter is populated by free agents (fully unified and equipped with robust basic rights) who *at a later stage* freely consent to establish legal institutions: "THE *natural liberty* of man is to be free from any superior power on earth, and not to be under the will or legislative authority of man, but to have only the law of nature for his rule."[321] Of course, Locke goes on to defend a conception of freedom that Philip Pettit rightly categorizes as republican and, hence, as ultimately opposing Bentham and Berlin's. In opposition to Filmer (who thinks that liberty is "not to be tied by any laws"), Locke contrasts civil liberty (under law) with the aforementioned natural freedom. Civil liberty consists in not being "subject to the inconstant, uncertain, unknown, arbitrary

---

318 Berlin 2002 (1969), pp. 166–217.

319 Berlin 2002 (1969), p. 170 fn. Berlin's two-part qualification concerning despotism and chaos is important for the overall alternative view defended in this book. For the current argument, however, we focus on the first part of his statement that submits that law *always* takes away from one's, pre-institutionally conceived, freedom.

320 Long 1977, p. 43.

321 Locke 2003 (1689), p. 109.

will of another man."[322] Hence, the Lockean conception of civil liberty, established and maintained in a commonwealth that is entered because of the inconveniences one is exposed to in the pre-legal state of nature, turns out to be very much in line with the non-domination view that will be presented later in this section as a rectification of the non-interference claim. However, the disagreement with Locke concerns the initial stages of his arguments, i.e., his conception of the pre-institutional state of nature. Conceptually (not psychologically, historically, etc.) the particular conception of *natural* liberty, that Locke adheres to, rests on a variety of the unqualified non-interference claim. Also for Locke, free agency (plus fully determined individual rights) in the state of nature is a perfectly coherent notion. And social institutions (especially those that enforce shared norms and practices) are not needed to create and maintain non-interference in this minimal sense.

The view critical of the non-interference claim can be put in the form of an oversimplifying slogan that regards the necessity of law differently: The law and individual freedom are two sides of the same coin. On the non-domination view the two concepts of freedom and external public norms are features of one overarching conception of (free) individual agency that emerge simultaneously (conceptually, not temporarily).[323] Locke, on the other hand, sharply distinguishes between liberty *per se* and *civil* liberty and refuses to conflate the two in the way that is suggested here. The former, a freestanding conception of natural liberty, is another expression of the non-interference claim and of its corollary that there can be a fully coherent conception of external freedom in the absence of shared public norms.[324]

It must first be admitted that the attempt to confront and undermine the non-interference claim, pursued in the next paragraphs, reminds us of an important way in which the argument from self-constitution has to be qualified. Even if the argument from self-constitution is correct, it cannot be taken to support an "all or nothing" conception of agency and freedom. Rather, freedom and

---

322 Locke 2003 (1689), p. 110. Notice the extent to which the adjectives used by Locke resemble those that were used to describe Anarchia.

323 An analogous and related discussion underlies the more common disputes concerning the permissibility of taxation. It seems natural to many that one's pretax income is a kind of "natural" baseline, a maximum that then gets reduced by a coercive government by means of collecting taxes. Any taxation then readily appears as an "unnatural" and, hence, unjustifiable reduction of this default maximum of one's pre-institutional private property. (See Nagel & Murphy 2002, p. 31–37 and Ripstein 2009, pp. 270–284.)

324 Thanks to Fred Miller for reminding me of the importance of the Lockean distinction between liberty *per se* and *civil* liberty, Pettit's republican reading of Locke notwithstanding.

agency come in degrees, i.e., the absence of modern legal institutions does not result in the *complete* impossibility of action and agency. The non-interference claim is right in attacking radical versions of the self-constitution argument and one would have to say much more about degrees of self-constitution and freedom at this point. This task has to be largely postponed for a later occasion when such things as deformed public identities under radically non-ideal public conditions are discussed. We will come back to one aspect of this issue in the next chapter though, when standards for the evaluation of legal orders are presented.[325]

This qualification notwithstanding, the argument from Anarchia, envisioning a breakdown of individual agency, can be put forward against the non-interference claim. As argued above, the thought experiment retains its force, unless we assume some version of individual determinism concerning social behavior, i.e., the view that individuals necessarily cannot interfere with one another. Another way to clarify this claim is to see how the thesis about the necessity of public norms contrasts with Madison's famous dictum that "if men were angels, no government would be necessary."[326] Madison's view informs a

325 On the relationship between corrupt political systems and individual agential freedom, see Patterson 1982; Sterba 1996; Rundle 2009. A related question that the argument from the external conditions of self-constitution has to confront is the one concerning the social and cultural history of the human species. This seems to be an especially acute issue because the view presented in the text has defended a distinctively modern (Kantian and Weberian) conception of those public norms that are necessary for agency. Simply put, what about humans who lived before the modern state (or comparable institutions) emerged? It seems quite a bullet to bite to say that these humans were not agents at all (in addition to the recurring chicken-egg problem of who "created" the modern state, if there were not any individual agents around to do so). Two ways of responding to this observation are a) by again admitting that one and the same universal conception of agency comes in degrees (in direct proportion to the historical presence of more or less stable and rule-governed social environments) or b) that the distinct historical conceptions of agency differ qualitatively, depending on the quality of the environment. The latter response would suggest that modern agency (under the rule of law, individual rights,...) is a variety of agency *sui generis*, without that necessarily implying that, for example, the Ancient Greeks were not (free) agents (as Hegel claims). These genealogical concerns about the origins of the modern individual are important and difficult. However, they can be put aside here, since the prime task of this essay is an internal, almost phenomenological, account of modern life and agency under its distinct social institutions. In other words, the project is similar to Rawls's concern about political stability in his later work that is *addressed at* citizens of modern constitutional democracies. His aim is not to convince outsiders to join such a regime but rather to ask those who are already insiders, "Do you have reasons to revise those public norms that constitute the institutions to which you are subject to?"
326 Madison 2003 (1788), p. 252.

common assumption about the law, namely that it present the solution to the "problem of bad character."[327] In other words, legal institutions compensate for the distrust and non-cooperative attitudes that make life in the state of nature uncomfortable and inconvenient (very much in the spirit of Locke's account of the state of nature). If men were nicer by nature we could perfectly well do without coercively enforceable public norms. The Kantian line taken here (and summarized in the *Doctrine of Right* quote at the beginning of this part) contrasts with this Madisonian (as well as Hobbesian, Lockean, and Humean) view concerning "the need" for law.[328] Entering and staying in a rightful condition (establishing legal institutions) is a practical necessity (and an obligation), regardless of the contingent psychological dispositions of those who populate the state of nature. Only if Madison's angels were determined (in the hard sense of determinism mentioned above), and hence unable to conceive of themselves as even capable of interfering with others, "no government would be necessary." Consider, in contrast, the starting point of Kant's legal and political philosophy:

> It is not experience from which we learn of human beings' maxim of violence and of their malevolent tendency to attack one another before external legislation endowed with power appears. It is therefore not some fact that makes coercion through public laws necessary. On the contrary, it still lies *a priori* in the rational idea of such a condition (one that is not rightful) that before a public lawful condition is established individual human be-

327 Shapiro 2011, pp. 173–175. (See also Raz 1990, pp. 157–161.)

328 This is not to say that empirically contingent reasons (and those that depend on our specific human weaknesses) for subjecting one's agency to the rule of law are not important and valid. On the contrary, even Kant pays a lot of attention to, for example, the assurance problem. However, even with respect to the assurance problem Kant's justification for its traditional solution (i.e., that legal institutions are needed to ensure widespread enough compliance with public norms) draws our attention to an *a priori* problem in the state of nature: "*I am therefore under no obligation* to leave external objects belonging to others untouched unless everyone else provides me assurance that he will behave in accordance with the same principle with regard to what is mine" (MM 6:256; my emphasis). The problem here is not only that the absence of enforcement mechanisms renders the complying party into an imprudent "sucker," like in traditional prisoner's dilemma approaches to state justification. (See Kavka 1986, pp. 139–140.) Rather, the problem is one of mutually restricting individual freedom and "the assurance argument shows that acquired rights [e.g., property rights] are not enforceable in a state of nature, so that any attempt to enforce them is unilateral force that *others may resist with right*" (Ripstein 2009, p. 160; my emphasis). Again, this line of argument is compatible with additional considerations from prudence, efficiency, and convenience that dominate the strategic approach underlying much of traditional contractarian thought. I thank Jonathan Miller for drawing my attention to the relevance of empirical considerations, especially with respect to Madison's claim about the necessity of law.

> ings, peoples, and states can never be secure against violence from one another, since each has its own right to do *what seems right and good to it* and not to be dependent upon another's opinion about this.[329]

The last part of this quote is especially crucial for our purposes. Kant identifies a conceptual incoherence in the state of nature between asserting one's external freedom (defined as "independence from being constrained by another's choice"[330]) on the one hand and the preference to remain in this lawless condition on the other. Robert Pippin summarizes the *a priori* problem with freedom in the state of nature succinctly. He uses the specific examples of why Kant believes that the institutions of property and contract cannot be coherently established in a lawless condition and in the absence of omnilaterally legitimized public institutions.[331] The problem with unilaterally (privately) delimiting and enforcing certain possessions as "mine" is not primarily that this is an inefficient or impractical ("inconvenient") way of making use of external objects; rather this unilateral acquisition purports to put all others under an obligation to abstain from using/taking the object(s) in question. The unilateral restriction of all others' freedom is incompatible with Kant's account of the right to freedom as independence ("each has its own right to do…"). As Pippin summarizes, the Kantian state of nature cannot generate natural liberties and rights (apart from the innate right to freedom in one's own person) because it is a state of two

> *incompatible commitments* – on the one hand, inescapably, to intelligible possession [property rights to objects that I do not currently physically (empirically) posses/hold; C.H.], and so a solution to the mine/thine indeterminacy, but, on the other hand, to a restriction in the state of nature to unilateralism that cannot establish this intelligible possession. Hence the *exeundum* claim [the "practical necessity" to enter a lawful condition; C.H.].[332]

We need not delve into all the complicated details of Kant's anti-Lockean theory of property rights here.[333] The point of looking at Kant's description of the state

329 MM 6:312.

330 MM 6:237.

331 Pippin 2006. For another recent presentation of Kant's account of property, see Hodgson 2010a.

332 Pippin 2006, p. 445.

333 The brief summary of Kant does not even give a full account of all "Three Defects in the State of Nature," which is impressively done by Ripstein. (See Ripstein 2009, pp. 145–181.) I focus on the problem of unilateral choice and its incompatibility with equal freedom and do not at all discuss the two other shortcomings that undermine, *pace* Locke, the possibility of conclusive property and contractual rights in the state of nature, i.e, the assurance problem

of nature is to present additional support for the claim that there is something inherently incorrect about the non-interference claim and its normative cousins in political philosophy. Most importantly, according to the interpretation employed in Kant's argument, it is not just actual interference (the act of actually dispossessing another in the context of possessions) that is the problem in the state of nature; rather, it is the normative contingency of the condition of not-being-interfered-with (the failure of a purely unilateral and private act of acquisition to put all others under a binding requirement to accept the infringement of their freedom to use particular external objects) that undermines the conceptual coherence of individual external freedom and a high degree of individual agency more generally there. Since a coherent regime of private property and conclusive sovereignty over external objects is, on the other hand, an *a priori* requirement, rooted in our nature as purpose-pursuing and end-setting beings, the state of nature puts us into a normatively contradictory status, completely independently of the character traits and the possibly good will of its inhabitants.[334]

Conceptually, and this is the main claim submitted in response to the non-interference claim, the "fact" that others do not actually interfere with my action-attempts is due to a positive, non-trivial, restraint on their part, which an entity like the Weberian state backs by providing a coercive public institutional apparatus. It is, of course, not the case that this restraint is constantly actively enforced by the legal institutions (a good legal system will not have to resort to force often because its citizens take the law into consideration when practically deliberating).[335] However, the presence of legal certainty and security (that a public authority stands ready to enforce one's status as an end-setting and pursuing agent) is necessary for non-interference to be ruled-out in the sense required for setting ends conclusively. The normative application of the non-interference claim ignores that as beings who conceive of themselves as free individuals, part of this self-conception is that we at least *could* constantly interfere with others' action-attempts, its empirical impracticability notwithstanding. And it is this fact about our self-understanding that suffices to undermine the default view on the abstract conceptual level currently discussed. The Anarchia thought experiment's purpose was to illustrate this empirically unlikely, but still conceivable, scenario in which would-be agents are not restrained

and the problem of interpretation and indeterminacy (of claims to property). For a Lockean defense, see Simmons 1999.

334 See also fn. 368.

335 On the role that law plays in individuals' practical deliberation, see section 8.2.

by publicly established norms from constantly impinging on each others' attempts to act. Psychological and sociological insights concerning interaction notwithstanding,[336] it is the option of externally completely unrestrained interference, open to each one, that undermines the capacity to sustain a high degree of a unified self-conception by means of performing actions in Anarchia.

An empirical consideration needs to be briefly mentioned at this point that has to do with the Kantian claim, defended here and below, that a modern Weberian state and its legal institutions are necessary to *conclusively* (as opposed to provisionally) set ends in the presence of others who could interfere with this activity.[337] It might be objected that no actually existing modern state can provide absolute stability and predictability concerning these external conditions for the unconditional possibility of agency. However well-run and good a job a legal order does in enforcing individual rights and liberties, there always seems to remain a rest of uncertainty und vulnerability to the interference by others. The degree interpretation of the central argument again helps here. However, the degree argument must be adapted a little bit in the face of the very plausible claim that no juridified state can completely escape the Anarchian condition.

The degree of successful self-constitution does, I have submitted, in fact go hand in hand with the degree to which public norms and institutions render the setting and pursuit of ends and projects reliable.[338] Hence, while agency and

336 In the same sense in which these *explanations* of non-interference are highly plausible the normative *justifications* for non-interference are extremely persuasive. As I try to make clear in the text, these explanations/justifications and their merits are not the crucial point when spelling out the shortcomings of the non-interference claim as a default view of the human condition.

337 I am indebted to Fred Miller's research group at BGSU for pressing this issue. Also of relevance in this context is Korsgaard's remark on the problem of our actions becoming/remaining "hostage to the [...] actions of others" that was discussed in the previous part in concluding the argument for the public identity claim. (See section 5.2.) A full reply to this concern has to wait until we discuss the nature of law in Chapter 8.

338 This gradual account of the connection between individual agency and public norms also helps to avoid the recurring chicken-and-egg problem that asks how the public norms that condition individuality can be created by non-agents in the first place. Of course, it would be worthwhile to look at Hegel's philosophy of history at this point, a task that cannot be undertaken here. (See Hegel 2011 (1837).) One might worry, however, that the gradual view leads to unacceptable conclusions concerning state authority, resulting in a totalitarian version of a modern Weberian state. The worry is that the degree argument, and the claim that agency is enhanced in proportion to which the rule of law is realized as a social institution, recommends a kind of utilitarian "maximization" of predictability and stability. Why not establish a police state that assigns a 24/7 "supervisor" to each citizen, thereby making compliance with the law

freedom under law remain two parts of one regulative ideal that can never be *fully* realized, its partial realization always tracks the parallel development of those social, political, and legal institutions that condition it. However, and this is the adaptation that the degree-version has to undergo, the claim that agency develops along a continuous spectrum and in the form of degrees does not rule out that we look at the very same development from a perspective that allows the incorporation of discrete steps, so to speak. It is such a discrete and unique step that the argument presented in this section defends, when it endorses Kant's story about the necessity of leaving the lawless state of nature. The correctness of the degree-version does not conflict with the claim that the status of citizens, understood as rights-holders and duty-bearers under the law, is a distinct normative achievement that emerges with passing a threshold point along the spectrum of degrees of agency. That a one hundred percent stability, predictability, and enforceability of the external conditions of agency is empirically impossible does, therefore, not undermine the force of the claim that entering a rightful condition establishes a qualitatively distinct status, and its corresponding normative self-conception, that cannot be sustained in Anarchia.

Actual vs. possible interference

Still, the unpersuaded defender of the non-interference claim might continue to object, a crucial part of the argument presented in this work rests on the idea that it is not just actual interference but the probable and unpredictable potential interference that has this catastrophic impact on the possibility of self-constituting action. But how can the mere threat of interference have such an impact on the possibility of a robustly unified self-conception of agents? And why do we need legal institutions and the rule of law to overcome this problem? Surely, more has to be said about this feature of the argument.

---

extremely reliable? The quick reply to this worry is that *even if* it were true that such a state would maximize "the goods" of predictability etc., there are clearly other considerations (not the issue of this essay) that militate against the creation of such a super state. Moreover, as will be spelled out in the next chapter, the claims about predictability and stability can be understood relative to a rather "small" Weberian state. In other words, the point of the argument for the public identity claim and the self-constitution argument is not necessarily to recommend a detailed regulation of all possible actions but rather to a) reliably enforce the law there is and b) to make sure that the legal norms in question are of a certain form as opposed to a specific content. (See the discussion of Fuller in section 8.1.)

In order to defend this aspect of the public identity claim we must return to the seven stage argument establishing it, presented in Part 2.[339] There, the conception of a practical identity was reformulated as a genuinely public one (at least insofar as we deal with an individual human being who constitutes herself in the societal condition). We can now apply this abstract story of how individual agency and social institutions are conditioning each other to the specific case of (modern) citizenship. This approach allows us to regard citizenship (in the sense of being subject to coercive public norms[340]) as an instantiation of this conception of public identity. According to the view presented, citizenship simply is an individual's normative self-conception as it is constituted under the law and legal institutions. Since the action-guiding principles constituting this identity necessarily include those enforceable public norms that make any action possible, a practical identity under the law is at the same time always also a public identity. When agents deliberate and choose a course of action they set ends. Conclusively doing so (that is, without them remaining dependent on the other individuals' choices), let alone successfully pursuing them by executing the related acts, requires the public establishment and maintenance of the status of an end-setter.[341]

339 See section 5.2.

340 Given the argument for the public identity claim and its main feature that action-descriptions "under the law" are the object of the choice that citizens deliberate upon in the course of self-constituting action, it will be quite obvious at this point that the resulting account of "citizenship" must be a fairly non-standard one. The issue of visitors, tourists, and even individuals residing outside a jurisdiction's immediate reach (and how all these groups do count to some degree as subjects to a particular legal order's public norms) will be discussed in section 8.2.

341 The term "conclusive" (sometimes "peremptory") is, again, crucial. Adapting and extending the line of argument in Kant's *Doctrine of Right* (there used in the context of distinguishing between provisional and conclusive property rights), it is here submitted that ends can be set only "provisionally" in the absence of the kind of publicly enforceable norms that are emphasized in the text. (See MM 6:257.) A public identity (that consists in those non-private principles that one endorses in the course of action in the presence of others (see section 5.2)) amounts to having the mutually acknowledged status of a person who can set her ends conclusively. For Kant the status of someone who has conclusive property rights consists in having transformed mere provisional possession (i.e., property holdings outside of a legal order) "into rightful possession through being united with the will of all in a public lawgiving [...]" (MM 6:257). The point at which I go beyond Kant, so to speak, is that I draw attention to the implications for an individual's self-understanding when she finds herself in such a provisional condition that leaves here choices and actions more generally (and not just those related to property) subject to the private will of others. I thank Jonathan Miller for suggesting to remind the reader of the specific role that *conclusively* performing actions plays at this crucial point.

Support for this seemingly collectivist view of individuality comes from Hayek. Just consider the following statement (not by Hayek but approvingly quoted by him) that can be readily incorporated into the action-theoretical account (with its emphasis of connecting individual agency and the law) defended here: "The rule whereby the indivisible border line is fixed within which the being and activity of each individual obtain a secure and free sphere is the law."[342] In the societal condition a particular feature of an individual's practical identity is non-contingent. This feature is expressed in the public declaration and maintenance of the "indivisible border" just mentioned. This border, that lays down the omnilaterally authorized and guaranteed limits of non-interference, takes on the form of public principles, i.e., laws and constitutional norms. And these public principles in turn are part of the endorsement-process that takes place when an agent chooses actions in the comprehensive sense described in Chapter 5. A complete description of a proposed action (its *logos* and maxim) includes the legal principles that establish and protect the action's very possibility. It is this necessary feature of an agent's normative self-conception, determining her standing vis-à-vis all others, which is her public identity. The self-conception of a citizen under the rule of law, then, simply is the first-personal manifestation of this general type of public identities. In other words, regardless of what particular practical identity one endorses by means of choosing and performing certain actions, one adopts at the same time a public identity that comprises those principles that we know as the law and that defines "a secure and free sphere" of non-interfered-with action. It is again Hayek who sums up succinctly what external conditions are necessary for the kind of action that constitute a high degree individual liberty (and, *a fortiori*, for the possibility of a high degree of individual self-constitution):

> The significance for the individual of the knowledge that certain rules will be universally applied is that, in consequence, the different objects and forms of action acquire for him new properties. [...] The effects of these man-made laws on his actions are of precisely the same kind as those of the laws of nature: his knowledge of either enables him to foresee what will be the consequences of his actions, and it helps him to make plans with confidence.[343]

Thinking of this account of citizenship as the answer to the question of why agency necessarily involves some form of public identity leads us back to the issue of actual and possible interference with action-attempts. The complete

342 Von Savigny in Hayek 1960, p. 148. Claims like these will also be crucial for the discussion of the total law thesis in the next section.
343 Hayek 1960, p. 153. See also ibid., p. 142.

absence of the law (as envisioned in the Anarchia thought experiment) constitutes a complete lack of a basis for developing and sustaining such a public identity. Another way to clarify this claim, that something essential for successful agency is lacking in the case of Anarchians, is to revisit the example of the "particularistic willer," discussed in section 4.2. Remember, that this case of failed agency exhibited the incapacity to endorse practical principles in an identity-constituting way because the individual in question did not at all conform her action-attempts to the *internal* constitutive principles of practical reason (the two Kantian imperatives). She failed to describe her actions' maxims in a minimally universalistic, principle-based, way.

Korsgaard's particularistic willer failed to *lead* a life and did not maintain a practical identity across time because of her incapacity to commit herself to any practical principles that reliably guide her actions in similar-enough circumstances. A desire pops up and immediately gets, without passing the "filter" of a practical identity and its action-guiding principles, transformed into a pseudo-reason for exactly this *one* particular action without, to put it in Joseph Raz's terms, "creating precedent, (and) setting and consolidating trends," all of which creates the "patterns of our lives (that) help us make sense of our lives and of ourselves."[344] In other words, the particularistic willer completely fails to legislate for herself – she is not a law to herself (again, that is all the version of the categorical imperative I am ready to endorse here requires an agent to do). In Chapter 4 it was argued that a "particularistic willer" in its extreme (!) version is inconceivable as an agent. A heap of unstructured desires and impulses is not an agent.

The kind of "particularity" involved in the argument from particularistic willing can be applied to the analysis of what the law means to those who are subject to it. Insofar as an individual finds herself in the societal condition (i.e., is not the kind of Robinson Crusoe described above) but this condition lacks any principle-based patterns that structure interpersonal interaction, this individual (since she is necessarily in need of public principles that acknowledge her standing vis-à-vis the others) cannot sustain a stable practical identity. This time the reason for this instability is not some internal deficiency on part of the agent, as in the case of radical violations of the categorical and hypothetical imperatives. In Anarchia the reason is that there simply are no public principles

---

344 Raz 1999, p. 242. And he continues, very much in the spirit of the argument presented in the text (but from rather different premises): "One way or another our past actions and decisions form us. They make us into who we are." (Ibid.) For the complex relationship between my (principle-focused) view of practical deliberation and action under the law and Raz's (reason-focused) account, see section 8.2.

that one could endorse in the course of deliberation and action. An agent's public identity, however, is the first-personal viewpoint from which such public principles (that regulate and confine the spheres of non-interfered-with action in Hayek's sense) figure in the agent's practical deliberation.

Eventually we come full circle then. As was argued in support of the argument for the public identity claim, the process of endorsing the practical principles that constitute a public identity simply consists in conclusively performing actions guided and conditioned by them. This process of self-constituting oneself into an agent (with a sophisticated and multi-layered practical identity) then necessarily involves the incorporation into practical reasoning of the law that structures one's standing with respect to all other individuals as the author of one's actions.[345] Since action (as the medium of successful self-constitution) is, however, non-contingently possible only when the law *ensures* non-interference, the necessity of engaging in self-constitution comes with a catalog of formal requirements that the law must meet in order to facilitate such a stable public structure of non-interference.[346]

Consider an example that illustrates these abstract claims about how practical identities in the modern state necessarily involve the law and, hence, are necessarily public identities according to the argument for the public identity claim. Take the practical identity of a mother.[347] It consists of action-guiding principles such as "in case of an emergency take care of my children first, before I rescue others," "in case my child has a severe illness, I make sure it receives sufficient medical attention," "when my child refuses to go to school, I make sure she goes," and so forth. As will become especially clear in the next section, where the total law thesis is introduced, even these seemingly non-public principles depend, for successfully playing their role in self-constitution, on the existence of "free spheres" of action that the modern state establishes and guarantees.[348] Hence, a mother's practical identity always also includes principles such as "I'll make sure that my child gets medical attention *and* all others will

---

345 In what exact sense agents necessarily "incorporate" the law into their practical deliberation and action, and what that implies for their freedom, is discussed in section 8.2.

346 This is the topic of section 8.1.

347 By means of choosing a practical identity that is seemingly far removed from the public sphere, I deliberately make the task of illustrating the argument for the public identity claim hard. If we can show that the practical identity of a mother is also (at least to some extent) incorporating the practical principles that constitute the law, the same will be true at least to the same extent for practical identities like "police officer," "teacher," etc. with respect to which the legal system's role is even more obvious.

348 Hayek's notion of legally "assured free spheres" is discussed in section 7.2.

not interfere with me doing so as a matter of publicly acknowledged right." In discussing the argument for the public identity claim it was emphasized that these higher-order practical principles have to be actualized in concrete actions. A seemingly non-public action like getting one's child to a hospital *does* include in its full description (its maxim and *logos*) the shared and publicly upheld practice of letting mothers do so. All that the critique of the non-interference claim says is that, amongst beings like us, this is a non-trivial achievement. We could interfere with others' actions if we wanted to and that part of our self-understanding is all that is needed to undermine the view that the condition of non-interference somehow establishes itself. And the juridified action-guiding principles incorporated in the law and in constitutional norms establish this non-interference in a unique way; a way that makes sure that these principles figure in all agents' practical deliberation, choice, and action as non-optional constraints.[349] That is why, in the modern state, all practical identities involve the law, some more so some less.

Non-dominated agency

In Anarchia, the relevance of the contrast between actual and potential interference gets diminished from the perspective of the individual that engages in practical reasoning and thereby (futilely) attempts to take into consideration her standing and status with respect to all the others around her. Starting from very different concerns and premises, namely consequentialist ones, Philip Pettit's critique of (negative) freedom as non-interference can be used to further clarify the argument presented in response to the common-sense objector who, in the grips of the non-interference claim, has claimed that contingent non-interference is sufficient for individuals to constitute themselves into well-unified agents. It is not necessary for conclusively performing self-constituting actions, the objector insisted, that this non-interference is established and secured in the form of legal norms.

In his *Republicanism* Pettit attempts to revive the republican conception of freedom as non-domination.[350] He contrasts this conception with (classical)

349 The general framework of planning rationality, inspiring the account defended in the text, is also indebted to Bratman 1987, 2000, 2009, 2011. For a recent attempt to use Bratman's account of rational planning for explaining the phenomenon of law (in a way different from mine though), see Scott Shapiro's "Planning Theory of Law." (See Shapiro 2011, pp. 118–192.)
350 Pettit 1999.

liberalism's core-commitment to freedom understood as non-interference.[351] As discussed above, the latter conception has its prominent origin in Hobbes. Freedom as non-interference did not gain superiority over the republican alternative, however, until Paley and especially Bentham promoted it in their work.[352] The basic conceptual difference between the two contrasting accounts of freedom is best summarized by using some of Pettit's clear examples.[353] According to freedom as non-interference, a slave can be perfectly free. If a slave is lucky and happens to end up with a master who does not actively interfere with the slave's choices and actions then her freedom does not differ from the non-slaves'. It is only actual interference with an agent's choices that the non-interference conception counts as a restriction and limitation of freedom. The flip side of this view is the one expressed in Bentham and Berlin's account of the law presented above: since the law often interferes with individuals' choices and actions it is *necessarily* a restriction of freedom. Such interference is *prima facie* problematic because it takes away a certain amount of the pre-institutional freedom every person naturally possesses; laws might be justified in order to maximize utility, for example, but juridified and democratically legitimized interference is interference nonetheless.

Now the republican conception of freedom contrasts exactly along these two dimensions when Pettit submits that freedom is, on the one hand, incompatible with certain scenarios of non-interference and compatible with certain forms of actual interference on the other.[354] He summarizes: "Domination [...] may occur without actual interference: it requires only the capacity for interference; and interference may occur without any domination: if the interference is not arbitrary then it will not dominate."[355] Pettit, arguing in a strictly consequentialist framework, does not discuss Kant's political philosophy. But the idea of freedom as non-domination can be further supported by considering Kant's insistence that a rightful condition cannot be based on a purely private agree-

351 Pettit is, of course, aware that the conceptual landscape of freedom is much more complex than I present it here for the sake of brevity. Most importantly, there is Berlin's influential distinction between positive and negative liberty. While negative liberty, according to Pettit, is closely aligned with the ideal of freedom as non-interference, it does not follow that his republican alternative, freedom as *non*-domination, is a positive conception of liberty. Republican freedom is itself a negative conception.

352 For a detailed historical account of the origins and context of Hobbes's conception of freedom, see Skinner 2008.

353 Pettit 1999, pp. 31–35.

354 Pettit 1999, pp. 63–66.

355 Pettit 1999, p. 272. For Pettit's clarification of the term "arbitrary," see Pettit 1999, pp. 55–58.

ment of non-interference, but must necessarily exhibit a public form.[356] Consider the above example of the mother's practical identity. The higher-order practical principles that define this particular practical identity take on a different content and form when they are applied to actions that are not merely non-interfered with but are so in a non-dominated action-context. The principle of "I'll make sure that my child gets medical attention *and* all others will not interfere with me doing so as a matter of publicly acknowledged right" can only apply to actions under the law. According to the argument for the public identity claim, only when this principle gets applied to concrete actions that incorporate the action's end in a non-private way, can this principle fulfill its function as a building block of a practical identity that is at the same time also a public one. Purely private arrangements of non-interference (like personal promises) suffice for establishing the *contingent* status of the mother's end – obtaining the medical attention for her child. However, this status is different from the one that the end has under the law that does not leave the mother (and her practical identity) hanging on the private good will of individual promisors and their non-interference.

Even more drastically, the problem with the "free" slave is that her "freedom," while indeed not actually interfered with, is subject to the private – "lawless" – will of her master. As mentioned above, Kant's definition of external freedom conceives of it as a status of "independence from being constrained by another's choice."[357] The slave-master relationship is the paradigmatic example of the negation of freedom so defined. This is not necessarily the case because the slave cannot go about his business uninterruptedly; actually that is quite possible when she is lucky enough to have a benevolent master. The repugnance of slavery that Kant and republicans so clearly saw lies not (only) in the constant and actual interference with the slave's attempts to act as a free agent. It is rather the status of being subject to the exclusively private will and choice of another person that undermines the independence and freedom of the slave and that constitutes the moral outrage of slavery.[358]

---

356 To my knowledge the only attempt to draw attention to the significant parallels between Kant's notion of external freedom and Pettit's consequentialist account of freedom as non-domination is presented in Hodgson 2010. The main claim presented by Hodgson is endorsed in this essay: "The two approaches have in common a crucial element: they both construe freedom as demanding not only the absence of interference with a person's choices but also a form of independence from the choices of others" (Hodgson 2010, p. 792).

357 MM 6:237.

358 The often smiled at views on sexuality and marriage presented by Kant (just think of Brecht's amusing Marxist sonnet "On Kant's Definition of Marriage" (Brecht 1987 (1938), p.

The flip side of the non-domination claim is especially crucial for the purpose of the current chapter, i.e., the defense of the rule of law as a constitutive feature of individual agency and freedom. Not every instance of actual interference is a restriction of freedom. According to Pettit, republican government and the rule of law does interfere with individuals' lives and actions. However, it does so non-arbitrarily. Putting interpersonal relations under enforceable public norms "means reducing other people's capacities for arbitrary interference in their lives, and will reduce their need for strategic deference or anticipation, as it will reduce the level of uncertainty with which they have to live."[359] Kant's non-consequentialist arguments support Pettit's conclusion very well at this point. Freedom as a political ideal is not restricted if interference takes on a certain form and is justified from a specific standpoint, namely the specifically *public* standpoint from which the law's authority and administration are generated. Interference with citizens' choices and actions that originates in the public (or as Kant, inspired by Rouessau, calls it "omnilateral") will and finds its expression in a republican constitution and the rule of law are not necessarily fetters of freedom as Bentham and Berlin claim. Pettit's preferred formulation at this point is that the rule of law and (republican) legal institutions "condition" citizens' freedom.[360]

The claim submitted in the previous paragraph, that interpersonal relations must be put under enforceable public norms, is open to the objection that mere publicity cannot be sufficient for the norms in question to provide the external preconditions needed for self-constitution. What if the public norms are issued by a sadistic dictator who indulges in arbitrarily thwarting her subjects' chances of leading a life according to a coherent plan?[361] This case seems to show that

312), in which Brecht interprets Kant as commodifying the use of sexual organs) are actually less backward and cranky once their underlying political assumptions are identified. As was pointed out recently by feminist Kant scholars, Kant's opposition against extramarital sex and prostitution are motivated by a genuine egalitarian concern for non-dominating relationships between men and women. For Kant on the institution of marriage, see Mendus 1992 and Kneller 2006. (This is, of course, not meant to deny the outrageously sexist comments by Kant in other contexts, well enumerated in Beiner 2010.) For a defense of the necessity of a legalistic understanding of private relationships along Kantian lines, see Waldron 1993, pp. 370–391 and the next section of this book.

359 Pettit 1999, pp. 86–87.

360 "Freedom as non-domination is compromised by domination and domination alone. [M]y freedom is not compromised, therefore, by a limitation in my ability to exercise it [...]; it conditions the freedom that I enjoy" (Pettit 1999, p. 76).

361 I am indebted to Fred Miller for suggesting to address the issue of *arbitrary* public norms directly and early on.

the presence of public norms *simpliciter* is not sufficient to provide the social background needed for successfully engaging in the self-constituting activity in the societal condition. This objection is absolutely on target and must be kept in mind until the next chapter, when the nature of legal norms is investigated within Lon Fuller's jurisprudential framework. This much has to be submitted at this point already though: according to the view of law's nature defended below (a view that presents the law as a particular instantiation of public norms) the dictator, to the extent to which she changes its subjects' legal circumstances willy-nilly, simply fails to create law.[362] Ultimately, this failure is the result of the dictator not addressing her subjects in a coherent way and making it hardly possible for them to complete actions uninterruptedly. The dictator is, in an important sense, putting her subjects into an environment that is the same as the one described in the two thought experiments. Notice, however, that the notion of non-arbitrary laws that underlies the criticism of the dictator is not a substantial moral criterion, distinguishing arbitrary from non-arbitrary public norms (as it is in Pettit (maximizing the common good) and Kant (rendering coherent the exercise of the external freedom of all agents)) but one that constrains what can count as law on the basis of the rational requirements that come with the nature of the law's addressees qua agents. These laws might turn out to be deeply unjust, but still non-arbitrary (in the non-moral sense of arbitrary) by enabling agents to plan and perform actions conclusively.

The introduction of law (understood as an instantiation of public norms) then does not take away from individuals' pre-legal heap of maximum freedom (as defenders of the non-interference claim would have it). Rather, assuming a pre-institutional maximum of individual freedom as a baseline ignores how freedom and successfully-constituted agency depend on guaranteed (not just conditional and private) non-interference. From the first-personal viewpoint, a non-dominated action is not the same as a non-interfered with action. Engaging in the former constitutes an agent with a public identity that is different from the one that is constituted by performing actions that are merely non-interfered with (without that non-interference being guaranteed by the law). The individual performing actions under the rule of law constitutes herself into an agent by means of choosing principles of action, the full account of which incorporates those public norms that structure the non-dominating social environment required for setting ends as a matter of right and not because other private parties

362 In this sense the dictator resembles King Rex in Fuller's thought experiment, discussed in section 8.1. However, King Rex honestly tries to create valid law and fails as opposed to the dictator, who deliberately undermines the possibility of the successful agency of her subjects.

just happen to let one do so. This is, it is submitted here, one way of understanding Hayek's point when he describes actions "acquiring new properties" when performed within a legal context.

All of this is not at all meant to deny that actual interference with an agent's action-attempts presents a significant infringement of her individual agency – also Pettit and Kant certainly agree with this observation.[363] Moreover, what renders private and unregulated interference problematic cannot exclusively be accounted for by the chanciness, randomness, etc. that reigns in Anarchia. After all, what about chancy, random, and unpredictable benefits that befall an agent? Imagine, receiving anonymous bank transfers from time to time and in accordance with a completely erratic pattern (or, rather, no pattern at all). That this instance of an unpredictable chain of events hardly counts as undermining agency shows that interference must be the ultimate concern, even for the alternative view that focuses on the notion of domination. Another way to underline this supposed conceptual priority of interference is to look at cases in which interference occurs on a perfectly predictable basis. What about a slave who is, contrary to the one in Pettit's example, reliably and constantly interfered with in her attempts to perform actions that, if they were successful, would constitute her as a human individual? Surely, these cases show, the worry concludes, that what is wrong with domination is not so much that one is subject to possible and chancy interference, but first and foremost it is actual interference (that is more likely to occur under certain conditions) that threatens the successful execution of self-constituting action.

In response to these observations one should acknowledge both points. Firstly, in many (maybe most) cases actual interference indeed undermines agency and, secondly, there is a certain conceptual priority of interference (over domination) underlying the non-domination paradigm defended in this chapter. However, and this is all we need for vindicating the general argument supported by Pettit and Kant, interference is neither a necessary nor a sufficient condition for constituting an infringement of the external conditions of the possibility of agency. It is not necessary because, as in Pettit's slave example, a person's agency might be held hostage by a lazy dominator who does not actually interfere. There is no actual interference happening there, but we still think that the subjects' agency is severely curtailed. The *status* of an agent is one that the lucky slave cannot coherently ascribe to herself, the absence of interference notwithstanding. On the other hand, interference (even if highly predictable

363 I am indebted to the members of Fred Miller's research group at BGSU for asking me to clarify this point concerning the issue of predictable interference.

and reliable) is not sufficient for counting as undermining agency. Following Pettit's remarks on non-arbitrary interference, interference might be well justified and actually enhance agency (as in the case of the state enforcing property rights against a burglar (whose action-attempts are, after all, interfered with and undermined by the police), for example).

Actual interference then does of course matter a lot for the prospects of successful self-constitution and for the stability of individual agency. But actual interference in and of itself does not provide an exhaustive basis for explaining what is necessary for the high degree of agency we are concerned with here. The status of being an agent is undermined when interference (and non-interference!) takes on a certain form (which it does in a scenario like Anarchia) and it is this dimension of the external conditions of agency that the traditional non-interference paradigm neglects. This qualification remains readily compatible with the claim that actual interference is a severe threat for agency.

Summary and a further note on slavery

After this brief account of the arguments by Pettit and Kant in support of freedom as non-domination, we can now summarize the response to the non-interference claim, according to which the contingent absence of non-interference is, firstly, an unexciting pre-institutional fact and, secondly, sufficient to let individuals in the societal condition constitute themselves into well-unified agents. Neither Kant nor Pettit address directly the impact that merely contingent non-interference has on action-attempts and the development and sustainability of an agent's public identity.[364] The "lawless freedom"[365] that

---

364 Surprisingly, given what is said in the text, it is consequentialist Pettit who has things to say that support identity-based arguments for the rule of law, whereas Kant's Doctrine of Right, exclusively concerned with *external* freedom, does not directly address the issue of what impact external conditions have on agents' practical reasoning and their will. (See fn. 367.)

365 MM 6:307. The notion of "freedom" employed in the specific context of Kant's discussion of the state of nature might be better understood as referring neither to "freedom as non-interference" nor to "freedom as non-domination" as narrowly defined in this section. Rather Kant's notion of "externally lawless freedom" is better captured by the notion of "licentiousness." I believe, though I am not fully arguing for this here, that the attempt to establish the parallel between the particularistic willer (who fails to give internal laws to herself) and Anarchia (in which agents collectively fail to legislate the external normative conditions of the possibility of their own agency) might provide a fruitful starting point for interpreting Kant's opaque notions of "lawless freedom" and "savage violence." Thanks to Fred Miller's research

individuals seem to enjoy in Anarchia (if they are lucky and end up in a condition of contingent non-interference) differs not just "quantitatively" from a "rightful condition." It is not just that they somehow have "less" freedom.[366] The normative self-understanding of individuals who are subject to the stability- and predictability-providing principles of the law differs qualitatively from the Anarchians because only the former can engage in self-determining practical reasoning with the knowledge that their status vis-à-vis all others is based on enforceable public (not private) norms.[367] This common knowledge, figuring in the activity of setting and pursuing *every* end, is the necessary ingredient in the process of self-constitution that is at stake in the argument defended here. It is also essentially related to the attitude of realizability presented in Part 2. This attitude, that comes with setting ends and settling on *determinate* personal plans, is not fully sustainable and justifiable *to* the agent (from her own first personal perspective) when non-interference lacks a non-contingent and rightful institutional backing.[368] The rule of law then is the external guarantee and

---

group at BGSU for urging me to make clear what is meant by "quantitatively" different conceptions of freedom.

366 It is, of course, not clear at all how one would go about quantifying freedom[s] in the first place here. The argument in the text just tries to accommodate views that take for granted notions such as "trade-offs" between liberty (and security), "compromising" freedom, etc. that seem to presuppose ways to come up with a continuous spectrum, along which quantities of freedom can be determined, aggregated, and exchanged.

367 Pettit presents psychological and empirical support for the claim that it is common and internalized knowledge of the fact that public norms rule that has an impact on agential self-understanding. (See Pettit 1999, pp. 58–61 and 70–73.) "This point is of the greatest importance, because it connects non-domination with subjective self-image and intersubjective status. It means that the enjoyment of non-domination in relation to another agent – at least when that agent is a person – goes with being able to look the other in the eye, confident in the shared knowledge that it is not by their leave that you pursue your innocent, non-interfering choices; you pursue those choices, as of publicly recognized right" (Pettit 1999, p. 71).

368 As Arthur Ripstein 2009 (pp. 86–106), Thomas Pogge 1988, and Paul Guyer 2005 have forcefully argued, Kant's defense of private property (and its dependence on public authority) is ultimately based on our nature as end setters and purpose-pursuing agents. Publicly enforceable sovereignty over external objects is a necessary condition for the rational adoption of plans and ends, very much in the spirit of the argument defended in the text. While disagreeing with the details of Guyer's interpretation, Robert Pippin summarizes this line succinctly: "[I]t is essentially the rule of law that allows us to engage at all in an activity that Kant at least once defines as the distinguishing mark of humanity itself: the setting and pursuit of our own ends. The [Guyer-style, C.H.] argument might go: without giving up the right to determine mine-thine in one's own case and without the rule of law, this faculty cannot be effectively exercised and so our basic humanity would go unrealized" (Pippin 2006, pp. 425–426). And later, in presenting his own interpretation, Pippin claims that "it is not *in principle* possible to establish *unilat-*

condition (in Pettit's sense) that potential agents require to conclusively (in Kant's sense) perform self-constituting actions, which sustain a public identity (in my sense of citizenship).

When some historians and sociologists regard slavery as "social death"[369] and as the negation of citizenship, this statement can be even better understood when looked at from the perspective of self-constituting action and agency defended here. It is of course true that third-personal accounts of slavery and its impact on well-being contribute a lot to explaining our moral outrage with respect to it. However, the argument from self-constituting action and public identity suggest that an important source of the unconditional condemnation of slavery lies in the denial of the status of being subject to public norms that put interpersonal relationships on a firm and predictable ground. This denial is not just instrumentally problematic (it surely is) but, and this is the contribution of the current argument, slavery is incompatible with the constitutive requirements of agency.[370] A public identity does not get off the ground (conceptually, not empirically) in a slave-master relationship. The slave's action-attempts, even if contingently "successful" because the master stays her hand, are not resulting in a coherent and stable self-conception as an agent in charge of her life. Since a legal framework is completely lacking *within* the slave-master relationship there simply is no "public" principles and norms the slave could endorse. And since a public identity (which is constituted by the endorsement of exactly such public principles and norms) is indispensible for having an identity at all (unless one is Robinson Crusoe) the condition of being subject to the possible caprice of the mere private wills of others is incompatible with being a well-constituted agent.[371]

erally the intelligible possession that is a necessary condition of the exercise of our rational agency in a finite world populated by other agents" (Pippin 2006, 433).

369 See Patterson 1982.

370 There have been attempts to make sense of the notion of (voluntary) "slave contracts." That a slave *contract* is a conceptually incoherent notion because it would require one party to the contract to completely (self-)annihilate its legal status (and the status of being such a legal subject is necessary in order to *uphold* any legal contract) is spelled-out along Kantian lines by Ripstein 2009 (pp. 133–143).

371 Of course, this is not to be understood as saying that the historical cases of actually existing slaves were not agents at all. The conceptual claims about (free) agency made in this essay always look at extreme and limiting cases that are (thankfully) empirically hardly realizable. Still, the point of the constitutivist explanation of why slavery is such an outrage consists in showing that the historical cases of slavery *partook* in a form of social relationship that, if driven to its extremes, would have annihilated agency completely. Even if this extreme case

It must be emphasized that the argument from public identity does not present an exhaustive account of all the things that are morally wrong with slavery. That a slave is subject to her master's will, and that her self-constituting actions remain thoroughly contingent on another private party's purposes and aims, is compatible with the important historical observation of the codification and institutionalization of slavery (legally granting slave owners absolute control over their slaves' lives and actions). One has to distinguish two levels of unpredictability and contingency here: on the one hand, there is the legal and public fact that establishes the two kinds of legal subjects of slaves and masters. This legal structure was in fact (unfortunately) extremely stable in certain parts of the world and, hence, seems to provide an instance of the kind of (public) predictability we are concerned with. On the other hand, however, such a legal regime is one of subjugation (of agents and their lives and actions) that codifies the slave's being completely subjected to her master's arbitrary and private interests and choices. It is in this sense, it is insisted, that slaves are denied the status of being subject to any public norms. The slaves' relationship to their master is deliberately kept outside of the reach of public legal norms *by the law itself*, so to speak.[372]

Anarchia, an extreme version of a lawless condition, condemned individual would-be agents to a global version of the slave-master relationship – with the only difference that in Anarchia all are both slaves and masters at the same time.[373] The clash of private wills, unregulated by any publicly acknowledged

---

does not apply to any actual case of slavery it still makes the wrongfulness of slavery more intelligible. Thanks to Jonathan Miller for asking me to clarify this point.

372 I am indebted to Albert Dzur for urging me to clarify the general argument with respect to the actual cases of, for example, the slave *laws* of Virginia that very much created an extremely stable and predictable legal framework that was, of course, morally unjustifiable. Also of relevance here is Kristen Rundle's illuminating discussion of what the introduction of the Nuremberg laws meant to the possibility of Jewish agency and life in the Third Reich. In a nutshell, Rundle's point (supported by autobiographical material by victims of the regime) is that the introduction of these laws was experienced as a "relief" on part of many German Jews because they clarified and stabilized (at least for the time being) their public standing and situation and, hence, made a (highly constricted) variety of Jewish agency and identity possible. Again, this does not at all amount to any kind of (all things considered) justification of these extremely unjust and discriminatory laws. Rundle's claim rather is that from the point of view of what is necessary for the possibility of agency, discrimination in legal and juridified form is "preferable" to discrimination that is completely random and arbitrary. (See Rundle 2009, pp. 89–103.)

373 This sweeping analogy between the state of nature and a global slave-master relationships might be considered inept. Again, the reason for this worry is that the historical cases of slavery have exactly been juridified institutions. The slave owner has a legally established right to interfere with her slaves, a right that cannot, by stipulation, be present in Anarchia. In line

norms and laws, does not result in universal unimpaired freedom but in the impairment of existing as one, well-unified, person across time. The publicly enforceable principles, settling what others can and cannot do to action-attempts as a matter of right (not as a matter of mere private fiat), are a necessary component of a well-unified agent's practical identity in the societal condition. That is the reason for why non-domination (not merely the fact of non-interference in its contingent form) is required for a high degree of self-constitution. It is not denied here at all that it is ultimately actual non-interference with one's actions that enables agents to sustain their practical identities. However, there is a substantial difference between this state of non-interference being the result of contingent restraint on the part of individuals on the one hand and that non-interference being established in the form of institutions that make this non-interference a matter of a practice that claims to be shared by all agents, on the other. This difference finds its expression in different degrees of agency – the actions performed under modern legal institutions being the most robust ones. The shortcoming of the non-interference claim is that it presumes that amongst free beings like us (i.e., beings that could, however empirically unlikely that is, constantly interfere with one another and thereby badly damage one another's identities) this condition of non-interference can be had without some shared principled restraint that is part of one's practical identity as an agent. The notion of non-domination provides this additional feature: under shared norms, the guarantee of which is no longer subject to the good-will of private individuals, the non-interference one enjoys when engaging in the self-constituting activity is put on a stable and predictable foundation that pays attention to the fact that non-interference is not the trivial and "natural" starting point in our human relationships but is itself an "artificial" practice and norm, limiting our lawless freedom to impinge on other's spheres of action.

Another passage from Hayek on coercion sums up the importance of discussing the non-interference claim (and supplementing it with the idea of non-domination) as presented in the course of this long section,

> It is because, and insofar as, we can predict events, or at least know probabilities, that we can achieve anything. And though physical circumstances will often be unpredictable,

---

with what has been argued above, the focus of the analogy therefore must lie on the action-theoretical characteristics *internal* to the slave-master relationship (i.e., the lack of any legally established constraints within it). I thank Jonathan Miller for urging me to keep in mind the important truth that "a slave or master under the law is not the same as a slave or master under no law."

> they will not maliciously frustrate our aims. But if the facts which determine our plans are under the sole control of another, our actions will be similarly controlled.[374]

7.2 The Total Law Thesis

By now the reader is hopefully sufficiently convinced by the argument just presented and agrees that contingent non-interference is not enough to put the necessary external conditions for individual self-constitution on a firm basis. Non-domination, established and secured by the rule of law, is the correct view of how interpersonal relations have to be structured, namely by public norms and principles which become part of an individual's public practical identity. Non-interference, in the complete absence of stable and predictable public laws, fails to provide this component of agents' practical deliberation in which they engage in the process of self-constituting action. "Freedom under the law"[375] is the state that successfully constituted agents with a public identity are in. Only these agents conceive of themselves as capable of conclusively setting ends in a world that they (necessarily and unavoidably) share with others who are, in principle, free to constantly interfere with their action-attempts. There is no default baseline of non-interference. There is a social dimension to the "human plight" of beings like us, whose dealings with the world are no longer determined by unalterable instincts. "Free" (in this sense of non-instinctually determined) humans are the kind of beings whose relations vis-à-vis one another are in need to be put on the firm foundation described by Kant and Pettit as the non-dominating relationship between independent citizens.

Even if this view about self-constituting action and its necessary public conditions is accepted, however, the common-sense objector might attack this argument from yet another angle. Especially modern liberal polities draw an important distinction between two spheres of interpersonal interaction. There certainly is the public sphere, the realm of political and legal institutions, where laws (and legal rights) are the essential elements of defining and structuring interpersonal relations among citizens. With respect to this sphere it has to be admitted, the objector continues, that a public identity can and must be sustained by means of self-constituting action. The public norms, that make possible to conclusively engage in action, figure in the practical deliberation of agents. When agents negotiate and honor contracts, for example, then the legal

---

374 Hayek 1960, p. 134.
375 Hayek 1960, p. 148.

principles and norms that are constitutive of this institution become elements in the contract parties' normative self-understanding. Moreover, individuals who *want* to play a more active role in the public sphere are certainly in need of endorsing the normative self-conception of being a subject to the rule of law and the reason-providing norms, standards, and principles it expresses and incorporates.[376] Citizen-agents' practical reasoning is necessarily informed by the law that puts their status as end-setters on a firm foundation and makes the self-constitutive actions possible in the "public arena" that would be chaotic in the complete absence of legal institutions.

However, there clearly is what we call the "private sphere" in modern societies as well, the objector argues. Independently of how narrowly one defines that sphere it certainly includes the realm of the family, but might be extended to all kinds of associations and activities that lie outside the narrow confines of government and its institutions. Some people consider the economic sphere of society as genuinely private in the sense of being independent from public affairs "regulated" by state-enforced norms (cf. "voluntary exchanges" in the "private sector").[377] Communitarian criticisms of liberalism similarly argue that an overly juridified conception of individual agency not only presents an *unnecessary* intrusion of public norms into intimate relationships; worse: that, for example, rights are structuring the institution of marriage undermines the affec-

376 Section 8.2, will discuss in more detail the minimal sense of "being subject to the law" that is definitive of an agent's public identity. Being subject to the law is primarily conceived of as incorporating public norms into one's practical deliberation. That this "incorporation" is fairly minimal will become obvious once we discuss the case of the sophisticated criminal and badly informed citizen, both examples leading to a rather unorthodox view of how to define (free) citizens.

377 Murray Rothbard's view develops this paradigm of privacy and privatization to its extreme normative conclusion: "The ultimate libertarian program may be summed up in one phrase: the *abolition* of the public sector, the conversion of all operations and services performed by the government into activities performed voluntarily by the private enterprise economy. [...] Abolition of the public sector means, of course, that *all* pieces of land, all land areas, including streets and roads, would be owned privately, by individuals, corporations, cooperatives, or any other voluntary groupings of individuals and capital. [...] What we need to do is to reorient our thinking to consider a world in which all land areas are privately owned" (Rothbard 1973, pp. 201–202). Jeremy Waldron's illuminating discussion of the status of homeless people identifies Rothbard's vision of a completely privatized world as incompatible with the concept of freedom. (See Waldron 1993, pp. 309–338.) A Kantian argument for the conceptual necessity of public spaces, very similar to Waldron's, is presented by Ripstein 2009 (pp. 232–266).

tive substance of the kind of loving and caring relationships that are supposed to lie at the heart of a good marriage.[378]

Moreover, empirically examining how real-world humans develop, the objector submits, my argument seems to get things exactly the wrong way around. Our lives, understood as the process of constituting ourselves into the particular persons we are, begin in the distinctively non-public sphere of the family. Only after an individual has constituted herself sufficiently does she enter the public sphere and develops the public identity of being a subject to the law. Therefore, the objector concludes, becoming and remaining an agent does not necessarily depend on the presence of public norms and principles, let alone them figuring in an agent's action-directed practical planning and reasoning. In addition, there is a priority of the private self, very much in the Lockean spirit discussed above. The rule of law appears artificial in the sense of "non-natural," especially when compared to the seemingly naturally grown "institution" of the family. The former must be created by already free agents, while the latter is the place where agents are *made* and become free.

The response to this common-sense view, let us call it the "primacy of the private" view, consists in what I am going to call the "total law thesis." The total law thesis submits that a correct analysis of the necessary conditions of the possibility of agency reveals a conceptual priority of the publicly acknowledged law over the private sphere. It states: *In the modern state* every *action falls under a description that includes those public principles and norms (i.e., the law) that make its non-dominated performance possible.* The view defended in response to the common-sense intuition is importantly not that there is no such thing as a private sphere – a view like that would render the total law thesis into the "totalitarian law thesis" indeed.[379] The total law thesis merely observes that, in the

---

378 For a summary of and reply to this particular criticism of liberalism, see Waldron 1993 (pp. 370–391). The reply presented in the text has a lot in common with Waldron's defense of rights and the former is therefore similarly critical of Marxian utopianism that expects the historically contingent institution of (bourgeois) rights to "wither away" once a classless society renders the need for enforceable public norms unnecessary. In other words, this essay can be read as a critique of Marx's historical relativism concerning the necessity of the state when my argument submits that individual agency and its constitution require enforceable public norms for its coherent possibility. Again, this is not a psychological claim but a conceptual one concerning external conditions of action in the societal condition (whether communist or not, does not matter for this conceptual necessity).

379 It should be mentioned (though this will only become fully clear towards the end of Chapter 8) that the juridification of human relationships is not a good to be "maximized" in the sense that we should always welcome more rather than less instantiations of it. There can, of course, be too much law and creating more and more legal norms is not an end in itself – rather

modern state, the institutions of the private sphere are both circumscribed and infused by the public norms and institutions of the law. Accepting the common-sense view is tempting because self-constitution seems to *begin* with the endorsement of what appears to be purely non-public practical norms, structuring and defining interpersonal relationships (e.g., the father's force-backed command, obligating his child to bring out the trash). How does the rule of law (and its institutional manifestation, the modern state) enter this relationship as a constitutive condition?[380]

The private family

In order to establish the total law thesis, let us revisit a footnote by Max Weber that was already briefly discussed in section 2.1. In the course of presenting his influential definition of the state (claiming "a monopoly over the legitimate physical coercion") Weber talks about the family. He says that "[t]oday, furthermore, 'legitimate' violence exists only to the extent that the state's laws

---

the end is a minimal degree of individual human agency and self-constituting action. Hence, the view defended in the text is compatible with those trends in recent legal scholarship, above all the critical legal studies movement, that complain that we have too much (criminal) law and demand the abolition of many (most) of the norms constituting it. It is true that the criminal law "creates" legal subjects in a stable and predictable manner but often does so in ways otherwise unjustifiable. The stability and order we gain by employing criminal law often rests on (morally) unacceptable categorizations of individuals and their behavior. However, this observation is compatible with both, the claim defended in the text that the general ideas of law and a legal system are inherently connected to individual human agency and, secondly, that removing spheres of behavior from direct juridical regulation (by decriminalizing it) does not relocate them "outside" the law. The latter issue is the subject of the current section. I thank Albert Dzur for directing my attention to the critical legal studies literature, which presents many more reminders concerning the non benign nature that the law too often exhibits and that is, for the most part, put aside in this exploration. For the account of criminal law, hinted at above, see Mathiesen 1974.

380 The discussion of the public and the private spheres will play a role also in the final replies to Kukathas in section 9.2. *The Liberal Archipelago* presents a definition of "community" (and "political community") that rests on the public vs. private distinction: "A community is *a collectivity of individuals who share an understanding of what is public and what is private within that collectivity*" (Kukathas 2003, p. 169). Importantly, Kukathas's definition seems to lend support to the claim defended in this section that the determination and acknowledgment of the borderline between the public and the private spheres is itself a shared public practice (and in the modern state that shared practice is taking on a juridified form) that does not rely on a pre-institutional and natural baseline of privacy.

permit or prescribe it – for example, the ‘right to discipline children’ is permitted to the father of the family.”[381] Hence, even if families are considered free to structure their internal dealings as they please, this is a legally sanctioned privilege and is not to be confused with a “natural” default setting. Analogous to the case of individuals in the societal condition, the fact that family members can structure their relations as they see fit is an achievement, conditional on the enforceable restraint of all others mediated by publicly enforceable norms.

The total law thesis’ insistence that privacy is a non-trivial social achievement becomes clearer when we think about how our common-sense objector conceives of rights *to* privacy and how the argument suggested here presents an alternative conception of this right.[382] In the same way in which individuals qua citizens need the law for setting ends in a norm-governed way that is not subject to the private wills of others, individuals qua family members need family-internal practical norms, which in turn, however, receive their *ultimate* authority from the public law. The question of the conceptual priority of the public standpoint is related to the discussion in the previous section. There the Lockean view concerning how individuals leave the state of nature by “giving up” some of their natural freedom was discussed. In a similar tone, a Lockean-style right to privacy will be regarded as a protection of a pre-institutional and pre-contractual maximum of privacy that then gets reduced when the law starts intervening with intra-familial affairs.

The total law thesis rests on a very different conception of the non-public realm. First of all, the thesis views privacy not as something to be protected *from* legal interference but as a legally constructed concept that is maintained and protected *by* the threat of sanctions directed at potential interferers. These sanctions are signposts and demarcation lines directed at all the other addressees within a particular legal system. The legal norms that, for example, protect the Smiths’ practice of saying grace at the dinner table imposes legal obligations on the Jones’s living next door. While it has been a traditional (and well-justified) liberal concern to worry about the state’s coercive institutions threatening the Smith’s practice, the view defended here reminds us to look at the situation from the alternative viewpoint concerning the relationship between the legal subjects and what their being subject to privacy-protecting laws means to them.

381 Weber 1978 (1921), p. 56.

382 For the philosophical equivalents of the common sense objector’s conception of the origins and status of rights to privacy (and “family autonomy”), see Glenn 2003, pp. 15–60. A recent attempt to combine moral and legal issues concerning privacy is presented in Moore 2011. The reference point for moral-philosophical discussions of privacy rights remains Thomson 1975.

From the latter viewpoint it becomes better visible that the necessity of law originates in defining and delimiting the private sphere of, for example, the family. That the Smith's are free to do what they do vis-à-vis the Jones's, and that this freedom is publicly acknowledged, is a feature of all legal subjects' self-understanding as agents under the law.

This is, again, not to say that there are not excellent moral and political arguments for legally constructing the private sphere in a particular (extensive) way; and, following that construction, there are excellent reasons for worrying that the state itself interferes into the private realm it so construes, thereby undermining the predictability and stability required for individual agency – classical liberals are certainly right about this. However, and that is the crucial point, the precise limits and boundaries of the private sphere remain the result of publicly authorized norms that constitute this realm in a particular way rather than another. Moreover, following from this two-sided claim about the law's circumscribing and infusing powers, the self-constituting actions that take place *within* the private sphere incorporate these public norms when they are described comprehensively in Aristotle's and Kant's sense defended in the argument for the public identity claim. Hence, even if Dad does not explicitly invoke them when he commands Billy to take out the trash, Dad *can* threaten Billy with (certain) sanctions in case the latter refuses to perform the action in question. Under the rule of law, Dad's authority is a post-institutional privilege. This privilege is not just legally "granted" by the Weberian state but is due to the legally enforceable restraint on part of all the other legal subjects that the rule of law guarantees.[383]

383 A strong empirical and historical case against the total law thesis is presented in Ellickson's *Order without Law*. (See Ellickson 1991.) In response to Ellickson's central claim, that small-scale communities regulate their affairs without anything resembling legal institutions as defined in the text, reviewer John Brigham refers to the case of the family in a way supporting the total law thesis: "We recognize that in property law and family law there are social relationships. [...] In a family, law is easier to see after divorce. In either case it is naïve not to see the law's role, but when we fail in this regard we are simply not getting the whole story. In a divorce, all the law that romance hides becomes more evident. There is a lot of romance in Ellickson's story, and the resulting view of law in cattle-country [Shasta County, CA; C.H.] is insufficient" (Brigham 1993, pp. 616–617).

An analogy: Scanlon on friendship

Even if the common-sense objector grants that there is this kind of conceptual priority of the publicly acknowledged legal framework over the private sphere concerning the separation and delimitation of the two spheres, she might continue to worry about the radical claim defended here for another reason. After all, the total law thesis is not merely saying that the line circumscribing the private realm is part of a legal structure, but that the law "permeates" the private sphere. Translated into our action- and identity-language, the total law thesis says that an individual's practical reasoning and deliberation (her setting of ends in the process of self-constituting action) can *never* be completely detached and performed independently from the legal norms and principles that put her interpersonal standing on a stable and predictable foundation. However, the common-sense objector continues her concern, does not it seem quite a stretch to imagine the actions within one's family to necessarily have anything to do with the rule of law? It seems far more plausible to say that even if actions' maxims are described comprehensively, these objects of self-constituting choice do not necessarily always involve the practical principles incorporated into a legal system. According to the account of agency presented here such a concession, in turn, would imply that a public identity is not a necessary feature of individual self-constitution in the societal condition. Even if the line separating the public from the private sphere is itself part of the legal system (and hence is in an important sense public), it must be the case that those dealings on the private end must be *purely* private.[384]

The total law thesis denies that this purity of privacy is possible in the societal condition. In order to show that the total law thesis is plausible, another analogy based on an argument in Scanlon's account of morality will be helpful. It is important to emphasize at the outset that the use of Scanlon's argument does not depend on the correctness of his ethical theory. Rather, the analogy

384 There is a certain ambiguity involved in the total law thesis and its central claim that the public has priority over the private in the modern state. "Public" can refer to two things: in a narrow sense it refers to "public legal norms" and it is this sense that is central to the claim in the text that the private sphere is itself a legally circumscribed and defined realm. On the other hand, however, the public sphere is on a par with the private sphere and both are autonomous arenas of self-constituting action. My claim is that these two notions of "public" are compatible. The discussion of Kukathas's definition of community in section 9.2 further elaborates this claim that the borderline between the public and the private sphere is itself negotiated and drawn in forums that are public without that reducing the private to "a mere epiphenomenon when it comes to agency" (Personal correspondence with Fred Miller).

isolates a particular argumentative move that Scanlon makes when he discusses the relationship between the core of his contractarian morality on the one hand and values that are seemingly detached from this morality on the other.[385] In chapter five of *What We Owe to Each Other*, Scanlon replies to the worry that his contractarian account of morality fails to leave enough room for interpersonal relationships such as friendship. This issue is part of the broader concern that Scanlon refers to as "the problem of priority." He says, "[t]his is the question of how the morality of right and wrong is related to our other values and how it could make sense to give it priority over them."[386] Friendship seems to be constituted by norms and principles of a distinctively non-contractarian kind. We see this when loyalty to friends and family (apparently) conflict with the demands of impersonal morality.[387] In addition, friendship (and comparable relationships like parental ones) involve sentiments and attitudes that cannot be exhaustively accounted for in the framework of Scanlon's "morality of right and wrong." In a nutshell, the objection to contractarian morality is that it fails to make room for a number of central phenomena that every reasonable conception of moral life should be able to account for.

Scanlon's reply is that also the personal and intimate relationship of friendship *incorporates* the principles and demands of contractarian morality. According to Scanlon, the moral norms and principles that consist, for example, in the requirement not to harm others, to keep promises, etc. constitute a common basis of all human relationships – public as well as private, to put it in the categories used in this section. It is not the case that the normative force of the requirement not to harm one's friend has a different source than the requirement not to harm a stranger. The same contractarian justification applies in both cases: "Friendship, [...], involves recognizing the friend as a separate person with moral standing – as someone to whom justification is owed in his or her own right, not merely in virtue of being a friend."[388] Friendship does, of course, involve more than that. However, and Scanlon's contractarian account is perfectly compatible with this, these non-contractarian additions are put on top of (and must not conflict with) the contractarian foundations that ought to structure all interpersonal relationships. The flip side of Scanlon's reply is, and this

385 Scanlon 2000, pp. 160–166.

386 Scanlon 2000, p. 160.

387 As Scanlon himself clarifies at the outset of dealing with the priority problem, his argument can be read as a reply to Williams' critique of utilitarian and Kantian conceptions of morality and their incapability to make sense of the particular reasons that love and friendship provide. (See Scanlon 2000, p. 160.)

388 Scanlon 2000, p. 164.

is the point crucial for using his move for our purposes, that, firstly, true friendship cannot occur where the contractarian morality is absent.[389] Secondly, there is a constitutive priority of impartial morality over the particularistic and affective additions definitive of a particular instance of friendship. Genuine friendship (and the practical identity that comes with being a friend) necessarily involves the norms of the morality of right and wrong and if they are absent then alternative sources cannot compensate for this specific lack. Sure, a true friend does not *only* treat you in a way required by morality; however, a true friend's actions do always *also* incorporate the principles required by the norms of impersonal morality. What appears to be a relationship that can rely on affection and sentiment alone does have to "involve recognizing the moral claims of friends *qua* persons, [...]. Compatibility with the demands of interpersonal morality is built into the value of friendship itself."[390]

Analogously, the form (not the value-theoretical substance) of Scanlon's argumentative strategy can be deployed in response to the common sense objection, according to which action in the private sphere can be conducted in complete isolation from the publicly enacted and shared legal norms surrounding it. Dad's command to take out the trash directed at Billy is not a purely private one. It does, of course, involve a richer interpersonal set of norms and principles than Dad's relationship with a random stranger walking by the house. (That Dad cannot command a stranger to take out the trash shows this.) Still, not only does a third-personal description of what is going on in this case remain incomplete when the pervasion of Dad and Billy's relationship by legal norms is neglected. Moreover, and this is the crucial point concerning public identity, from the perspective of the deliberating agent, the law (that declares a parent's use of "violence"[391] legitimate) informs and constrains her practical deliberation,

389 Scanlon's kidney example illustrates the point in the text well. "There would, for example, be something unnerving about a 'friend' who would steal a kidney for you if you needed one. This is not just because you would feel guilty toward the person whose kidney was stolen, but because of what it implies about the 'friend's' view of your right to your own body parts: he wouldn't steal them, but that is only because he happens to like you" (Scanlon 2000, pp. 164–165).

390 Scanlon 2000, p. 165.

391 The term violence is put in scare quotes here because of our heightened intolerance with respect to inner familiar physical and other violence against children. Weber's notion of violence must be read more broadly as the privilege to extract compliance with one's commands by threatening to impose corporal sanctions of some kind. That certain forms of physical violence have now not only been identified as morally repugnant but are outlawed further illustrates how the legal delimitation of "private" institutions has the priority that is argued for in the text.

choice, and action. As in Scanlon's discussion of friendship this will not always be the case in a full-blown conscious way. Dad will not always explicitly appeal to the authority of the rule of law. The transfer of law's authority to his action of coercing Billy will not always take center stage in his justifications for why he commands his son the things he does.[392]

The seemingly private practical identity of a father and its constitutive normative principles are necessarily (also) public ones. The publicly established legal norms and principles, structuring and stabilizing interpersonal affairs on the most general level, permeate what the common-sense objector identified as purely private normative self-conceptions. In modern societies with their characteristic legal institutions, therefore, the self-constituting activity in the private sphere not only takes place within the framework of legal norms but is informed by them via the agents' choice of actions. A complete and exhaustive description of Dad's actions and practical plans includes the law.

Hayek on "free spheres"

Let us conclude our discussion of the non-interference claim and the total law thesis by looking at how these two claims are related with one another. It is again Hayek who provides a rich starting point for supporting the claim that the non-domination and the independence that we enjoy in the private sphere are not to be taken for granted. In discussing the importance of an "assured free sphere" for the non-contingent standing as an agent among others, Hayek stresses the point concerning non-domination, made along Kant and Pettit's line above: "The assurance that he can count on certain facts not being deliberately shaped by another can be given to him only by some authority that has the necessary power. It is here that coercion of one individual by another can be prevented only by the threat of coercion."[393] The importance of the idea of a

392 However, once we are old enough to make sense of such arguments, our parents do appeal to the legal responsibilities they have with respect to their minors' actions. Their claims are public ones and further reveal that the family cannot be conceived of as a purely private institution.

393 Hayek 1960, p. 139. This passage is very close to Kant's account of the circumstances, under which a public authority is entitled to use coercion: "[I]f a certain use of freedom is itself a hindrance to freedom in accordance with universal laws (e.g., wrong), coercion that is opposed to this (as a *hindering of a hindrance to freedom*) is consistent with freedom in accordance with universal laws, that is, it is right" (MM 6:231).

private sphere lies in the role it plays in making action possible by allowing individuals to set and pursue ends without the arbitrary interference of others.

The interesting turn that Hayek attaches to this standard liberal claim is that he seems to believe in a view very similar to what has been called "the priority of the public law" in this section. Firstly, Hayek reminds us that the protection we enjoy in our private sphere makes us overlook the non-trivial conditions required to establish such a free sphere. Later in *The Constitution of Liberty* he says that "[o]ur familiarity with the institutions of law prevents us from seeing how subtle and complex a device the delimitation of individual spheres by abstract rules is."[394] This misguided (common sense) impression of taking the existence of private spheres as a default condition (stressed above) is noticeable when, for example, the term "coercion" oftentimes gets defined in terms of interference with a seemingly pre-institutional private sphere. Correcting this view, Hayek says: "The existence of such an assured free sphere seems to us so much a normal condition of life that we are tempted to define 'coercion' by the use of such terms as 'the interference with legitimate expectations,' or 'infringement of rights,' or 'arbitrary interference.'"[395] According to Hayek, these faulty definitions of coercion presuppose the existence of the very institutional structures that were introduced to solve the problem of coercion in the first place.[396] The mistake involved in these definitions is that the appeal to "legitimate expectations" and "rights" in order to define coercion gets it the wrong way round, so to speak. "[I]n defining coercion we cannot take for granted the arrangements intended to prevent it."[397] Rather than simply presupposing the demarcation line of the free private sphere and define coercion as actions that transgress it, Hayek claims, the invoked notions (i.e., legitimate expectations etc.) "are the result of the recognition of such a private sphere. [...] Only in a society that has already attempted to prevent coercion by some demarcation of a protected sphere can a concept like 'arbitrary interference' have a definite meaning."[398]

In the same way in which the total law thesis and the critique of the non-interference claim have identified the law as a necessary component of a non-

394 Hayek 1960, p. 148.
395 Hayek 1960, p. 139.
396 Hayek's argument is very Rawlsian at this point. Especially Rawls's critique of invoking notions of pre-institutional desert in order to determine legitimate expectations to be generated by a society's basic institutional structure comes to mind here. (See Rawls 1999 (1971), pp. 272–276.)
397 Hayek 1960, p. 139.
398 Hayek 1960, p. 139.

dominating societal environment, Hayek's argument concerning the conditions for establishing "free spheres" concludes with the necessity of general enforceable rules. The key idea in the above quote is the bit emphasizing the "recognition of a private sphere."[399] The borders of the private sphere, but also the rights and legitimate expectations structuring it internally, are always subject to a restraint on part of all the others who populate the societal condition with oneself. Free private spheres are a non-trivial normative achievement. And in order for this achievement to be "assured" in the sense of a non-dominated interpersonal relationship, the law must make sure that the limits of this sphere are not dependent on the will and choices of the other private parties. Rather, "[t]he solution that men have found for this problem rests on the recognition of general rules governing the conditions under which objects or circumstances become part of the protected sphere of a person or persons."[400] This recognition of public principles that Hayek alludes to is the crucial element of an agent's public identity. Practical deliberation and action incorporate these norms and when an agent acts on these principles, even seemingly private actions constitute her identity into a necessarily public one. Free citizens are those that are successful as agents, and the latter task requires the recognition of enforceable norms that make the setting and pursuit of ends, in a publicly acknowledged free sphere, possible.

Summary

We have worked our way from the very general idea of social practices and institutions back to the issue of seemingly private associations and the Weberian state. This direction towards political-philosophical issues indicates that we are now almost at the end of this project and can eventually show why Kukathas's utopia is a conceptually unstable version of a liberal society. Before doing so, however, revisiting a paradigmatic account of the nature of law will help to further support the claim that the unifying train of thought underlying the total law thesis and the attack on the non-interference claim is correctly identified as the response to a set of problems that Scott Shapiro, inspired by Hume and

---

399 Again, Kukathas's definition of community, discussed in section 9.2, pays similar attention to the fact that the borderline between the public and the private rests on a shared recognition of that very boundary: "A political community continues to exist for as long as its members generally recognize the conventions that define it – conventions which identify the commonly accepted understanding of the public concerns of the polity" (Kukathas 2003, p. 172).
400 Hayek 1960, p. 140.

Rawls, labels the "circumstances of legality."[401] The law provides a basic building block of the solution to the unavoidable problem of action that was initially presented as "the human plight." This genuinely human challenge defines us, the beings who must confront the task of self-constitution by means of performing actions that are chosen in the course of practical reasoning. A public practical identity, the normative principles that guide the actions of planning creatures like us, is both a condition and a result of this process of maintaining our agency in the societal condition. The way in which the total law thesis and the idea of non-domination have established the link between the law and individual agency does not remain without consequences for what legal norms can and cannot be. The next chapter shows that our nature as planning and acting agents suggests a certain set of "inner" features and standards of the law, which *all* legal norms have to live up to in order to play the role in the process of identity-constituting action defended here.

401 Shapiro 2011, pp. 170–173. "The circumstances of legality obtain whenever a community has numerous and serious moral problems whose solutions are complex, contentious, or arbitrary. In such instances, the benefits of planning will be great, but so will the costs and risks associated with nonlegal forms of ordering behavior, such as improvisation, spontaneous ordering, private agreements, communal consensus, or personalized hierarchies" (Shapiro 2011, p. 170).

Chapter 8: The Nature of Law Revisited

This chapter further clarifies the account of law as an external condition of self-constituting action and the role that an agent's public identity plays in this process. The account is clarified by looking at an influential account of the nature of law, namely Lon Fuller's. The purpose of this critical exposition is to show that the argument presented in the previous chapters can both enlighten Fuller's theory of law's nature as well as itself be further clarified and strengthened by studying Fuller. Fuller's "internal morality of law" can be interpreted as being ultimately concerned with the conditions that are necessary for action and with the manifestation of these conditions in the form of the law. However, instead of viewing Fuller's eight principles as defining law's "inner morality," they will be presented as rational standards that legal norms must conform to in order to play their role as external conditions of self-constituting action. The concern, therefore, is to defend certain formal requirements that a system of public norms must satisfy in order to count as law as opposed to arbitrary and chaotic pronouncements. While these standards do not get us all the way to "just" and "morally right" law, they still conceptually delimit what can count as law. These formal limits have something to do with the norms in question being capable of figuring in citizens' practical deliberation and action.

Adopting Fuller's account in a way that makes law fit a citizen-centered perspective (as opposed to legal positivism's focus on how officials recognize the law as valid) will lead to the discussion of another objection to the view presented here, namely that it results in an overly demanding account of citizenship. Section 8.2 deals with the following questions: Does the idea of the necessity of a public identity, conditional on the incorporation of legal norms and principles into one's practical reasoning, require ordinary legal subjects to become legal experts on a par with the officials administering the legal system they are subject to? And what about, for example, criminals who pay a lot of attention to those norms that structure their public relationships (and define their legal standing) but use this knowledge to pursue illegal ends? The slogan "*Know* your rights!" is just one popular way of expressing the claim concluding this chapter that is presented in the course of answering these questions. Agency and freedom *are* demanding regulative ideals. Self-constituting action sustains a free agent more successfully when the public laws that apply to her inform to a larger degree the process of practical deliberation resulting in those very actions.

8.1 The Internal Rationality of Law

Lon Fuller's attack on legal positivism in *The Morality of Law* attempts to show that the idea of law comes with certain normative commitments.[402] If norms fail with respect to a specific set of eight formal requirements (discussed below) then they do not count as law. Since Fuller regards legality as consisting in the adherence to these formal requirements that, at the same time, enables the achievement of certain *moral* ends he concludes that all law (deserving that label) necessarily overlaps with the realm of morality.[403] Fuller thereby attacks the positivists' "separability thesis"[404] concerning law and morality. The separability thesis' most famous formulation is as simple as it has been influential. H.L.A. Hart insists that "[I]t is in no sense a necessary truth that laws reproduce or satisfy certain demands of morality, though in fact they have often done so."[405]

Law's rationality vs. law's morality

As important as the issue of law's relationship to morality is, it will not be the crucial one for the purpose of this chapter, *viz.*, illustrating the role that law plays in the process of individual self-constitution. Getting clear on why Fuller labels his eight standards of law "moral" is necessary, however, because of the following considerations. In discussing Fuller, a strategy similar to the one adopted in Part 2 is deployed where Korsgaard's version of the categorical and hypothetical imperatives were discussed. In the same way in which the above exposition parted company with Korsgaard when she claims that the normativity of these two constitutive principles of practical reason necessarily get us into moral territory, it is now claimed that, while Fuller's account presents a strong

---

402 Fuller 1969.

403 See Fuller 1958, pp. 644–648. Scott Shapiro summarizes Fuller's rationale for labeling the internal standards of legality as "moral" in the following way: "It is a *morality* on his view because its observance necessarily generates certain moral goods: any system that obeys the Rule of Law will provide its citizenry with a fair opportunity to obey the law" (Shapiro 2011, p. 394).

404 See Raz 1979, pp. 37–38, Coleman 1998, p. 5, Waldron 1999, p. 169. For a skeptical view concerning the widespread strategy to distinguish legal positivists from natural law theorists by means of their stance towards the separation of law and morality, see Coleman 2002, pp. 336.

405 Hart 1994 (1961), pp. 185–186.

argument for the necessarily normative character of law, this does not establish a direct[406] and necessary link between law and morality.[407] It is for this reason that the section heading changes the label attached to Fuller's account, replacing the internal morality of law with "law's internal rationality."[408]

We will discuss the implications of this shift from morality and justice on the one hand towards law's rationality on the other for reassessing Kukathas's *Liberal Archipelago* in the next chapter. It should be noted at this point that this shift seems to constitute a significant concession to Kukathas. After all, by admitting that even fairly unjust laws can sufficiently well provide the necessary external conditions for self-constituting action, the Fullerian story is less demanding than, for example, Rawls's account of an overlapping consensus concerning issues of basic *justice*.[409] However, this concession to Kukathas does not invalidate the critique of his visions of liberal society and state. The problem with Kukathas's monolithic and uncompromising conceptions of freedom of conscience and exit rights renders unstable a legal order *simpliciter*, not just

406 By saying that there is no direct relationship between law's internal formal conditions and substantial morality the option is left open, not pursued in this essay, that there might be an indirect relationship. What I have in mind is that *moral* agency (a substantial view of what a morally good/right agent looks like) has as one necessary condition of its possibility the successful constitution of agency *simpliciter*. The argument in the text is concerned with the latter and might therefore be indirectly necessary for giving a full account of the former. However, the point remains valid that (contrary to Korsgaard and Fuller) morally bad acts and unjust acts of legislation are compatible with the account of self-constitution presented. However, the same is not true of rationality, in the sense of the necessary conditions of the possibility of self-guided action. The rationality-requirements incorporated into Fuller's eight principles are related to the concept of law in the same way in which the two Kantian imperatives' (categorical and instrumental) rationality is necessary for the internal prerequisites of self-constitution.
407 Recently, there have been several attempts to show that Fuller's account is committed to substantial ideas of justice. Colleen Murphy 2005 and Jennifer Nadler 2007 argue that implicit in Fuller's internal morality of law is a commitment to substantial conceptions of democracy, transparency, and self-determination. The relationship of these interesting essays to the argument in the text is similar to the one adopted with respect to Korsgaard's substantial moral argument: It is not denied that more robust conceptions of moral rightness and public justice can be put on top of the inner rationality of law. However, the argument pursed here remains agnostic with respect to these more ambitious substantial moral conclusions and arguments.
408 See Bratman 2011, p. 74, where Bratman introduces this label in a discussion of Scott Shapiro's planning theory of law and its relationship with Bratman's account of practical rationality. Bratman acknowledges Fuller as his inspiration for this label.
409 See Rawls 1993, Lecture IV.

those that are erected on the foundation of a substantial moral conception of justice that claims to be shared by all. More on this below.[410]

To some extent then the reading of Fuller presented here agrees with his positivist critics and the separability thesis. Labeling his eight formal principles of legality "moral" has been one of the main sources of dispute between Fuller's defenders and their critics.[411] In what follows these issues are sidestepped as much as possible by the relabeling just suggested. Let us try to remain agnostic concerning the question of whether or not Fuller's eight principles are inherently related to let alone guarantee justice and legitimacy. Nothing that is said in this chapter shows that a conceptual analysis of law, that situates it within the framework of self-constituting action, necessarily gets us into genuine moral territory. However, as the label "internal rationality of law" tries to convey, the question of what law is can only be answered when certain formal standards are paid attention to – that these standards are not necessarily moral ones does not diminish their status as normative constraints on what law-makers and law-administrators (can) do.

Law's addressees: officials vs. citizens

Before we have a look at Fuller's eight principles, yet another preliminary remark is necessary. This remark concerns the addressees of the law and the way they figure in jurisprudential accounts. Whether or not a legal system exists has been considered (especially by legal positivists) to depend on legal officials recognizing the law's authority – a perspective uncongenial to the argument from citizenship qua public identity pursued in this essay. Fuller's account, while being itself in need of modifications concerning the issue of the law's addressees (discussed promptly), at least takes steps into the right direction.[412]

---

410 I am indebted to Fred Miller for pointing out that my attempt to render the idea of law less morally demanding, has important repercussions for my disagreements with Kukathas.

411 The classic replies to Fuller concerning the question of whether or not his eight principles identify law's internal *morality* are Dworkin 1965; Raz 1979, pp. 223–226; Hart 1983; Kramer 2003; Simmonds 2007.

412 On the problematic aspects surrounding this choice of the law-givers' perspective (as opposed to the perspective of those who are subject to the laws, i.e., the citizens), see Allan 2001, p. 55. The claim that even Fuller was "pushed" into adopting this perspective is extensively discussed by Nadler: "[A]dopting the perspective of the law-giver was a rhetorical strategy of Fuller's, for it was an attempt to refute the positivist theory on its own terms" (Nadler 2007, pp. 23–30).

Very much in the language adopted in the arguments presented here, the law, according to Fuller, fulfills a fundamental function in structuring human relationships in general: "law is the enterprise of subjecting human conduct to the governance of rules."[413]

The focus on legal officials for determining whether or not a system of public rules counts as a legal system, leads to an incomplete and underdeveloped account of what law is. To see that Hart's view ("a great proportion of ordinary citizens – perhaps a majority – (will) have no general conception of the legal structure or of its criteria of validity"[414]) causes a problem for accounts of law's nature, we need to turn to some recent critiques of legal positivism.[415] In his response to an essay by Kenneth Einar Himma[416] (basically saying that legal positivism culpably ignores the question of how the law relates to ordinary citizens as a normative feature of their environment), Jules Coleman provides a succinct justification for why legal positivists restrict their focus to legal officials' relationship to the law. Coleman admits that Himma's observation is correct but at the same time unproblematic from the perspective of jurisprudence (as opposed to political philosophy, for example). Coleman says that "[r]ightly or wrongly, fairly or not, I have narrowed my focus accordingly. Indeed all positivists do. The focus is on official behavior both as a condition of the possibility of law and as to the normativity of law."[417] Coleman then distinguishes two questions that can be asked with respect to the law: "part of the standard framework of positivism is the importance of distinguishing between the validity of a norm as law and its legitimacy [...]."[418] Now Coleman's major claim is that jurisprudence is concerned with the first question only while delegating the second one (law's legitimacy) to political philosophy. In conjunction with the claim that the first issue ("the validity of a norm as law") *can* be answered by ignoring the role of citizens entirely, Coleman concludes that jurisprudence should not be blamed for ignoring how the law can figure in individual citizens' practical deliberation, let alone for not explaining how the law obligates them in a normatively rich sense (in the sense of citizens taking on the internal point of view with respect to these legal norms, to put it in Hart's terms).

---

413 Fuller 1969, p. 46.

414 Hart 1994 (1961), p. 114.

415 In addition to the essay by Himma, see Delacroix 2006, pp. 174–183; and Bertea 2009, pp. 94–96

416 Himma 2002.

417 Coleman 2002, p. 342.

418 Coleman 2002, p. 342.

However, Coleman's defense of jurisprudence's focus on official behavior does not undermine the project pursued in this chapter. In order to understand the phenomenon of law we must, *pace* Coleman, take into consideration the role that citizens are supposed to play in a legal system. There are two reasons for remaining dissatisfied with Coleman's defense of legal positivism's narrow focus on officials. Firstly, making sense of the law as a necessary external condition of self-constituting action does not necessarily have to concern itself with how the law obligates citizens and, related to this, with just law's legitimacy (remember the remarks concerning the separability thesis above). Hence, even the project of conceptualizing the law, pursued in this chapter, does not deal with the substantial moral issues that Coleman thinks are the exclusive domain of political philosophers as opposed to legal philosophers. In other words, and in line with his categorization of philosophical disciplines, the following exegesis and reinterpretation of Fuller in terms of law's internal rationality remains within the narrow confines of jurisprudence. However, secondly, the major response to Coleman is the following: even if we ignore the substantial issues of law's moral quality (the issues Coleman happily pushes aside and leaves to political philosophers), and indeed exclusively focus on *his* question of what constitutes "the validity of a norm as law," we still cannot answer it by ignoring the role that law is supposed to play in individual citizens' practical reasoning and action. The fact that citizens are the ultimate addressees of a legal system and that it is the citizens who have to take up the law in their practical deliberation and planning activities, must be taken into account when Coleman's normative ("validity"!) question is answered.[419]

Fuller's theory of legality is more open to looking at the legal-subjects' role as law's addressees. Moreover, Fuller understood that an account of legal validity must ultimately rest on a certain "view of man implicit in the internal morali-

419 It is, of course, true that many legal norms are not addressed at citizens. There are laws explicitly concerned with officials' action (e.g., the laws determining the authority of judges, the legal norms and statutes regulating the legislative details of law-making). Two quick replies to this correct observation: 1. The law, in its general form discussed in the text, does not consist only of laws concerned with how officials relate to the law and to one another. A legal system that were only concerned with addressing the officials who make and administer its norms would not be a legal system playing the role in our lives described in the text. 2. Even if the focus on legal officials were accepted, the relationship between those officials would itself remain a prime example of a "shared activity of social planning" (Shapiro 2011, 195) and, hence, subject to the analysis defended in the text, i.e., the view that the crucial feature of the law is the principles and reasons that it provides in the course of practical deliberation and action (in this case the deliberation and action of officials).

ty of law."[420] It has been stressed recently that Fuller's jurisprudence is more sympathetic to taking the citizens' perspective into account at especially two points:[421] firstly, when he distinguishes law from "managerial direction"[422] and, secondly, when he insists that legal relationships are characterized by a certain ideal of "reciprocity"[423] (as opposed to mere efficacy) between legal officials and the law's subjects. Fuller's discussion of these two related points is getting very close to the main line of argument pursued in this book when he summarizes the reciprocal legal relationship between citizens on the one hand and law-makers and law-administrators on the other in the following way:

> [L]aw is not, like management, a matter of directing other persons how to accomplish tasks set by a superior, but is basically a matter of providing the citizenry with a sound and stable framework *for their interactions with one another*, the role of government being that of standing as a guardian of the integrity of this system.[424]

Another way to clarify the notion of law's addressees is to compare the relationship between legal institutions and their subjects on the one hand to that between a superior commander and her subjects in, for example, a prisoner of war camp on the other.[425] The system of rules that applies to the prison inmates differs from a legal system exactly because it rests on a different conception of who it is that the instructions are directed to. The eight internal principles of legality, that will be spelled out promptly, assume a conception of man that "involves of necessity a commitment to the view that man is, or can become, a responsible agent, capable of understanding and following rules, and answerable for his

420 Fuller 1969, p. 162. The importance of an account of agency for law's form is stressed in Kristen Rundle's work on Fuller. (See Rundle 2009 and 2012.)

421 See Murphy 2005, p. 241; Nadler 2007, pp. 18–20; Fox-Decent 2008, pp. 553–554; Rundle 2009a, pp. 78–81.

422 Fuller 1969, 207–213.

423 Fuller 1969, p. 61. "[T]here is a kind of reciprocity between government and the citizen with respect to the observance of rules. Government says to the citizen in effect, 'These are the rules we expect you to follow. If you follow them, you have our assurance that they are the rules that will be applied to your conduct'" (Fuller 1969, pp. 39–40).

424 Fuller 1969, p. 210 (my emphasis). And a bit earlier in *The Morality of Law* Fuller gets even closer to the focus of my argument on citizens' interpersonal relationships: "The rules of a legal system, […], normally serve the primary purpose of setting the citizen's relations with other citizens and only in a collateral manner his relations with the seat of authority from which the rules proceed. (Though we sometimes think of the criminal law as defining the citizen's duties toward his government, its primary function is to provide a sound and stable framework for the interactions of citizens with one another.)" (Fuller 1969, pp. 207–208).

425 I am indebted to Fred Miller for providing this example and for urging me to further clarify the notion of law's addressees.

defaults."[426] Now a system of prison rules and commands certainly resembles a legal system. It too assumes the human capacity to at least understand and act upon instructions and commands. However, as Fuller himself notes in accordance with his view that the existence of a legal order is a matter degree,[427] there is a direct relationship between the degree to which a system of instructions respects the conception of man just described on the one hand and the extent to which this system counts as a legal system on the other. And in the limiting case (e.g., an especially barbarous version of the POW camp) the respective conception of the addressees deteriorates so much that "even the verb 'to judge' becomes itself incongruous in this context; we no longer judge a man, we act upon him."[428]

It is in the context of passages like this one that Fuller attempts to move away from the narrow focus on legal officials' deliberation and reasoning, dictated by legal positivism, and moves towards the question of how successful legal institutions have an influence on the subjects' lives and actions. That Fuller pays attention to citizens' normative self-conception is also clear in his discussion of legal obligation. Fuller rejects the view that legal obligation can be conceived in Hobbesian and Austinian terms, i.e., as a one-way and bottom-down relationship without imposing any standards on the institutions and individuals creating and administering the law. In *The Morality of Law* Fuller sums up his main answer to the question of why (and to what extent) legal subjects have an obligation to obey the law in basically contractarian language: "[T]his notion of a contract between state and citizen is capable of indefinite extension. [...], the state's position of superior power rests ultimately on a tacit reciprocity. This reciprocity, once made explicit, can be extended to all eight of the principles of legality."[429]

A "reductionist" strategy

With this brief acknowledgement of Fuller's appreciation of the legal subject in mind we are in a position to adopt his jurisprudence within the framework of

426 Fuller 1969, p. 162.
427 Fuller 1969, pp. 122–123.
428 Fuller 1969, p. 123. See also my remarks on war and slavery in section 7.1. The same point applies to the POW camp and the idea of institutional deprivations of freedom more generally: one (certainly not the only) of their rationales is that these systems of norms target the development/maintenance of efficient and well-constituted individual agency.
429 Fuller 1969, p. 61.

self-constituting action and public identity. In order to show that the argument from necessary external conditions for the possibility of individual agency constrains what can and cannot count as law, a "reductionist strategy" is defended. Contrary to what Fuller's aforementioned claims concerning reciprocity might suggest on a superficial reading, it is not primarily the relationship between legal officials and legal subjects that accounts for why the eight principles of law's internal rationality are constitutive of the law-making and administering activity. Rather, it is the interpersonal relations between the legal subjects that ultimately account for the internal normative standards that law must adhere to. In other words, the reasons for why legal officials are constrained by the eight Fullerian principles in question (and not by others) can be *reduced* to the need of the subjects qua agents to have their standing vis-à-vis others established and maintained in a stable and reliable manner. Directing attention to the idea that the concept of law comes with certain formal (though normative) requirements *because* the law is a necessary external condition of a high degree of self-constituting action, allows us to establish an explanatory priority for the citizens' over the legal officials' processes of practical deliberation and reasoning.

Fuller was on the right track (especially in comparison to the positivists' account of the nature of law) when he envisioned the frustrated response on the part of Rex's subjects (discussed promptly) when their King clumsily engages in the process of law making. Transferred to the Anarchia-scenario, employed in Part 2, an extreme case of Rex would not so much be guilty of a *moral* failure when he corrupts and undermines the efficacy and predictability of his legal-officials' actions (this is, of course, a big problem too); much worse, Anarchian Rex would fail to provide the external conditions necessary for individuals to rationally structure their end-setting under his laws. Erratic decisions of legal institutions are bad for agency but at least equally detrimental is the (related) possible and actual interference on part of the subjects with respect to one another that results when legal institutions completely fail to produce and administer law.

The inner rationality of law can therefore be ultimately anchored in the requirements related to the legal subjects' process of self-constitution and their performance of actions. This remains true, the reductionist strategy insists, even if the eight principles are primarily addressed to those who make and administer the law. As Nadler points out, Fuller's standards put constraints on what rules can be proper objects of recognition by legal officials.

> Whereas Hart [...] treated the rule of recognition as being entirely open to any content whatsoever, Fuller shows that this cannot be true. The rule of recognition cannot be, for

> example, 'whatever the Queen says is law.' For if the Queen fails to pay proper attention to law's internal morality, what she decrees will not be law.[430]

Now my addition to this line of argument is that the Queen's failure to make law rests in her insufficiently addressing her subjects' need to confront the inescapable human challenge, described as the "human plight" above. As will be shown by examining Fuller's principles in more detail, legal norms have to live up to these principles not in order to achieve genuinely moral ends (at least not directly); rather, conformity with these eight principles discharges law's function of providing the kind of interpersonal relationships that make self-constituting action possible. This is the reason for why an exclusive focus on legal officials' relationship to the law is deficient. What law is, is necessarily partly determined by the fact that the law has to rationally figure in citizens' practical deliberation. And, according to the interpretation defended here, Fuller's achievement has been to have identified the minimal formal standards that law must satisfy to do so.[431]

Rex and the eight principles

That Fuller assumes a conception of law's addressees that is much closer to the one defended here than positivism's, becomes visible in *The Morality of Law's* famous argumentative device, the case of lawmaker Rex.[432] Hapless Rex illustrates the eight ways in which an entity in charge of legislating and administering public norms, intended to guide their subjects' behavior, can fail to do so.[433] The allegory of Rex establishes formal and procedural principles that lawmakers have to conform to if their enactments are to deserve the label "law." These principles are normative because they prescribe to lawmakers what they have to do in order to enact valid law. These prescriptions are, however, entirely formal

---

430 Nadler 2007, pp. 19–20.

431 Despite his commitment to legal positivism, Scott Shapiro's "planning theory of law" rests on views very similar to the Fullerian conception defended here. Just consider the following passage by Shapiro: "There is no mystery about why plans are needed to regulate individual actions in communal settings. When people occupy the same space and share a common pool of resources, certain courses of action will result in clashes between individual pursuits, while others will avoid them. Planning is often necessary to ensure that those who live together do not undermine each other's ends" (Shapiro 2011, p. 152).

432 Fuller 1969, pp. 33–38.

433 It is an important assumption of the Rex thought experiment, that Rex sincerely *tries* to make law.

because they merely consist of those normative principles that are "internal" to achieving the end of lawmaking, i.e., giving citizens a reasonable chance to comply with the law's demands. The internal "morality" of law is, consequently, opposed to external moral conceptions that identify the law's purpose in achieving substantial conceptions of social and political justice. Fuller agrees with the positivist that there cannot be a necessary connection between the activity of lawmaking on the one hand and the norms and principles of controversial external moralities defining legislative purposes on the other. However, such a necessary connection does exist between law and its internal (constitutive) norms.

What does this internal rationality of law(-making) consist in? What norms and principles does Rex fail to adhere to when he futilely embarks on declaring rules that structure his subjects' external conditions of action? There are, according to Fuller, "eight distinct routes to disaster,"

> The first and most obvious lies in a failure to achieve rules at all, so that every issue must be decided on an ad hoc basis [i.e., a failure to satisfy the generality requirement; C.H.]. The other routes are: (2) a failure to publicize or at least to make available to the affected party, the rules he is expected to observe; (3) the abuse of retroactive legislation, which not only cannot itself guide action, but undercuts the integrity of rules prospective in effect, since it puts them under the threat of retrospective change; (4) a failure to make rules understandable; (5) the enactment of contradictory rules or (6) rules that require conduct beyond the powers of the affected party; (7) introducing such frequent changes in the rules that the subject cannot orient his action by them; and, finally, (8) a failure of congruence between the rules as announced and their actual administration.[434]

Fuller's conclusion concerning Rex is strong. In order to fail to constitute a proper legal system, the norms declared by Rex only need to fail with respect to any single one of the eight internal principles of law: "A total failure in any one of these eight directions does not simply result in a bad system of law; it results in something that is not properly called a legal system at all, [...]."[435]

Let us begin with the generality requirement.[436] The generality of rules allows their application to a set of cases that overlap to a sufficient extent concerning some relevant properties. Rex's first and most fundamental failure upon assuming the role of law giver consists in two successive steps. Firstly, Rex ("trained as a lonely prince") is imagined as simply being incapable of declaring propositions of a general form: "Though not lacking in confidence when it came

434 Fuller 1969, p. 39.
435 Fuller 1969, p. 39.
436 Fuller 1969, pp. 46–49.

to deciding specific controversies, the effort to give articulate reasons for any conclusion strained his capacities to the breaking point."[437] After having realized that his utterances utterly fail to constitute law, Rex decides to reduce his role to that of an arbitrating judge. The result is devastating (for both him and his subjects): "After he had handed down literally hundreds of decisions neither he nor his subjects could detect in those decisions any pattern whatsoever. [...] Such tentatives toward generalization [...], *gave false leads to his subjects* and threw his own meager powers of judgment off balance in the decision of later cases."[438]

The emphasis in the quoted passage suggests that the generality requirement *is* one that can get assimilated into the self-constitution framework. The law, as the feature of the societal condition that makes the conclusive setting of ends and their pursuit possible, fails to guide action if it "gives false leads to its subjects." A lawgiver who is incapable of even formulating rules with a general scope reminds one of the conditions depicted in the Anarchia thought experiment. Extreme particularism and unpredictability with respect to official judgments (the lack of a "pattern") go hand in hand. The outcome of Rex's incapacity to issue any rules whatsoever, ultimately consists in a failure to provide the "legal signposts" that can guide his subjects' actions. Rex, to put it in Bratman and Shapiro's planning-language, "was unsuccessful in his legal endeavors because *he was not a social planner at all.* He simply lacked the dispositions that human beings, as planning agents, normally possess."[439] Hence, even honoring the generality requirement can be shown to be a necessary condition of lawmaking because "rules" that result in a constant need to decide cases on an *ad hoc* basis corrupt the external conditions of the kind of environment that is necessary for action. There simply are no persisting public propositions that figure in the individuals' practical reasoning and, therefore, no public identity that establishes and maintains her standing vis-à-vis all others in terms of legal norms.

However, there is a different reading of the generality requirement, the violation of which is less radical than the one Rex is guilty of. It is this alternative reading (that Fuller sometimes seems to prefer in his exposition)[440] that might

437 Fuller 1969, p. 34.

438 Fuller 1969, p. 34 (my emphasis).

439 Shapiro 2011, p. 395.

440 Fuller's discussion of the generality requirement is not fully consistent. In his "Reply to Critics," published in the second edition of *The Morality of Law*, Fuller revisits the principle of generality and seems to reject the permissibility of highly individualized "special legislation" – even if only the internal rationality of law is considered: "Applying rules faithfully implies, in

make one doubt whether all of Fuller's eight principles can be explained in terms of self-constituting action. It is a common view in jurisprudence that one of law's defining features is that it does not single out specific individuals as addressees, i.e., it does not use proper names in its formulations.[441] There is a specific idea of equity and fairness that many believe comes with the formal requirement that rules have to be formulated in general terms in order to be law. At one point, Fuller himself categorizes this reading of the generality requirement as belonging to the external morality of law, i.e., the (more) controversial norms of substantial justice that are used to flesh out the abstract and internal requirements presented as his eight principles. Whereas the internal generality requirement, discussed in the previous two paragraphs, states that laws are necessarily rules of some kind ("however fair or unfair they may be") Fuller identifies the external reading of the generality requirement

> to mean that the law must act impersonally, that its rules must apply to general classes and should contain no proper names. Constitutional provisions invalidating 'private laws' and 'special legislation' express this principle. But the principle protected by these provisions is a principle of fairness, which, in terms of the analysis presented here, belongs to the external morality of the law.[442]

In line with what has been argued in the previous chapters, the discussion of the two readings of the generality requirement suggests that the argument from the necessary conditions for self-constituting action is limited in ways similar to the way Fuller's distinction between external and internal legal moralities is. In the same way in which Fuller's internal version of the generality requirement is

---

turn, that rules will take the form of general declarations; it would make little sense, for example, if the government were today to enact a special law whereby Jones should be put in jail and then tomorrow were 'faithfully' to follow this 'rule' by actually putting him in jail" (Fuller 1969, p. 210). It is not entirely clear to me what Fuller means by "make little sense" here. If he means that such laws would be gravely unjust, impractical etc. then, of course, I agree. However, if Fuller now argues that such a law is incompatible with the first principle of the *internal* rationality of law I disagree. A law singling out Jones, as long as it conforms to the other seven principles and does not undermine the necessary conditions of Jones's ability to plan and perform actions on the grounds of those expectations created by legal institutions, is not ruled out by the argument defended in the text.

441 As Colleen Murphy rightly points out this reading of the "generality requirement is consistent with general injunctions on behavior being issued to specific individuals or groups. […], laws need not apply to the entire population" (Murphy 2005, p. 240). On the generality of laws (in the second sense discussed in the text), see Hayek 1960, pp. 151–153; Hart 1994, pp. 20–25; Raz 1979, pp. 215–216.

442 Fuller 1969, p. 47.

compatible with great inequity (because laws can be particularized but at the same time predictable and stable rules), the task of individual self-constitution is *not* undermined in case Rex successfully creates a highly individualized legal system. That a satisfying completion of such a questionable feat is unrealistic does not undermine the conceptual point. A legal system that issues individualized laws to each citizen is most likely intrusive, discriminatory, highly paternalistic etc. but it does not necessarily conflict with individuals maintaining a sustainable public identity and a stable public standing vis-à-vis all other individuals.[443] The scenario of highly diverse laws applied to *different* individuals at the *same time* (Smith's speed limit is 38 mph, Jones's is 35, Brown's is 50, etc.) cannot be ruled out as conflicting with law's inner rationality (and with what is necessary for self-constituting action).[444] However, highly particularistic and diverse laws, unpredictably applied to *one and the same* individual (Smith's speed limit is 38 mph now, ten minutes later it gets changed to 20 mph, another 7 minutes later it is 40 mph, etc.) does exactly amount to a Rex-like violation of the first principle of Fuller's internal standards of legality. Such a violation of the generality requirement threatens to undermine the self-constituting activity of the law's addressees because setting and pursuing ends is rendered impossible in the circumstances created by such "laws."

Law-makers therefore count as adhering to law's internal principle of generality even if they subject every individual to *her* personalized legal code. Of course, with respect to the main concern argued here (i.e., that citizens get clear about their standing vis-à-vis *all* others) such a highly individualized system of laws must conform to the other seven principles that Fuller presents (another reason for declaring such a system utterly unrealistic). Smith not only needs to know the legal standards and principles defining her public identity but needs to know those (possibly very different ones) that apply to every single other individual who possibly interferes with her actions. Reliable guidance of

---

443 See, however, fn. 445.

444 Needless to say that such laws *can* be ruled out on different grounds, namely those that Fuller calls the "external morality of law." Similarly, the argumentative framework in the text does not purport to settle all (not even all the important) questions concerning how agents' interpersonal relationships should be structured by the law. This is also the reason for why neither Fuller's nor my story about the nature of law can ground anything close to an all-things-considered obligation to obey the law. Our accounts simply leave too many questions concerning "good"/"just" and "bad"/"unjust" laws unanswered. Still, the argument from self-constituting action can be developed into a free standing argument in support of a *prima facie* obligation to obey the law, anchored in a transcendental argument from what is a necessary condition for such action.

Smith's actions requires that this interpersonal dimension of her legal standing is known to her when she practically reasons about what and what not to do. If every individual is subject to a highly "customized" set of legal norms this might well become practically impossible.[445]

When wrapping up the discussion of the principle of generality we see that even this element of Fuller's internal morality of law can, to a limited degree, be supported by an argument from self-constitution and public identity.[446] Let us conclude the discussion of Fuller by discussing the other principles of the internal rationality of law. The remaining seven principles differ in how well they fit arguments from self-constitution and public identity but since all of them receive their ultimate justification from the fact that they render the law into a reliable action-guiding device the following illustration can be completed quickly.

---

445 Fred Miller is therefore absolutely right when he suggests that my concession (that the internal rationality of law cannot rule out highly particularistic traffic rules) might have been premature. After all, the point of public regulation is to *facilitate* some minimum level of cooperation and coordination and that goal seems to necessitate rules' generality. Take for example the right of way at an intersection and the overly complex set of rules, considering every possible encounters at intersections, that would have to be created in the highly individualized legal regime that Rex creates in the text. Each individual would have to get assigned her unique rank in a complete hierarchy of rights of way and would have to keep in mind, when approaching an intersection, what her ranking-position is relative to the others who approach the intersection at the same time – a highly bizarre and impractical arrangement given the limited cognitive resources and information at our (and Rex's) disposal.

446 Commentators have expressed puzzlement concerning this choice and the ranking motivating it (i.e., the ranking of Fuller's eight principles in accordance with their amenability to my framework). Is not Fuller's third principle – the prohibition of retroactive laws (Fuller 1969, pp. 51–62) – actually the one least susceptible to get incorporated into an argument concerning what is necessary to perform (self-constituting) *future* action? After all, these commentators submit, retroactive laws do not interfere with the planning activity and practical reasoning of acting agents. That's why they are called *retro*active laws. I disagree with the claim that such laws do not have an impact on the process of self-constitution. As always, this point becomes readily visible when the legal and institutional practice of retroactive laws is not used sporadically but is imagined as a universally, though unreliably, executed policy, thereby becoming part of the shaky expectations of the subjects and their normative self-conceptions. The Chaotica and Anarchia thought experiments were supposed to show that what Dworkin calls the "integrity" of a legal system (sufficiently undermined when retroactive laws are enacted willy-nilly) is a necessary condition for the constitution of a public identity and its normative principles guiding interpersonal relationships. I also believe that an argument like this one underlies Kant's defense of the private law institutions of contract and private property. I cannot expand upon this interpretation here. Dworkin's account of legal integrity is discussed in section 9.2.

In order to figure in the agents' practical reasoning and inform their setting of ends, enforceable external normative structures have to be knowable by the subjects (the publicity-requirement).[447] Obviously, secret laws cannot inform the subjects' normative self-conception vis-à-vis their fellow citizens. Such legal norms cannot figure in the formulation of supposed actions' *logoi* and maxims and, hence, cannot guide their choice of self-constituting actions. Retroactive law, according to Fuller, "not only cannot itself guide action, but undercuts the integrity of rules prospective in effect, since it puts them under the threat of retrospective change."[448] Retroactive laws can be justified on other grounds, as the well-discussed case of the Nuremberg Trials illustrates. We cannot go into the extremely intricate jurisprudential details surrounding these debates. It must suffice to submit that the argument from self-constitution can be used to establish the *prima facie* impermissibility of retroactive legislation under ideal conditions (in stable constitutional democracies, for example).[449] Things are even more straightforward with respect to the principles of understandability[450] (a particular law, A, has to be formulated in a way that suits the reasoning-capacities of its addressees), the principle of consistency in legislation[451] (law A must not outlaw φ when, at the same time, law B requires φ), and the principle of laws not requiring the impossible[452] (law A must not outlaw φ when addressees cannot not- φ). The last principle that Fuller presents is not so much internal to the process of legislation but concerns the "congruence between official action and declared rule."[453] Also with respect to this formal requirement it is clear that its continuous violation undermines the interpersonal conditions, necessary for the indispensible task of figuring out what ends can be set and what actions embarked on by individual agents.

The principle that best illustrates how the law constitutes such an interpersonal condition of agency, however, is the principle of temporal constancy.[454] This requirement best sums up the way in which the Anarchia thought experiment has been driven by similar basic assumptions as Fuller's argument for the

447 See Fuller 1969, pp. 49–51. Whether or not citizens have to actually know all the intricate details of public law in order to have an authentic public identity (and be free) will be discussed in the next section.

448 Fuller 1969, p. 39. See Fuller 1969, pp. 51–62.

449 On a recent explication of the ideal/non-ideal distinction, see Simmons 2010.

450 See Fuller 1969, pp. 63–65.

451 See Fuller 1969, pp. 65–70.

452 See Fuller 1969, pp. 70–79.

453 See Fuller 1969, pp. 81–91.

454 See Fuller 1969, pp. 79–81.

internal requirements of law-making. Confronted with Rex's decision to render his laws as flexible as possible, by subjecting them "to a daily stream of amendments," his subjects protest: "A law that changes every day is worse than no law at all."[455] Hence, despite the fact that Anarchia on the one hand and an overregulating Rex on the other lie at the two exact opposite extremes of the spectrum of legal intervention, the consequences for agents' prospects of successful self-constitution are the same in the two cases. Whereas Anarchia fails to put one's relationship concerning those around oneself on any foundation, Rex's regime renders this relationship utterly unstable and unpredictable by constantly changing its terms. It was argued in the previous part that the incorporation of the principles that legally establish and maintain one's standing amongst all others into one's action-guiding practical reasoning is a necessary condition for agency. To the extent to which erratic changes of the former principles take place in Rex's empire then the results are undermining his subjects' attempts to perform actions and, therefore, their attempts to constitute themselves into unified agents existing across time.

Summary

It is again important to stress the extreme character of both the Anarchia thought experiments and Fuller's Rex. Even frequent changes, democratically legitimized and embedded in a well-ordered constitutional order, do of course not undermine agency; on the contrary (though this is a set of complex issues that cannot be pursued here) legislation can and often must rectify past and current injustice by disrupting the constancy of the law. The worry that the thought experiments (and the extreme violations of law's constitutive norms taking place there) inevitably lead us to embrace an overly conservative account of a social and legal order are unwarranted. In his summary of Fuller, Shapiro puts it well: "While it is impossible, indeed undesirable, that each principle [of Fuller's eight; C.H.] be fully satisfied by any legal system (imagine the deficiency of a legal system whose rules are so stable that they never change), the wholesale flouting of any particular principle results in the failure to create or maintain an existing legal system."[456] Also, Madison (quoted in Fuller's discussion of the constancy principle) is certainly right when he says the following: "They ['the sober people of America'; C.H.] have seen with regret and indigna-

455 Fuller 1969, p. 37.
456 Shapiro 2011, p. 394.

tion that sudden changes and legislative interferences...become ...snares to the more-industrious and less-informed part of the community."[457]

The last remark concerning the "less-informed" legal subjects is interesting for another reason. Many a reader will already have wondered about the high standard that the foregoing argument from self-constitution imposes on legal subjects. Is not it utterly unrealistic and overly demanding to expect ordinary citizens to make knowledge of the law a necessary component of their normative self-conception?

8.2 An Overly Demanding Conception of Citizenship?

The shift towards the legal subjects' perspective ("what the law means to them"), was supposed to establish a priority over the perspective of legal officials. The reductionist strategy, applied to Fuller's internal morality of law, showed that the concept of law comes with certain formal but nevertheless normative requirements. Because of its ultimate addressees' need to plan and perform actions, the law's standards of legal validity receive their normative authority from the necessary role that the law must play in providing the background for its subjects' practical reasoning and action. In criticizing Hart, Shapiro sums up well the shift of focus that informs the view of law and citizenship presented here: "Hart's account [...] misconstrues the intended audience of the law. Subjects, not officials, are the primary objects of legal guidance and evaluation. Thus, when officials guide and evaluate conduct, they form judgments and make claims about the conduct their subjects should perform."[458]

The central element of the view defended here, therefore, is that citizens incorporate the law into their practical deliberation and self-constituting actions when they set and pursue ends under its authority. The maintenance of the citizens' public identity (which they must *have* in one form or the other in the societal condition) as legal subjects is conditional on the law conforming to the minimal Fullerian requirements of legality though. Fuller's eight principles of law's inner rationality describe public norms insofar as they play this role of informing the citizens' self-understanding relative to their co-citizens when each decides what ends to set and what actions to perform.

---

457 Madison in Fuller 1969, p. 80.
458 Shapiro 2011, p. 115.

Law and reasons for action

All this talk about incorporating law into practical reasoning and deliberation will sound familiar to those who know Joseph Raz's influential account of legal authority. Their impression is correct. Just consider this programmatic statement by Raz and compare it with the account of law's nature and function presented in this essay: "Our understanding of law is greatly defective unless it includes and is based on a sound view of the role of law in practical reasoning. The first precept of legal theory is that law is practical, that its essential function is to play a role in its subjects' reasoning about what to do."[459] Doing justice to Raz's enormously complex work on law's nature, its authority, and its relationship to practical reasoning will be impossible in the limited space available. Hence, instead of trying to present a comprehensive account of all the points at which Raz's views on practical reasoning and mine coincide, the following discussion focuses on just one theme that Raz introduces in his theory of law's authority – authority that asserts to make a practical difference in the deliberation and actions of agents.

Raz uses the term "service conception"[460] to label his account of practical (and legal) authority. The "service" that a well-functioning legal system provides, is that it is an instrument that enables the law's subjects to better conform with reasons for action that apply to them (independently of the law). The central element in Raz's account of how the law makes a difference in the action-directed deliberation of legal subjects is his distinction between reasons for action that apply to agents independently of an authority's directives (henceforth, "independent reasons") on the one hand and "dependent reasons" (provided by, for example, a legal directive) on the other.[461] In the context of the law, the distinction between independent and dependent reasons works as follows: Independent reasons for action are those considerations that apply to agents *before* (conceptually, not necessarily temporarily, speaking) legal authorities provide any directives that claim to determine (for those agents) whether or not to act on the balance of the independent ones. A legal authority issues (second-order) reasons that "pre-empt" its subjects from appealing to the independent reasons (that applied to them if the authority did not exist) as the basis of deciding what to do. The justification of legal authority is that its pronouncements are issued on the basis of identifying and coordinating, in a way that is more

459 Raz 1989, p. 1154.
460 My summary of Raz's conception of practical authority is based on Raz 1986, pp. 38–69.
461 Raz 1986, p. 41.

reliable than the agents themselves would be able to, the independent reasons that apply to its subjects.

The service conception of practical (and hence, legal) authority consists of three theses that clarify and summarize the way that Raz thinks the law claims to have an impact on its subjects' reasons for action. The three theses are:

> The dependence thesis: "*all authoritative directives should be based on reasons which already independently apply to the subjects of the directives and are relevant to their action in the circumstances covered by the directive.*"[462]

> The normal justification thesis: "*the normal way to establish that a person has authority over another person involves showing that the alleged subject is likely better to comply with reasons which apply to him (other than the alleged authoritative directives) if he accepts the directives of the alleged authority as authoritatively binding and tries to follow them, rather than by trying to follow the reasons which apply to him directly.*"[463]

> The pre-emptive thesis: "*the fact that an authority requires performance of an action is a reason for its performance which is not to be added to all other relevant reasons when assessing what to do, but should exclude and take the place of some of them.*"[464]

An example will help to clarify what the two different kinds of reason in play here are and the sense in which they figure in relationships of authority.[465] Imagine two persons who cannot agree upon their vacation destination, Paris vs. the Caribbean. There is a plethora of reasons that the two persons weigh against each other and that informs their deliberation, for example financial considerations, the time of the year (are many other tourists likely to go to the two destinations?), and the weather forecast. The two persons agree to invest a third person, an arbitrator, to authoritatively settle their dispute. According to the service conception of practical authority, the reasons just mentioned are the independent reasons that pertain to the two travelers' deliberation. In addition, these independent reasons are the basis on which the arbitrator provides a dependent reason for action for the two travelers.[466] Importantly, the function of the arbitrator is to decide the question of where the two litigants should vacate

---

462 Raz 1986, p. 47.
463 Raz 1986, p. 53.
464 Raz 1986, p. 46.
465 Raz 1986, p. 41. The general framework of the arbitrator case is Raz's; the details of the example (the specific dispute concerning a travel destination) are mine.
466 As Raz makes clear: "The dependence thesis does not claim that authorities always act for dependent reasons, but merely that they should do so. Ours is an attempt to explain the notion of legitimate authority through describing what one might call an ideal exercise of authority" (Raz 1986, p. 47).

on the basis of the independent reasons. Raz summarizes the gist of the dependence thesis in the following way: "The arbitrator's decision [of whether the two go to Paris or to the Caribbean; C.H.] is meant to be based on the other reasons, to sum them up and to reflect their outcome."[467] Once the arbitrator has reached a decision, it provides a dependent (second-order) reason for the disputants to act in a specific way (going to Paris, for example) without them any longer referring to the independent reasons that had pertained to their dispute before the arbitrator issued her decision.

Let us consider this example further in order to get clearer about the other two theses, constituting Raz's service conception of the law. First, concerning the normal justification thesis, consider the arbitrator being a travel agent, i.e., a professional and expert who can be trusted to be in possession of information and expertise that makes her, under *normal* circumstance, better at adjudicating among the conflicting considerations that apply to her customers' considerations for and against a particular course of action. Insofar as this is the case, and the authority of the travel agent is *justified* by means of showing that her costumers better comply with their independent reasons when they act on the former's directives, the pre-emptive thesis applies: from the perspective of the two travelers/customers appeal to the independent reasons for action is now pre-empted. Hence, the travel agent's directive to go to Paris, while itself being dependent on the independent reasons that are supposed to provide the basis for her judgment, rules out that the two travelers take the financial, prudential etc. reasons as *their* reasons for action. This does not mean that the two travelers must no longer reflect on the basis of their independent reasons; rather it "is merely action for some of these [independent; C.H.] reasons which is excluded. [...] The point is that reasons that could have been relied upon to justify action before his [the arbitrator; C.H.] decision cannot be relied upon once the decision is given."[468]

This then is the service that the law provides according to Raz: It helps agents to better comply with the practical reasons that apply to them independently of the law's pronouncements (like the reasons for and against going to Paris or to the Caribbean, in our example). The justification of the binding directives to act/not to act on these independent reasons is that the directives claim to be connected to these independent reasons for action in a particular way. The law is the paradigmatic social institution that generates dependent reasons that pre-empt its subjects to act on considerations that would otherwise

467 Raz 1986, p. 41.
468 Raz 1986, p. 42.

(i.e., in the absence of the authority in question) apply to them directly. Raz's service conception of the law can therefore be considered an "instrumentalist" conception. As becomes most visible in the normal justification thesis, legal systems (and efficient practical authorities more generally) are useful instruments of personal and social organization, since they provide the service of making its subjects comply better with respect to the independent reasons for action that apply to them anyways. According to this instrumentalist justification, "law [...] is a tool in the hands of men differing from many others in being versatile and capable of being used for a large variety of proper purposes."[469] When the arbitrator in our example decides that the better vacation destination is Paris, then our litigants have a dependent reason to go to Paris. The force of this reason rests on the two litigants being better off because the arbitrator does a superior job in evaluating and balancing the reasons that constitute their disagreement.

Raz's service conception of the law and constitutivism

Having outlined Raz's service account of practical authority we can now look at how his view relates to the constitutivist argument for law's normative impact on practical reasoning defended in this investigation. Let us focus on his account of practical reasons.[470] As was discussed above, Raz draws a distinction between dependent reasons (paradigmatically, but not exclusively, provided by the law) on the one hand, and the reasons on the basis of which the dependent reasons claim to be formulated on the other. Importantly, the independent reasons would apply to the law's subjects even if legal norms and institutions were not present. It is this dichotomy of independent, understood as pre-legal, reasons on the one hand and dependent, understood as juridified, reasons on the other, underlying especially the dependence thesis, that the constitutivist account wants to reconsider. Whereas, according to Raz, the addressees of legal norms are subject to independent reasons that are detached from the institutions in charge of assisting them to better comply with them, the constitutivist alternative considers most (including many of the most important) independent reasons as at least co-determined by social practices and norms, the characteristically modern one being the legal system. The relationship between the two

---

469 Raz 1979, p. 226.

470 For his most comprehensive statement concerning the nature of reasons, see Raz 1999 and Raz 2009.

types of Razian reasons is a complex one; one that renders problematic the "independence" of the one from the other. In order to clarify this claim we need to compare Raz's view of the role and origin of reasons with the one that has been endorsed in this essay.

In a recent publication Raz defines reasons for actions as "facts which constitute a case for (or against) the performance of an action."[471] In contrast to this view, and as was mentioned in Chapter 5, the conception of action underlying the defended account of law's nature regards practical reasons to be non-foundational normative considerations.[472] Different from, among many others, Scanlon, Parfit, and Raz the Neo-Aristotelian and Neo-Kantian action-theory proposed by Korsgaard submits that the concept of a reason for action cannot be explicated without considering the more fundamental unit of a practical principle. Whereas Raz treats practical reasons as elementary facts that we encounter in the course of practical reasoning, the Kantian alternative conceives of these reasons as the *result* of a constructivist deliberation-process. An incentive can only become a reason for action once it is endorsed on the basis of a practical identity, that is, the description under which we value ourselves as persons who chose certain courses of action rather than others. And when we say that an agent acts for a reason this always means that a subjective principle of action (Aristotle's *logos*, Kant's maxim describing an act that is performed for the sake of an end) has been chosen on the basis of those abstract and higher-order principles that constitute her deliberative standpoint. According to the view that differs from Raz's, the reason for performing an action is not a fact that is "external" to the chosen action so conceived; rather, the form of the specific maxim constitutes the reason for performing (or not performing) it when an agent chooses it in accordance with her practical identity.[473] A practical reason

---

471 Raz 2009, p. 37.

472 This diagnosis of the difference between Korsgaard's account of practical reasons and the alternative view is indebted to Pauer-Studer 2009, p. 400. With respect to his analysis of law's authority Raz says the following: "The preference for a reason-based explanation is motivated by the belief that reasons provide the *ultimate* basis for the explanation of *all* practical concepts, namely, that all must be explained by showing their relevance to practical inferences" (Raz 1979, p. 12; my emphases). For Raz's comprehensive statement concerning the relatively minor role that practical principles play for his view, see his account of "Putting Principles in their Place." (See Raz 1999, pp. 225–228.)

473 Importantly, this view does not collapse into some kind of moral subjectivism – after all, nothing could be more alien to a broadly Kantian view. It makes perfect sense, for the Kantian, to criticize an agent in terms of "not having recognized a reason that she should have recognized." The distinctive feature of the view that opposes Raz's account is that this criticism can always be reduced to the complaint that the criticized agent should have made certain identity-is the result and end point of a deliberative and constructive process – not a basic fact that provides its starting point. The reason for driving up to Cleveland to visit my sick friend, for example, is not a fact "external" to the action, e.g. her well-being. According to the view adopted here, the reason rather is the result of employing one's higher-order identity-constituting practical principle of valuing oneself as the kind of person who shoulders some burden to support a friend in need, to the specific action of driving-to-Cleveland-to-visit-my-friend. Of course, my friend's well-being plays a role in explaining and justifying my action in the form of providing the action's end and purpose; but it is not the reason for my action (in the technical sense of "whole action packages" endorsed above). In short, without the complex interplay between my identity-constituting principles and my proposed actions, there are no reasons for action (understood as plain facts).[474]

Now let us take this difference concerning the nature of practical reasons for granted and let us assume that the view of the primacy of practical principles (and the non-foundational character of reasons) is defensible. What does this alternative view imply with respect to Raz's aforementioned claim that independent reasons are those reasons that apply to us in the absence of the legal institutions that are supposed to render compliance with these reasons more successful and reliable? In order to answer this question recall two things: firstly, the so-called total law thesis, introduced and defended above.[475] And, secondly, the more general tenet defended in this work, namely that the practical principles that are the sources of our reasons are at the same time the building blocks of our practical identities as agents.[476]

There the claim was that, at least in the societal condition, successful actions (i.e., actions that constitute their authors into well-unified agents) are dependent for their possibility on the shared acknowledgement of some minimum of practical principles of intersubjective restraint and/or cooperation. It was then argued that an especially highly-developed instantiation of these pub-

---

constituting principle her own. (Morally) objective reasons are, therefore, perfectly compatible with the constitutivist view. However, these reasons are not foundational facts in Raz's sense. Rather, they are the result of practical deliberation in terms of practical principles that an agent can be criticized for in case she fails to endorse them.

474 "To believe in a principle is just to believe that it is appropriate or inappropriate to treat certain considerations as counting in favor of certain acts. Because that's what a principle is: a principle is a description of the mental act of *taking* certain considerations to count in favor of certain acts" (Korsgaard 2008, pp. 227–228).

475 See section 7.2.

476 See the seven stage argument for the public identity claim in section. 5.2.

lic principles is the law that subjects citizens of modern states to enforceable norms and awards them fundamental legal rights.[477] Since practical deliberation and the choice of actions is the moment of self-constitution, it was argued that a practical identity that is constituted in the course of performing actions within these institutions is a public one. The practical identity of agents in the societal condition is constituted in the process of performing actions and since the principles describing these actions include the norms and public principles that restrain all others from interfering with their actions, the resulting identity is to some extent always necessarily a public one. It is constituted by practical principles that have a public side to them simply because the process of self-constitution is conditioned by others' action (and inaction) in the sense that underlies Hayek's claims concerning the recognition of individual agential "assured free spheres" *under* the law.

It should become clearer where Raz's service conception of law differs from the constitutivist alternative presented here. Raz regards the law merely as a useful instrument that helps an agent to coordinate her practical deliberation in a way that makes her conform better to the reasons that apply to her independently of these public norms. The constitutivist account of the law's role in practical reasoning, on the other hand, suggests that the law already figures in the emergence of independent reasons. This is the case, and now the alternative view of practical reasons comes into play, because the practical principles that are the source of reasons for actions are themselves in part constituted by the public norms that render self-constituting action possible in the first place. The independent reasons that apply to us and that are in need of efficient coordination by the law (following Raz) are not only non-foundational elements of the deliberation about our actions (following Korsgaard); moreover, these "independent" reasons are not "lawless" (in the sense of being completely independent from the legal circumstances within which an agent deliberates and acts) because of the public nature of the principles that they are partly conditioned by.

---

477 This is a good point to remind us that the claim in the text cannot be the paradoxical one, according to which modern legal institutions historically *precede* individual agents (that need to be around in order to create these institutions). In the course of the development of our species instinctual restraint (not to interfere with others) got slowly transformed into the highly complex regimes of legal principles that we mostly take for granted – and will probably get transformed even further, into something that is yet unthinkable for us. Still, and already this claim will be too controversial for many, this process is presented as one that stands in a direct relationship to the manifestation of degrees of well-unified individual agency.

Consider again our initial example about the two travelers who were unable to agree on a vacation destination. Many reasons pertained to this dispute: financial considerations, the expectations concerning whether or not many other people will go to these destinations at the same time, and such things as the weather forecast. With respect to all of these reasons the argument from the public identity claim and the total law thesis suggest that even these seemingly brute "facts" do not turn into reasons for/against action unless they are taken up in practical deliberation about those facts. And it is this kind of deliberation that can only be conducted from within a particular practical standpoint and identity. In the first two cases (financial considerations and the expectations concerning the behavior of others) the role of public principles like the law is more readily visible than in the third. These reasons depend on an institutional and juridified background (like the legal right to travel, systems of monetary exchange) that conditions their status as considerations relevant for deciding what to do.

However, even the weather does provide a reason for action only for those individuals who conceive of themselves as agents with a particular practical identity, an identity that is, at least for citizens of modern states, the result of self-constituting activity under public principles. It is in the following sense then that external norms (and in the case of modern citizenship this is in an important way the law) are implicated in the emergence of *all*, in Razian terms, independent reasons: the practical identities of the two travelers are necessary for the weather forecast to be regarded as a reason pertaining to their proposed actions. Since, as was argued above, every practical identity is (at least in the societal condition) also a public one, the independent reasons like the weather in Paris depend for their *status as reasons* on the presence of those principles that make the successful constitution of such an identity possible in the first place. And in the context of life in the modern state, these principles are partly provided by the legal system, that provides them in the unique form of publicly acknowledged and enforceable law. In the case of the weather qua reason for action this role of the law is admittedly a very indirect one. Still, that legal principles partly constitute every practical identity of citizens of modern states is sufficient to qualify Raz's suggestion that there is a clear disconnect between the system of legal norms on the one hand and many of our (independent) reasons on the other.

Despite this point of disagreement, the Razian service conception of the law shares much more with the constitutivist account than it disagrees with it about. This is so for two reasons. Firstly, Raz acknowledges that our reasons, actions, and our goals are "dependent on existing social forms" and institutions.[478] He says: "[...] individual behavior would not have the significance it has but for the existence of social forms. [And] even if the first were not the case, individuals would not have been able to acquire and maintain their goals except through continuous familiarity with the social forms."[479] And with respect to my total law thesis consider the following statement: "Activities which do not appear to acquire their character from social forms in fact do so."[480] Since the view defended here regards "legal forms" (i.e., the legal norms that condition life and action in the modern state) as an instantiation of Raz's social forms, we see that Raz's view is not, after all, hostile to the claim that our reasons are at least partly the result of external normative conditions.

Secondly, and now my view moves closer to Raz's, even the constitutivist account of how practical principles generate reasons does not deny that there is a genuine role to play for legal systems in the Razian sense of being the source of dependent directives and reasons. Much more would have to be said about how these dependent reasons function in the principle-based constitutivist alternative view of law. This task cannot be pursued here. It should merely be submitted that the above claims about how even Raz's independent reasons arise out of a legally structured context, do not imply that these reasons cannot be the subject of the service conception of legal regulation and adjudication. The concern here has been with the nature of independent reasons and with the sense in which even their origin is not entirely isolated from legal norms. This second qualification highlights that Raz's account of law qua useful tool is not incorrect; rather, it is merely incomplete as an account of law's significance. Accordingly, the constitutivist account does not deny the importance of the instrumental benefits that legal systems provide.

The demandingness of being a (free) legal subject

After this excursus dedicated to Raz's account of how (and why) the law figures in citizens' practical reasoning we can now return to another objection to the view that has been presented as constitutivist. One might object that the self-constitution account of law comes with a conception of individual agency (and, hence, of a necessary component of individual freedom) that results in an overly

---

478 Raz 1986, pp. 308–313.
479 Raz 1986, p. 310.
480 Raz 1986, p. 311.

demanding and utterly unrealistic conception of what it means to be subject to public, agency-enabling, norms. Different from Raz's view, in which the law plays a coordinating role in already well-constituted agents' practical reasoning, the argument presented here makes practical deliberation dependent on being related to the law in a particular, constitutivist, way. If sufficient (or even maximum) awareness and knowledge of the enforceable law is necessary for a high degree of agency in the societal condition, then free agency is threatened whenever individuals have to keep themselves alert and updated (and may fail to do so) concerning the complexities of the legal system that applies to them – a task that will turn out enormously time- and resource-consuming. And, given its demanding implications, does not the view defended here lead to an unintended comeback of positivistic jurisprudence's primacy of the legal experts' perspective – this time in terms of certain individuals simply knowing the law much better than the rest and therefore performing self-constituting actions with a greater awareness of how the legal order conditions this process? What does this imply about the freedom of those citizens who do a bad job with respect to understanding the legal norms that structure the public realm within which they perform their self-constituting actions? Hart refers to these addressees of the law as the "great proportion of ordinary citizens – perhaps a majority – (that will have) no general conception of the legal structure or of its criteria of validity."[481]

Before qualifying the argument from law's role regarding self-constitution in a way that makes it more suitable to mundane conceptions of citizenship I want to make a case for the strong, ideal-type, version first. The strong version insists that it is in fact the case that citizens' attempts at self-constituting action are *prima facie* more successful when these actions incorporate the legal facts determining one's standing amongst all other agents who might potentially interfere with these actions. Note, however, that law's incorporation into practical deliberation does not necessarily amount to the endorsement of the law as legitimate, right, or justified all things considered. The strong thesis rests on a view similar to the Hayekian one quoted at the end of Chapter 6, saying that public laws are to be treated like "natural obstacles that affect my plans"[482] and that separate those proposed actions that an agent can see herself performing from those that she cannot. Hence, given the current line of argument, a criminal who orients her actions by carefully maneuvering in a legally informed matter fares quite well – at least with respect to the self-constituting activity that

481 Hart 1994 (1961), p. 114
482 Hayek 1960, p. 142.

takes place under the law. As will be discussed below, in one sense the (sophisticated) criminal does constitute herself into an agent more successfully than a legal subject who more or less accidentally conforms to legal requirements when performing her actions. Moreover, given the assumption that there is a connection between successful self-constitution and individual freedom (a connection merely stipulated here), it seems as if the criminal is more free than the legally uninformed citizen who performs actions that contingently conform with the legal requirements that apply to her. The former incorporates the law that makes her actions possible into her deliberation, the latter does not do so to the same degree.

The first thing to say in response to the criminal case is to emphasize the qualification, not just added in the current context. The seven stage argument for the public identity claim has been concerned with a necessary but non-moral condition for agency in the societal condition. Morally deficient and morally corrupted individuals are still agents.[483] It was a deliberate choice that each of the seven stages of the argument has left unspecified the specific form that an agent's identification with *her* legal norms is going to have. And the morally corrupted individuals stand in a relationship to the law that is one of mere acknowledgement instead of endorsement. But even the sophisticated criminal has to formulate her actions' maxims on the basis of those normative public principles that she expects others to endorse in their actions. The ends that the criminal sets and the acts she performs are then dependent for their possibility upon the presence of public norms and institutions in a relevantly similar way in which the non-criminal agents' ends are.[484] Consequently, the criminal's practical identity consists of normative principles that are sensitive to the public prerequisites of her (illegal) actions – and that is all that the public identity claim has purported to show. It follows that even if the criminal deliberately violates exactly those public norms that make these actions possible, her self-constituting actions incorporate the law, though in a rather perverted and inverted sense.

The last conclusion points towards the stronger replies to the case of the criminal that I am presenting here. The argument defended in this essay has emphasized the necessity of sustaining a *public* identity that consists in incor-

483 It is, of course, at this point that Kantians and Platonists would most strongly object to my interpretation of what is going on in the case of the sophisticated criminal. (See Korsgaard 2009, chs. 7, 8, and 9.) The argument in the next paragraph in the text moves closer to the Kantian/Platonic claim that the disunified agent is also one that is unjust but it still falls far short of a fully developed moral critique of the criminal.

484 See especially stage 5 of the argument for the public identity claim.

porating those legal norms that clarify one's standing vis-à-vis others into the processes of practical reasoning and action. The criminal, by deliberately violating the norms that make her actions possible in the first place (the role of the criminal is parasitic on the stable and predictable non-interference by others, so to speak), ends up with a "strained" and "divided" practical identity. At least in a well-ordered legal structure and society one defining feature of crime is that it comes with an identity antithetical to publicity and transparency.[485] The public identity of our criminal, while very well-informed concerning the law, is an internally divided one. Her actions, while relying on the predictability and stability provided by the legal institutions she is subject to, do incorporate subjective principles that do not survive their public declaration.[486] It may sound a bit dramatic and mysterious but the criminal is in a certain sense "divided against herself" when she deliberately and secretly violates those public norms that render her actions possible. This line of argument is, of course, a variation of standard universalizability and public reasons arguments (that come with the well-known cohort of standard objections).[487] Still, the self-constitution/public identity version of such arguments adds something important and new when directed at the deliberating perspective of the legally informed criminal. That the criminal's proposed actions (if performed by all others) undermine the necessary conditions of her own agency does provide a unique *prima facie* reason against engaging in such actions.[488]

Still, there remains a sense in which the law-acknowledging criminal is more of a unified agent (and more free) than the law-conforming "citizen" who

---

485 Fred Miller presented the interesting case of undercover police officers and espionage agents (for a just regime) as a challenge to this view. In response, one should keep in mind that the argument for the public identity claim rests on very idealized assumptions, i.e., conditions under which good citizens (like the police officers) need not deceive others in order to protect the constitutional order. Still, there remains *something* wrong about wiretapping and undercover police action, even if this wrong is outweighed by the benefits it produces under non-ideal conditions. And this "something" can, again, be spelled out in terms of taking away a bit of free agency from the legal order's citizens.

486 This is, of course, the thought that underlies both, Kant's Kingdom of Ends version of the categorical imperative as well as the *Doctrine of Right*'s "Universal Principle of Right." The latter says: "Any action is *right* if it can coexist with everyone's freedom in accordance with a universal law, or if on its maxim the freedom of choice of each can coexist with everyone's freedom in accordance with a universal law" (MM 6:230).

487 See Pettit 2000.

488 Another looming problem for the view defended in the text further justifies the *prima facie* qualifier. It seems as if my argument (at least the self-constitution part) cannot sufficiently differentiate between the sophisticated criminal and a person engaged in an act of civil disobedience when the latter finds herself in radically non-ideal legal circumstances.

merely accidentally avoids its violation and stumbles through the legal order without *any* knowledge of the law whatsoever. When looking at yet another case, getting rid of the intuitive immorality of the sophisticated criminal, the plausibility of the controversial claim, according to which knowledge of the law contributes to an increased degree of maintaining a coherent public identity, becomes stronger. Let us add to our duo, populating a specific legal order, the "informed citizen" and compare the latter to the completely ignorant citizen and the sophisticated criminal. Consider how the three individuals *do* with respect to the task of self-constitution. The informed citizen is not merely aware that there are some external public conditions of her actions; rather, the law and what it means for the task of setting and pursuing ends, are distinct elements in her processes of practical reasoning and action. When the informed citizen engages in the task of planning in the course of her life, she does so with a self-understanding of someone who has a publicly maintained standing. Her free sphere of agency is guaranteed as a matter of legal right and not as an arbitrary coincidence – and she *understands* that and why that is so. The informed citizen takes on fully what Hart called the "internal point of view."[489] Only she adopts a stance towards the law that sees how its "rules function as rules in [her life; C.H.] [...]." The informed citizen uses these rules, "in one situation after another, as guides to the conduct of social life, as the basis for claims, demands, admissions, criticisms, or punishment, viz., in all the familiar transactions of life according to rules."[490] The completely ignorant citizen, on the other hand, cannot take on the internal point of view simply because the rules, responsible for her social environment's stability and predictability, remain, for whatever reason, unknown to her.

Importantly, according to Hart's interpretation of his distinction, also our sophisticated criminal counts as failing to adopt the internal point of view with respect to the law.[491] Regarding the sophisticated criminal, then, the informed citizen differs to the extent that only the latter regards the enforceable public principles that she is subject to as reason-providing *for herself*. The criminal

---

489 Hart's discussion of what "constitutes the normative structure of society" in terms of those individuals who take on merely the "external point of view" towards social rules and those who adopt the "internal point of view" is important for the discussion in the text. (See Hart 1994 (1961), pp. 88–91.)

490 Hart 1994 (1961), p. 90.

491 "The external point of view may very nearly reproduce the way in which the rules function in the lives of certain members of the group, namely those who reject its rules and are only concerned with them when and because they judge that unpleasant consequences are likely to follow violation" (Hart 1994 (1961), p. 90).

looks at the very same principles from a merely external perspective and acknowledges them as the immediate source of reasons *for others*. Since it is, however, the others' behavior that the sophisticated criminal is interested in (in order to plan her own actions), the public principles of the law nevertheless figure in her practical deliberation in a way that they do not in the case of the ignorant citizen. The ways in which public principles play a role in self-constituting processes take on very distinct forms in the three cases. It is only in a very weak sense that these norms "figure" in all three agents' practical deliberation: to the least extent this is the case with the ignorant citizen who is merely lucky not to perform actions that conflict with the law that applies to her. Her freedom is only conditional since she lacks the public identity that is dependent on actively incorporating the norms that make non-interfered-with action possible. The object of her choices (her actions' maxims and *logoi*) fail to incorporate the norms that guarantee her "assured free sphere." Consequently, as was argued in section 7.1, the essential part of her normative self-understanding, that was identified as necessary for non-dominated (as opposed to merely non-interfered with) agency, is completely absent in the case of the ignorant citizen.[492]

While the ignorant citizen *is* subject to the coercively enforced public norms that make her conclusively setting ends possible, she fails to incorporate that fact into her normative self-conception at all. The ignorant citizen completely misses out on the recognition of the reasons constituted by the law and the acts she engages in remain severely underdescribed in more than a gradual sense. Given that we are talking about an individual in the societal condition, this extreme version of the ignorant citizen seems almost incoherent and more difficult to envision than it might seem at first sight. (Remember the similar difficulties regarding Robinson Crusoe.) Insofar as something resembling an identity were to be constituted in such a case, it would lack its essential public features. The extreme case of the ignorant citizen (if it turns out to be a coherent self-conception at all) would be another case of self-deception if she considers herself to be a free agent. The discussion of our three cases allows us to restate the main task of this work from yet another angle then: Once the existence of other individuals is acknowledged, agents face a qualitatively different challenge with regard to the task of self-constituting agency than if they were to populate

492 It is important to keep in mind that the ignorant citizen is ignorant in an extreme way and, therefore, an empirically highly unlikely case. As soon as an individual knows at least a little bit about the legal regime she is subject to, she counts as incorporating public norms into her practical identity. Still, the case of the ignorant citizen presents an interesting limiting case and a challenge to the view presented in this essay.

the universe alone. Acknowledging these other persons, however, comes with the recognition of those public norms that structure and delimit these agents' "assured free spheres," within which ends can be set and pursued (and within which the process of self-constitution can take place). Hence, in the societal condition (upon realizing that there is this other person) the completely ignorant citizen, i.e., the one without any public identity, is hard to conceive as a unified agent who conclusively sets ends and performs actions.

The sophisticated criminal, on the other hand, incorporates the principles that constitute her legal system into her actions and, hence, maintains a public identity. She does so, however, in an indirect and skewed way, i.e., by considering how those principles structure the actions and reactions of the agents around her. Law's principles and reasons (and the agents taking them into account directly) become part of the criminal's practical deliberation that leads up to the crime and, via this detour, the law becomes part of her normative self-conception too. Furthermore, the informed citizen directly takes law's reason into consideration when she engages in the process of performing those actions that determine her identity. Raz's three main theses concerning law's authority (the dependence, preemption, and normal justification theses) discussed above best apply to the informed, "normal," citizen and her actions. Of course, the informed citizen *also* does what the criminal does with the law, i.e., also the former incorporates the public norms into her practical reasoning indirectly, when expecting others to perform actions in a predictable manner. However, the informed citizen makes the practical principles and reasons incorporated in the law her own in a way that renders this incorporation into her practical standpoint a public one – a standpoint that endorses the fact of how law is necessary for her actions in the first place. The informed citizen abides by the law whereas the sophisticated criminal merely recognizes it.[493]

493 This is the point at which one should introduce a further stage completing the argument from self-constitution and law-conditioned freedom. This additional step would consist in a defense of public autonomy and democratic self-determination. In other words, the argument in the text does not in and of itself establish that it does make a difference whether or not the law is self-imposed by those individuals who are subject to it. Concerning the completion of this project, I am convinced that the argument from self-constituting action and public identity can be further developed to show two things at the same time: firstly, it supports the claim that government by the rule of law has to be connected to the subjects' agency and will in a non-dominating way. At the same time, secondly, since individual agency is constituted by action, that in turn is successful only when performed in a framework of public norms, democratic will-formation is itself conditional on the law being in place. For a recent defense of a specifically democratic justification of legal norms and citizenship in the juridical state along Kantian lines, see Stilz 2009.

Some political implications

We should briefly acknowledge some practical implications that follow from the defense of the informed citizen as the most unified agent when judged in accordance with the standards of self-constituting action. These practical implications are not fully spelled out here. Rather, in order to wrap up this chapter on the internal rationality of law and the demandingness objection, let us just consider some interesting consequences for the politics and policies of citizenship that are suggested by the arguments presented here.

If it is in fact the case that living up to the slogan of "knowing one's rights" is connected to the possibility of agency (and freedom) in the way defended here, then making sure that those who are subject to the law also sufficiently understand this social fact becomes a personal as well as a public concern. The idea of citizenship education and the public provision of basic legal information and representation gains support, when the addressees of the law are identified as being in need of a stable public identity. Even though this legal education need not necessarily be provided by a public agency the approach defended here is closely enough related to the idea of "legal centralism"[494] that it will require the adherence to some basic, content-based, standards that teaching citizenship involves and that are not negotiable with those who teach the legal system to (future) citizens. In this sense the argument presented here is certainly demanding with respect to its policy-related implications. However, at the same time it is not an infringement of liberty (even if we take Bentham and Berlin's conceptions of liberty as the standard). Making those who are subject to the law – i.e., those public norms that make their free lives possible – aware of this fact does not diminish agency and freedom but puts them on a coherent and transparent foundation. Just by briefly recalling the summary of Kukathas's views in Chapter 2, we already see the extent to which his views on the one hand and the argument from self-constitution on the other stand in a strained relationship. Settling these theoretical (and practical) disagreements will be dealt with in more detail in the concluding chapter.

However, and this much should be submitted at this point already, despite the significant disagreements with Kukathas concerning the importance of a legal system's integrity, the state, and citizenship, other practical consequences

494 Ellickson 1991, pp. 137–147. "Oliver Williamson has used the phrase *legal centralism* to describe the belief that governments are the chief sources of rules and enforcement efforts. The quintessential legal centralist was Thomas Hobbes, who thought that in a society without a sovereign, all would be chaos" (Ellickson 1991, p. 138).

of the argument defended are quite congenial to many conclusions in *The Liberal Archipelago*. Kukathas's skepticism concerning communitarian and nationalistic views regarding (enforced) solidarity and social cohesion is more than compatible with the individualistic argument from self-constitution and public identity presented here.[495] Moreover, Kukathas's critique of perfectionist and overly moralized conceptions of political society are continuous with the moral austerity characteristic of the previous chapters. Both theories share the enlightenment conviction that pluralism and diversity are facts of the modern condition that render certain visions of political order unfeasible and unjustifiable. However, what critics of legal centralism (and Kukathas is one of them) have called "an overlegalized conception of modern society"[496] is exactly part of the solution to the problem of how diverse individuals and groups have to organize their lives on the basis of principle-based public norms. The assumption that lies at the heart of the disagreement between the view defended here and that of critics of the modern state like Kukathas is that individuals who find themselves in the societal condition *have to* settle on such public norms. As was argued above, the anarchist's belief that the societal condition comes with a natural and default maximum of liberty rests on turning a blind eye on the complicated issue of how agency is dependent on interpersonal norms that make action possible. The alternative constitutivist view comes across as "overlegalized" only when the regulation and juridification of human relationships is regarded as something optional.

There are other practical implications resulting from the view defended here. Citizenship is not to be conceived of as some kind of innate property but consists in the performance of actions based on a public identity that incorporates the practical principles that regulate the interpersonal realm that one shares with one's co-citizens. Given the way citizenship is defined today, the limits of applying such an "internal" and first-personal conception of citizenship become obvious very quickly though. Were the public-identity theory of citizenship adopted, neither *jus sanguinis* nor *jus soli* policies of determining citizenship status would be directly relevant to discriminating between citizens

495 My view is individualistic in the same, robust, sense in which Hegel's is, the widespread view that his account of the citizen-state relationship is unacceptably collectivistic and organicistic notwithstanding. The *loci classici* of this highly influential Hegel-interpretation are Popper 2003 (1945) and Berlin 2003 (1952), pp. 74–104. This influential view is summed up in "Russell's famous quip that Hegelian freedom is the freedom to salute the police" (Pippin 2008, p. 26). For recent rectifications of this view, see Pippin 2008 and Honneth 2010.
496 Baumgartner 1993, p. 336.

and non-citizens of a particular legal order.[497] Since citizenship is a status that the state has traditionally been awarded on the basis of "external" and "third-personal" criteria, i.e., criteria that are identified independently of the (potential) citizens' practical standpoint and her normative self-conception, the practical realizability of the alternative account of citizenship-requirements presented here seems meager.[498] However, and this is the modest claim defended here, if it were somehow possible to determine whether or not individuals incorporate the law into their practical deliberation and actions (like the informed citizen did), this would be a superior criterion to award and maintain their status as members of a particular legal order.

Summary

Where do these reflections concerning the practical implications of the presented theory of citizenship leave us with respect to the question motivating this section? We have been asking whether an account of citizenship that consists in individuals incorporating the law into their actions results in an overly demanding picture of practical reasoning. We now see that this question cannot be as straightforwardly answered as might have seemed after we revisited law's internal rationality and how the latter's norms are necessary external conditions of the possibility of agency. The balance sheet is mixed with respect to the demandingness objection: on the one hand, the view defended in fact claims that the reflective endorsement of those public laws that structure one's standing vis-à-vis all others does stand in a directly proportional relationship with agency and, ultimately, individual freedom. The better informed a citizen is with

---

497 For the legal and political dimensions of defining citizenship, see Kymlicka and Norman 1994; Safran 1997; Janoski 2010.

498 The exception is naturalized citizens in certain countries who are required to publicly commit themselves to the constitutional values and principles of their new home country. As should be clear by now the conception of citizenship defended in the text is sympathetic to this approach. It would, however, even extend it to individuals born in the country in question. This extension does, of course, point towards another practical limitation of this citizenship-theory: if we require those who were born and grew up in a certain state to show, by means of passing some sort of test, that they have incorporated the law into their practical identity to a sufficient degree then what are we going to do with those who fail to do so, i.e., those who cannot/refuse to incorporate the law into their public identity (if that turned out to be possible at all)? Should a legal order expel those who refuse to accept its authority? This is certainly another indication that the view of citizenship presented in the text cannot present a complete practical account.

respect to the legal system, and the better she understands the sphere of possible actions that she can and cannot perform, the freer she is and the less self-deceptive is her public identity as an agent. This claim led to a couple of conclusions and implications that many might find counterintuitive. A sophisticated criminal, cunningly maneuvering through the intricacies of the law, is more of an agent than a legally completely ignorant person and a badly informed citizen. Overall, a first-personal account of citizenship (and, more generally, of what it means to be subject to public norms) has limited practical appeal. This concession does not, however, diminish its theoretical adequacy: citizens are those human beings who know the rights and liberties (and those of their fellows) that apply to them *qua* subjects to a particular legal order. They incorporate this knowledge into their practical outlook as agents when performing actions under the law. Our nature as planning and acting creatures requires the stability that the law is supposed to guarantee and we better make sure we sufficiently understand how *our* laws achieve this goal.

Chapter 9: Reply to Kukathas

It is now time to use the arguments presented above to revisit Kukathas's liberal archipelago and the claims concerning citizenship and liberal legal institutions made there. As we saw in part one, Kukathas finds contemporary defenses of the latter ideas wanting and believes that his account of an open liberal society does a superior job in accommodating the core liberal values of tolerance and freedom of conscience. Since *The Liberal Archipelago* is not primarily a legal-philosophical work, Kukathas's remarks on the role of legal systems in the modern world are few in number. However, they provide central elements for his argument and deserve close examination.

The response to Kukathas, based on the conception of public identity and citizenship defended above, shows that the rule of law and the modern Weberian state cannot be dismissed as a merely contingent and insignificant historical artifice – as is suggested in *The Liberal Archipelago*. Building on the provisional replies to Kukathas that were discussed in Chapter 3, this chapter's first section looks at Kukathas's views concerning the internal institutional structure of those associations that constitute the liberal archipelago. It will be argued that Kukathas is suspiciously silent when it comes to spelling out how the individual associations go about ordering their internal affairs. What were called mini-states in the initial replies will now be reintroduced as small-scale legal communities, themselves monopolizing the use of legitimate coercion used to enforce public norms. The need for such institutional structures inevitably arises in *every* societal condition because the possibility of successfully constituted individual agency requires them.

The final section (9.2) looks at issues of institutional design and examines how federalist solutions to the need for social order can be incorporated into the self-constitution paradigm. It revisits Kukathas's critique of mainstream liberalism, especially Dworkin's notion of "law's integrity." After having identified a misunderstanding on Kukathas's part, a reading of Dworkin is defended that emphasizes the importance of law's vertical as well as horizontal integrity. This defense of Dworkin leads back to the issue of citizenship and concludes with the claim that a coherent public identity is not undermined by federalist legal structures that divide and devolve the monopoly of legitimate violence, as long as the resulting institutional arrangements are themselves constituted in a legal form.

9.1 Kukathas and the Law

At the beginning of the chapter "Freedom of Association and Liberty of Conscience" Kukathas engages in the task of defining the term "society."[499] This task is crucial because the main goal of *The Liberal Archipelago* is to present a vision of what a liberal *society* should look like. We have already seen that Kukathas conceives of a liberal society as a political association which is constituted by the diverse associations that exist more or less independently from each other and whose coexistence is supervised by the umpire, i.e., the liberal state.[500] Kukathas says "that a society is a form of association made up of people who belong to different communities or associations which are geographically contiguous."[501] Let us keep in mind that Kukathas does not do away with the liberal state altogether and that in accordance with the state's role as an umpire, "[i]ts only concern ought to be with upholding the framework of law within which individuals and groups can function peacefully."[502] The umpire is introduced as a law-governed and law-enforcing institution that necessarily, to put it in terms that Kukathas tries to avoid, "unifies" the associations "below" it, even if only in a very thin sense. More will be said about the legal norms that rule at the level of the umpire and what they mean to the members of particular associations promptly.

Before looking at the liberal archipelago's rule of law, let us return to Kukathas's definition of society. With respect to the question of what role and importance the liberal archipelago assigns to the law, Kukathas's conception of society rests on the thought that "[s]ince *all* societies are governed by law, the move from one *legal jurisdiction* is, to some extent, a move from one society to another."[503] However, it is in his discussion concerning the issue of jurisdictional borders of societies that Kukathas's definition of society becomes puzzling and unclear. In short, the problem is that in the passage under discussion Kukathas seems to switch between two distinct objects of analysis, namely legal jurisdiction as referring to the broader liberal society (ruled by the umpire) on the one hand and legal jurisdictions as referring to the individual associations populating a specific liberal society on the other. We need to know if the archipelago's associations are themselves legal orders in order to answer the ques-

499 Kukathas 2003, pp. 77–78.
500 See Chapter 1.
501 Kukathas 2003, p. 77.
502 Kukathas 2003, p. 249.
503 Kukathas 2003, p. 77 (my emphasis).

tion of whether or not the envisioned liberal society can provide the necessary external conditions for self-constituting action.

In order to further illustrate why Kukathas's definition of "society" is puzzling consider statements like the following: "For a society surely exists when there is some established set of customs or conventions or legal arrangements specifying how the laws apply to persons whether they stay put or move from one jurisdiction to another within the greater realm."[504] Here the suggestion seems to be that there are a number of jurisdictions "within the greater realm" of the liberal archipelago and movement between these jurisdictions (that each have internal laws of their own) is governed by "customs or convention or legal arrangements" with respect to which the liberal umpire is in charge. Since these sub-jurisdictions *are* jurisdictions though, it follows that they also have to count as societies in accordance with the above definition ("a move from one legal jurisdiction is, to some extent, a move from one society to another"). If X is a society, then X is (necessarily) a jurisdiction.

Things get confusing when Kukathas illustrates his definition of society by discussing the millet system.[505] This legal arrangement, privileging the Jewish, Muslim, and Christian communities of Medieval Spain to take into their own hands certain aspects of their legal affairs, is presented as a paradigmatic example of a (one) society. What remains unclear in Kukathas's discussion is the extent to which the religious associations in question are themselves sovereign jurisdictions and, therefore, count as independent societies. The millet system allowed for the coexistence of the three groups "under elaborate legal arrangements specifying the rights and obligations individuals had within their own religious communities, and as outsiders within the others."[506] Here too it remains unclear where in the system legal sovereignty is located. The passage makes it sound as if, with respect to the "elaborate legal arrangements" *under* which the three religious associations co-existed, the ultimate authority rests squarely with the (liberal) umpire, making it the case that only the millet system as a whole deserves the label "society."

However, the concluding discussion of his society-definition makes it again sound as if such religious associations are themselves separate jurisdictions *but not* societies, contradicting the initial definition of societies *in terms of* legal unity and independence. The final version of the definition summarizes the puzzling conceptual landscape that Kukathas leaves us with: "[A] society will

504 Kukathas 2003, pp. 77–78.
505 Kukathas 2003, p. 78.
506 Kukathas 2003, p. 78.

be taken to be a region of contiguous jurisdictions related by law. Societies can be distinguished from one another by jurisdictional separateness."[507] In the second sentence it remains unclear what the referent of the term "societies" is. Does Kukathas apply this term to entities like the liberal archipelago? Or are the archipelago's individual associations themselves societies? Does the term "society" apply to both kinds of entity, because both are law-governed jurisdictions?

Now the definition of society quoted in the previous paragraph, in order to be rendered consistent with the earlier definition ("a move from one legal jurisdiction is, to some extent, a move from one society to another"), would have to replace "societies" in the second sentence with "associations." A (liberal) society would then be defined as a region of contiguous associations (i.e., small-scale jurisdictions) which are related by (the liberal umpire's) law. The associations can be distinguished from one another by their jurisdictional separateness. However, and this seems to be the source of the confusion, these associations are now themselves fully legally independent and self-sufficient *societies* since the latter have been defined as such jurisdictional units.

Those who remember the initial replies to Kukathas presented in chapter 1.3 will already have a suspicion for why I engage in such a nitpicking exegesis of Kukathas's handling of the notion of "society." There, Walzer's claim was defended that the liberal archipelago is much less revolutionary than it might appear at first sight. The major observation was that the archipelago already exists in the form of the international state system (the international *society*) that is maximally tolerant and leaves sovereign societies (and their internal legal arrangements) benignly neglected. Now the unclarity of Kukathas's definition of society (especially his reluctance to admit that the archipelago's associations turn out to be legal orders and, hence, are in an important sense sovereign) may well have its source in the correctness of Walzer's observation. When in *a* liberal society the overarching legal institutions get reduced to the umpire-role, then the associations will have to fill in public norms of their own. That Kukathas's account does not acknowledge this outcome is understandable. Recall that the major motivation for defending the liberal archipelago as a superior vision of liberal politics was *individual* freedom of conscience. If associations are coercive enforcers of laws we run into the very same problem that the liberal archipelago was supposed to solve in the first place, i.e., that a legal regime (in Weber's sense of the state) sometimes/often forces subjects to act against their conscience. Kukathas cannot explicitly affirm that the archipelago's associations become jurisdictional units themselves (i.e., units internally

507 Kukathas 2003, p. 78.

governed, not just externally related to other units, by law) because that would be tantamount to pushing the very problem of coercively enforcing public norms to the level of these associations.

As will be remembered from the discussion of Kukathas's dilemma above, there is of course the alternative horn he can take, *viz.* individualist anarchism[508] in the sense of each individual person forming her own legally sovereign "association." The claim that this option is not really an option and that Kukathas's liberal archipelago is therefore left with the other horn (resulting in "legal associations") has been argued for by making use of the argument from self-constitution and public identity. In fact, the main claim is that the anti-anarchist horn of the dilemma is not actually the horn of a dilemma at all but just an expression of the basic circumstances of our shared human condition. That the liberal archipelago's associations cannot avoid the task of settling the issues of delimiting and guaranteeing (by law) free spheres etc. is required by our natures as end-setting and pursuing agents in the presence of others.

Let us focus on another interesting passage in *The Liberal Archipelago* in order to highlight the conceptual limits of Kukathas's overall argument. Again, the following passage is picked because it is among the few that clarify the liberal archipelago's relationship to the rule of law. In the course of discussing objections to his conception of liberal toleration and the exit principle, Kukathas considers the worry caused by "individuals who choose to reject the

508 As was briefly explained in fn. 281, my usage of the term "individualist anarchism" is directed at a moving target. In the seven stage argument for the public identity claim and in the Anarchia thought experiment, the target was a view that denies the necessity of *any* social practices and institutions for the process of action qua self-constitution. The current reply to Kukathas focuses on the particular instantiation of these external features in the form of political and legal institutions. I can therefore not claim that Kukathas's liberal archipelago undermines every possible form of social practices and institutions. However, his views concerning exit rights and freedom of conscience undermine the possibility of the modern juridified state, in the Kantian sense defended in section 7.1. The degree interpretation of self-constitution again helps here: what Kukathas denies the populace of his ideal liberal society is the conclusive (in Kant's sense) juridification of their (unavoidable) interaction and, hence, the external conditions that are necessary for a *high* degree of self-constitution. Kant too, does not contrast this juridified condition with the state of nature understood as a condition of permanent injustice – rather it is a condition "devoid of justice" (MM 6:312). This captures very well the general point of this essay: it has not been claimed that the absence of social practices and institution (such as the modern state) *must* result in permanent interference ("injustice"); this absence, however, amounts to the lack of the possibility of settling disputes by means of investing a public authority with the power to do so, which in turn has the envisioned impact on one's self-conception as an agent in charge of one's actions. I will return to these issues in the conclusion.

authority of the wider society or the state and withdraw into communities as small as a single family (or individual). Are they not licensed, under the present defense of toleration, to reject the authority of the law and to do entirely as they please?"[509]

Kukathas's response to this objection is admirably frank as usual: "it must be conceded that this is, in principle, quite possible."[510] The liberal archipelago (and its central legal institution, the liberal umpire) do in fact not have any resources to prevent this in-principle possibility of the archipelago splitting-up into individualized associations and "jurisdictions." It has been this possibility that motivated the first horn of the dilemma, i.e., individualist anarchism. In other words, the liberal umpire (and its constitutive associations and communities) do not have the power to issue laws that are *prima facie* unconditionally binding. Instead, the "laws" in question have the form: "You are obligated to φ, unless you don't want to φ." Kukathas, realizing that his account is in danger of undermining any legal cohesion whatsoever (and some level of cohesion is necessary even for his utopia's existence to be possible) is quick to help himself to standard cost-benefit arguments in order to identify the anarchist option as unbearably costly. Let us pay particular attention to what he says about the law here:

> The cost of such a move [exiting all authority-relationships; C.H.], however, would make this *extremely unlikely* since the individuals or families 'seceding' in this way would, in effect, sentence themselves to the status of 'out*law*'. In repudiating the authority, they would deny themselves the protection of any legal community.[511]

Kukathas then observes that another reason for why individual secession "is not a very likely outcome of strong principles of toleration" is the historical fact that "outlawry" has always been considered an especially harsh form of punish-

509 Kukathas 2003, p. 135. With respect of the Kantian view that there is an unconditional duty to enter a "rightful condition" (a condition in which our interpersonal relationships are put on the basis of law that is *omnilaterally* authorized) it is noteworthy that Kukathas summarizes the objection under consideration in the following way: "Yet if we tolerate communities of people who reject the authority of the wider society, [...], what is to prevent individuals from *unilaterally* rejecting all authority and withdrawing into communities of one – or perhaps, communities comprising only a single family" (Kukathas 2003, p. 139; my emphasis). Kant would respond that such individuals wrong (not necessarily harm!) each other "to the highest degree" because they undermine their innate right of humanity, i.e., freedom understood as independence from other individuals' private (unilateral) choices. For an illuminating account of Kant's argument, see Varden 2008.

510 Kukathas 2003, p. 139.

511 Kukathas 2003, pp. 139–140 (my emphasis).

ment.[512] Actually, in concluding his brief reply to the problem of individual secession, Kukathas comes very close to subscribing to the view about the constituting role of the law defended here. He acknowledges "that there is already a substantial pressure toward conformity exerted by the fact of human interdependence."[513]

Still, Kukathas's reply to the worry that his archipelago allows for the possibility of dissolving into one-man associations and the dissolution of any law-governed institutions must leave one dissatisfied. That individualist anarchism is empirically unlikely because costly does not go deep enough as an answer, so to speak. It has been the task of this essay to show that the proper reason for why, on the level of the archipelago's associations, something like the rule of law has to be institutionalized is a non-historical and non-empirical one. The transcendental argument defended here claims that "the move" into individualist anarchy and lawlessness is an action which conceptually undermines the necessary external conditions of the high degree of individual agency that can only be achieved under the law's guarantees and protection. The *option* of a complete withdrawal from any such legal authority (however unlikely and impractical it is) that Kukathas grants the populace of the liberal archipelago is tantamount to such an undermining of what is necessary for a non-dominated public identity, and *a fortiori*, a high degree of self-constituted agency in the presence of other agents. Coercive laws, understood as those normative principles that figure in an agent's practical reasoning and constitute her public identity in a way that only the law can provide, are simply absent when the authority issuing them always (and on the basis of the principle of toleration) attaches the qualifier "unless you see conflicts with your conscience" to them. It is the publicly acknowledged option to return to the state of nature that has this actual impact on the normative self-conception as someone who can set ends conclusively in the societal condition. Legal security requires external mechanisms that ensure that individuals do not pull out of the legal guarantees they acknowledge with respect to each other. Our activities as planning agents remain inconclusive when this legal security is absent and our standing as end-setters hinges (exclusively) on the private conscience of our fellows.

Kukathas might refer us to yet another passage in which he talks about the law, its authority, and whether they are practically necessary.[514] There, Kukathas again makes clear that in the liberal archipelago the right to exit is the

512 Kukathas 2003, p. 140.
513 Kukathas 2003, p. 140.
514 Kukathas 2003, pp. 143–144.

fundamental one and "there is no association or community from whose authority an individual or group of individuals may not withdraw."[515] However, especially given the example of real-world states, Kukathas claims that it is not easy to escape the reach of any authority-structures whatsoever entirely. The interesting feature of this qualification are the facts responsible for the difficulty to exit all authorities. Kukathas gets very close to what has been said in this third part:

> Unless individuals or groups intend to live in isolation, which in the modern world is not an option readily available, they will have to coexist with others, and find some *modus vivendi*. To the extent that they will have to interact, they will have to abide by mutually accepted laws, and to accept the authority of some third party who will adjudicate disputes. Nor will they always be able to simply move in and out of membership to suit their convenience, as if changing banks to get a better interest rate.
>
> The point of all this is to say that, in a society governed by toleration, it is not going to be possible for individuals or groups easily to arrogate to themselves the power to do entirely as they wish with others – including their children. For they will be bound by the norms or conventions or the laws of the communities to which they belong – which may in turn be shaped by requirements laid down by other associations of which these groups are themselves parts.[516]

There are a lot of details in these two paragraphs worth discussing. Again, notice the language expressing the historical and empirically contingent unlikelihood of ending up with individualist anarchism. What is *not* going to be *possible* in the societal condition is that individuals (or groups) *easily* declare full individual sovereignty and thereby assume the status of an, in principle, unpredictable force outside the law. Still, and this follows from the foundational status of the right to exit, it is possible for the liberal archipelago's people "uneasily" to do so and this is, in accordance with the major argument defended here, enough to deprive the law of the function that it plays with respect to self-constituting action. The last sentence of the first paragraph is absolutely right and in line with the conclusion defended here: individuals will not be able to

515 Kukathas 2003, p. 143.

516 Kukathas 2003, p. 143–144. This passage is also interesting because the last sentence vindicates the reading according to which Kukathas implicitly acknowledges that all of the archipelago's associations will be norm-governed. But even in this passage he does not fully commit himself to the claim that the communities are necessarily "legal communities" – as suggested by his puzzling definition of "societies" in terms of "jurisdictional units" discussed above. Kukathas is clearly influenced by the work of Benson 1990 and Ellickson 1991 who make the, empirical and historical, claim that "Order without Law" is quite possible.

simply move in and out of membership at will. However, it is difficult to see any principled basis for Kukathas submitting this claim if the right to exit is as absolute as he insists throughout *The Liberal Archipelago*. Withdrawing from the reach of any authority, also for reasons of convenience and however difficult it is in the modern interdependent world, remains an option for all Archipelagoans all the time. That this mere possibility undermines what Kant calls a "rightful condition" (especially the core legal guarantees expressed in the institutions of private property and contracts) should by now be clear. The conditional laws structuring interpersonal relationships in the liberal archipelago's associations, as well as those issued by the umpire, are not really laws. In other words, the residents of the liberal archipelago basically remain in a lawless condition that undermines the necessary prerequisites of a free life.[517]

But what about the other (improbable) option hinted at in the long quote, i.e., that it is in principle possible to "intend to live in isolation?" Kukathas is certainly right when he reminds us that such an isolationist solution is hardly realizable under modern conditions. But still we seem to be able to realize individualist anarchy if we intended to turn our backs to each other, walk away in opposite directions, and live our lives in isolation from each other ever after. If we really wanted to, we could do without legal institutions and without any *modus vivendi*, the isolationist would insist.

An empirically non-contingent response to the possibility of living a life in complete isolation utilizes the discussion of the non-interference claim execut-

---

517 A reading like this one also helps making (more) sense of Kant's controversial views concerning a right to revolution. (See MM 6:318–623 and TP 8:298–8:300.) Similar to the infamous right-to-lie essay, the crucial aspect that is often overlooked is the term "right" and the legal-philosophical (as opposed to moral-philosophical) context of the debates. If we keep in mind what a right implies, and that Kant argues that conclusive contractual and property rights are to be maintained by a public authority in order to be legitimate, it becomes more understandable why he believed a *right* to revolution, granted by the very authority that demands obedience to the law, to be an incoherent notion. No law-issuing and administering authority *can* grant its subjects the legal (again, not moral) right to obey the law only to the extent that they (i.e., private individuals) unilaterally decide to do so. The point argued in the text is similar but approaches the issue from the perspective of what is necessary for being a well-unified agent. In both, Kant's and my, cases the arguments presented do not establish all-things considered moral requirements to obey all laws all the time. However, and this will be too much for Kukathas already, there is always *some* wronging involved when the law is broken (and there is always *some* reason to follow the law's demand) having to do with the external conditions of agency presented in this work and law's constitutive, non-instrumental, function. For recent work on Kant's attitude toward revolution see, for instance, Korsgaard 2008, pp. 233–262, Flikschuh 2008 & 2008a, Ripstein 2009, pp. 325–352, and Byrd and Hruschka 2010, pp. 90–91.

ed above.[518] Remember that part of the argument against that claim purported to show that even a society of hermits, each of whom determined not to interact with any other individual at all, cannot avoid to somehow arrange their standing and status vis-à-vis all others. The mere mutual awareness of other individuals, understood as potential interferers with one's action-attempts, confronts us with an inescapable problem. The above discussion of the non-interference claim then committed itself to the even more ambitious conclusion that actual non-interference is not enough to provide all the necessary external conditions for maintaining the kind of public identity that life in the societal condition requires (and with respect to which citizenship was presented as the paradigmatic exemplar). The distinction between non-interference and non-domination (inspired by Pettit and Kant's conceptions of freedom) does apply to the long passage in *The Liberal Archipelago* just quoted. Hermits are also in need of such a public identity; they are in need of public (not merely private) normative principles that clarify what they and others can rightfully do and cannot do. Hence, the fact that modern life makes it difficult and therefore unlikely that individuals withdraw from all law-governed associations is certainly a plausible claim. However, such contingent qualifications of *The Liberal Archipelago's* main thesis leave out the more fundamental conceptual issues. The impact on action and agency discussed here not only ensues when individuals, despite the high costs related to exiting, actually withdraw from all law-governed associations but even when this possibility is merely granted as a matter of principle in the liberal society envisioned by Kukathas.

9.2 Law's Integrity and Federalism

In order to conclude our discussion of Kukathas's arguments this section looks at two more concrete and practical issues discussed in *The Liberal Archipelago*. In the course of criticizing contemporary liberalism and its central notions of legal unity, citizenship, and the rule of law, Kukathas presents the liberal archipelago as a genuinely open society. The prime target of Kukathas's critique is Rawls's "closed society," unified under one consistent liberal constitutional and legal structure. A crucial feature of this critique of contemporary liberalism's legal institutions is their supposed intolerance towards legal diversity, a diversity that will inevitably develop in pluralistic societies, according to Kukathas. *The Liberal Archipelago* dedicates a number of passages to Ronald Dworkin's

---

518 See section 7.1.

Law's Empire, especially the chapters therein that defend the idea that a legal system has to exhibit a certain degree of principled integrity.[519] Dworkin claims that we have good reasons to reject so-called "checkerboard solutions" to legal and political disputes and he argues that only integrity understood as a separate and freestanding value (in addition to justice and fairness) can account for this rejection. Based on his critique of Dworkin, Kukathas argues that contemporary liberalism gravitates towards legal centralism and fails to remain compatible with federalist alternatives worthy of that name. While there is much to say in support of Kukathas's critique of liberal political and legal institutions, his interpretation of Dworkin is imprecise and his criticisms inadequate. The possibility of a multilayered public identity, based on the argument from self-constitution and agency defended in this book, can demonstrate that federalist views and legal integrity are not in principle at odds with each another.

First, let us have a closer look at Kukathas's criticisms of Dworkin. According to Kukathas's reading, checkerboard solutions to fundamental moral and political disputes settle the latter "differently in different jurisdictions, so that laws on, say abortion, might be different from one province, or state within the nation, to the next."[520] When Kukathas interprets the passages in *Law's Empire* that identify checkerboard solutions as based on "unprincipled" political and judicial decisions, he understands the violation of integrity in play to consist in a conflict between local legal regimes with the norms (like constitutional ones) at a higher level of the legal system.[521] Dworkin, according to this reading, is willing to restrict local jurisdictions' legal sovereignty for the sake of the value of overall institutional integrity and coherence. Since such policies, dedicated to the enforcement of legal unity, will necessarily involve coercive action by the overarching political entity (the liberal state), it follows that the integrity of a constitutional order is likely to violate the association-members' right to associate on only those terms they acquiesce to. Based on this reading, Kukathas then presents the liberal archipelago as allowing exactly such a legal pluralism in which different, contiguous, jurisdictions decide issues as they see fit. This approach results in a plurality of legal communities that might hold mutually contradictory public norms: "According to the idea of liberal toleration defend-

519 Dworkin 1986, pp. 176–224 and pp. 225–275.

520 Kukathas 2003, p. 180.

521 Dworkin presents the idea of law's integrity in two different, but related, contexts: "integrity in legislation" and "integrity in adjudication." The first is concerned with those whose job it is to make coherent law (Dworkin 1986, p, 176), the second is addressed at judges and the procedures of their legal reasoning (Dworkin 1986, p. 217). The line of argument pursued in the text is more concerned with the first conception of integrity.

ed here, however, the checkerboard solution is a principled solution to the problem of disagreement over fundamental questions of morality that might be found in any political society."[522]

It is necessary to stop at this point and have a closer look at Kukathas's reconstruction of Dworkin's notion of "integrity." We need to pay particular attention to how the passages quoted above understand the notion of an "unprincipled decision" of legal issues. Again, for Kukathas, Dworkin means by "unprincipled" a conflict between two legal systems that are unified into one larger federal structure. The example that Kukathas has in mind here is the constitutional order of the United States, in which the federal constitution imposes a certain pressure towards unity on the lower levels of legislation (e.g., the States). Such a reading would be adequate if Dworkin had, for example, presented as a checkerboard solution the case of Alabama adopting a law concerning racial discrimination that substantially differs from the one its neighboring states enact. Sure, this *is* a kind of checkerboard system and we'll return to this case below. However, the scenario in which Alabama and Tennessee have different, and incompatible, laws is not the violation of integrity that worries Dworkin in the passages in *Law's Empire* discussed by Kukathas. It must be admitted that Dworkin's account of integrity is not particularly clear and the fact that one of the examples involves Alabama and the issue of racial discrimination makes it tempting to expect the integrity-issue to be concerned with the conflicts between federal and state legislation in American jurisprudence. But let us look in more detail at the two checkerboard examples that Dworkin actually presents to illustrate why we have to reject such legal settlements as unprincipled and as lacking integrity.

> Do the people of Alabama disagree about the morality of racial discrimination? Why should *their* legislation not forbid racial discrimination on buses but permit it in restaurants? Do the British divide on the morality of abortion? Why should *Parliament* not make abortion criminal for pregnant women who were born in even years but not for those born in odd ones?[523]

Especially the second example makes it quite clear what sense of "unprincipled" legislative and juridical decisions Dworkin is concerned with in his discussion of law's integrity. The issue is not one of, as I want to call it, "vertical integrity" but one of "horizontal integrity." The two checkerboard solutions are rejected not because the Alabamian racist legal norms conflict with some "high-

522 Kukathas 2003, p. 180.
523 Dworkin 1986, p. 178 (my emphasis).

er" law but because *within* one legal community (Alabama) a fundamental and disputed political issue is settled arbitrarily by "their legislation." It is this alternative meaning of "unprincipled" (synonymous with "arbitrary") that Kukathas ignores and that makes all of a difference when interpreting Dworkin. It is horizontal lack of integrity of the Alabama/British law that makes us reject the arbitrary solutions to the disputed issues. Satisfying British pro-choice advocates and pro-lifers by splitting the female population into two groups on utterly arbitrary grounds is an unacceptable, because unprincipled, way of regulating this contested issue. Our rejection of unprincipled law-making and administration is motivated not merely by justice and fairness (though this is also true according to Dworkin) but because checkerboard solutions violate the freestanding legal standard of integrity: "it [a checkerboard solution; C.H.] simply affirms for some people a principle it denies to others"[524] and this results in a legal order that "endorses principles to justify part of what it has done that it must reject to justify the rest."[525] This is the central claim that Dworkin is concerned with in the passages discussed by Kukathas. The concern is not, as Kukathas claims, that checkerboard statutes create a plurality of neighboring legal systems but rather that *within* one of these local systems fundamental legal issues (Rawls's "constitutional essentials" and "matters of basic justice"[526]) must not be settled arbitrarily, i.e., without recourse to any unifying legal principles and reasoned justification.[527] Now compare what has been said here with Kukathas's initial characterization of what he thinks Dworkin refers to when the rejection of checkerboard solutions is discussed. Kukathas explicitly refers to the abortion issue and claims that what is unacceptable to Dworkin is

---

524 Dworkin 1986, p. 183.
525 Dworkin 1986, p. 184.
526 Rawls 1993, pp. 227–230.
527 This is also the reasons for why, at least from the perspective of integrity, a checkerboard solution ranks below even a morally wrong settlement. With respect to the Alabama example this means that the unprincipled statute, arbitrarily allowing racial discrimination *tout court* in restaurants but outlawing it on buses, ranks below a settlement that allows racial discrimination in buses as well as restaurants and thereby conclusively sides with the principle that allows it. (See Dworkin 1986, p. 182.) However, Dworkin is clear that both legislators and judges must not regard integrity as an absolute value that can never be overridden. The standard of integrity is "not absolutely sovereign over what judges must do at the end of the day," because "other and more powerful aspects of political morality might outweigh this requirement in particular and unusual circumstances" (Dworkin 1986, pp. 218–219).

that laws "might be different from one province, or state within the nation, to the next."[528]

At this point at least Kukathas is attacking a straw man then. Horizontal checkerboards, so to speak, are o.k. with Dworkin as long as self-contained jurisdictions (e.g., US states) conduct their juridified internal affairs on the basis of public principles. However, even if this alternative interpretation of Dworkin's views on checkerboard solutions turns out to be adequate, we also have to consider Kukathas's critique of contemporary liberalism's adherence to vertical integrity. It is certainly true that many liberals object to checkerboard statutes (concerning fundamental rights) that lead to an incoherence between different *levels* of legislation and not merely to such incoherence on one particular level. In order to illustrate the difference between horizontal and vertical integrity, and in order to show in what way liberals are right to insist on both, let us turn to two hypothetical examples. The discussion of these examples shows that vertical integrity and coherence are part of the internal rationality of law that planning creatures like us require to set ends and perform actions. It will also show that such an account of integrity is well compatible with federalist legal structures as long as the latter do not result in contradictory laws addressed to an individual agent.

In both examples we imagine a society similar to the one Kukathas envisions in his *Liberal Archipelago*. There is one overarching umpire "U" on the one hand and two associations/jurisdictions (with their own legal norms) "A" and "B" on the other. In the first example A and B have mutually exclusive legal norms, L_A and L_B. Let us say that L_A and L_B are legal norms concerning painting fences so that L_A says to its addressees (A's association-members) "Fences are to be painted blue but not red" whereas L_B says "Fences are to be painted red but not blue." The umpire for his part issues a fence-painting law too, L_U, "Fences are to be painted either blue or red." The umpire's subjects are all the members of A and B and they are, therefore, subjects to L_U (and are U's citizens).

With respect to this first example a couple of issues, related to Dworkin's notion of integrity, can be illustrated. A first complication and ambiguity that arose concerns the notion of horizontal integrity. There are two varieties of horizontal integrity involved in the example, one within the two associations respectively, the other concerning the interassociational relationship between A and B. Whereas (different from Dworkin's examples of Alabama and Britain)

528 Kukathas 2003, p. 180. A bit further in the text I will present additional, textual, evidence that Dworkin's value of integrity is not incompatible with the kind of checkerboard solution that Kukathas refers to in the quote.

horizontal integrity is respected *within* A and B respectively (*all* of A's citizens are subject to the same laws and the issue of painting fences has been settled in a principled manner there), Kukathas might object that Dworkin cannot be happy with the overall legal structure depicted in the example. After all, since A and B issue mutually exclusive fence-painting laws, but are still both part of the same liberal society (U), this arrangement constitutes a checkerboard solution according to Kukathas's reading of *Law's Empire*.

However, as was mentioned, the violation of this second variety of horizontal integrity is not a problem for Dworkin and he is fairly clear about this. Even with respect to a fundamental issue such as abortion, the value of integrity does not necessarily rule out a pluralistic solution in the liberal archipelago's sprit. He says, explicitly contradicting the passage by Kukathas mentioning abortion and quoted above, "[t]hat suggestion [that the abortion-issue should be decided by each US state and not on the federal level; C.H.] is not itself a checkerboard solution: each state would retain a constitutional duty that its own abortion statute be coherent in principle, and the suggestion offers itself as recognizing independent sovereigns rather than speaking for all together."[529] This passage further supports the reading of Dworkin defended above, according to which horizontal integrity matters within each US state but not between them, in the example under consideration. Horizontal integrity among the states is not a requirement of legislation and adjudication in a liberal and federal order.[530] Applied to our analogous case, the fact that A and B have mutually exclusive fence-painting laws does not in and of itself constitute a condition that liberals have to object to in the name of (horizontal) integrity.

Let us now look at vertical integrity. After all, A and B's citizens are subject to two law-issuing and law-administering authorities. L_A and L_B both cohere with L_U. Dworkin and other liberals will insist that this vertical integrity is re-

---

529 Dworkin 1986, p. 186. It would be unfair not to mention that Dworkin immediately goes on to qualify the statement just made. He notes that "a question of integrity remains" and that, in the actual US case, one has to ask the question related to what is called "vertical integrity" in the text, i.e., how US constitutional norms cohere with the proposed state laws on abortion. However, this qualification does not undermine the more general point that the emergence of 50 fundamentally different abortion laws (some outlawing it completely) does not "itself" constitute a checkerboard solution in Dworkin's sense. And this is enough to undermine Kukathas's reading, according to which contemporary liberalism is incompatible with true legal federalism.

530 Things are of course more complicated especially once citizens of A and B start interacting with one another. For the sake of argument it is assumed that A and B are isolationist associations without any interaction going on. This possibility, while empirically unlikely, is not ruled out by Kukathas's scheme.

spected in a federal system and it is at this point that Kukathas parts company, because of expected conflicts with individual freedom of conscience. A clear passage is the following in which Kukathas addresses Dworkin's notion of a legal order understood as a "community of principle" directly. Kukathas believes that Dworkin's conception of a liberal society "will not tolerate a variety of competing legal authorities except insofar as they are subordinate to the principal authority. It will not readily countenance different legal jurisdictions which uphold different laws on fundamental issues."[531]

The notion of "competing legal authorities" is key here. In order to see that Dworkin is correct to insist that a multilayered legal system must not consist of such competing and incoherent levels of law, let us discuss a second version of the hypothetical example presented above. In this new version all remains the same as in the first version except for association B now issuing L_B^* "Fences are to be painted yellow." Concerning horizontal integrity nothing has changed. L_B^* still satisfies horizontal integrity vis-à-vis B's citizens since all of them are subject to the same legal requirement. L_B^* also stands in the same horizontal relationship with respect to its neighboring jurisdiction A; L_B^* contradicts L_A but, as was argued above, that's not the kind of incoherence that Dworkin is worried about and does not itself present a checkerboard solution concerning the issue of fence-painting legislation.

However, the second version of the example introduces a violation of vertical integrity that is absent in the first. L_B^* competes with L_U in the sense of issuing public norms that contradict U's. If this kind of competition is regarded as characterizing the liberal archipelago then this should give us a reason to reject Kukathas's vision of a liberal society. Vertical integrity is an important feature, not only of our legal and political practices, but even an intricate part of the concept of law itself. First, remember one of the features of the internal rationality of law discussed above, namely the one ruling out contradictory laws.[532] In the discussion of Fuller's eight principles the central claim was that certain formal requirements have to be adhered to if the law is to fulfill its function of guiding practical deliberation and action. It was argued that the rationality-requirements expressed in the eight principles ultimately gain their normative force (addressed at legislators, judges, and, importantly, citizens) from law's role in the process of individual self-constitution.

Without repeating all the details of this argument from public identity and self-constitution we can briefly apply it to the issues of law's integrity and fed-

531 Kukathas 2003, p. 192.
532 Fuller 1969, pp. 65–70.

eralism, thereby showing, once again, why Kukathas's liberal archipelago is erected on premises that undermine its coherence as a political ideal. In a nutshell, vertically competing legal authorities are incompatible with the task of providing the external conditions for self-constituting action. They fail to do so in the same way in which one single authority that issues contradictory norms does. The citizen of B, asking herself what color to paint her fence, does not get a clear and action-guiding answer when inquiring the law that is supposed to structure her interpersonal standing with respect to all others in a reliable and predictable way. A contradictory version of such an external norm-structure is figuring in B's citizens' practical deliberation in the form of providing contradictory principles ("paint the fence yellow" vs. "don't paint the fence yellow").

Since the argument defended in this essay rests on the assumption that individuals constitute themselves into agents with particular practical identities by means of performing actions (and that such a performance is conditional on conclusively setting ends), an extreme version of such an incoherent legal order, ridden by competing and contradictory norms, will at a maximum succeed in causing its subjects "to have a nervous breakdown."[533] Fuller's use of psychological language is adequate here. If a legal "order" were to adopt Kukathas's vision of a federal and multilayered system and adopted as its public fundamental principle and universal policy the idea of "competing legal authorities" this would lead to a weakening of individual agency and not just to the collapse of legal authority. A legal system taking on the form of a vertical checkerboard, so to speak, would indeed undermine the individual agent's ability to maintain a stable and unified public identity. Only an unprincipled set of norms figures in her practical reasoning. This arbitrariness leads to the same consequences as do interpersonal relationships that are not structured by any public norms at all.

Vertical integrity in the sense defended by contemporary liberals is then, contrary to what Kukathas claims, an inherent feature of the ideal of the rule of law that also the liberal archipelago and its constitutive associations have to honor. *If* individual citizens are subject to different legal authorities (as is the case with the associations of the liberal archipelago that acquiesce to L_U) then they must not compete with each other in the sense of issuing contradictory norms as a matter of principle.[534] That this view, concerning the internal rationality of law, does not rule out legal pluralism and federalism has not only been

533 Fuller 1969, p. 66.

534 Things are of course different *if* associations secede from the liberal archipelago and become fully sovereign legal authorities of their own. I have discussed the problems that come with the option of secession (down to the level of the individual agent) at several points and insert a brief final remark on secession at the end of this section.

shown by re-visiting Dworkin's remarks on law's integrity. Moreover, the two versions of the fence-painting example above were supposed to show that a citizen's public identity can be multilayered – neither Dworkin's argument nor mine present any in-principle objection to this kind of identity that citizens of contemporary states have. Citizens are subject to different levels of legislation, law-enforcement, and judicial adjudication that, in order to figure in their practical reasoning in a choice- and action-guiding way, must cohere to a degree that make them reliable conditions for setting and pursuing ends.

Problematic are those situations in which a citizen sees herself confronted with a plurality of legal authorities that issue incompatible but equally binding laws concerning a particular action the citizen is deliberating about. It is of course possible that the authority concerning fence-painting-laws is unambiguously and completely located within the two jurisdictions, A and B, respectively. B would then be authorized to issue whatever fence-painting laws it wants to – simply because U does not issue its own, potentially conflicting, ones.[535] However, if B remains part of the liberal archipelago, this choice is itself a public decision that must cohere with U's public norms (in this case U's remaining silent concerning fence-painting regulation altogether) and to this extent the view defended here adheres to legal centralism. A federal structure has to get clear on the question of what legal and political issues are to be settled by which of the authorities that constitute this structure.[536]

Another way to defend the norm of vertical integrity, and how it constrains federalism, is to pay attention to the fact that we encounter writ-large versions of the rejection of the non-interference claim and the defense of the total law

535 However, notice how this move leads us to the common problem implicit in Kukathas's view and discussed at several points. Relocating the final say concerning fence-painting laws just shifts the problem to a more local level but does not get rid of the problem of ensuring "legal unity," unless we go all the way down to one-man associations (and individualist anarchy). Just because B is now sovereign with respect to a particular legal issue does not dissolve the problem that Kukathas is so worried about, i.e., the latent conflicts between binding public norms and *individual* conscience.

536 For a good illustration of the issue of where to locate legal authority (concerning one specific subject matter of legislation) in the US legal system, see Shapiro 2011, pp. 220–224. Shapiro agrees with a constitutional version of the total law thesis, when he introduces the notion of a "self-certifying planning organization." Such an organization is defined as a rule-issuing social institution that "enjoys a general presumption of validity from all superior planning organizations" (Shaprio 2011, p. 221). In order to fulfill its function as a planning device, a legal system must unambiguously clarify what institutions are such self-certifying entities that enjoy this presumption of validity (e.g., US-states) and which are not (e.g., a condominium board).

thesis at this point. When B is left alone to regulate/not regulate its fence-painting policies this is not the natural default condition of U's non-interference. If association B is embedded in the wider legal order of a liberal society (as Kukathas assumes) then what aspects of its societal condition B is and is not authorized to structure, is always the subject of public justification and choice vis-à-vis U. In order for B's freedom from U's interference to be a lawful (i.e., non-dominated) one their relationship has to be juridified, something that has been done traditionally by adopting a constitution. That even the maximally tolerant liberal archipelago is such a "community of [legal; C.H.] principle," the Dworkinian notion that Kukathas rejects because it exhibits too much of a centralizing tone, is implicit in one of the initial descriptions of his ideal of a liberal society. The liberal archipelago is "a collection of communities (and, so, authorities) *associated under laws* which recognize the freedom of the individual to associate as, and with whom, they wish."[537] Ensuring that the non-interference amongst communities (as well as individuals) is not a contingent and unpredictable state of affairs is the constitutional law's job. The non-domination claim, that was presented as a supplement to the non-interference claim above, can be applied to the associations of the archipelago. Kukathas recognizes the need for the rule of law at many points but he neither fully acknowledges the fundamental reasons underlying this need ("the human plight") nor is he willing to accept the implications that come with the unavoidable task of having to satisfy it (i.e., satisfying vertical integrity among the authorities an individual agent is subject to).

Furthermore, in line with the total law thesis, U's authority does extend *into* the associations A and B in the same way in which Dad's, seemingly "private," command directed at Billy is not uttered in a legal vacuum. The historical fact that A and B are often the "prior" units, that at a later point unite into one liberal archipelago (just think of the *United* States and the European *Union*) must not be confused with the issue of conceptual priority. The conceptual point rests on the claim that once multiple authorities address *one* individual there is pressure on these authorities, originating in law's nature as a rational planning institution, to structure their relationships on a legal basis ("under law"). Just because the archipelago's umpire might come "later" in the historical process does not in itself settle the question of where ultimate legal authority rests once a variety of authorities are in place.

Kukathas discusses this issue concerning what was called the "priority of the public" (in the sense of a priority of the law enforced by the modern state) in

537 Kukathas 2003, p. 19 (my emphasis).

the following passage in which he criticizes Brian Barry for uncritically assuming that final authority regarding a broad range of issues rests squarely with the liberal state. Kukathas admits that "[i]n one sense, *of course*, final authority will rest with the state to the extent that, since it is charged with keeping the peace among communities, it is up to it to determine what is needed to keep the peace."[538] Kukathas does qualify this statement by insisting on the importance of the separation and devolution of power(s) and the fact that a liberal state is itself constrained by law, defining ideas of (classical) liberalism.[539] Most importantly, however, Kukathas is quick to point out that, contrary to Barry, the umpire's final authority does not extend into the associations' internal affairs.

Still, the statement about the umpire's monopoly with respect to at least the issue of peace and the determination of "what is necessary to determine what is needed to keep it"[540] is important in making again clear that Kukathas's vision of a liberal society shares a critical feature with his contemporary liberal nemeses, Rawls, Kymlicka, and Dworkin.[541] It is the liberal legal and constitutional order (the state/umpire) that authoritatively determines what is needed to keep the archipelago stable and internally peaceful. Even the liberal umpire's powers, even if defined much more narrowly than Barry's social democratic state, must be codified in something like a political constitution in order to be nonarbitrary and predictable. Devolution, federal structures, and the "principle of subsidiarity"[542] (as long as they do not result in providing reasons for mutually

538 Kukathas 2003, p. 147 (my emphasis). The passage from which the quoted sentence is taken, is unclear. The second half of the paragraph makes clear that Kukathas rejects Barry's view, according to which it is *obvious* that final authority must rest with the state as opposed to the associations. However, the sentence quoted ("of course"), since it refers to the state being "charged with keeping the peace among communities" and having the power "to determine what is needed to keep the peace," has Kukathas admit that "[i]n one sense" the umpire/state *is* the final authority in the liberal archipelago, at least with respect to the issue of upholding peace. This reading is also supported by the transition in the paragraph beginning with "[l]eaving this complication aside." *This* complication, I take it, is the special case of the umpire's monopolized power to regulate interassociational peace. I am indebted to Fred Miller for paying attention to the broader context of this quote.

539 See Pincione 2011.

540 This formulation is vague. The umpire might deem many things "to be needed" to ensure interassociational peace (who decides whether or not the umpire interprets this privilege correctly?). This is just one of the many points at which Kukathas's description of the liberal archipelago reminds one of, for example, the complex relationship between the federal government of the United States (the umpire) and the 50 states (the associations).

541 One must not forget that the umpire is in charge also of enforcing the right to exit.

542 The principle of subsidiarity is a central and binding tenet in the EU's *Treaty on European Union*: "Under the principle of subsidiarity, in areas which do not fall within its exclusive

exclusive courses of the citizens' actions) are not incompatible with the account of legal institutions presented here. The total law thesis and the rejection of the non-interference claim highlight, however, that there are limits to legal pluralism that have their source not just in practical issues (consistent property and contractual rights, for example). Rather, the archipelago's associations and more importantly all its citizens (understood as agents who are subject to multiple action-guiding structures) depend for a non-dominated existence on the stability provided by enforceable law.

To conclude, there is actually much that the argument from self-constitution and practical identity defended here shares with Kukathas's view. His criticisms of strong communitarian visions of national cohesion and of the enforcement of perfectionist public norms by the state are well compatible with the austere conception of the citizen qua legal subject presented in this book.[543] In the societal condition, those who are subjects to coercive legal institutions understand themselves as planning agents and subject to practical norms that necessarily have a public side to them which defines and regulates each individual's sphere of action. A thick and rich conception of political community is not necessary for the external stability and predictability that agents require to develop and sustain a normative self-conception by means of setting ends and

competence, the Union shall act only if and insofar as the objectives of the proposed action cannot be sufficiently achieved by the Member States, either at central level or at regional and local level, but can rather, by reason of the scale or effects of the proposed action, be better achieved at Union level" (European Union 2008, p.18). The crucial point to emphasize here is that the subsidiarity principle is itself endorsed and executed by the European Union and its institutions. It is the latter that ultimately has the authority to decide what issues and tasks are covered by this principle and which are not. The case of the European Union is more complicated though since individual nation states (especially the strongest and most influential ones) in turn determine much of the European Union's policy. This might create similar problems in the liberal archipelago: will the umpire itself not be subject to pressures from the powerful and influential member-associations to adjust its laws according to their preferences? For a similar response, see Spinner-Halev 2005.

543 I am indebted to Albert Dzur for reminding me that much more would have to be said about the relationship between the account of public identity (and the way in which legal institutions condition individuality) and communitarianism, especially as presented by Charles Taylor and Michael Sandel. I hope that the remarks in the text help clarifying the main claim with respect to communitarian critiques of liberalism, i.e., that, despite my adherence to a view that emphasizes the interplay between individuality and societal norms, the conception of public identity defended here will be way too thin to excite communitarians and other advocates of robust notions of political solidarity and loyalty. The "community of principle," membership in which is defended as constitutive of agency, is first and foremost a legal community (but does not, of course, preclude the evolution of much thicker public norms and identities).

performing self-constituting actions. I therefore have sympathies for Kukathas's worries and criticisms directed at mainstream liberalism when he reminds Rawls, Dworkin, Galston, and Kymlicka that the liberal rule of law's purpose must not necessarily be the active promotion of substantial moral conceptions and ways of life. Promoting such collective moral ends and purposes (above and beyond what is necessary for individual self-constitution) is certainly not sufficiently supported by the argument defended in this essay (the promotion of such ends is not, however, ruled out by that argument either).

Remember the example of the French *niqab* controversy, discussed in Chapter 1.[544] What does the argument from self-constitution recommend with respect to this issue and the substantial egalitarian republicanism that the French government has appealed to when justifying the ban of wearing the *niqab* in public places? The answer that can be submitted must remain general and abstract. As the discussion of Fuller's account of the internal rationality of law suggested, the argument from self-constitution does not provide a rich enough basis for judging specific laws as just or unjust ones. The *niqab* ban might well be unjustified all things considered but the jurisprudential argument defended above does not provide the kind of moral basis that is needed to establish that claim (or its opposite). The self-constitution account has merely insisted that even if such a ban is not in place, the identities of those who wear a *niqab* (and those who expect them to do so) are constituted under legal norms that permit doing so and that are authorized by public institutions. This was the central thought of the total law thesis. It is merely in this very thin sense of shared legal practices then that this account overlaps with the Rousseauian idea of a general will that figures prominently in the French self-understanding, motivating the policy criminalizing wearing the *niqab*. As long as not outlawing this religious practice does not amount to a complete annihilation of the external conditions of agency (which would make "acquiescing" in Kukathas's sense impossible), the argument from self-constitution, since it remains on such a general and abstract level, remains silent on the specific content of the legal norms that define what is and what is not left to individuals' choices in the private realm.

Kukathas does ask a question, however, his negative answer to which seems to suggest that his view is not that readily compatible with the view presented here:

> The centrally important point of contention is the relationship between the individual and the community and, more specifically, the question of whether the individual is shaped or

---

544 See section 1.1.

> constituted by the community, or whether the community is something to which individuals merely belong or are attached. The issue here is one of identity.[545]

It is with respect to passages like this one that the argument defended here seems to be at odds with Kukathas's liberal archipelago. But is this actually the case? The argument presented in this essay indeed insists that in an abstract and formal sense the individual is constituted by her *legal* community's public norms and principles (i.e., its laws). However, even with respect to the question concerning the relationship between individual and community, the gap between this view and Kukathas's is much smaller than it seems. This is notable when Kukathas briefly comments on the debate between liberals and communitarians that has circled around the question of the extent to which individuals are constituted by their communities.[546] The result of this debate, most notably between Sandel and Rawls, is that communitarians and liberals have more or less ended up agreeing that individuality is the result of life within specific, often overlapping, attachments. However, this is only partly so. At the end of his discussion of the notion of community, Kukathas seems to agree with this qualified view, when he says that "community membership is only partly constitutive of identity; [...]."[547]

The self-constitution account of legal communities is perfectly compatible with such a qualified view about the relationship between individual and community. It would be bizarre to claim that the principles defining a legal order, characteristic of life in the modern state, fully and completely constitute the practical identities of its citizens. The enforceable public normative principles (the law, in the modern state) that provide the external preconditions for non-dominated self-constituting action are *necessary* for having a robust practical identity in the societal condition; yet these principles are by no means sufficient to account for all the features of our individual practical identities.

That Kukathas's framework is not entirely incompatible with the argument from public identity, has to do also with his definition of political community (and community more generally). He says that "[a] political community is essentially *an association of individuals who share an understanding of what is public and what is private within that polity*."[548] As was briefly mentioned above, when the total law thesis was presented,[549] the existence of a private sphere (with its

545 Kukathas 2003, p. 167.
546 Kukathas 2003, p. 168.
547 Kukathas 2003, p. 171.
548 Kukathas 2003, pp. 171–172.
549 See section 7.2.

own identity-constituting norms and principles) is not denied at all when the law is identified as the means by which the private sphere is defined and delimited in a public way. Actually, Kukathas makes a very similar observation when he notes that "a matter is of public interest or concern if it is something that is *generally regarded* as an appropriate subject of attention by the political institutions of the society."[550] In the modern state, with its characteristic feature of the rule of public law, the instrument that is used to formulate and settle what is "generally regarded" as the limit between the public and the private spheres is itself cast in a legal (very often, constitutional) form.

The total law thesis merely insisted on that point and on its action-theoretical corollary, i.e., that even actions *within* the private sphere bear the mark of those public norms that circumscribe the "assured free spheres" of the citizens' private lives. Such a claim does not imply that actions within that sphere are *fully* determined by these public norms – that would amount to a totalitarian version of the public identity argument indeed. Kukathas is therefore right when he says: "In recognizing this [that there is a private sphere; C.H.], communities make clear that they are, ultimately, only partly involved in the identities of the individuals who make them up."[551] Again, the only thing that the constitutivist view adds to this statement is that the recognition of this private sphere that Kukathas talks about must itself be a public practice and in the modern state this collective and shared recognition is incorporated into legal protections.

The discussion of Kukathas's insightful work, that has motivated this entire project, can thus be concluded in the following way. It is in fact the case that the legal orders that modern individuals find themselves subjected to partly constitute their identities as agents. By means of (necessarily) incorporating public norms into their practical reasoning when deliberating about the actions they perform, they turn into the particular agents they are. The public norms, the law in the case of modern citizens, inform how an individual perceives herself as such an agent when she successfully sets and pursues ends in a stable and predictable environment (knowing that others will do the same as a matter of non-contingent public right). For individual human beings in the societal condition this incorporation of the norms that settle and clarify one's standing vis-à-vis all others is inevitable. By means of performing actions in a world that she does not populate alone, then, the norms that first-personally determine what an agent considers to be her practical options, necessarily exhibit this public element.

---

550 Kukathas 2003, p. 172 (my emphasis).
551 Kukathas 2003, p. 171.

The realization of this necessity and non-optionality is the element of an agent's self-understanding that constitutes her public identity as a citizen – an agent performing actions under law.

Conclusion

The purpose of this essay was to present a particular conception of citizenship and to defend it against views that regard the modern state (the institutional arrangement central to this notion of citizenship) as neither necessary nor desirable. The constitutivist and Neo-Kantian strategy employed in the previous nine chapters conceives of citizenship as a distinctively modern instantiation of what has been called a public identity. To have such an identity is necessary for all of us because it presents the answer to a problem that we cannot escape: As human beings we face the inevitable task of leading (as opposed to merely undergoing) a life and to constitute ourselves as unified agents in the course of performing actions.[552] A unified agent is one whose practical standpoint (her first personal perspective on who she is) consists of a well-structured and coherent ensemble of practical principles that guide her practical deliberation and action across time. The only way to acquire these principles and to maintain the unity as a practical agent is to perform actions. Inspired by Christine Korsgaard's programmatic slogan "action is self-constitution," this book looked at the *external* conditions that have to be in place for the possibility of engaging in action so understood and, hence, for the possibility of successfully constituting individual agency.

The constructivist process of employing practical principles in one's deliberation, choices, and actions is not just dependent on the adherence to certain internal standards of self-constitution (the two Kantian imperatives); moreover, and this was the main feature of the argument for the public identity claim defended in Chapter 5, the environment external to the agent too has to be of a "legislated" and "juridified" from. It is at this point that the critique of anar-

---

552 For a challenge of this claim about the inescapability of the task of agency that has not been dealt with at all in this essay, see Velleman 2006a and, of course, Parfit 1984, Part 3. Velleman addresses the view that is taken as a starting point in this exploration directly: "Philosophers as diverse as Christine Korsgaard and Daniel Dennett have claimed that the self is something that we must invent or construct. But these philosophers believe that inventing or constructing a self is a wonderful accomplishment of which we should be proud, whereas the Buddhists believe that it is a tragic mistake that we should try to undo" (Velleman 2006a, p. 2). I am indebted to Jonathan Miller, and his expertise, for the following written comment: "Buddhists do not deny that the self exists in a conventional sense, and indeed it is precisely this conventional self which enables moral evaluation of persons. Even an enlightened being such as the Buddha still constitutes himself in the conventional sense, so there may be less of a gap between Buddhism and these other theories than there seems to be at first."

chism (in the broad sense employed in Part 2)[553] is supposed to get traction because a world without any such external structure lacks a necessary prerequisite for action and, hence, of a unified practical standpoint. Part of the task of providing the kind of external stability and predictability necessary for action (especially for *setting* and *willing* the ends that actions necessarily involve) is taken care of by nature and its regularities. However, as creatures who conceive of ourselves as radically free (i.e., even free to undermine each other's action attempts) humans face the unique problem of having to legislate their interpersonal standing and relationships vis-à-vis one another. A legal system (Kant's "rightful condition") provides a distinct solution to this problem and does so in a particular way, namely in the form of norms that are created and administered by a public authority.

We took as our starting point an extensive discussion of Kukathas's critique of contemporary liberalism (and of the idea of a unified legal system in the form of the Weberian state). The major objection to Kukathas's alternative view of society, the liberal archipelago, was that his attempt to overcome the liberal dilemma (social unity vs. freedom of conscience) undermines the public authority that a legal system rests upon, which in turn amounts to undermining the external conditions necessary for unified agency and public identity as defended in Parts 2 and 3 of the book. If freedom of conscience and the right to exit legal associations trump societal unity unconditionally, the liberal archipelago necessarily rests on a contingent basis – the private choices of its inhabitants remain sovereign, rendering incoherent, for example, rights to property, contracts, etc.

The liberal archipelago (and its possible end-state, i.e., individualist anarchism) never gets us out of the state of nature and into, what Kant calls, a "rightful condition." The latter is a condition which, it must be admitted, might end up conflicting with what some individuals consider (or claim to consider) dictates of their conscience. The balancing act between social (or rather, legal) unity in the form of a minimally homogenous legal order on the one hand and respect for individual conscience on the other remains a continuous and difficult task that (liberal) politics has to deal with. Contrary to what Kukathas concludes in the face of this difficulty, however, this essay argued that we cannot simply give up on the goal of unity entirely and thereby overcome the dilemma he so sharply identified. Individuality, selfhood, agency, and freedom themselves require a minimally coherent and unified social environment. And in order to achieve such a condition individuals must "externalize" certain aspects

---

553 See fn. 508.

of their private wills. A (necessarily) public authority that legislates and executes law on the one hand and that provides binding adjudication concerning private disputes on the other does just that.

One of the most remarkable historical examples of such a process remains the "We the People" moment in American history (notwithstanding the fact that, at that time, the actual "We" excluded too many that should not have been). Even if many Americans will probably find a Kantian and Rousseauian interpretation of this moment foreign,[554] this essay tried to strengthen the point that the endorsement of a political *constitution* does not merely amount to the creation and establishment of certain institutional arrangements (though it certainly does that too). The public act of putting themselves under the authority of shared institutions and legal norms is also the moment in which individuals constitute themselves into agents of a new kind, agents with a public identity that they could not have had before that act.[555] The practical principles composing the constitution and the associated legal order are those features of their self-constituting actions that are now performed under the authority and protection of these public institutions. By means of endorsing the practical principles of their constitution, the inhabitants of the thirteen colonies did not merely constitute a set of institutions; they constituted themselves as American citizens with a particular public identity.

I want to conclude by briefly drawing attention to the relationship of the account defended here to some competing lines of argument in support of the necessity of law and the modern Weberian state. This will help to highlight the kind of contribution this exploration is making. The claim is not that these diverse alternative accounts of justifying the idea of public regulation are incorrect, but rather that they fail to see one important rationale for why a coherent and consistent system of law is needed and has emerged in the course of human history.[556] The distinctive nature of the constitutivist picture concerning the

554 See Cushing 2006, pp. 229–230.

555 Of course, like all historical illustrations of the self-constitution model, also the American one shows that the main conceptual claims defended in this essay do not apply in their ideal and pure form to actual cases. The 13 colonies, uniting and constituting themselves into the United States, were themselves already legal orders and the individual identities constituted within these public institutions are part of a process as opposed to popping into existence out of nowhere.

556 For an illuminating account of invisible hand versions of the emergence of the state (as represented by Nozick's Lockean argument for the minimal state), see Gaus 2011. A possible future research project, expanding on the constitutivist model, would look at the relationship between the account of legal ordering presented in this essay and invisible hand/spontaneous

relationship between public institutions and individual agency becomes especially visible when we consider consequentialist (e.g., utilitarian) and instrumentalist (also Lockean natural-rights justifications of the state count as such) accounts of the advantages of maintaining institutions that provide security and stability.[557] The non-private nature of law-creating and administering institutions, that was defended along Kantian lines in this essay, necessarily remains an empirically contingent feature when the rule of law is considered a neutral instrument, employed to enable individuals to efficiently pursue their pre-institutionally conceived goals and projects. One corollary of such an instrumentalist account is that the requirement to establish and maintain public authorities remains conditional on empirical facts such as those concerning human motivation (to reliably cooperate or not,...) and resource-related features of the environment (limited scarcity,...). If alternative ways of structuring the societal realm and our interpersonal standing (such as Rothbard's regime of privatized legality) turn out to do a more *efficient* job in producing a pre-institutionally defined state of affairs, for example a maximum of aggregate welfare, then also entirely non-juridified solutions to the distinctly human challenge of action in the presence of others seem sufficient.

The constitutivist alternative is distinctively non-consequentialist and non-instrumentalist. As discussed in Chapter 4, there is of course a sense in which even the constitutivist argument in support of social institutions *is* consequentialist in the "minimal sense" discussed there. We are required to juridify our relationships *in order to* create an environment that provides the external conditions for attaining the highest degree of individual agency and identity. If consequentialism is conceived that broadly, every theory (also Kant's and Aristotle's ethics, for example) count as its instances.[558] However, the distinctive point

order explanations of how the Weberian state emerges *without* anyone directly intending its creation.

557 See Ripstein 2009, pp. 7–11 and 52–56. "Bentham's utilitarianism provides a particularly stark example of this idea. He argues that the purpose of legal and political institutions, [...], is to approximate a moral result – the greatest happiness of the greatest number – which could in principle be specified without any reference to institutions or rules. [...] The only basis for setting up legal institutions is that they are likely to produce the right results, as identified by external criteria, more often than they get the wrong ones." And natural rights theories "claim that persons have fully formed moral rights in a state of nature, and [...] the only legitimate purpose of legal institutions is to solve problems of self-preference or insufficient knowledge in the application of these rights to particulars. [...] [I]f people knew more, cared more about the moral considerations that apply independently of institutions, or were more fair-minded in their judgments about particulars, legal institutions would not be required at all."

558 See Brown 2011 and Portmore 2011 .

about the constitutivist approach is that the public principles, that enable individuals to set ends and pursue actions, are partly but necessarily defining the very ends and activities that are engaged in under/within them. As beings who are inevitably entangled in the process of constituting themselves in the presence of other agents, the commitment to upholding some set of public norms is built into that very activity in the same way in which a commitment to the logical form of *modus ponens* is built into the process of theoretical reasoning. Sure, we can also say that the most fundamental rules of logical inference are a good instrument and mechanism to "produce" good cognitive consequences, i.e., holding as many true beliefs as possible; however, this is not the same as recognizing that the very same norms are constitutive principles of the subject engaged in the activity of reasoning. In the same way, this essay argued, public institutions and norms are not merely instruments employed to efficiently produce as much as possible a pre-institutionally determined state of affairs.[559]

The relevance of the distinctive features of the view defended here becomes especially evident when one considers the in-principle reservations that the constitutivist has with respect to a full privatization of the legal order.[560] Even if private arrangements turned out superior according to other, possibly very important, parameters (such as relieving pressure from a state's budget, for example), these arrangements cannot, by definition, provide the kind of public standing that was identified with Kant as a genuine external condition for unified agency as described above. In the complete absence of public entities that, for example, enforce contracts and authoritatively settle disputes concerning their content, even the most efficient privatized law system falls short of establishing the status of legal persons who pursue their actions and life plans as a matter of right. Of course, and we have seen that too many times in the history of the modern state, the monopolization of legitimate violence that was defended here as the necessary feature of a public environment that renders individuals independent from the good will of all other private parties, is at the same time the source of its greatest danger. When public institutions are used in the perverted way of promoting exclusively private interests, then this is rightly identified by the constitutivist as the paradigmatic instance of corruption. Since those institutions that establish and maintain the public standpoint are run by mortal and fallible individuals, this non-public exploitation of the state-apparatus remains

---

559 See Korsgaard 2009, pp. xii–xiii.

560 See Rothbard 1973 and Stringham 2007.

a constant threat to the agency of the law's subjects.[561] Obviously, in a thoroughly privatized world this kind of abuse of *public* power can indeed not happen; however, individuals who fail to enter a rightful condition and do not establish a juridical state wrong one another in a different, deeper, sense. In one of the *Doctrine of Right's* critical passages, this thought takes center stage:

> Given the intention to be and to remain in this state of externally lawless freedom, human beings do *one another* no wrong at all when they feud among themselves; [...] But in general they do wrong in the highest degree by willing to be and to remain in a condition that is not rightful, that is, in which no one is assured of what is his against violence.[562]

The constitutivist argument defended in this essay allows to read passages like this one in a new light. Applied to the issue of private law associations – in principle a legitimate contender for the consequentialist/instrumentalist about legal institutions mentioned above – Kant's point is that there is no wronging involved in case property and contractual arrangements are unilaterally dissolved in a condition in which merely private actors engage in them. As discussed in Chapter 7, every unilateral attempt to put others under enforceable requirements to abstain from insisting on their external freedom to use specific objects, necessarily fails. Agreements between private actors, in the absence of a public authority, cannot overcome these problems, the moral stringency of, for example, promises notwithstanding. Property and contract qua legal relationships can only put private parties under mutual obligations when an institution outside of these parties stands ready to apply the norms of a public legal system to the particular case at hand. The complete privatization of a legal order would be tantamount to regressing into a condition in which individuals are exclusively subject to others' private unilateral judgments and choices.[563] The

---

561 Kukathas is certainly right to recommend federalism and the separation of powers (very much in Kant's sense) as an important remedy against this inherent problem of the Weberian state. As discussed in Chapter 9, the view defended in this work does not have any problem with these suggestions – as long as they do not amount to a market-style competition amongst law-makers and enforcers. It is, however, exactly the latter that Kukathas and Rothbard allow (and advocate).

562 MM 6:308.

563 Again, Gaus's analysis of Nozick's path-dependent (and invisible hand) account of the state presents a different perspective on the status and relationship of individuals in a condition of pure private morality. (See Gaus 2011, pp. 117–119.) Importantly, Nozick's account of the state gets off the ground only if a robust and comprehensive Lockean "moral filter" is employed with respect to these relationships and interactions that then, unintentionally, result in the emergence of the minimal state. It is, of course, these assumptions that the Kantian does not share. Gaus summarizes Nozick's account: "The legitimate state is an emergent pattern

wrongdoing involved in the refusal to enter a juridical state that Kant refers to is such "in the highest degree" because it violates the one thing we owe to each other even in the state of nature, namely to put our status as free agents into the hands of a public authority that acts in the name of all who are its subject. The argument defended here (especially in Chapter 6) showed that this Kantian point can be spelled out in the framework of the external conditions of action and agency.

Rothbardian libertarians, for example, will insist that the "services" of legal authorization and adjudication can be provided by a third-party arbitrator that has been agreed to by the participating parties in a purely private contract.[564] However, it is exactly this private-contract solution that the Kantian must reject. More generally, this rejection is based on the observation that the very private "contract," supposed to establish the office of the third-party arbitrator, already *presupposes* what it claims to establish in the first place, namely conclusive contractual rights and, hence, a rightful condition of publicly established and enforceable norms. The Kantian claims that "[...] the creation of a rightful condition cannot require a private transaction of any sort, because the rightful condition is the only context in which procedures can be valid [...]."[565] Helga Varden summarizes another related Kantian line of criticism directed at the attempt of privately establishing legal institutions (there are many more):

> [T]here may arise conflicts over whether an agreed-upon arbiter performs his duty. In this case, the parties need another arbitrator to solve the dispute about whether or not the first arbiter appropriately exercises his entrusted task – resulting in an infinite regress of arbitration. The third-party, private solution therefore is not sufficient for *enforceable* contract right: it amounts to a contractual solution to the problem of contracts, which merely generates the contractual problem once again.[566]

Moreover, although economic rationality and self-interested market-behavior suggest that private parties will do both, enter and stick to their agreements, this does not solve the problem the constitutivist is concerned with. It is certainly right that it would be in the economic self-interest of, for example, private security companies to serve *all* of those who are willing and able to pay for their services. However, also these economic considerations (and let us grant that

produced by the prosaic actions by reasonable and rational Lockeans" (Gaus 2011, p. 138). (See also section 7.1 of this book.)

564 See Rothbard 1973. Thanks to Jonathan Miller for urging me to make more explicit the Kantian objections to Rothbard's version of anarchism.

565 Ripstein 2009, p. 190.

566 Varden 2008, pp. 20–21.

they are adequate) are not sufficient to overcome the problem that this investigation emphasized and the reason for why this is so highlights the in-principle deficiency of a purely private solution to the problem of societal ordering. Imagine the case of a stateless condition in which private law agencies refuse to serve a certain subgroup of the population – for whatever reason. According to Kant, none of these private agencies is required to serve the members of the group in question. (Unless, of course, there is some legal regulation in place that coerces them to do so. But then we are, of course, already talking about the juridified condition.) Again, it is not denied here that there are extremely compelling economic incentives for each of the private agencies to provide the service for this particular group; however, it is the condition of remaining subject to the private wills of others that constitutes "the wrong in the highest degree" that Kant talks about. In the absence of a juridified condition that establishes what rights and obligations come with being the entity of a law agency the exclusion of certain individuals as customers is nothing a private party can be justifiably blamed for. Also remember that the sheer possibility of ending up in the same position as the minority in our example has an *actual* effect on the status of all the current customers. They remain exclusively subjected to their provider's choices (as do the providers to their customer's by the way). It is the disappearance of this condition that the option of entering a rightful condition presents and which at the same time reveals the in principle difference between a citizen and a customer.[567]

The important instrumental benefits (solving coordination problems, overcoming the issue of bad character by threatening punishment,...) of juridifying our relationships are important arguments in support of establishing a structure of legally enforceable rights and obligations; however, the constitutivist strategy strove to find an even more stringent and non-contingent justification for the same institutional arrangements. It is hoped that this book highlighted such an argument, one that is not dependent for its validity on future developments in economics, psychology, and other empirical sciences. It is the features of hu-

567 Of course, one might reply, the history of the state clearly shows that *it* has been the worst perpetrator of discrimination and exclusion from legal standing. That is true, but the point is that in the case of the state the Kantian framework has the resources for showing that a wrong is involved when a legal order refuses to acknowledge some of its subjects as legal ones (after all, the discriminating state fails to act in accordance with the omnilateral will of all of those individuals that constitute it). A private actor in the Kantian state of nature, on the other hand, cannot be so charged (in the same way in which a private company cannot be coerced to do business with specific clients or groups of clients); what it can be charged with though is the refusal to enter a rightful condition.

man agency and our nature as individuals in need of a coherent identity that ultimately necessitates the answer to Kukathas's challenge that insisted on a minimal degree of homogeneity in the social realm. The specific (moral) qualities and the details of the processes of spelling out the features of this homogeneity (direct vs. representative democracy, the role of judicial review, etc.) have not been the subject of this essay. Especially the controversial details concerning the specification of the essential ideas of property and contractual rights, for example, have been bracketed since they are the subject matter of political morality and of political deliberation. Given Kukathas's correct observation that pluralism about the right and the good is a social fact that is here to stay, the straining processes of politically negotiating the external norms of self-constitution is an inescapable task – simply because the activity of leading a human life in the presence of others is. Also the inhabitants of the liberal archipelago cannot evade this challenge.

Recall the reflections on the French *niqab* controversy, discussed in section 1.1 and "resolved" in section 9.2. A distinguishing feature of the self-constitution account is that it presented a mere formal reply to the conflicting claims that the parties to this dispute often submit. On the one side are people like Kukathas who consider it an unacceptable violation of free conscience for a legal order to prescribe republican and egalitarian norms. On the other side are those, like Rawls, who claim that some minimal consensus concerning justice must be upheld in order for a stable political society to exist. The constitutivist alternative agrees and disagrees with both sides of the dispute: while a (moral) consensus concerning justice is in fact not required for individuals to lead *some* form of life in the societal condition, a shared consensus concerning *some* public norms is always needed and a necessary component of any solution to the inescapable challenge of self-constitution in the presence of others. The worry concerning Kukathas's view was that his premise concerning the option of exiting associations (the liberal state included) undermines the possibility of even this minimal (non-moral) consensus. The constitutivist account, maybe exactly because it is located between Kukathas's and Rawls's positions, cannot provide a clear cut answer to the question of whether or not the French *niqab* ban is justified all things considered. It can submit, however, that there is simply no way around the task of settling this question some way or the other and in a *public* manner (Kant's "omnilateral authorization"[568]). Among other ideas, Hayek's notion of a

568 Ripstein 2009, p. 24.

legally created and assured "free sphere" was discussed in order to illustrate the inescapability of this task.[569]

The point established in this work was more abstract and on a meta-level with respect to these specific political and legal debates: a full specification of legal rights, obligations, and of our status as legal subjects more generally (all parts of the set of public principles that agents need in order to perform actions as a matter of a publicly acknowledged entitlement), is inconclusive if merely conducted between two (or more) private individuals. It was submitted that Kukathas's monolithic and unconditional defense of freedom of conscience results in a variety of exit rights that amounts to a full privatization of these interpersonal prerequisites of individual agency. The specific moral qualities of the public arrangements in question and many related issues have to be dealt with at other occasions when the constitutivist picture gets further developed into a comprehensive theory of society and politics.

569 See section 7.2.

References

Kant's works: References to Kant's works are given by the page numbers of the relevant volume of *Kant's gesammelte Schriften*. For the translations quoted, see this section's entries for "Kant."

G	*Groundwork of the Metaphysics of Morals*
MM	*The Metaphysics of Morals*
PP	*Perpetual Peace*
TP	"On the common saying: That may be correct in theory, but it is of no use in practice"
WE	"What is Enlightenment?"

Adorno (2002 (1944)), Theodor W. and Max Horkheimer: *Dialectic of Enlightenment: Philosophical Fragments*. Edited by Gunzelin Schmid Noerr. Translated by Edmund Jephcott. New York NY, Cambridge University Press.

Agnew (2009), John: *Globalization and Sovereignty*. Lanham MD, Rowman and Littlefield.

Allan (2001), Trevor R.S.: *Constitutional Justice*. New York NY, Oxford University Press.

Anderson-Gold (2009), Sharon: "The Cosmopolitan Foundations of the (Kantian) State", in: *Contemporary Readings in Law and Social Justice*. Vol. 1, No. 1, pp. 20–27.

Apel (2004), Karl-Otto: "Kant, Hegel, and the Contemporary Question Concerning the Normative Foundations of Morality and Right", in: Robert Pippin and Otfried Höffe (eds.): *Hegel on Ethics and Politics*, pp. 49–77.

Applbaum (2007), Arthur Isak: "Forcing A People to Be Free", in: *Philosophy and Public Affairs*, Vol. 35, No. 4, pp. 359–400.

Arendt (1976), Hannah: *The Origins of Totalitarianism*. New York NY, Harcourt.

Aroles (2007), Serge: *L'Enigme des Enfants-Loups*. Paris, Edition Publibook.

Auxter (1981), Thomas: "Kant's Conception of the Private Sphere", in: *The Philosophical Forum*, Vol. 12, No. 4, pp. 295–310.

Babbitt (1984), Susan E.: "Personal Integrity, Politics, and Moral Imagination", in: Samantha Brennan et al. (eds.): *A Question of Values*, pp. 107–131.

Bader (2011), Ralf M. and John Meadowcroft (eds.): *The Cambridge Companion to Nozicks* Anarchy, State, and Utopia. New York NY, Cambridge University Press.

Baer (2001), Josette: "Book Review: Bird's *The Myth of Liberal Individualism*", in: *Ethical Theory and Moral Practice*, Vol. 4, pp. 191–192.

Ball (2003), Terence (ed.): *The Federalist. With Letters of Brutus*. New York NY, Cambridge University Press.

Barandalla (2011), Ana and Michael Ridge: "Function and Self-Constitution: How to make something of yourself without being all that you can be. A commentary on Christine Korsgaard's The Constitution of Agency and Self-Constitution", in: *Analysis*, Vol. 72, No. 2, pp. 364–380.

Barry (2001), Brian: *Culture and Equality: An Egalitarian Critique of Multiculturalism*. Cambridge UK, Polity Press.

Bauman (1989), Zygmunt: *Modernity and the Holocaust*. Ithaca NY, Cornell University Press.

Baumeister (2006), Andrea: "Book Review: Kukathas's *The Liberal Archipelago*", in: *Ethnic and Racial Studies*, Vol. 29, No. 4, pp. 749–752.

Baumgartner (1993), M. P.: "On the Overlegalized Conception of Modern Society", in: *Contemporary Sociology*, Vol. 22, No. 3, pp. 336–337.

Baumgarth (1978), William P.: "Hayek and Political Order: The Rule of Law", in: *Journal of Libertarian Studies*, Vol. 2, No. 1, pp. 11–28.

Baynes (1989), Kenneth: "Kant on Property Rights and the Social Contract", in: *The Monist*, Vol. 72, pp. 433–453.

Beiner (2010), Ronald: "Paradoxes in Kant's Account of Citizenship", in: Gorana Ognjenovic (ed.): *Responsibility in Context: Perspectives*, pp. 19–34.

Benhabib (2004), Seyla: *The Rights of Others: Aliens, Residents, and Citizens*. New York NY, Cambridge University Press.

Benson (1990), Bruce L.: *The Enterprise of Law: Justice Without the State*. San Francisco CA, Pacific Research Institute for Public Policy.

Bentham (1843), Jeremy: *The Works of Jeremy Bentham*. Vol. 2, Part 2, Edinburgh, William Tait.

Berlin (2002 (1969)), Isaiah: *Liberty: Incorporating Four Essays On Liberty*. New York NY, Oxford University Press.

Berlin (2003 (1952)), Isaiah: *Freedom and Its Betrayal: Six Enemies of Human Liberty*. Princeton NJ, Princeton University Press.

Bernstein (2010), Alyssa: "Book Review: Ripstein's *Force and Freedom*", in: *Journal of the History of Philosophy*, Vol. 48, No. 4, pp. 531–532.

Bertea (2009), Stefano: *The Normative Claim of Law*. Portland OR, Hart Publishing.

Bertea (2011) Stefano and Georgios Pavlakos (eds.): *New Essays on the Normativity of Law*. Portland OR, Hart Publishing.

Bicchieri (2006), Cristina: *The Grammar of Society. The Nature and Dynamics of Social Norms*. New York NY, Cambridge University Press.

Bierce (2008 (1890)), Ambrose: *The Complete Short Stories of Ambrose Bierce*. Stilwell KS, Digireads.

Bird (1999), Colin: *The Myth of Liberal Individualism*. New York NY, Cambridge University Press.

Bird (2007), Colin: "Harm Versus Sovereignty: A Reply to Ripstein", in: *Philosophy and Public Affairs*, Vol. 35, No. 2, pp. 180–194.

Blake (2001), Michael: "Distributive Justice, State Coercion, and Autonomy", in: *Philosophy and Public Affairs*, Vol. 30, No. 3, pp. 257–296.

Bohman (2009), James: "Living without Freedom. Cosmopolitanism at Home and the Rule of Law", in: *Political Theory*, Vol. 37, No. 4, pp. 539–561.

Brandom (1979), Robert: "Freedom and Constraint by Norms", in: *American Philosophical Quarterly*, Vol. 16, No. 3, pp. 187–196.

Brandom (2007), Robert: "The structure of desire and recognition. Self-consciousness and self-constitution", in: *Philosophy & Social Criticism*, Vol. 33, No. 1, pp. 127–150.

Bratman (1987), Michael E.: *Intention, Plans, and Practical Reason*. Cambridge MA, Harvard University Press.

Bratman (2000), Michael E.: "Reflection, Planning, and Temporally Extended Agency", in: *Philosophical Review*, Vol. 109, No. 1, pp. 35–61.

Bratman (2009), Michael E.: "Agency, Time, and Sociality", in: *Proceedings and Addresses of the APA*, Vol. 84, No. 2, pp. 7–26.

Bratman (2011), Michael E.: "Reflections on Law, Normativity, and Plans", in: Stefano Bertea and Georgios Pavlakos (eds.): *New Essays on the Normativity of Law*, pp. 73–85.

Brecht (1987 (1938)), Bertold: *Poems 1913–1956*. London, Methuen.

Brennan (1984), Samantha, Tracy Isaacs, Michael Milde (eds.): *A Question of Values: New Canadian Perspectives in Ethics and Political Philosophy*. Atlanta GA, Radopi.

Brennan (1985), Geoffrey and James M. Buchanan: *The Reason of Rules. Constitutional Political Economy*. New York NY, Cambridge University Press.

Brigham (1993), John: "*Order without Lawyers: Ellickson on How Neighbors Settle Disputes* ", in: *Law & Society Review*, Vol. 27, No. 3, pp. 609–618.

Broadie (2010), Sarah: "Book Review: Korsgaard's *The Constitution of Agency*", in: *Social Theory and Practice*, Vol. 36, No. 4, pp. 705–711.

Broome (1999), John: "Normative requirements", in: *Ratio*, Vol. 12, pp. 398–419.

Brown (2011), Campbell: "Consequentialize This", in: *Ethics*, Vol. 121, No. 4, pp. 749–771.

Brudner (2011), Alan: "Private Law and Kantian Right", in: *University of Toronto Law Journal*, Vol. 61, pp. 279–311.

Brudney (1993), Daniel: "Two Links of Law and Morality", in: *Ethics*, Vol. 103, No. 2, pp. 280–301.

Buchanan (2000 (1975)), James M.: *The Limits of Liberty. Between Anarchy and Leviathan*. Indianapolis IN, Liberty Fund.

Byrd (2006), B. Sharon and Joachim Hruschka (eds.): *Kant and Law*. Aldershot, Ashgate.

Byrd (2010), B. Sharon and Joachim Hruschka: *Kant's Doctrine of Right. A Commentary*. New York NY, Cambridge University Press.

Calhoun (1995), Cheshire: "Standing for Something", in: *The Journal of Philosophy*, Vol. XCII, No. 5, pp. 235–260.

Campbell (2002), Joseph Keim, Michael O'Rourke, and David Shier (eds.): *Law and Social Justice*. Cambridge MA, MIT Press.

Candlish (2009), Stewart and George Wrisley: "Private Language", in: *The Stanford Encyclopedia of Philosophy (Winter 2009 Edition)*, Edward N. Zalta (ed.), URL = http://plato.stanford.edu/entries/private-language/

Cervantes Saavedra (1979 (1605)), Miguel de: *Don Quixote of La Mancha. Translated and with an Introduction by Walter Starkie*. New York NY, New American Library.

Chappell (2010), Timothy: "Book Review: Korsgaard's *Self-Constitution*", in: *Philosophy: The Journal of the Royal Institute of Philosophy*, Vol. 85, No. 333, pp. 424–432.

Cholbi (1999), Michael J.: "Egoism and the Publicity of Reason: A Reply to Korsgaard", in: *Social Theory and Practice*, Vol. 25, No. 3, pp. 491–517.

Chrisafis (2011), Angelique: "Full-face veils outlawed as France spells out controversial niqab ban", in: *The Guardian* (retrieved 2.14.2012), URL = http://www.guardian.co.uk/world/2011/mar/03/niqab-ban-france-muslim-veil

Clayton Coleman (2005), Mary: "Public Reasons and Practical Solipsism", in: *The Southern Journal of Philosophy*, Vol. XLIII, pp. 317–336.

Cohen (1996), G. A.: "Reason, humanity, and the moral law", in: Christine M. Korsgaard: *The Sources of Normativity*, pp. 167–188.

Coleman (1998), Jules: "Incorporationism, Conventionality, and the Practical Difference Thesis", in: *Legal Theory*, Vol. 4, pp. 381–425.

Coleman (2002), Jules: "Facts, Fictions, and the Grounds of Law", in: Joseph Keim Campbell et al. (eds.): *Law and Social Justice*, pp. 327–351.

Cox (2009), Damian, Marguerite La Caze, and Michael Levine: "Integrity", in: *The Stanford Encyclopedia of Philosophy (Winter 2009 Edition)*, Edward N. Zalta (ed.), URL = http://plato.stanford.edu/entries/integrity/

Crary (2000), Alice and Rupert Read (eds.): *The New Wittgenstein*. New York NY, Routledge.

Crary (2000a), Alice: “Wittgenstein’s philosophy in relation to political thought”, in: Alice Crary and Rupert Read (eds.): *The New Wittgenstein*, pp. 118–145.
Crowe (2007), Jonathan: “Dworkin on the Value of Integrity”, in: *Deakin Law Review*, Vol. 12, No. 1, pp. 167–180.
Cushing (2003), Simon: “Justification, Legitimacy, and Social Embeddedness: Locke and Rawls on Society and the State”, *The Journal of Value Inquiry*, Vol. 37, pp. 217–231.
Darwall (1983), Stephen: *Impartial Reason*. Ithaca NY, Cornell University Press.
Darwall (2007), Stephen: “Law and the Second-Person Standpoint”, in: *Loyola Law Review*, Vol. 40, No. 2, pp. 891–909.
Defoe (1994 (1719)), Daniel: *Robinson Crusoe: An Authoritative Text, Backgrounds, Sources, and Criticism*. Michael Shinagel (ed.). New York NY, Norton.
Delacroix (2006), Sylvie: *Legal Norms and Normativity. An Essay in Genealogy*. Oxford, Hart Publishing.
Doomen (2010), Jasper: “Book Review: Korsgaard’s *Self-Constitution*”, in: *Dialogue: Canadian Philosophical Review*, Vol. 49, No. 2, pp. 317–321.
Douglas (2007), Ian R.: “Globalisation and the End of the State?”, in: *New Political Economy*, Vol. 2, No. 1, pp. 165–177.
Dworkin (1965), Ronald: “The Elusive Morality of Law”, in: *Villanova Law Review*, Vol. 10, p. 631–639.
Dworkin (1986), Ronald: *Law’s Empire*. Cambridge MA, Belknap Press.
Dusza (1989), Karl: “Max Weber’s Conception of the State”, in: *International Journal of Politics, Culture, and Society*, Vol. 3, No. 1.
Dyzenhaus (1997), David: “Legal Theory in the Collapse of Weimar: Contemporary Lessons?”, in: *The American Political Science Review*, Vol. 91, No. 1, pp. 121–134.
Edmundson (1993), William A.: “Rethinking Exclusionary Reasons: A Second Edition of Joseph Raz’s ‘Practical Reason and Norms’”, in: *Law and Philosophy*, Vol. 12, No. 3, pp. 329–343.
Edmundson (1998), William A.: *Three Anarchical Fallacies. An Essay on Political Authority*. New York NY, Cambridge University Press.
Edmundson (2010), William A.: “Book Review: Ripstein’s *Force and Freedom*”, in: *Ethics*, Vol. 120, No. 4, pp. 869–873.
Eley (2008), Goeff and Jan Palmowski (eds.): *Citizenship and national identity in twentieth-century Germany*. Stanford CA, Stanford University Press.
Ellickson (1991), Robert C.: *Order without Laws: How Neighbors Settle Disputes*. Cambridge MA, Harvard University Press.
Emmet (1975), Dorothy: *Rules, Roles and Relations*. Boston MA, Beacon Press.
Enoch (2006), David: “Agency, Shmagency: Why Normativity Won’t Come from What Is Constitutive of Action”, in: *Philosophical Review*, Vol. 115, No. 2, pp. 169–198.
Enoch (2009), David: “Can there be a global, interesting, coherent constructivism about practical reason?”, in: *Philosophical Explorations*, Vol. 12, No. 3, pp. 319–339.
Estlund (1996), David: “The Survival of Egalitarian Justice in John Rawls’s *Political Liberalism*”, in: *The Journal of Political Philosophy*, Vol. 4, No. 1, pp. 68–78.
European Union (2008): “Consolidated version of the Treaty on European Union”, in: *Official Journal of the European Union*, Vol. 51, pp. 13–45.
Ferrero (2009), Luca: “Constitutivism and the Inescapability of Agency”, in: *Oxford Studies in Metaethics*, Vol. 4, pp. 303–333.
FitzPatrick (2005), William J.: “The Practical Turn in Ethical Theory: Korsgaard’s Constructivism, Realism, and the Nature of Normativity”, in: *Ethics*, Vol. 115, No. 4, pp. 651–691.

Flathman (1994), Richard: "Liberalism and the Suspect Enterprise of Political Institutionalization: The Case of the Rule of Law", in: Ian Shapiro (ed.) *The Rule of Law*, pp. 297–327.
Flikschuh (2000), Katrin: *Kant and Modern Political Philosophy*. New York NY, Cambridge University Press.
Flikschuh (2008), Katrin: "Reason, Right, and Revolution: Kant and Locke", in: *Philosophy and Public Affairs*, Vol. 36, No. 4, pp. 375–404.
Flikschuh (2008a), Katrin: "Side-stepping Morality: Korsgaard on Kant's No-right to Revolution", in: *Jahrbuch für Recht und Ethik*, Vol. 14, pp. 127–145.
Fox-Decent (2008), Evan: "Is the Rule of Law Really Indifferent to Human Rights?", in: *Law and Philosophy*, Vol. 27, 533–581.
Frankfurt (1988), Harry G.: *The importance of what we care about: philosophical essays*. New York NY, Cambridge University Press.
Fried (2003), Barbara H.: "'If You Don't Like It, Leave It': The Problem of Exit in Social Contractarian Arguments", in: *Philosophy and Public Affairs*, Vol. 31, No. 1, pp. 40–70.
Fukuyama (2011), Francis: *The Origins of Political Order*. New York NY, Farrar, Straus and Giroux.
Fuller (1958), Lon L.: "Positivism and Fidelity to Law – A Reply to Professor Hart", in: *Harvard Law Review*, Vol. 71, No. 4, pp. 630–672.
Fuller (1969), Lon L.: *The Morality of Law. Second Edition*. New Haven CT, Yale University Press.
Gaus (1994), Gerald F.: "Public Reason and the Rule of Law", in: Ian Shapiro (ed.) *The Rule of Law*, pp. 328–363.
Gaus (2011), Gerald F.: "Explanation, justification, and emergent properties: an essay on Nozickian metatheory", in: Ralf M. Bader and John Meadowcroft (eds.): *The Cambridge Companion to Nozick's* Anarchy, State, and Utopia, pp. 116–142.
Gert (2002), Joshua: "Korsgaard's Private-Reasons Argument", in: *Philosophy and Phenomenological Research*, Vol. 64, No. 2, pp. 303–324.
Gibbard (1990), Allan: *Wise Choices, Apt Feelings. A Theory of Normative Judgments*. Cambridge MA, Harvard University Press.
Gibbard (1999), Allan: "Morality as Consistency in Living: Korsgaard's Kantian Lectures", in: *Ethics*, Vol. 110, No. 1, pp. 140–164.
Glenn (2003), Richard A.: *The Right to Privacy. Rights and Liberties under the Law*. Santa Barbara CA, ABC-CLIO.
Gowans (2002), Christopher W.: "Practical Identities and Autonomy: Korsgaard's Reformation of Kant's Moral Philosophy", in: *Philosophy and Phenomenological Research*, Vol. LXIV, No. 3, pp. 546–570.
Gowans (2010), Christopher W.: "Book Review: Korsgaard's *The Constitution of Agency* and *Self-Constitution*", in: *International Philosophical Quarterly*, Vol. 50, No. 1, pp. 117–129.
Giudice (2011), Michael: "Joseph Raz's Legal Philosophy", in: *IVR Encyclopaedia of Jurisprudence, Legal Theory and Philosophy of Law (Summer 2011 Edition)*, URL = http://ivr-enc.info/index.php?title=Joseph_Raz%27s_Legal_Philosophy
Guyer (1992), Paul (ed.): *The Cambridge Companion to Kant*. New York NY, Cambridge University Press.
Guyer (2000), Paul: *Kant on Freedom, Law, and Happiness*. New York NY, Cambridge University Press.
Guyer (2005), Paul: *Kant's System of Nature and Freedom*. New York NY, Oxford University Press.

Guyer (2006), Paul (ed.): *The Cambridge Companion to Kant and Modern Philosophy*. New York NY, Cambridge University Press.

Harrison (1960), Paul M.: "Weber's Categories of Authority and Voluntary Associations", in: *American Sociological Review*, Vol. 25, No. 2, pp. 232–237.

Hart (1958), H. L. A.: "Positivism and the Separation of Law and Morals", in: *Harvard Law Review*, Vol. 71, No. 4, pp. 593–629.

Hart (1983), H. L. A.: *Essays in Jurisprudence and Philosophy*. New York NY, Oxford University Press.

Hart (1994 (1961)), H. L. A.: *The Concept of Law*. Second Edition. New York NY, Oxford University Press.

Hawkins (2004), Deborah: "Book Review: Kukathas's *The Liberal Archipelago*", in: *Social Theory and Practice*, Vol. 30, No. 4, pp. 589–598.

Hayek (1960), F. A.: *The Constitution of Liberty*. London, Routledge.

Hegel (1991 (1821)), G. W. F.: *Elements of the Philosophy of Right*, ed. A. Wood, trans. H.B. Nisbet. New York NY, Cambridge University Press.

Hegel (2011 (1837)), G. W. F.: *Lectures on the Philosophy of World History, Vol. I: Manuscripts of the Introduction and the Lectures of 1822–3*, eds. & trs. R. F. Brown and P. C. Hodgson. New York NY, Oxford University Press.

Hekman (2004), Susan J.: *Private selves, public identities: reconsidering identity politics*. University Park PA, Pennsylvania State University.

Heyes (2003), Cressida J. (ed.): *The Grammar of Politics: Wittgenstein and Political Philosophy*. Ithaca NY, Cornell University Press.

Himma (2002), Kenneth Einar: "Conceptual Jurisprudence and the Intelligibility of Law's Claim to Obligate", in: Joseph Keim Campbell et al. (eds.): *Law and Social Justice*, pp. 311–326.

Hobbes (1994 (1651)), Thomas: *Leviathan*. Indianapolis IN, Hackett.

Hodgson (2010), Louis-Philippe: "Kant on the Right to Freedom: A Defense", in: *Ethics*, Vol. 120, No. 4, pp. 791–819.

Hodgson (2010a), Louis-Philippe: "Kant on Property Rights and the State", in: *Kantian Review*, Vol. 15, No. 1, pp. 57–87.

Hohfeld (1978 (1913)), Wesley Newcomb: *Fundamental Legal Conceptions as Applied in Judicial Reasoning; edited by Walter Wheeler Cook; with a new foreword by Arthur L. Corbin*. Westport CT, Greenwood Press.

Holtman (2002), Sarah Williams: "Revolution, Contradiction, and Kantian Citizenship", in: Mark Timmons (ed.): *Kant's Metaphysics of Morals: Interpretive Essays*, pp. 209–231.

Holton (2011), Robert J.: *Globalization and the Nation State (2nd edition)*. London, Palgrave Macmillan.

Honneth (2010), Axel: *The Pathologies of Individual Freedom. Hegel's Social Theory*. Princeton NJ, Princeton University Press.

Horstmann (2004), Rolf-Peter: "The Role of Civil Society in Hegel's Political Philosophy", in: Robert Pippin and Otfried Höffe (eds.): *Hegel on Ethics and Politics*, pp. 208–238.

Hume (2000 (1739)), David: *A Treatise of Human Nature*. Edited by David Fate Norton and Mary J. Norton. New York NY, Oxford University Press.

James (2007), Aaron: "Legal and Other Governance in Second-Person Perspective", in: *Loyola Law Review*, Vol. 40, No. 2, pp. 101–127.

Janoski (2010), Thomas: *The Ironies of Citizenship: Naturalization and Integration in Industrialized Countries*. New York NY, Cambridge University Press.

Johnson (2008), Robert: "Kant's Moral Philosophy", in: *The Stanford Encyclopedia of Philosophy (Summer 2010 Edition)*, Edward N. Zalta (ed.), URL = http://plato.stanford.edu/entries/kant-moral/

Kalberg (2005), Stephen: "Authority in the Modern Epoch", in: Max Weber: *Readings and Commentary on Modernity*, pp. 173–178.

Kant (1996), Immanuel: *Practical Philosophy* (The Cambridge Edition of the Works of Immanuel Kant). Translated and edited by Mary J. Gregor. New York NY, Cambridge University Press.

Kavka (1986), Gregory S.: *Hobbesian Moral and Political Theory*. Princeton NJ, Princeton University Press.

Kelly (2003), Duncan: *The State of the Political: Conceptions of Politics and the State in the Thought of Max Weber, Carl Schmitt and Franz Neumann*. New York NY, Oxford University Press.

Kelsen (2002 (1934)), Hans: *Pure Theory of Law*. Translation from the Second (Revised and Enlarged) German Edition by Max Knight. Union NJ, The Lawbook Exchange.

Kersting (1992), Wolfgang: "Kant's Concept of the State", in: Howard Williams (ed.): *Essays on Kant's Political Philosophy*, pp. 143–165.

Kersting (1992a), Wolfgang: "Politics, Freedom, and Order: Kant's Political Philosophy", in: Paul Guyer (ed.): *The Cambridge Companion to Kant*, pp. 342–366.

Ketcher (2010), Tim: "Book Review: Korsgaard's *Self-Constitution*", in: *Philosophical Investigations*, Vol. 33, No. 4, pp. 384–386.

Kleingeld (2012), Pauline: *Kant and Cosmopolitanism : The Philosophical Ideal of World Citizenship*. New York NY, Cambridge University Press.

Klosko (2005), George: "Democracy and Liberty: Extending the Paradigm", in: *The Review of Politics*, Vol. 67, No. 1, pp. 135–152.

Kneller (2006), Jane: "Kant on Sex and Marriage Right", in: Paul Guyer (ed.): *The Cambridge Companion to Kant and Modern Philosophy*, pp. 447–476.

Korsgaard (1996), Christine M.: *The Sources of Normativity*. New York NY, Cambridge University Press.

Korsgaard (1996a), Christine M.: *Creating the Kingdom of Ends*. New York NY, Cambridge University Press.

Korsgaard (2002), Christine M.: "Internalism and the Sources of Normativity", in: Herlinde Pauer-Studer (ed.): *Constructions of Practical Reason*, pp. 50–69.

Korsgaard (2008), Christine M.: *The Constitution of Agency. Essays on Practical Reason and Moral Psychology*. New York NY, Oxford University Press.

Korsgaard (2008a), Christine M.: "Ethics at the Intersection of Kant and Aristotle. An Interview with Christine M. Korsgaard by Ana Marta González", in: *Anuario Filosófico*, Vol. XXXVI, No. 3, pp. 775–794.

Korsgaard (2009), Christine M.: *Self-Constitution: Agency, Identity, and Integrity*. New York NY, Oxford University Press.

Korsgaard (2009a), Christine M.: "Natural Motives and the Motive of Duty. Hume and Kant on our Duties to Others", in: *Contemporary Readings in Law & Social Justice*, Vol. 1, No. 2, pp. 8–35.

Kramer (2003), Matthew H.: *In Defense of Legal Positivism*. New York NY, Oxford University Press.

Kukathas (2003), Chandran: *The Liberal Archipelago. A Theory of Diversity and Freedom*. New York NY, Oxford University Press.

Kukathas (2009), Chandran: "One Cheer for Constantinople: A Comment on Pettit and Skinner on Hobbes and Freedom", in: *Hobbes Studies*, Vol. 22, pp. 192–198.
Kukathas (2011), Chandran: "*E pluribus plurum*, or, How to fail to get to utopia in spite of really trying", in: Ralf M. Bader and John Meadowcroft (eds.): *The Cambridge Companion to Nozick's* Anarchy, State, and Utopia, pp. 289–302.
Kymlicka (1994), Will and Wayne Norman: "Return of the Citizen: A Survey of Recent Work on Citizenship", in: *Ethics*, Vol. 104, No. 2, pp. 352–381.
Kymlicka (1995), Will: *Multicultural Citizenship: A Liberal Theory of Minority Rights*. New York NY, Oxford University Press.
Laden (2005), Anthony Simon: "Evaluating Social Reasons: Hobbes Versus Hegel", in: *The Journal of Philosophy*, Vol. CII, No. 7, pp. 327–356.
Landy (2008), David: "Hegel's Account of Rule-Following", in: *Inquiry*, Vol. 51, No. 2, pp. 170–193.
LaVaque-Manty (2002), Mika: *Arguments and Fists*. New York NY, Routledge.
LaVaque-Manty (2011), Mika: "Our Kant. Review Essay", in: *Political Theory*, Vol. 39, No. 2, pp. 261–275.
Lavin (2005), Douglas: "Practical Reason and the Possibility of Error", in: *Ethics*, Vol. 114, No. 3, pp. 424–457.
LeBar (2001), Mark: "Korsgaard, Wittgenstein, and the Mafioso", in: *Southern Journal of Philosophy*, Vol. 39, No. 2, 261–271.
Leiter (2007), Brian and Neil Sinhababu (eds.): *Nietzsche and Morality*. New York NY, Oxford University Press.
Levey (2004), Geoffrey Brahm: "Book Review: Kukathas's *The Liberal Archipelago*", in: *Perspectives on Politics*, Vol. 2, No. 3, pp. 573–574.
Locke (2003 (1689)), John: *Two Treatises of Government and A Letter Concerning Toleration*. New Haven CT, Yale University Press.
Long (1977), Douglas C.: *Bentham on Liberty*. Toronto ON, University of Toronto Press.
Mackie (1980), John Leslie: *The Cement of the Universe: A Study of Causation*. Oxford, Clarendon Press.
Maclure (2011), Jocelyn and Charles Taylor: *Secularism and Freedom of Conscience*. Cambridge MA, Harvard University Press.
Madison (2003 (1788)), James: "The Federalist No. 51", in: Terence Ball (ed.): *The Federalist*, pp. 251–255.
Mandle (2010), Jon: "Book Review: Ripstein's *Force and Freedom*", in: *Dialogue: Canadian Philosophical Review*, Vol. 49, No. 3, pp. 479–487.
Mathis (2000), Stephen: "Korsgaard, Normativity, and the Publicity of Reasons", in: *Southwest Philosophy Review*, Vol. 17, No. 1, pp. 75–83.
McCarty (2009), Richard: *Kant's Theory of Action*. New York NY, Oxford University Press.
McDonald (2010), Fritz: "Agency and Responsibility", in: *Journal of Value Inquiry*, Vol. 25, No. 2, pp. 199–207.
McDonald (2010a), Fritz: "Book Review: Korsgaard's *The Constitution of Agency*", in: *Ethical Theory and Moral Practice*, Vol. 13, pp. 235–236.
McDowell (1996), John: *Mind and World: With a new Introduction*. Cambridge MA, Harvard University Press.
Mendus (1992), Susan: "Kant: 'An Honest but Narrow-Minded Bourgeois'?", in: Howard Williams (ed.): *Essays on Kant's Political Philosophy*, pp. 166–190.

Meyer (2003), Lukas M., Stanley M. Paulson, Thomas Pogge (eds.): *Rights, Culture, and the Law: Themes from the Legal Philosophy of Joseph Raz.* New York NY, Oxford University Press.

Michelman (1996), Frank I.: “Parsing ‘A Right to have Rights’”, in: *Constellations*, Vol. 3, No. 2, pp. 200–208.

Milgram (2009), Elijah: "Practical Reason and the Structure of Actions", in: *The Stanford Encyclopedia of Philosophy (Summer 2009 Edition)*, Edward N. Zalta (ed.), URL = http://plato.stanford.edu/archives/sum2009/entries/practical-reason-action/

Mill (1998 (1861)), John Stuart: *Utilitarianism*. New York NY, Oxford University Press.

Miller (2002), Alexander and Crispin Wright (eds.): *Rule-Following and Meaning*. Montreal, McGill-Queen’s University Press.

Miller (1995), David: *On Nationality*. Oxford, Clarendon Press.

Mitnick (2006), Eric J.: *Group-Differentiated Rights in Liberal Theory*. Aldershot, Ahsgate.

Moon (2003), Donald J.: “Liberalism, Autonomy, and Moral Pluralism”, in: *Political Theory*, Vol. 31, No. 1, pp. 125–135.

Moon (2005), Donald J.: “Book Review: Kukathas’s *The Liberal Archipelago*”, in: *Ethics*, Vol. 115, No. 2, pp. 422–427.

Moore (2011), Adam D.: *Privacy Rights: Moral and Legal Foundations*. University Park PA, Pennsylvania State University Press.

Morris (1998), Christopher W.: *An Essay on the Modern State*. New York NY, Cambridge University Press.

Murphy (2005), Colleen: “Lon Fuller and the Moral Value of the Rule of Law”, in: *Law and Philosophy*, Vol. 24, pp. 239–262.

Murphy (2002), Liam B. and Thomas Nagel: *The Myth of Ownership. Taxes and Justice*. New York NY, Oxford University Press.

Nadler (2007), Jennifer: “Hart, Fuller, and the Connection Between Law and Justice”, in: *Law and Philosophy*, Vol.27, pp. 1–34.

Nagel (1979), Thomas: *Mortal Questions*. New York NY, Cambridge University Press.

Nagel (1996), Thomas: “Universality and the Reflective Self”, in: Christine M. Korsgaard: *The Sources of Normativity*, pp. 200–209.

Nagel (2005), Thomas: “The Problem of Global Justice”, in: *Philosophy and Public Affairs*, Vol. 33, No. 2, pp. 113–147.

Newton (2004), Michael: *Savage Girls and Wild Boys: A History of Feral Children*. New York NY, Picador.

Nicholson (1992), Peter P.: “Kant, Revolutions and History”, in: Howard Williams (ed.): *Essays on Kant’s Political Philosophy*, pp. 249–268.

Noe (1991), R. A.: “Did Kant Anticipate Wittgenstein’s Private Language Argument?”, in: *Kant Studien*, Vol. 82, No. 3, pp. 270–284.

Norman (2000), Richard: “Public Reasons and the ‘Private Language’ Argument”, in: *Philosophical Investigations*, Vol. 23, No. 4, pp. 292–314.

Norton (2003), Andrew: “Book Review: Kukathas’s *The Liberal Archipelago*”, in: *Policy*, Vol. 19, No. 4, pp. 57–58.

Nozick (1974), Robert: *Anarchy, State, and Utopia*. New York NY, Basic Books.

Nozick (1981), Robert: *Philosophical Explanations*. Cambridge MA, Harvard University Press.

Oakeshott (1975), Michael: *On Human Conduct*. Oxford, Oxford University Press.

Oakeshott (1983), Michael: *On history and other essays*. Totowa NJ, Barnes and Noble.

O'Day (1998), Ken: "Normativity and Interpersonal Reasons", in: *Ethical Theory and Moral Practice*, Vol. 1, pp. 61–83.
Ognjenovic (2010), Gorona (ed.): *Responsibility in Context: Perspectives*. Dordrecht, Springer.
O'Hagan (2004), Emer: "Practical Identity and the Constitution of Agency", in: *The Journal of Value Inquiry*, Vol. 38, pp. 49–59.
O'Neill (1989), Onora: *Constructions of Reason: Explorations of Kant's Practical Philosophy*. New York NY, Cambridge University Press.
O'Neill (1992), Onora: "Reason and Politics in the Kantian Enterprise", in: Howard Williams (ed.): *Essays on Kant's Political Philosophy*, pp. 50–80.
O'Neill (1996), Onora: *Towards Justice and Virtue. A Constructive Account of Practical Reasoning*. New York NY, Cambridge University Press.
O'Neill (2000), Onora: *Bounds of Justice*. New York NY, Cambridge University Press.
Pakulski (1986), Jan: "Legitimacy and Mass Compliance: Reflections on Max Weber and Soviet-Type Societies", in: *British Journal of Political Science*. Vol. 16, No. 1, pp. 35–56.
Pallikkathayill (2010), Japa: "Deriving Morality from Politics: Rethinking the Formula of Humanity", in: *Ethics*, Vol. 121, No. 1, pp. 116–147.
Parfit (1984), Derek: *Reasons and Persons*. Oxford, Clarendon Press.
Patterson (1982), Orlando: *Slavery and Social Death*. Cambridge MA, Harvard University Press.
Pauer-Studer (2003), Herlinde (ed.): *Constructions of Practical Reason: Interviews on Moral and Political Philosophy*, Stanford CA, Stanford University Press.
Pauer-Studer (2009), Herlinde: "Book Review: Korsgaard's *The Constitution of Agency*", in: *Kant Studien*, Vol. 100, No. 3, pp. 395–401.
Pauer-Studer (2011), Herlinde and J. David Velleman: "Distortions of Normativity", in: *Ethical Theory and Moral Practice*, Vol. 14, No. 3, pp. 329–356.
Pavlakos (2008), George: "Non-Individualism, Rights, and Practical Reason", in: *Ratio Juris*, Vol. 21, No. 1, pp. 66–93.
Penner (2003), J. E.: "Legal Reasoning and the Authority of Law", in: Lukas H. Meyer et. al. (eds.): *Rights, Culture, and the Law: Themes from the Legal Philosophy of Joseph Raz*, pp. 71–97.
Pettit (1996), Philip: *The Common Mind. An Essay on Psychology, Society, and Politics*. New York NY, Oxford University Press.
Pettit (1996a), Philip and Michael Smith: "Freedom in Belief and Desire", in: *The Journal of Philosophy*, Vol. XCIII, No. 9, pp. 429–499.
Pettit (1999), Philip: *Republicanism. A Theory of Freedom and Government*. New York NY, Oxford University Press.
Pettit (2000), Philip: "Non-Consequentialism and Universalizability", in: *The Philosophical Quarterly*, Vol. 50, No. 199, pp. 175–190.
Pettit (2001), Philip: *A Theory of Freedom. From the Psychology to the Politics of Agency*. New York NY, Oxford University Press.
Pettit (2008), Philip: *Made with Words. Hobbes on Language, Mind, and Politics*. Princeton NJ, Princeton University Press.
Pettit (2009), Philip: "Response to Commentaries on *Made with Words*", in: *Hobbes Studies*, Vol. 22, pp. 208–218.
Pincione (2011), Guido: "Rule of Law – Philosophical Perspectives", in: *IVR Encyclopaedia of Jurisprudence, Legal Theory and Philosophy of Law (Summer 2011 Edition)*, URL = http://ivr-enc.info/index.php?title=Rule_of_Law_-_Philosophical_Perspectives

Pippin (2001), Robert B.: "A Mandatory Reading of Kant's Ethics?" (Review of Guyer's *Kant on Freedom, Law, and Happiness*), in: *The Philosophical Quarterly*, Vol. 51, No. 204, pp. 386–393.

Pippin (2004), Robert B. and Otfried Höffe (eds.): *Hegel on Ethics and Politics*. New York NY, Cambridge University Press.

Pippin (2006), Robert B.: "Mine and Thine? The Kantian State", in: Paul Guyer (ed.): *The Cambridge Companion to Kant and Modern Philosophy*, pp. 416–446.

Pippin (2008), Robert B.: *Hegel's Practical Philosophy – Rational Agency as Ethical Life*. New York NY, Cambridge University Press.

Pitkin (1985), Hanna: *Wittgenstein and Justice: On the Significance of Ludwig Wittgenstein for Social and Political Thought.* Berkeley CA, University of California Press.

Polanyi (1951), Michael: *The Logic of Liberty*. Chicago IL, University of Chicago Press.

Pogge (1988), Thomas W.: "Kant's Theory of Justice", in: *Kant-Studien*, Vol. 79, pp. 407–433.

Popper (2003 (1945)), Karl: *The Open Society and Its Enemies*. London, Routledge.

Porter (2009), Thomas: "Book Review: Kukathas's *The Liberal Archipelago*", in: *Contemporary Political Theory*, Vol. 8, No. 3, pp. 365–367.

Portmore (2011), Douglas W.: *Commonsense Consequentialism: Wherein Morality meets Rationality*. New York NY, Oxford University Press.

Railton (1999), Peter: "Normative Force and Normative Freedom: Hume and Kant, but not Hume *versus* Kant", in: *Ratio (new series)*, Vol. XII, pp. 320–353.

Rauscher (2009), Frederick: "Kant's Social and Political Philosophy", in: *The Stanford Encyclopedia of Philosophy* (Winter 2009 Edition), Edward N. Zalta (ed.), URL = http://plato.stanford.edu/entries/kant-social-political/

Rawls (1993), John: *Political Liberalism*. New York NY, Columbia University Press.

Rawls (1999 (1971)), John: *A Theory of Justice*, revised edition. New York NY, Oxford University Press.

Raz (1979), Joseph: *The Authority of Law*. New York NY, Oxford University Press.

Raz (1986), Joseph: *The Morality of Freedom*. New York NY, Oxford University Press.

Raz (1989), Joseph: "Facing Up: A Reply", in: 62 *Southern California Law Review*, pp. 1153–1235.

Raz (1990), Joseph: *Practical Reason and Norms*. Princeton NJ, Princeton University Press.

Raz (1990), Joseph and Avishai Margalit: "National Self Determination", in: *The Journal of Philosophy*, Vol. LXXXVII, No. 9, pp. 439–461.

Raz (1994), Joseph: *Ethics in the Public Domain*. New York NY, Oxford University Press.

Raz (1999), Joseph: *Engaging Reason*. New York NY, Oxford University Press.

Raz (2003), Joseph: *The Practice of Value. With Christine Korsgaard, Robert Pippin & Bernard Williams*. New York NY, Oxford University Press.

Raz (2009), Joseph: "Reasons: practical and adaptive", in: David Sobel and Stephen Wall (eds.): *Reasons for Action*, pp. 37–57.

Reath (2006), Andrews: *Agency and Autonomy in Kant's Moral Theory. Selected Essays*. New York NY, Oxford University Press.

Ripstein (2004), Arthur: "Authority and Coercion", in: *Philosophy and Public Affairs*, Vol. 32, No. 1, pp. 2–35.

Ripstein (2006), Arthur: "Beyond the Harm Principle", in: *Philosophy and Public Affairs*, Vol. 34, No. 3, pp. 215–245.

Ripstein (2006a), Arthur: "Private Order and Public Justice: Kant and Rawls", in: *Virginia Law Review*, Vol. 92, No. 7, pp. 1391–1438.

Ripstein (2007), Arthur: "Legal Moralism and the Harm Principle: A Rejoinder", in: *Philosophy and Public Affairs*, Vol. 35, No. 2, pp. 195–201.

Ripstein (2009), Arthur: *Force and Freedom. Kant's Legal and Political Philosophy*. Cambridge MA, Harvard University Press.

Risse (2007), Mathias: "Nietzschean 'Animal Psychology' versus Kantian Ethics", in: Brian Leiter et al. (eds.): *Nietzsche and Morality*, pp. 57–82.

Robinson (2009), Christopher C.: *Wittgenstein and Political Theory: The View from Somewhere*. Edinburgh, Edinburgh University Press.

Roth (2011), Klas: "Principles of the Unification of our Agency", in: *Education Philosophy and Theory*, Vol. 43, No. 3, pp. 283–297.

Rothbard (1973), Murray: *For a New Liberty*. New York NY, Mcmillan.

Rundle (2009), Kristen: "The Impossibility of an Extermination Legality: Law and the Holocaust", in: *University of Toronto Law Journal*, Vol. 59, pp. 65–125.

Rundle (2009a), Kristen: *"Forms Liberate": Reclaiming the Legal Philosophy of Lon L. Fuller*. University of Toronto, Doctoral Thesis.

Rundle (2012), Kristen: *Forms Liberate: Reclaiming the Jurisprudence of Lon L. Fuller*. Portland OR, Hart Publishing.

Safran (1997), William: "Citizenship and Nationality in Democratic Systems: Approaches to Defining and Acquiring Membership in the Political Community", in: *International Political Science Review*, Vol. 18, No. 3, pp. 313–335.

Sandel (1998), Michael J.: *Liberalism and the Limits of Justice (2nd edition)*. New York NY, Cambridge University Press.

Scanlon (2000), Thomas: *What We Owe to Each Other*. Cambridge MA, Harvard University Press.

Schapiro (2001), Tamar: "Three Conceptions of Action in Moral Theory", in: *NOÛS*, Vol. 35, No. 1, pp. 93–117.

Schlosser (2011), Markus: "Book Review: Korsgaard's *Self-Constitution*", in: *The Philosophical Quarterly*, Vol. 61, No. 242, pp. 212–214.

Schlösser (2011), Ulrich: "Book Review: Korsgaard's *Self-Constitution*", in: *European Journal of Philosophy*, Vol. 19, No. 1, pp. 160–164.

Schmidtz (2006), David: *Elements of Justice*. New York NY, Cambridge University Press.

Searle (2010), John: *Making the Social World: The Structure of Human Civilization*. New York NY, Oxford University Press.

Shapiro (1994), Ian (ed.): *The Rule of Law*, NOMOS XXXVI. New York NY, New York University Press.

Shapiro (1997), Ian and Will Kymlicka (eds.): *Ethnicity and Group Rights*, NOMOS XXXIX. New York NY, New York University Press.

Shapiro (2011), Scott: *Legality*. Cambridge MA, Harvard University Press.

Shattuck (1994), Roger: *The Forbidden Experiment*. New York NY, Kodansha International.

Shelton (2003), Mark: "Obligation as Self-determination: A Critique of Hegel and Korsgaard", in: *Pacific Philosophical Quarterly*, Vol. 84, pp. 155–174.

Sher (2001), George: "Book Review: Bird's *The Myth of Liberal Individualism*", in: *Mind*, Vol. 110, No. 437, pp. 171–174.

Shoemaker (1996), David W.: "Theoretical Persons and Practical Agents", in: *Philosophy and Public Affairs*, Vol. 25, No. 3, pp. 318–332.

Siep (2004), Ludwig: "Constitution, Fundamental Rights, and Social Welfare in Hegel's *Philosophy of Right*", in: Robert Pippin and Otfried Höffe (eds.): *Hegel on Ethics and Politics*, pp. 268–290.

Simmonds (2007), Nigel E.: *Law As a Moral Idea*. New York NY, Oxford University Press.

Simmons (1999), A. John: "Justification and Legitimacy", in: *Ethics*, Vol. 109, No. 4, pp. 739–771.

Simmons (2010), A. John: "Ideal and Nonideal Theory", in: *Philosophy and Public Affairs*, Vol. 38, No. 1, pp. 5–36.

Skinner (2008), Quentin: *Hobbes and Republican Liberty*. New York NY, Cambridge University Press.

Skinner (2009), Quentin: "Reply", in: *Hobbes Studies*, Vol. 22, pp. 199–207.

Skorupski (1998), John: "Rescuing Moral Obligation", in: *European Journal of Philosophy*, Vol. 6, No. 3, pp. 335–355.

Sobel (2009), David and Stephen Wall (eds.): *Reasons for Action*. New York NY, Cambridge University Press.

Spinner-Halev (2005), Jeff: "Book Review: Kukathas's *The Liberal Archipelago*", in: *The Journal of Politics*, Vol. 67, No. 2, pp. 595–597.

Sterba (1996), James P.: "Understanding Evil: American Slavery, the Holocaust, and the Conquest of the American Indians", in: *Ethics*, Vol. 106, No. 2, pp. 424–448.

Stevenson (1982), Leslie: "Wittgenstein's Transcendental Deduction and Kant's Private Language Argument", in: *Kant Studien*, Vol. 73, pp. 321–337.

Stilz (2009), Anna: *Liberal Loyalty: Freedom, Obligation, and the State*. Princeton NJ, Princeton University Press.

Stringham (2007), Edward P. (ed.): *Anarchy and the Law*. New Brunswick NJ, Transaction Publishers.

Surprenant (2005), Chris W.: "A Reconciliation of Kant's Views on Revolution", in: *Interpretation: A Journal of Political Philosophy*, Vol. 32, No. 2, pp. 151–169.

Swanson (1992), Judith A.: *The Public and the Private in Aristotle's Political Philosophy*. Ithaca NY, Cornell University Press.

Taylor (1985), Charles: *Philosophy and the Human Sciences. Philosophical Papers 2*. New York NY, Cambridge University Press.

Tenenbaum (2011), Sergio: "Book Review: Korsgaard's *Self-Constitution*", in: *Ethics*, Vol. 121, No. 2, pp. 449–455.

Thompson (2008), Michael: *Life and Action. Elementary Structures of Practice and Practical Thought*. Cambridge MA, Harvard University Press.

Thomson (1975), Judith Jarvis: "The Right to Privacy", in: *Philosophy and Public Affairs*, Vol. 4, No. 4, pp. 295–314.

Thomson (2008), Kevin: "Sovereignity, Hospitality, and Commerce: Kant and Cosmopolitan Right", in: *Jahrbuch für Recht und Ethik*, Vol. 16, pp. 305–319.

Thurber (2008 (1939)), James: *The Secret Life of Walter Mitty*. Mankato MN, Creative Education.

Timmons (2002), Mark (ed.): *Kant's Metaphysics of Morals. Interpretive Essays*. New York NY, Oxford University Press.

Tubert (2011), Ariela: "Korsgaard's Constitutive Arguments and the Principles of Practical Reason", in: *The Philosophical Quarterly*, Vol. 61, No. 243, pp. 343–362.

Varden (2008), Helga: "Kant's Non-Voluntarist Conception of Political Obligation; Why Justice Is Impossible in the State of Nature", in: *Kantian Review*, Vol. 13, No. 2, pp. 1–45.

Velleman (1992), J. David: “What Happens When Someone Acts?”, in: *Mind*, Vol. 101, No. 403, pp. 461–481.
Velleman (2006), J. David: *Self to Self*. New York NY, Cambridge University Press.
Velleman (2006a), J. David: “So It Goes”, in: *Amherst Lecture in Philosophy*. Vol. 1, pp. 1–23.
Waldron (1989), Jeremy: “The Rule of Law in Contemporary Liberal Theory”, in: *Ratio Juris*, Vol. 2, No. 1, pp. 79–96.
Waldron (1993), Jeremy: *Liberal Rights. Collected Papers 1981–1991*. New York NY, Cambridge University Press.
Waldron (1993a), Jeremy: “Special Ties and Natural Duties”, in: *Philosophy and Public Affairs*, Vol. 22, No. 1, pp. 3–30.
Waldron (1994), Jeremy: “Why Law – Efficacy, Freedom, or Fidelity?”, in: *Law and Philosophy*, Vol. 13, pp. 259–284.
Waldron (1996), Jeremy: “Kant’s Legal Positivism”, in: *Harvard Law Review*, Vol. 109, No. 7, pp. 1535–1566.
Waldron (1999), Jeremy: “All We Like Sheep”, in: *Canadian Journal of Law and Jurisprudence*, Vol. XII, No. 1, pp. 169–186.
Waldron (2002), Jeremy: “Is the Rule of Law and Essentially Contested Concept (in Florida)?”, in: *Law and Philosophy*, Vol. 21, pp. 137–164.
Waldron (2008), Jeremy: “Positivism and Legality: Hart’s Equivocal Response to Fuller”, in: *New York University Law Review*, Vol. 83, pp. 1135–1169.
Wallace (2001), R. Jay: “Normativity, Commitment and Instrumental Reason”, in: *Philosophers’ Imprint*, Vol. 1, No. 4, pp. 1–26.
Wallace (2009), R. Jay: “The Publicity of Reasons”, in: *Philosophical Perspectives*, Vol. 23, No. 1, pp. 471–497.
Wallimann (1980), Isidor, Howard Rosenbaum, Nicholas Tatsis, George Zito: “Misreading Weber: The Concept of Macht”, in: *Sociology*, Vol. 14, No. 2, pp. 261–275.
Walzer (1997), Michael: “Response to Kukathas”, in: Ian Shapiro and Will Kymlicka (eds.) *Ethnicity and Group Rights*, pp. 105–111.
Watson (1975), Gary: “Free Agency”, in: *The Journal of Philosophy*, Vol. 72, No. 8, pp. 205–220.
Weber (1971), Max: *Gesammelte Politische Schriften. Johannes Winckelmann ed. 3., rev. Aufl.* Tübingen, Mohr.
Weber (1978 (1921)), Max: *Economy and Society. An Outline of Interpretive Sociology. Edited by Guenther Roth and Claus Wittich. 2. vols.* Berkeley CA, University of California Press.
Weber (1994), Max: *Political Writings* (Cambridge Texts in the History of Political Thought). Edited by Peter Lassman and Ronald Speirs. New York NY, Cambridge University Press.
Weber (2005), Max: *Readings and Commentary on Modernity* (edited by Stephen Kalberg). Malden MA, Blackwell.
Weinrib (1992), Ernest J.: “Law as Idea of Reason”, in: Howard Williams (ed.): *Kant’s Political Philosophy*, pp. 15–49.
Weinrib (2008), Jacob: “Kant on Citizenship and Universal Independence”, in: *Australian Journal of Legal Philosophy*, Vol. 33, pp. 1–25.
Weinrib (2008a), Jacob: “The Juridical Significance of Kant’s ‘Supposed Right to Lie’”, in: *Kantian Review*, Vol. 13, No. 1, pp. 141–170.
Williams (1983), Howard L.: *Kant’s Political Philosophy*. New York NY, St. Martin’s Press.
Williams (1992), Howard L. (ed.): *Essays on Kant’s Political Philosophy*. Chicago IL, The University of Chicago Press.

Willigenburg (2002), Theo van: “Shareability and Actual Sharing: Korsgaard’s Position on the Publicity of Reasons”, in: *Philosophical Investigations*, Vol. 25, No. 2, pp. 172–189.

Wisconsin v. Yoder (1972), 406 U.S. 205.

Wittgenstein (2009 (1953)), Ludwig: *Philosophische Untersuchungen. Philosophical Investigations: The German Text, with a Revised English Translation*. Translated by G. E. M. Anscombe, P. M. S. Hacker and Joachim Schulte. Malden MA, Blackwell.

Wolf (2001), Martin: “Will the Nation-State Survive Globalization”, in: *Foreign Affairs*, Vol. 80, No. 1, pp. 178–190.

Wolff (2004), Michael: “Hegel’s Organicist Theory of the State: On the Concept and Method of Hegel’s ‘Science of the State’”, in: Robert Pippin and Otfried Höffe (eds.): *Hegel on Ethics and Politics*, pp. 291–322.

Wolff (1998 (1970)), Robert Paul: *In Defense of Anarchism. With a New Preface*. Berkeley CA, University of California Press.

Wood (2008), Allen W.: *Kantian Ethics*. New York NY, Cambridge University Press.